D1201227

HOOVER AND THE
UN-AMERICANS

The FBI, HUAC, and the Red Menace

HOOVER AND THE UN-AMERICANS

The FBI, HUAC, and the Red Menace

Kenneth O'Reilly

TEMPLE UNIVERSITY PRESS

PHILADELPHIA

Temple University Press, Philadelphia 19122
© 1983 by Temple University. All rights reserved
Published 1983
Printed in the United States of America

Library of Congress Cataloging in Publication Data

O'Reilly, Kenneth.
    Hoover and the un-Americans.

    Bibliography: p.
    Includes index.
    1. Subversive activities—United States—
History—20th century. 2. Hoover, J. Edgar (John
Edgar), 1895–1972. 3. United States. Federal
Bureau of Investigation—History—20th century.
4. United States. Congress. House. Committee on Un-
American Activities—History—20th century. 5. Com-
munism—United States—1917–.   I. Title.
E743.5.O73   1983   322.4′2′0973   83–491
ISBN 0-87722-301-7

to my mother and father

Contents

Preface

Dozens of books and literally thousands of newspaper and magazine articles have chronicled the stormy career of the House Committee on Un-American Activities (HUAC). One Committee alumnus, after all, rode the Communist issue, and in particular HUAC's investigation of former State Department official Alger Hiss, into national prominence eventually, some argue, into the Oval Office. Moreover, the current President of the United States, Ronald Reagan, once appeared before the Committee as a "friendly" witness. Indeed, HUAC had hunted Communists in and out of government long before Joseph R. McCarthy entered the chase in February 1950, and it continued to promote the red menace long after the Junior Senator from Wisconsin was forcibly retired. It was the Committee that policed the headline-grabbing Hollywood blacklists, not Senator McCarthy, whose contribution to the anticommunist political style to which others gave his name was more dramatic than innovative. This is not to minimize Senator McCarthy's contribution, only to place it in perspective. Quite simply, the fixation of historians and others on "Tailgunner Joe's" career and style has obscured our understanding of the nature of McCarthyism.

The same thing can be said for much of what has been written about the Committee on Un-American Activities. Both Senator McCarthy and HUAC belong on center stage, but they must share it with FBI Director J. Edgar Hoover and FBI Assistant Directors Louis B. Nichols and Cartha DeLoach. Never content to confine FBI investigations to bona fide Communist party members, Hoover, Nichols, DeLoach, and other senior Bureau officials sought to gain acceptance for their own political belief that radical political and economic reforms were "subversive," as were those who questioned the emerging anticommunist consensus and those who condemned the cultural pollution and blacklists of the so-called McCarthy era.

To explain the origins and resilience of the Cold War on the home front solely by reference to the actions and decisions of a single political elite, no matter how highly motivated and resourceful, would be naive. The FBI's impact, however, was considerable and, arguably, of more importance than the efforts of any other anticommunist interest group. FBI officials had their own vision of a better society, the will to make their vision a reality, and the resources to challenge traditional American values in virtually every home in the nation. The Bureau, after all, not only underwrote much of HUAC's politics of exposure but also supported the similar efforts of Senator McCarthy and many of the era's most influential newspaper columnists. One thing is certain. Had former FBI Director Hoover and his top public relations specialists, FBI Assistant Directors Nichols and DeLoach, been content with mere bureaucratic empire building, the political phenomenon known as McCarthyism would have been far different and far less capable of proscribing debate and limiting national options than it was.

Though this study attempts to describe FBI officials' role in the evolution of the anticommunist or McCarthyite political style, my original purpose was to write exclusively about the FBI's relationship with the Committee on Un-American Activities. But for various reasons, this book does more—and less—than that.

First of all, my Freedom of Information Act (FOIA) request (dated March 15, 1978) for the FBI's voluminous file on the Committee remains open. To date, I have received thousands of documents from this file, but the FBI continues to withhold others on "national security" grounds. Second, a full understanding of the shadowy FBI-HUAC relationship requires complete access not only to the HUAC file, but to the files of those FBI informers who appeared before the Committee and, as well, the individual case files of those who were named Communists, fellow travelers, Stalinist stooges, or whatever. Informant files, however, are generally inaccessible under the FOIA, and the Bureau's files on individual HUAC witnesses would no doubt total more than one million—perhaps several million—pages. According to one estimate, the FBI currently produces 400,000 documents daily and presides over some 500,000 individual case files. No matter how revealing, the FBI's file on the Committee might only constitute the tip of the proverbial iceberg, since Bureau leaks to HUAC were frequently recorded only in informant or individual case files. Third, the documentary trail of the covert FBI-HUAC relationship is strewn with fraudulent denials, phony paper records, and—something Lewis Carroll would have loved—"Do Not File" files.

It is not my intention to make excuses for any shortcomings in this study. Rather, my purpose is to point out that the political activities of FBI officials were probably much more pervasive than is generally known and that historians still have a great deal to examine. The history of the Cold War and McCarthyism, let alone the history of the Un-American Activities Committee, needs to be rewritten.

The following is an attempt to start in the right direction. To those who encouraged and supported my effort, I wish to express my appreciation. I particularly want to thank Marquette University for providing me with the time to write and the financial support, primarily through the Cyril Smith Research Scholarship Fund, to pursue my topic in nearly two dozen archives. The Herbert Hoover Presidential Library Association, the Eleanor Roosevelt Institute of the Franklin D. Roosevelt Library, the Harry S Truman Library Institute, and the Lyndon Baines Johnson Foundation also provided generous grants. For research assistance I am in debt to the archivists, too numerous to mention by name, at the twenty libraries and research institutions I visited. Charles Elston of the Marquette University Archives, Sandra Raub of the Franklin D. Roosevelt Library, Dennis Bilger of the Harry S. Truman Library, Stanley Mallach of the University of Wisconsin–Milwaukee Area Research Center, and Pearl Hefte of the Karl E. Mundt Library were particularly helpful. I should also acknowledge the assistance of R. Lawrence Angove, executive director of the Hoover Library Association, William R. Emerson, secretary of the Roosevelt Institute, Benedict K. Zobrist, director of the Truman Library, John E. Wickman, director of the Dwight D. Eisenhower Library, and Martin I. Elzy of the Johnson Library.

William Adams, George Corsetti, Alan McSurely, John T. Elliff, Douglass Cassel, Frank Wilkinson, Richard Criley, Richard Gutman, Robert F. Drinan, S.J., Henry S. Reuss, Frank J. Donner, Kenneth Waltzer, George Reedy, and Percival Bailey all shared their insights into FBI activities in Cold War America and helped me solve several research problems. Nancy Kramer, executive director of the Committee for Public Justice, Frank Wilkinson of the National Committee Against Repressive Legislation, and the board of the Chicago Committee to Defend the Bill of Rights granted me access to the FBI's files on their respective organizations. I reviewed other FBI files with the permission of Curtis D. MacDougall, Thomas I. Emerson, Milton Cohen, David R. Luce, Richard Criley, and Quentin Young.

The Freedom of Information Act is a valuable tool. But beyond delays, bureaucratic cover-ups, and the frustrating, capricious deletions made by magic-marker-wielding censors, it has an additional drawback—namely, cost. The FBI charges ten cents per page for documents released under FOIA and demands money up front and a written commitment to assume the burden of full payment. For a large file, such as the Bureau's HUAC file, these costs can be prohibitive. Without the aid of David R. Luce, Richard Criley, Rachel Rosen DeGolia, and John Henry Faulk I could not have raised the needed funds. The following people also made generous contributions: Mr. and Mrs. James Shellow, William O. Brown, Walter and Bette Johnson, Jan Kinnaman, John Corcoran, W. H. Ferry, Robert Havighurst, Peter and Rachel Rosen De-Golia, Quentin Young, Webster Woodmansee, Jan and Richard Criley, Stanford Luce, Boris Brail, Lambert King, Sidney Peck, Elizabeth Balanoff, J. R. Parten, Edward Blackorby, Bobette and Jack Zacharias, Daniel Peisch, and Leonard Sorkin.

I would also like to acknowledge Athan Theoharis, Robert P. Hay, Francis Paul Prucha, S.J., Karel D. Bicha, and William D. Miller of Marquette University, Michael Ames and Zachary Simpson of Temple University Press, and Kenneth Arnold for the long hours they spent with earlier drafts of this book. Their comments have greatly improved my work, both in content and in style. I owe the greatest debt to my dissertation director, Professor Theoharis, who planted the seed that led to this study and was always available and willing to talk and to share the fruits of his own research.

Portions of chapters I and II were published in the *Journal of American History* (December 1982) as "A New Deal for the FBI: The Roosevelt Administration, Crime Control, and National Security," and in *Congress and the Presidency* (Spring 1983) as "The Roosevelt Administration and Legislative-Executive Conflict: The FBI vs. the Dies Committee." Chapters III and IV include material from "The FBI and the Origins of McCarthyism," *The Historian* (May 1983). And chapter X is based on a short article, "Artful Dissemination: The F.B.I.—HUAC's Big Brother," that originally appeared in *The Nation* (January 19, 1980). I am grateful to the editors of these journals for permission to draw upon these articles.

Finally, I would like to thank, for their patience, my wife Maureen, who read every word in this book at least twice, and my son Eamon, who, upon discovering the FBI files I kept bringing home with me at night, instinctively reached for his crayons.

HOOVER AND THE
UN-AMERICANS

The FBI, HUAC, and the Red Menace

Introduction

Knowledge, as the old saying goes, is power. But if this political adage was true even in the days of Thomas Jefferson, not until the twentieth century would political elites institutionalize information gathering or intelligence functions by first creating mammoth bureaucracies, then charging them with a multitude of open-ended missions ranging from surveillance to covert action (whether to overthrow unfriendly governments abroad or to neutralize dissent at home), and last insulating them from external scrutiny.

Responsible elected officials, in turn, relied increasingly on faceless intelligence agency bureaucrats for information when making decisions. In theory, this reliance seemed rational to twentieth-century Americans grown accustomed to the less democratic, deferential politics of a complex technological society. It was also appealing to ambitious leaders as diverse as Franklin D. Roosevelt and Dwight D. Eisenhower, both of whom were sometimes impatient with public debate and other perceived inefficiencies of the democratic system. In reality, things did not work out as planned. Never content merely to gather information and to present "facts" to elected officials, intelligence bureaucrats very often used their agencies' resources to further their own political objectives regardless of the announced priorities of whoever happened to occupy the White House.

The intelligence community's well-publicized mission to protect the national security has been of only secondary importance for much of the recent past. The Central Intelligence Agency and Army Intelligence, among others, have

3

sometimes been more concerned with educating Americans for life in the Cold War. In 1958, for instance, a National Security Council directive, intended to propagandize the dangers of subversion rather than the threat of Soviet military power or the geopolitical struggle between two rival empires, enlisted the resources of the U. S. Army "to arouse the public to the menace of Communism." While Army G-2 intelligence operatives compiled dossiers on critics of the program and investigated speakers to insure "quality control," the Army sponsored a series of seminars across the country that featured such right-wing publicists as Dr. Fred C. Schwarz of the Christian Anti-Communist Crusade and Birch Society advocate E. Merrill Root, author of *Collectivism on the Campus*.[1] Similarly, the CIA produced, subsidized, or sponsored well over 1,000 books as part of what the Senate Select Committee to Study Intelligence Activities characterized in 1976 as "an attempt to lay an intellectual foundation for anti-communism around the world."[2]

In fact, the intelligence community devoted a good portion of its resources to subverting traditional American values, literally "targeting" (in the jargon of the community) dissident activists and not simply spies and saboteurs. A classified report of a special committee, chaired by celebrated World War II General James Doolittle, who was appointed in 1954 by President Eisenhower to study CIA covert activities, sums up this mentality:

> It is now clear that we are facing an implacable enemy whose avowed objective is world domination by whatever means and at whatever cost. There are no rules in such a game. Hitherto acceptable norms of human conduct do not apply. If the United States is to survive, long-standing American concepts of "fair play" must be reconsidered. . . . We must learn to subvert sabotage and destroy our enemies by more clever, more sophisticated and more effective methods than those used against us. It may become necessary that the American people be made acquainted with, understand and support this fundamentally repugnant philosophy.[3]

Intelligence agency bureaucrats were fully cognizant of an immediate political problem: for their own political objectives to be facilitated, both public opinion and the priorities of official Washington had to move right. Not surprisingly (as the CIA was not established until 1947), the first intelligence agency bureaucrats to realize this need and to further the process were Army officers and, more importantly, officials of the Federal Bureau of Investigation. Intermittently between World War I and the onset of the Cold War, and more systematically thereafter until the early 1970s, FBI officials consciously promoted the fear of a Communist menace to (1) convince the American people that domestic Communists and other dissidents posed a serious threat to the national security and (2) influence the national political debate on the Communist issue.

Prior to the Cold War, FBI efforts were restrained and had limited success. Nonetheless, the Bureau's domestic intelligence activities expanded with the help of a liberal Democratic President, Franklin D. Roosevelt, and a formidable public relations machine capable of promoting the FBI's apolitical image and of assuming more ambitious (what FBI officials called "educational") tasks. In February 1946, with the Cold War only in its embryonic stage, the Bureau launched a program intended to publicize the dangers of Communist subversion and to undermine traditional liberal tolerance of radical dissent. Ten years later, the FBI initiated another even more pervasive program—the first of the counterintelligence programs—and in 1958 began cooperating with the U.S. Army educational program.

All this does not imply a "conspiracy" theory of history. J. Edgar Hoover and his top aides primarily acted not as conspirators but as skillful bureaucrats equipped with the patience and resources needed to build an independent constituency, a shrewd understanding of the decision-making process, and a cool contempt for constitutional, moral, or legal restraints. The suggestion that FBI officials' intentions transcended bureaucratic self-interest and that the FBI was to some extent successful in shaping values and dictating national priorities may sound even more conspiracy-oriented, particularly to those who see American democracy as representative. In any event, the FBI hierarchy had little use for the pluralist myth. Rival interest groups were not to be bargained

5

with but to be destroyed, if possible, or crippled and then banished as pariah groups that supposedly represented the interests of Moscow and not the legitimate interests of a segment of the American people. The man in the street was not to be heard from but to be manipulated by a media program that probably made the Bureau the biggest "advertiser" in the nation. The FBI, however, was not selling soap. It was selling its own brand of anticommunisn. And if FBI officials spent millions of tax dollars each year to circulate their message, they did not have to buy time on Paul Harvey's radio show or space in the columns of Fulton Lewis, Jr. Such services, including the ostensibly independent editorial blessings of media allies like Harvey and Lewis, were free.

FBI officials' political activities had a considerable influence on American society during the Cold War years, but not simply because the global confrontation between the United States and the Soviet Union provided a context in which the Bureau's political objectives could develop and flourish. Many Americans had associated closely with Communist party (CPUSA) members and Communist fronts during the popular front era of the 1930s. And the CPUSA, with its wooden rhetoric (American Communist Israel Amter once opened a New York meeting with the words "Workers and Peasants of Brooklyn . . .") and tireless defense of Soviet imperialism, was vulnerable. FBI officials had nonetheless concluded that the Cold War rivalry would not inevitably lead to a McCarthyite politics with a narrow focus on dissident associations rather than on issues. This focus attributed such complex foreign policy failures as the "loss" of China or the "sell out" of Eastern Europe at the Yalta summit conference of 1945 to a domestic conspiracy rather than the limits of America's power.[4]

Instead, FBI officials reasoned, they would have to cultivate a McCarthyite politics on the home front. Thus their February 1946 decision was to (1) aid those who hunted subversives in and out of government, (2) hound the hunted as well as those who questioned the emerging McCarthyite politics, and (3) influence the debate within the liberal community between "First Amendment extremists" and Cold War liberals who believed Communist party members were not entitled to traditional constitutional protections. With or without the FBI, the Cold War would have developed. Its domestic fallout, however, would have been far different if FBI officials had not worked to nurture an anticommunist consensus by underwriting such McCarthyites as the junior Senator from Wisconsin and HUAC—a Committee that radical journalist I. F. Stone condemned in 1947 as "the John the Baptist of American fascism."[5]

If Stone erred, he was not far from the truth. HUAC very often spoke for others, and particularly for FBI officials eager to exploit its public forum. The Committee captured newspaper headlines and promulgated antiradical fears by transforming (or laundering) classified information from the Bureau's confidential files into widely disseminated "public source" information, without compromising the FBI's image of a disinterested, nonpartisan, investigative agency. Organized as a Special Committee to Investigate Un-American Activities in 1938 and chaired by a conservative Texas Democrat, Martin Dies, HUAC became a standing committee of the House in 1945 and was only abolished formally, under an altered name, in January 1975. During the dog days of the Cold War, the Committee specialized in blacklists and what *Nation* editor Victor S. Navasky called "degradation ceremonies." Those who were summoned faced the choice of informing, joining the ranks of the "Fifth Amendment Communists," or imprisonment. The Committee's spectacular hearings—notably its investigations of communism in Hollywood and of former State Department official Alger Hiss—brought the red menace to the attention of millions.

Whether relying on information supplied directly by the FBI or on the testimony of FBI informers, HUAC's mission remained remarkably consistent. The purpose of the Committee and its constituency, chiefly conservative journalists and other publicists, was not to investigate subversive activities but to disseminate information already known to the FBI. As HUAC member Karl E. Mundt (R., S. D.), a frequent recipient of Bureau leaks, said in 1946, "the extreme privilege of free press and free speech" would not stop the Committee from exposing those "engaged in actions which are un-American

7

even though their activities are legal." Echoing these sentiments the next year, FBI Director J. Edgar Hoover commended this politics of exposure: "Committees of Congress have served a very useful purpose in exposing some of these activities which no Federal agency is in a position to do, because the information we obtain in the Bureau is either for intelligence purposes or for use in prosecution, and committees of Congress have wider latitude in that respect."[6]

HUAC's personnel also lent some credence to Stone's characterization. The Committee provided a home for John ("Lightnin'") Rankin, a Mississippi Democrat and an explicit anti-Semite who in 1945 promised that HUAC would serve as a "grand jury." Two other HUAC members, Kit Clardy (R., Mich.) and Donald L. Jackson (R., Cal.), were troubled by the activities of "professional Negroes" and later joined the John Birch Society. J. Parnell Thomas (R., N. J.), who came into the world with the politically disadvantageous name of John Patrick Feeney and yet loved to rail at Communist party functionaries' frequent use of aliases, ran a kickback and payroll–padding operation on the side. In 1949, Thomas was tried and convicted on a charge of defrauding the government. Staff director Richard Arens also operated as a paid consultant for New York millionaire Wycliff Draper on a project to prove that blacks were genetically inferior.[7] Forced to resign from the Committee's staff in September 1960, Arens became a commissioner of the United States Court of Claims.

Other controversial persons associated with the Committee were chief investigator Louis Russell and Richard Roudebush (R., Ind.), whose bid in 1970 for Vance Hartke's Senate seat included a variety of Watergate-style dirty tricks. (Among other operations, a microphone was planted in Hartke's conference room with the receiver and recorder tucked safely away in the office of a Roudebush campaign official at the Indianapolis Republican State headquarters.) Russell, a ten-year FBI veteran who joined HUAC's staff in May 1945, lost his job as chief investigator in January 1954—but not for spying—although he did—on elected HUAC members and secretly forwarding executive session minutes to his former colleagues at the Bureau. Russell was fired because he borrowed $300 from a HUAC witness, actor Edward G. Robinson. He was then hired by another ex-FBI agent, Robert Aime Maheu, a high-profile "clandestine celebrity." Later, Russell went to work for James McCord's investigative service and then on to the General Security Services Company, whose responsibilities included security at the Watergate apartment complex. Russell was also allegedly involved in Republican National Committee investigations and, according to one unnamed source, present at the command post in the Howard Johnson motel at the time of the Watergate burglary. He died a few months after the break-in, and his pallbearers included CREEP (Committee for the Re-Election of the President) security chief McCord and another high-powered private sector "spook," Ken Smith, chief investigator for Bernard Fensterwald's Committee to Investigate Assassinations.[8]

A year earlier, in the summer of 1971, the special White House investigative unit known as the Plumbers had solicited the assistance of HUAC's successor, the House Internal Security Committee. On June 13 the *New York Times* began publishing the Pentagon Papers, the classified history of the Vietnam war, leaked by Daniel Ellsberg. President Nixon reacted by forming the Plumbers, placing John Ehrlichman in charge, and directing them to discredit Ellsberg by linking him to a New Left-Communist conspiracy. For the always-embattled Nixon, there was a sense of *déjà vu*. "I went through all this on the Hiss case and we won that," the President said when he and Ehrlichman developed a strategy to smear Ellsberg. This crisis, too, could be "won in the press" if "[we] mobilize our friends" and "leak stuff out." Reflecting on the Hiss investigation (as a freshman congressman he had worked closely and secretly with FBI Assistant Director Louis B. Nichols), Nixon realized he would again "need Hoover's cooperation" so that Ellsberg, like Hiss, could "be tried in the papers" and convicted "before a committee."

To accomplish this, "the stuff" uncovered by the FBI and the Plumbers linking Ellsberg to a "conspiracy" or revealing "domestic communist ties" would be passed on to the House Internal Security Committee. "Can [HISC Chairman Richard H.] Ichord [D., Mo.] do it?", Nixon wanted to know. Can we "call people before it," "make up a list," have "our men push HUAC and the bureaucracy"? Nixon seemed to think so. It had, after all, worked once before. And, as the President noted, the "FBI [was] going all out now." (In late June, for instance, Thomas E. Bishop, FBI Assistant Director for Crime Records, leaked derogatory information on Ellsberg's attorney, Leonard B. Boudin, to the Washington bureau chief of the Copley News Service. At Hoover's direction, Bishop then sent a copy of the resultant article by Ray McHugh to H. R. Haldeman and John Mitchell.) Ehrlichman directed Charles Colson, the master Plumber, to work up a "game plan."[9]

Colson worked through HISC staff member Bill Hecht, "a Republican hard-liner" who was "very close to Ichord." In a July 14 memorandum to Ehrlichman, Colson recommended that Hecht "act as the principal coordinator from the Hill end in the Ellsberg operation," the "contact through whom [E. Howard] Hunt," the ex-CIA man then working with the Agency on Operation Ellsberg, "would feed material and in turn . . . see that Ichord, [HISC member] Fletcher Thompson [R., Geo.] and others used it properly."

At the time, however, Ichord was thinking of running for Governor of Missouri and was reluctant to launch a sensational series of hearings, having concluded that it might cost him dearly in the Democratic primary. On the other hand, according to Hecht, "Ichord is first and foremost a patriot and . . . if the President personally were to tell Ichord that this was a matter 'important to the national security' Ichord would order the hearings immediately." The President, Colson cautioned, should not "make the call unless he could cover it in such terms that it would never come back to haunt him. Secondly, we must be certain that we have a very good case to give Ichord" or "the whole exercise could backfire." Attorney General Mitchell, moreover, did not consider the HISC chairman to be very reliable. He recommended working through House Armed Services Committee Chairman F. Edward Hébert (D., La.), a former HUAC member, or James Eastland (D., Miss.) and the Senate Internal Security Subcommittee.

Though insistent ("we'll not deny Ichord the stuff") and

willing to "get Eastland in too," Nixon, for whatever reasons, did not make the necessary phone call to Ichord. The HISC hearings were never held.[10] Instead, as Colson had predicted, the Plumbers' not-very-discreet search-and-destroy operation eventually came unglued. The formal prosecution of Ellsberg collapsed during the 1973 trial in Los Angeles after the government admitted that the White House had burglarized the offices of Ellsberg's psychiatrist, Dr. Lewis Fielding, and, further, that Ellsberg had been overheard on an illegal FBI wiretap. The integrity of the trial judge, W. Matt Byrne, Jr., was also compromised. Byrne had met secretly with Nixon and Ehrlichman in San Clemente (and again with Ehrlichman in a Santa Monica park), while the Pentagon Papers trial was in progress to discuss his possible appointment to the directorship of the FBI.

It was fitting, then, that the Watergate scandal ultimately embraced the Committee on Un-American Activities along with its most distinguished alumnus, Richard M. Nixon, who indirectly contributed to the House's decision of January 1975 to abolish HUAC's successor. Because of Watergate it was possible for the first time to write about the FBI's efforts to influence national politics and to shape public opinion through collaboration with the Committee and its constituency.[11] The scandal demonstrated that executive privilege claims were often intended to cover up embarrassing or illegal political activities rather than to prevent the release of information (to Congress, the courts, or the public) that could be damaging to the national security.

Watergate led Congress in 1974 to pass extensive amendments to the Freedom of Information Act (FOIA) of 1966. These amendments, for the first time, allowed scholars and others to request the release of intelligence agency files.[12] In the good old days, of course, it had been the Right (whose political descendants now want to gut the FOIA) who demanded access to intelligence agency files. They were convinced that these files would reveal either the incompetence of the Roosevelt and Truman administrations when confronting the domestic Communist threat or their complicity in an international

Communist conspiracy. McCarthyites claimed that loyalty files were withheld from Congress because the Democrats were engaged in a cover-up. Ironically, they were dead wrong about the reasons for the cover-up but, as Watergate demonstrated two decades later, they were right about the general issue—specifically, the inherent danger for a democratic society in accepting sweeping claims of executive privilege.

Watergate led a skeptical Congress to launch a series of investigative hearings into intelligence community affairs. The reports of the Senate Select Committee to Study Intelligence Activities—the so-called Church Committee—publicly disclosed the common thread of intelligence agencies' reliance on bugs, taps, break-ins, and mail openings and thus revealed that the adventures of Richard Nixon's Plumbers were not atypical. Aided by the FOIA amendments, the Church Committee exposé shattered the "national security game" and besmirched, as one neoconservative commentator recently said of Senator Joseph R. McCarthy, "the good name of anti-Communism."[13]

CHAPTER I

Federal Surveillance
and the Menace, 1919–1940

Both Congress and the Bureau of Investigation (renamed the Federal Bureau of Investigation in 1935) had investigated subversive activities long before the House of Representatives established a Special Committee to Investigate Un-American Activities in May 1938. Prior to that time, however, Congress had been reluctant to probe the affairs of Communists and other dissidents on a full-time basis. This congressional ambivalence was not shared by Bureau of Investigation officials, who curtailed their domestic intelligence investigations only after the Teapot Dome scandals compromised some of their most explicitly political activities. Thereafter, Bureau officials' urge to plunge headlong into the nether world of "un-American" activities was counterbalanced only by J. Edgar Hoover's conviction that the overt resumption of pervasive undercover activities could lead "to charges . . . of alleged secret and undesirable methods."

Concerned exclusively with possible criticism of the Bureau, Hoover never questioned the need "to secure a foothold in Communistic inner circles" in order to become "fully informed as to the changing policies and secret propaganda on the part of Communists."[1] Thus, when the Dies Committee began holding hearings in August 1938, the FBI once again geared up its surveillance machinery and began seeking suitable outlets to disseminate whatever political information it acquired through its domestic intelligence investigations.

The Dies Committee ultimately made the investigation of "un-American" activities a function of the House of Representatives for nearly forty years. Prior to 1938 congressional interest had been sporadic. During hearings held by a Senate subcommittee chaired by Lee S. Overman (D., N.C.) in January 1919, former Bureau of Investigation agent Archibald E. Stevenson challenged the loyalty of *Nation* editor Oswald Garrison Villard, historian Charles Beard, social workers Jane Addams and Lillian D. Wald, and many other prominent Americans. Bureau Director A. Bruce Bielaski also accused civil libertarian Roger Baldwin of being "actively disloyal."[2] Despite these sensational charges and mounting postwar antiradicalism, Congress soon lost interest in the Overman Committee's hearings. The Senate's later request that the Attorney General, A. Mitchell Palmer, report on Department of Justice efforts to suppress subversive activities suggested congressional deference to the executive during the nation's first major red scare.[3]

Another brief investigative excursion occurred in 1923 when a subcommittee of the Senate Foreign Relations Committee held hearings on whether the United States should recognize the six-year-old Soviet government. During these hearings, J. Edgar Hoover discovered his considerable talent for influencing national politics. The future FBI Director, then head of the Bureau radical squad, appeared at the witness table alongside the Secretary of State, Charles Evans Hughes, who successfully argued against recognition by highlighting the connection between native Communists and Soviet revolutionaries. Hughes's eloquent arguments were based on a report on Bolshevik tactics prepared by Hoover's General Intelligence Division (GID).[4]

Thereafter, Congress temporarily lost interest in subversive activities. The Senate ordered the printing of a United Mine Workers pamphlet charging a Communist conspiracy to seize the American labor movement in order to give its ideas wider currency, but the fate of a 1927 House joint resolution calling for a probe of native Bolsheviks better indicated congressional inattentiveness during the 1920s. Referred to the Committee on Rules, this resolution was never reported out.[5] Congressional interest revived in May 1930 following publicity generated by a series of documents connecting the Soviet Union's purchasing agent in the United States, the New York City–based Amtorg Trading Corporation, with the dissemination of Bolshevik propaganda.

Grover Whalen, then police commissioner of New York, first produced these seemingly incriminating documents during his executive session testimony before the House Committee on Immigration. Though Congressman Fiorello La Guardia (Republican-Progressive, N.Y.) later proved Whalen's documents were forged (a fact unknown to the police commissioner at the time), the allegations against Amtorg, combined with an ongoing Bureau of Investigation lobbying effort, prompted the House Rules Committee to authorize an investigation of bolshevism. Despite objections from La Guardia and other congressmen who predicted that the proposed probe would lead to "witch hunting," the House established a Special Committee to Investigate Communist Activities by a lopsided vote of 210 to 18. Hamilton Fish, a New York Republican who proposed to relieve the nation's crushing unemployment problem by deporting "every single alien Communist," was named Committee chairman.[6]

The so-called Fish Committee heard testimony from a leading Communist party functionary, William Z. Foster, but devoted most of its time to the alarmist rhetoric of such committed anticommunists as Father Edmund Walsh of Georgetown University, AFL President William Green, *National Republic* editor Walter Steele, and the head of the Daughters of the American Revolution (DAR), Mrs. Sherman Walter, as well as dozens of policemen from state and local red squads. One policeman, William F. Hynes of Los Angeles, inserted 1,514 pages of documentary evidence into the record. J. Edgar Hoover, appearing in closed session, affirmed the subservience of American Communists to the Soviet Union and urged the Fish Committee to recommend legislation proscribing radical propaganda. Such testimony prompted the Fish Committee to recommend legislation to deny Communists use of the mails and to create a special division within the Bureau of Investigation (the GID had been abolished in 1924) to investigate "revolutionary activity."[7]

None of the Fish Committee's proposals were enacted. Even Hoover opposed the recommendation that Congress grant the Bureau of Investigation formal authority to investigate subversive activities. Instead, he announced his desire to restrict the Bureau's investigative authority to criminal investigations, again advising Fish that "it would be better to make it a crime to participate in such activities."[8]

When Congress next assumed the burden of probing subversive activities, Communists and other left-of-center dissidents shared the limelight. In January 1934, Representative Samuel Dickstein (D., N.Y.) offered a resolution to investigate "Nazi propaganda" and all other "subversive propaganda that . . . attacks the principle of the form of government as guaranteed by the constitution." Members of the House voted 168 to 31 in favor of Dickstein's resolution and appropriated $10,000 for a Special Committee to Investigate Un-American Activities. They approved an additional $25,000 after Chairman-designate John McCormack (D., Mass.) noted Hoover's contention that more money would be needed to conduct even a preliminary probe.[9] The McCormack-Dickstein Committee then held hearings and issued its report in February 1935. And despite Hoover's tacit approval, the Committee apparently labored without Bureau assistance.[10]

Of the McCormack-Dickstein Committee's numerous legislative recommendations, two were eventually enacted. One required the registration of foreign agents distributing propaganda in the United States. The other extended congressional subpoena power to committee hearings outside the District of Columbia. The McCormack-Dickstein Committee also created a precedent by presenting Congress with a list of organizations that the Committee deemed subversive, without granting the pariah groups a hearing or the chance for rebuttal.

Unlike Congress, the Bureau of Investigation was not reluctant to devote substantial resources to the investigation of American dissidents. Formed in 1908 by Attorney General Charles J. Bonaparte, a grandnephew of Napoleon I, the Bureau had few investigative duties until the advent of World War I. An undisciplined, somewhat ineffectual, highly politicized organization during the war, the undermanned Bureau cooperated with the American Protective League (APL) and other private vigilante organizations when pursuing people suspected of disloyalty. Bureau-orchestrated slacker raids, for instance, led to the wholesale arrests of alleged draft dodgers by quasi-official APL volunteers scarcely concerned with such constitutional niceties as due process.[11] Following the formation of the special GID antiradical component on April 1, 1919, Bureau agents were directed to gather all possible information regarding sedition—specifically "evidence which may be of use in prosecutions . . . under legislation . . . which may hereafter be enacted." Reflecting these priorities, the GID concentrated on Communists and Socialists and within two-and-one-half years held files on some 450,000 persons.[12]

Domestic intelligence investigations continued unchecked into the early 1920s. Under William J. Burns, the former head of the Burns Detective Agency, the Bureau's announced mission was to "drive every radical out of the country and bring the parlor Bolsheviks to their senses." Predictably, then, Bureau surveillance extended to such nonradical groups as the National Association for the Advancement of Colored People (NAACP) and the American Civil Liberties Union (ACLU). Dossiers were also compiled on prominent individuals, including Felix Frankfurter, Zechariah Chafee, Jr., Frank Walsh, Roscoe Pound, and House Rules Committee Chairman Philip Campbell (R., Kans.). One Bureau report of May 1920 described Frankfurter as a member of the "Jewish element furnishing the brains for the radicals."

17

More importantly, Bureau officials routinely shared information from these investigations with conservative politicians and such private sector countersubversives as R. M. Whitney of the American Defense Society and Ralph Easley of the National Civic Federation.[13]

The Bureau's extensive political spying and crude attempts to shape public opinion finally came under close scrutiny during congressional investigations of the Harding Administration. The Teapot Dome scandal critically damaged the credibility of federal red-hunters when it engulfed President Harding's Attorney General, Harry M. Daugherty. Forced to resign in 1924 by a coalition of senators led by Burton K. Wheeler (D., Mont.), Daugherty retaliated by labeling Wheeler "no more a Democrat than Stalin, his comrade in Moscow." Caught in the middle, Bureau officials moved against their critics by wiretapping their telephones and breaking into their offices. Among other operations, Bureau agents attempted, unsuccessfully, to discredit Wheeler by luring him into a compromising situation with a young woman in a hotel room.[14]

These and other questionable activities led to executive reform. As a first step, in March 1924 President Coolidge appointed Harlan F. Stone, a former Columbia Law School dean, to replace Daugherty. Stone, in turn, fired Burns and appointed J. Edgar Hoover acting director of the Bureau of Investigation. Henceforth the Bureau would "be strictly limited to" investigating violations of federal statutes. To prevent future abuses, Stone then announced a series of reforms which prohibited wiretaps, dissolved the GID, ended Bureau ties with private detective agencies, and forbade dissemination of antiradical propaganda. Significantly, both the House and the Senate failed to act on pending bills that called for legal rather than voluntary constraints.[15]

Despite Stone's restrictions and later FBI assurances, the Bureau continued to collect political intelligence after 1924. Bureau agents, for example, spied on the ACLU throughout the 1920s by placing its meetings under surveillance and by monitoring bank deposits. In September 1924, one month before Stone made Hoover's appointment permanent, the

Bureau's Los Angeles office reported on an organization seeking employment for blacklisted radicals. The Bureau also received information on dissident activities from Captain Hynes of the Los Angeles Police Department, one of Hoover's informal contacts, and continued surveillance of the defense committee set up to aid jailed labor radicals Tom Mooney and Warren K. Billings.[16]

Moreover, Bureau officials began to service White House requests for political information during Herbert Hoover's presidency. A few of these requests were channeled through the Justice Department, but for the most part the Bureau Director had direct contact with senior White House aides— including presidential secretary Walter Newton, press secretary Theodore Joslin, and President Hoover's personal secretary, Lawrence Richey.[17]

Assistance to the Hoover White House began in November 1929 when the President received a letter from Alexander Lincoln, a Republican, prominent Boston attorney, and president of the Sentinels of the Republic. Founded during the postwar red scare and composed mainly of wealthy patriots, the Sentinels were dedicated to opposing the spread of radicalism and the increasing centralization of power in the federal government. Lincoln and other members of the Sentinels' executive committee were troubled by President Hoover's recent appointment of a Child Health Commission mandated "to investigate matters outside of the jurisdiction of the Federal Government." Richey responded by requesting that the Bureau compile a report on the Sentinels, and two agents of the Bureau's Washington, D.C., office were assigned to the investigation.[18]

Thereafter, White House aides Newton, Joslin, and Richey routinely solicited Bureau reports on groups and individuals who wrote letters to the President. The Hoover White House received dossiers on liberal organizations (the ACLU, the NAACP, and the Foreign Policy Association) as well as obscure far-right groups (the Federation of Lictor and the American Citizens Political Awakening Association).[19] On other occasions, Bureau dossiers were compiled at the direct request of businessmen and Republican party officials. On one occasion in October 1931, Joseph R. Nutt, chairman of the board of the Union Trust Company and treasurer of the Republican National Committee, wrote Joslin to complain about a newsletter being distributed by George Menhinick in Syracuse, New York. Aptly entitled *Wall Street Forecast* and based in large part on information culled from the *Wall Street Journal*, Menhinick's newsletter emphasized the dismal situation facing American bankers and investors. Describing the *Wall Street Forecast* as "the most vicious thing that has yet come to my notice," Nutt specifically requested that Menhinick be "reached." J. Edgar Hoover responded, when the Attorney General, William D. Mitchell, apprised him of Nutt's request, by dispatching five agents to Syracuse to investigate and perhaps intimidate Menhinick. Later an agent described him as "thoroughly scared" and not likely to "resume the dissemination of any information concerning the banks or other financial institutions."[20]

When responding to White House requests for domestic political intelligence reports and other forms of assistance, senior Bureau officials relied on a wide variety of investigative techniques. These included library research, pretext interviews, confidential access to the records of the Bureau of Internal Revenue, and quite possibly mail intercepts and break-ins. One investigation that probably included illegal techniques involved the Navy League of the United States, a civilian lobby seeking an increase in defense appropriations. League activists, a predictable mixture of superpatriots, former Navy officers, and businessmen from the ship building, munitions, and armor plate industries, were persistent critics of President Hoover's naval arms limitation initiatives. The President responded to the "big Navy lobby" by directing the Bureau to investigate it. The White House was particularly interested in knowing the size of the League's membership, even though J. Edgar Hoover had advised Richey on October 30, 1931, that such "information is possessed by only a few persons and seems extremely difficult to obtain confidentially." Two days later, Bureau agents in New York City surmounted this problem by securing "confidential access" to an internal Navy League financial report listing the total number of dues-paying members. (The Bureau routinely disguised illegal investigative techniques by blandly referring to "highly confidential sources," "anonymous sources," and similar terms of art.)[21]

If more restrained than the earlier GID exploits, the Bureau of Investigation's covert political activities continued into the mid-1930s, since senior Bureau officials invariably serviced White House requests for political information (thus suggesting that the relationship between J. Edgar Hoover and Herbert Hoover had more to do with politics and power than personal loyalty). In 1933, for instance, the Bureau investigated a milk strike in New York City at the request of the Roosevelt administration. The next year, press secretary Stephen Early solicited Bureau reports on the ACLU and on the members of a committee to honor slain Chicago Mayor Anton Cermak, who had lost his life during the attempted assassination of President-elect Roosevelt.[22]

Bureau of Investigation officials, moreover, continued to investigate radical groups and individuals based on their *own* priorities. In 1933, the Bureau unilaterally decided to begin what became an eight-year investigation of a Writers' Union Group in Oklahoma after learning that the group had worked with a radical activist, "Mother" Ella Reeves Bloor, to instigate a farmers' march for a state mortgage moratorium. The Bureau also investigated CPUSA efforts in mid-1934 to provide legal assistance to the Scottsboro boys; monitored Congressman Jerry J. O'Connell's (D., Mont.) 1937 speech protesting the treatment of Tom Mooney at San Quentin prison; and opened a file in the 1930s on Arthur Goldberg, a future National Lawyers Guild activist and Supreme Court Justice.[23]

Thereafter, the Bureau's political activities accelerated when the Roosevelt administration offered the Bureau of Investigation an opportunity to legitimize its domestic intelligence operations. First, in early May 1934, FDR ordered the Bureau to investigate the Nazi movement in America.[24] Then, in August 1936, following a meeting between Hoover and Roosevelt at the White House, the President directed the FBI to develop more systematic intelligence about "subversive activities in the United States, particularly Fascism and Communism." Roosevelt, as Hoover later put it, wanted "a broad picture of the general movement and its activities as [these] may affect the economic and political life of the country as a whole."

In a limited sense, this aim was already established FBI practice, with Hoover reporting to Roosevelt in August 1936 on CPUSA efforts to infiltrate various executive departments and labor unions. The FBI Director, nonetheless, promptly expanded the Bureau's surveillance of dissidents. In a memorandum of September 5, in language strikingly similar to Hoover's 1919 directive requiring his GID agents to forward all information ("whether hearsay or otherwise") concerning radical activity, the FBI Director ordered all field offices

> to obtain from all possible sources information concerning subversive activities being conducted in the United States. . . . It is desired, accordingly, that you immediately transmit to the Bureau any information relating to subversive activities on the part of any individual or organization, regardless of the source from which this information is received.[25]

Whether or not Roosevelt would have approved this sweeping order, he was committed to using FBI resources for political as well as national security purposes. Two weeks after Hoover issued his directive, FDR asked Attorney General Homer Cummings to investigate the political strategy of the CPUSA presidential candidate, Earl Browder.[26]

Following Roosevelt's September 1939 directive instructing the FBI "to take charge of investigative work in matters relating to espionage, sabotage, and violations of the neutrality regulations" and to receive "any information obtained by" other law enforcement officials "relating to espionage, sabotage, subversive activities, and violations of neutrality laws," White House abuse of the FBI again escalated dramatically.[27] The scope of this abuse is suggested by an FBI memorandum forwarded to the White House in October 1940—a time when Martin Dies and other anti-New Deal conservatives were complaining of a serious sabotage threat and the inadequacy of the Bureau's counterespionage program. "Because of the FBI's friendly relationships over a period of many years with various banking establishments," the President learned,

> excellent cooperation is received from financial institutions. This monitoring program of course produces much valuable information not only from the standpoint of detecting espionage, sabotage and similar activities for which the funds may be used, but also develops data and information of interest to the Treasury Department in reaching administrative decisions with reference to desirable legislation, etc.[28]

FBI assistance was not limited to financial policy. Just as Herbert Hoover had relied on J. Edgar Hoover during his confrontation with the Navy League, Roosevelt also looked to the FBI Director for assistance in countering critics of his own defense policy. But where the pacifist Hoover had sought arms reduction, Roosevelt favored policies (such as the destroyer-bases deal with Great Britain) deemed too interventionist by a broad spectrum of influential public and congressional leaders.

On one occasion in the fall of 1941, FDR sought to counter the isolationist *Chicago Tribune* by directing the FBI to contact numerous small-town publishers and urge them to support Marshall Field's bid to secure an Associated Press franchise for his newly founded *Chicago Sun*.[29] More often, Roosevelt, like his predecessor, responded to criticism by investigating his critics. In May 1940, Stephen Early sent the FBI Director several lists of individuals and institutions who had sent messages to the White House criticizing Roosevelt's fireside chat on national defense. The next month, Early sent another list of people who had commended Charles Lindbergh's recent critique of the President's foreign policy. Hoover responded by returning reports on these critics—including a brief dossier on the City College of New York—to the White House. This promptness inspired FDR to direct White House aide Edwin

Watson to "prepare a nice letter to Edgar Hoover thanking him for all the reports on investigations he has made." The next year, the FBI serviced another White House request for information on people who had spoken out against the pending Lend-Lease Bill by launching a sweeping investigation which included wiretaps, bugs, and physical surveillance.[30]

Nor were members of Congress or the press immune. FBI reports to the White House on the America First Committee contained political intelligence on isolationist Senators Wheeler and Gerald P. Nye (R., N.D.).[31] In October and again in November 1940, the FBI advised the White House of telephone conversations (intercepted either by the Bureau or by Military Intelligence) between Mrs. Hamilton Fish and Elly Colonna, the wife of the Italian ambassador in Washington, regarding their mutual hatred of the New Deal. Another FBI report of August 1941, based on "a source close to Honorable Gerald P. Nye," highlighted the attitude of Senators Alva B. Adams (D., Col.) and Francis Maloney (D., Conn.) toward Lend-Lease, expected gasoline shortages, and a proposed Senate subcommittee investigation of cinema propaganda. In May 1940, after a San Francisco radio station repeated the Japanese claim that the native population in the East Indies would soon revolt against Dutch colonialism, Roosevelt ordered Hoover to make "a careful check . . . on the ownership and management of this Station." A few months later, the President requested a probe of left-wing journalist George Seldes and his publication, *In Fact*.[32]

The White House also initiated FBI investigations of businessmen and others who promoted "nationalism . . . over internationalism."[33] In July 1940, FDR even ordered the FBI to investigate former President Hoover and Lawrence Richey after receiving a tip from columnist Marquis Childs. Childs told the President that Hoover and Richey, when attending the recent Republican National Convention, had sent cablegrams to Vichy France in hope of provoking a statement from former Premier Pierre Laval that would indicate Roosevelt had already made "definite commitments" to send United States soldiers abroad. Assistant Secretary of State Adolf A. Berle, Jr., relayed FDR's request for an FBI check to Edward A.

Tamm, an FBI Assistant Director.[34] Thereafter, Hoover may have been kept under some type of surveillance. In February 1941 the FBI Director sent a report to the White House detailing the former President's luncheon conversation with the British ambassador, Lord Halifax, regarding Winston Churchill's opposition to Herbert Hoover's proposed plan to send food and supplies to unoccupied France. Ironically, Churchill was also the subject of a later FBI report, with the Bureau reporting to the White House on his drinking habits.[35]

Once the United States became involved in the war, critics of the Roosevelt administration were subjected to more intensive surveillance. The Justice Department made a content analysis of the Hearst press, the *New York Journal American*, the *New York Daily News*,[36] the *Chicago Tribune*, and Father Charles Coughlin's *Social Justice* to see if their editorial "lines" were similar, as British Intelligence claimed, to themes favored by Nazi radio.[37] Following the charge by *Hour* editor Albert E. Kahn that pro-Hitler propagandist George S. Viereck had worked closely with Senator Robert R. Reynolds (D., N.C.), Chairman of the Military Affairs Committee, prior to America's entry into the war, in May 1942 Roosevelt wrote Attorney General Francis Biddle:

> Please read this number of "THE HOUR" of May second and return for my files. I think very definitely that the F.B.I. can run down things like this. Senators and members of Congress are, of course, protected in a sense by the Constitution, but this must be strictly construed. There is absolutely no valid reason why any suspected subversive activities on their part should not be investigated by the Department of Justice or any other duly constituted agency.[38]

On the other side of the political spectrum, Roosevelt received unsolicited reports from the FBI Director on the alleged communist and leftist associations of Senators Elbert D. Thomas (D., Utah), Claude Pepper (D., Fla.), and James M. Mead (D., N.Y.), New York City Mayor Fiorello La Guardia, and Congressman Vito Marcantonio (American Labor, N.Y.).[39]

The Bureau's services, moreover, were used to prevent potentially embarrassing situations from getting out of hand

25

and to facilitate the implementation of administration policies.[40] The White House also received FBI reports on such topics as the attitude of CIO leaders John L. Lewis[41] and Sidney Hillman toward Roosevelt's decision to run for a third term; the political associations of former Attorney General Cummings; a proposed "March on Washington" by civil rights leader A. Philip Randolph; the political climate in Italian, Yugoslav, German, Polish, and Czech communities throughout the country; allegations that Thomas E. Dewey was not qualified to be president; and various Republican party strategies. In 1943, for instance, Hoover reported on the formation of the Chicago-based Polish-American Congress and its anticipated criticism of Roosevelt's policy toward Poland. According to the FBI's informant, the Republican party financed this new organization in the hope of swinging the Polish-American vote away from the Democrats.[42]

JOHN DILLINGER AND J. EDGAR HOOVER

Another legacy of the Roosevelt administration and its special relationship with the FBI was the development of a formidable public relations machinery within the Bureau. FDR and Attorney General Homer Cummings actively supported the Bureau's first major effort to mold public opinion as part of the administration's broader effort to extend federal jurisdiction in the area of crime control.[43] This effort ultimately transformed the Bureau from a relatively minor federal agency, staffed by only 266 special agents and 60 accountants when Roosevelt took office, into one of the most powerful and politically motivated federal bureaucracies.

The movement to nationalize crime control had its roots in the Progressive Era, with the formation of the Bureau of Investigation as the first national police force in 1908. At the time, however, the Bureau's criminal jurisdiction had been sharply limited. It was not until passage of the White Slave Traffic Act (also known as the Mann Act) in 1910 that Progressive Era legislators began to chip away at a states' rights tradition that confined law enforcement responsibilities to local and state police agencies. The Mann Act expanded the Bureau's jurisdiction by making it a federal crime to transport a woman across a state line for immoral purposes. Relying on the Constitution's interstate commerce clause, Progressive Era lawmakers had made prostitution, traditionally a local crime, a national one. By similar reasoning, the Dyer Act of 1919 forbade interstate transportation of a stolen motor vehicle.

During the New Era, Bureau scandals precluded further expansion of federal police power. But by October 10, 1924, after seven months service as Harlan F. Stone's reform candidate, Hoover had begun to weed out the political hacks and to upgrade the Bureau's seedy public image. Stone responded by making Hoover's appointment permanent. During Herbert Hoover's presidency, the Bureau assumed additional duties, including the gathering of uniform crime statistics and the compilation of a single, national fingerprint file. Though a states'-righter on crime, President Hoover appointed a Commission on Law Observance and Enforcement, chaired by former Attorney General George W. Wickersham, to make an exhaustive study of national crime. In the private sector, the National Crime Commission (NCC) called for an increased federal presence through a sophisticated and emotional public relations campaign. The NCC executive committee included conservative businessmen and a smattering of former public officials—including the Democratic party's recent vice-presidential candidate and soon-to-be-elected governor of New York, Franklin D. Roosevelt.

Though supported by some Progressives and hard-boiled conservatives, none of whom were squeamish about calling on the federal government to solve problems, the movement to federalize crime control still lacked popular support. Public sentiment swelled in 1932 following the kidnapping of Charles Augustus Lindbergh, Jr., the infant son of the aviation hero. The official response, in contrast, was relatively restrained. Congress passed two statutes extending federal criminal jurisdiction to kidnapping and to sending ransom demands through the mail (the so-called Lindbergh Law of 1932 and a companion act).

When FDR assumed the presidency, the FBI still suffered

lingering fallout from its indiscreet past and remained a relatively obscure division within the Justice Department. Therefore, it was widely believed that Roosevelt would fire that "soft-shoe relic of the A. Mitchell Palmer days," J. Edgar Hoover. The President's choice for Attorney General, Senator Thomas J. Walsh (D., Mont.), had led an investigation of corruption in the Harding administration's Justice Department. Walsh was also very close to the junior Senator from Montana, Burton K. Wheeler—yet another scourge of Teapot Dome. And when the Justice Department sought revenge against Wheeler in 1924, by indicting him in Montana on a bogus influence-peddling charge, Walsh served as defense counsel. During the trial the federal prosecutor filed nightly reports to Hoover at Bureau headquarters—a fact known to both Montana Senators. Wheeler was acquitted.[44]

The rumors regarding the Bureau Director's future continued even after Walsh died, a few days before FDR's inauguration, and after Roosevelt had nominated a Hoover partisan to serve as Attorney General. Later, Hoover met privately with Wheeler, attempting to convince him that he had only been following orders in 1924 and had no role in framing the Senator. "I didn't believe him," Wheeler later claimed, "but I decided not to block him . . . besides, I thought Farley's man would be no damn good, too political." Thereafter, and despite the Senator's tendency to continue criticizing Hoover, the Bureau treated Wheeler as an ally. Even after leaving the Senate in 1947 Wheeler was provided, upon request, with confidential data from FBI files.[45]

The man behind the alleged plot to get Hoover, Postmaster General James A. Farley, reportedly was tailed by Bureau agents and his phone tapped, à la Teapot Dome. Whether or not Farley intended to effect Hoover's retirement, the Bureau did investigate Val O'Farrell, the flamboyant head of a private detective agency in New York City, who was Farley's choice to head the Bureau of Investigation.

Though the rumor that the Bureau Director would be fired had little substance after Walsh's death, it was taken quite seriously by J. Edgar Hoover—and by Herbert Hoover, who put in a good word for his friend while riding with FDR from the inaugural ceremonies in 1933. Hoover had close allies in Roosevelt's innermost circle, including Watson and Early, and had the President's backing. On one occasion in April 1933, both FDR and Felix Frankfurter were concerned that Hoover was unhappy with the administration and would soon resign. Roosevelt checked the rumor with Hoover and Attorney General Cummings and then reported happily back to Frankfurter that the rumor was untrue.[46]

Roosevelt and Cummings had ambitious plans for Hoover and the Bureau. Even if Herbert Hoover had not mobilized public opinion for a war on crime following the Lindbergh kidnapping, Roosevelt would have, and he did exploit other sensational crimes in pursuit of specific legislative objectives. And the early New Deal years offered an abundance of grisly capers and colorful hoodlums: George "Machine Gun" Kelly, Bonnie Parker and Clyde Barrow, Charles "Pretty Boy" Floyd, Alvin "Old Creepy" Karpis, and Kate "Ma" Barker and her son Fred. They provided a hit parade of Public-Enemy-Number-One types from 1933 to 1935.

Gangsters of the 1930s were mobile, opportunistic, and itching for something to do. After the repeal of prohibition, they exploited the limited jurisdiction of local and state police by fleeing across city, county, and state lines after robbing banks and trains. The most colorful gangster of all, John Dillinger, robbed at least ten banks between May and October 1933. Following several spectacular jail breaks, where Dillinger and his confederates alternately rescued each other, the FBI was finally called in—but only because Dillinger had fled to Chicago in a stolen car after escaping from the "escape proof" Crown Point County Jail in Indiana.

Roosevelt responded to the wave of crimes on January 3, 1934, in his annual message to Congress, by identifying crime as a threat to "our security." "These . . . violations of ethics," Roosevelt added, "call on the strong arm of Government for their immediate suppression; they call also on the country for an aroused public opinion."[47] Cummings was even more explicit. "We are now engaged in a war that threatens the safety of our country," he announced to the DAR in a widely publicized speech, "a war with the organized forces of crime."

Then, at the height of the Dillinger investigation, Cummings issued a stark order to Bureau agents: "Shoot to kill—then count ten."[48]

In the supercharged anticrime climate, the Attorney General also succeeded in pushing the Roosevelt administration's crime control package through Congress. Only a few congressmen objected, complaining of yet another New Deal assault on states' rights.

In May 1934, Congress approved six bills requested by Cummings and drafted by the Justice Department without even taking a record vote. In June, three more bills passed giving Bureau agents full arrest power and the authority to carry any kind of firearm. More importantly, the Bureau's jurisdiction was radically expanded. The Fugitive Felon Act prohibited accused criminals from fleeing across state lines to avoid prosecution, and the Lindbergh Law was amended to allow the Bureau to become involved in kidnapping cases automatically after seven days—even without proof that the victim had been transported to another state. The Stolen Property Act extended provisions of the Dyer Act to include all stolen property valued at $5,000 or more, while the Anti-Racketeering Act made it a federal crime to extort money or other valuables by telephone or through the mails. An amendment to the federal bank robbery statute extended federal jurisdiction to any bank insured by the Federal Deposit Insurance Corporation. The National Firearms Act, which granted the Bureau secondary jurisdiction, provided for the collection of a federal tax on machine guns, silencers, sawed-off shotguns, and rifles; the licensing of arms dealers and the registration of weapons; and restrictions on the importation of all weapons. Penalties for violating any of the new federal laws were significantly higher than under most state laws, and federal prosecutors were empowered to take charge of specific cases at their discretion.[49]

The results of the New Deal campaign to arouse the nation to confront the crime problem were not confined to legislative reforms. Roosevelt's successful effort to bring "the Federal Government's anti-crime machinery up to date" was supplemented by his drive to make the Bureau of Investigation "as

effective an instrumentality of crime detection and punishment
as any of the similar agencies of the world." "Federal men are
constantly facing machine-gun fire in the pursuit of gangsters,"
the President said when signing the New Deal crime control
legislation, "and gangster extermination cannot be made
completely effective so long as a substantial part of the public
looks with tolerance upon known criminals . . . or applauds
efforts to romanticize crime."

The administration's efforts to secure passage of crime
control reforms and, concomitantly, to "build up a body of
public opinion . . . sufficiently active or alive to the [crime]
situation in which we find ourselves," were not limited to
FDR's or Cummings's public lobbying.[50] Acting on the suggestion of Fulton Oursler,[51] the editor of *Liberty* magazine and a
friend of the Attorney General and the President, Cummings
launched an ambitious public relations campaign as part of the
New Deal crime control program. Oursler's idea, aptly described by Stephen Early as a "plan to publicize and make the
G-men heroes," was "put over for the F.B.I." by Henry
Suydam, the former Washington correspondent for the
Brooklyn Eagle. At the recommendation of a group of Washington newspapermen, Cummings hired Suydam in 1933 as a
special assistant to the Attorney General in charge of em-
bellishing the Bureau's image. When Suydam left his post in
1937, he received a personal letter from FDR thanking him for
services rendered.[52]

By the time Suydam returned to newspaper work the FBI
had developed a formidable public relations capability.
Though lamely professing an aversion to becoming a symbol of
the New Deal crime control crusade, Hoover quickly and
enthusiastically accepted this new responsibility. And the
Bureau's publicity efforts continued long after Congress
passed the Justice Department's crime bills in May and June
1934. The era's most notorious gangster, for instance, met an
untimely end in July—gunned down near Chicago's Biograph
Theater by some fifteen Bureau agents directed by Melvin
Purvis. (The Bureau agents had gathered outside the Biograph
waiting for the feature film, *Manhattan Melodrama* with Clark
Gable and William Powell, to end and John Dillinger to come

out into the street.) Hoover responded, according to one critic, by hanging "up Dillinger's picture, like a scalp, in [Bureau] offices all over the country and [posing] for the newspapers with Dillinger's hat, gun, and perhaps an ear."[53]

From there, and with Roosevelt's support, the Bureau and its Director became immersed in the world of public relations and opinion molding. Articles glamorizing the Bureau's machine-gun-toting war on crime appeared under Hoover's signature—sixteen, with titles like "Gun Crazy," appeared in *American Magazine* alone between February 1934 and August 1936. Most of these articles were written by Hoover's chief ghost writer, Courtney Ryley Cooper, a former *Denver Post* staff writer. Cooper was eventually put on the Justice Department's payroll to help carry out Henry Suydam's public relations coup. Cooper also wrote the introduction for Hoover's first book, *Persons in Hiding*. The FBI Director, in turn, wrote the introduction for Cooper's *Ten Thousand Public Enemies*.[54]

Hoover cooperated with movie producers, radio executives, fiction writers, newspaper and magazine reporters, and virtually any other publicist interested in "authentic source material taken from the files of the Federal Bureau of Investigation." The FBI Director was "chummy," as one critic put it, with many prominent Washington newspapermen, and most of his New York City friends were "writers and Broadway columnists." (He met Walter Winchell at the Stork Club.) According to conservative columnist Westbrook Pegler, who later became a recipient of information leaked from Bureau files, Hoover had a stable of "pet writers, or stooges, who scratch his back in return for material that glorifies Edgar Hoover and the G's." (On the other hand, beginning in the mid-1930s, the FBI routinely investigated publicists who continued to criticize the Bureau.) Manufacturers began to market G-man pajamas and toy machine guns, and pulp magazines regularly ran features lionizing the FBI Director. Comic strips were another Hoover favorite. He closely monitored two G-man strips, "Dick Tracy" and "Secret Agent X-9," while his aides supervised the production of at least one other strip. Hoover's personal friend, newspaper reporter Rex Collier, gained privileged access to the Bureau's closed case files for his syndicated "War on Crime," which was publicized as "part of a National educational movement to stamp out crime in America."[55]

The program to sell the FBI also included tours of FBI headquarters in Washington, where the public was treated to such contrasting sights as a plastic replica of Dillinger's death mask and Bureau agents poring over microscopes and finger-print indices. For those who could not make the FBI tour, Hoover took to the speaking circuit. His speeches before groups such as the DAR and the American Legion were often broadcast over national radio networks and were invariably reproduced and disseminated by the Bureau's sophisticated mass-mailing operation. By 1940 Hoover had built up a publicly funded component within the FBI that, according to Senator George Norris (R., Neb.), was charged with "writing speeches for him to make or for anyone else to make who will take the speeches."[56]

In July 1935 the FBI opened a National Police Academy— "the West Point of Law Enforcement." In the first ten months of 1936, senior Bureau officials helped organize or participated in more than seventy conventions of state and local law enforcement officials. In short, the Bureau emerged "as a clearing–house of information about criminals," acquiring in the process a bipartisan constituency in Congress. After the House approved a record $6,025,000 FBI budget in 1936 (more than double the Bureau's budget when Roosevelt took office), the Senate Appropriations Committee called for a $225,000 reduction. This modest effort to trim the FBI budget was defeated by an unlikely combination of New Deal Democrats and New Deal–hating Republicans led by Senator Arthur Vandenberg (R., Mich.).[57]

By 1937, as a Brookings Institution analyst noted, "the metamorphosis . . . was complete." The FBI's "agents, the 'G-men,' no longer 'examiners,' were now armed, trained, mobile, active in the pursuit of criminals, rapidly developing a legend of invincibility, and kept in the spotlight, sometimes to their embarrassment, by a remarkable propaganda policy."[58] Although the Bureau's public relations machinery had osten-sibly been created to make the New Deal crime control program more attractive, little else about the Roosevelt administration pleased the conservative FBI Director. Eventually, despite Hoover's willingness to put the Bureau's services at the disposal of the White House, the crows would come home to roost. By 1938 even Cummings became concerned about the FBI's publicity activities and ordered Hoover to limit—but not eliminate—them.[59] The Bureau maintained its high-powered, high-profile self-promotion work in the years to come but added a new dimension. FBI bureaucrats soon became more interested in public and congressional attitudes toward dissidents and internal security policy than gangsters and crime control.

THE PRIVATE SECTOR

During the Cold War the FBI consciously exploited information gathered during its investigations of subversive activities to pursue policy objectives that went far beyond self-promotion. Typically, the Bureau dispensed derogatory information on individual activists or dissident organizations to carefully selected journalists, congressmen, and private anticommunist interest groups. During the years from Attorney General Stone's restrictions of 1924 to the formation of the Dies Committee in 1938, these activities were apparently restrained—limited, in most cases, to servicing White House requests for sensitive political information. The FBI also accommodated select blacklisters, such as former U.S. Army G-2 intelligence officer Ralph Van Deman, though he was the exception rather than the rule.

While the FBI did not generally support charges of Communists-in-government and other red-baiting tactics by private sector and congressional anticommunists until the Cold War, without regular FBI assistance the anticommunist politics favored by these groups would not have gained legitimacy. If the 1930s was a decade of hard times for interest groups who sought to exploit the Communist issue as part of a conservative anti–New Deal politics, the private sector kept a formidable anticommunist nucleus intact. Corporate labor spies abounded, and in November 1934 the Hearst press announced a campaign to alert Americans to the threat posed by the CPUSA and its fellow travellers. In an effort to gather information for this campaign, Hearst "operatives" successfully "penetrated" Syracuse University and Columbia University. Other anticommunist journalists, such as Westbrook Pegler, established close ties with the red- and Nazi-hunting congressional committees of the 1930s. Police reports and congressional committee documents were routinely leaked to Pegler.[60]

In January 1934 the American Legion launched its own anticommunist educational campaign by indiscriminately listing people and organizations whose politics were radical and whose loyalty was therefore suspect. By the mid-1930s such listings were common. Elizabeth Dilling's *The Red Network* was perhaps the single most irresponsible example. Aiming directly at the "communistic" New Deal, Dilling accused some 500 organizations and 1,300 persons, from Eleanor Roosevelt to Chiang Kai-Shek, of participating in an international Communist conspiracy.[61]

Other special interest groups eager to exploit the Communist issue included the National Association of Manufacturers (NAM) and various chemical munitions firms. As part of a campaign to instruct Americans regarding the dangers posed by New Deal reforms and organized labor, the NAM worked with *New York Herald Tribune* reporter George Sokolsky. As a special consultant for the public relations firm Hill and Knowlton, Sokolsky received some $28,000 (at least $6,000 directly from NAM) between June 1936 and February 1938 as compensation for publicizing the red menace over the radio and on the speaking circuit.[62] Federal Laboratories, Inc., which had a sixty percent share of the domestic tear gas market and distribution rights to the Thompson submachine gun, used the Communist issue for an even more explicit purpose—to increase its chemical munitions sales to strikebreakers. Federal Laboratories distributed to prospective customers copies of Dilling's *Red Network*, which it advertised as "a handbook for the purchasers of tear gas," and sundry clippings from the

Hearst press. It also commissioned the production of other anticommunist literature. In April 1933, however, Federal Laboratories demonstrated its one-dimensional attitude toward the red menace by selling $339.43 worth of tear gas and accessories to the Amtorg Trading Corporation.[63]

Federal Laboratories' shallow anticommunism was not unusual. Most private sector red-baiters and congressional red-hunters were motivated by bread-and-butter objectives. And anticommunism was generally recognized for what it was—a conservative anti–New Deal politics. Red-baiting, in short, was favored only by the far-right fringe and a scattering of respectable publicists. Beginning with the seven-year reign of Martin Dies, however, an alternative emerged, and the American polity took a giant step toward what eventually became known as McCarthyism.

CHAPTER II

The Dies Committee

When Martin Dies introduced a resolution to establish yet
another special committee to investigate un-American activities, it was by no means certain the anticommunist political
style would work. If the Hearst press, the American Legion, the
NAM, and Federal Laboratories were veteran red-baiters, their
successes had been modest. And if at times the FBI was
reluctant to cooperate with the temperamental Dies or to
support indiscriminately his all-out assault on the New Deal's
programs, personnel, and constituency, nonetheless the Bureau
intermittently furnished his Committee carefully selected
information from FBI files—thereby setting a precedent for
the more formal relationship that evolved between the Bureau
and the Dies Committee's successor. Though unable to forge
an anticommunist consensus, the Committee developed a
formidable constituency. With the help of "educational materials" prepared and disseminated by the FBI, this constituency found new and unaccustomed respectability during
the Cold War years. As for the irrepressible Martin Dies, his
heirs did not hail him as either a prophet or a trailblazer but
rather condemned him for sullying the good name of anticommunism.

Since there was no anticommunist consensus in 1938, the
House, ironically, favored Dies's resolution principally because
of concerns over subversion by the Right. Samuel Dickstein,

for instance, was troubled exclusively by native Nazi and other far-right movements. Yet Dickstein supported Dies's call for the formation of a special committee to investigate "the extent, character, and object of un-American propaganda activities in the United States." To mobilize support for the proposed committee, Dickstein dusted off the McCormack-Dickstein Committee's sealed files and began reading the names of suspect Nazi spies, smugglers, and sympathizers into the *Congressional Record.* Astutely concluding that Dies intended to investigate the New Deal, a coalition of Republicans and conservative southern Democrats also rallied behind the resolution. The events of the previous year, notably the Supreme Court packing fight, the sit-down strikes by automobile workers, and the onset of a severe recession, increased congressional conservatives' dissatisfaction with the New Deal. This dissatisfaction determined their support for Dies's resolution.

Backed by conservatives and those, like Dickstein, who wanted to expose anti-Semites, the House overwhelmingly approved the resolution. Dies himself, when arguing for his proposed committee, conceded that he did not know "whether we can legislate effectively in this matter." Instead, he championed exposure as "the most effective weapon . . . in our possession," promising to bring "the light of day . . . to bear upon" un-American activities and to allow "public sentiment to do the rest." Under Dies, the new Committee membership—Arthur D. Healey (D., Mass.), John J. Dempsey (D., N.M.), Joe Starnes (D., Ala.), Harold G. Mosier (D., Ohio), Noah M. Mason (R., Ill.), and J. Parnell Thomas (R., N.J.)— proceeded to act on his directive. But the triumphant Dickstein enjoyed a Pyrrhic victory. Not among those appointed to the new committee, he soon emerged as one of its chief critics.[1]

THE BUND AND THE RADICAL RIGHT

Dickstein's opposition was understandable, though the Dies Committee did not ignore the Right, and the FBI and the Justice Department often assisted the Committee's investigations of rightwing organizations.[2] In early 1938 the FBI submitted to the Justice Department a detailed report on the German-American Bund, the largest and most boisterous native fascist organization. The FBI probe then "came to a dead end," according to the FBI's quasi-official historian, Don Whitehead, until the Dies Committee called upon the Justice Department to investigate Bund members' alleged violations of criminal statutes. Whitehead implied that pressure from the Dies Committee forced the Justice Department to resume its investigation of the Bund, an assertion seemingly confirmed by his privileged access to FBI files. In addition, the first serial in the Bureau's file on the Dies Committee, dated the day after the House passed Dies's resolution, concerned the Committee's anticipated request to review the FBI's report on the Bund and possible plans to subpoena the agents who had compiled it.[3]

On June 17, and again on July 6, Dies requested the Justice Department to make available all reports in its possession relating to Nazi activities in the United States. Acting Attorney General Robert H. Jackson responded on August 13 by forwarding to Dies the FBI's report and accompanying exhibits on the Bund. The day before, during its very first day of public hearings, the Dies Committee heard the testimony of John C. Metcalfe, who had infiltrated the Bund in 1937 on behalf of the *Chicago Daily Times*. Metcalfe's brother, James J., an ex-FBI agent who had followed John into the Bund, also appeared before the Committee. Shortly after testifying, John Metcalfe was hired as an investigator and the Dies Committee continued to pay intermittent attention to the Bund and other native fascist groups. Meanwhile, the Bureau and the Justice Department regularly reviewed the Committee's files on the Bund. In February 1940, furthermore, Dies Committee member Joe Starnes requested and received from Jackson "the results" of the FBI's probe of William Dudley Pelley and his Silver Shirts.[4]

Eventually, the Bund leader, Fritz Kuhn, was arrested for misappropriating Bund funds, and in March 1942 Attorney General Francis Biddle began a systematic campaign to denaturalize Bund members. Kuhn, for one, was deported to Germany. His successor, William Kunze, and other Bund members were among the thirty native fascists unsuccessfully prosecuted from July 1942 to April 1944 by the Justice Department under the Espionage and Smith Acts. Department attorneys led by O. John Rogge reviewed Dies Committee files when prosecuting Kunze and other native fascists, selecting some 900 documents for use in preparing the government's case.[5]

The Dies Committee, however, quickly parted company with countersubversives like Metcalfe, who sought to link several large American corporations with the Nazi party in Germany. Their investigations of the Bund and other right-wingers were, as Walter Goodman wrote, "like the comic who pops out between burlesque skits with a broom and sets diligently to sweeping up the stage until he is kicked off so that the show may proceed."[6] Dies (and FBI Director Hoover, for that matter),[7] often charged ahead blindly when probing the Left, but they were considerably more circumspect when probing the other end of the political spectrum. Even if *Nation* editor Freda Kirchwey erred in labeling Dies "our little Texas Himmler" for fraternizing with the Right, many native fascists and other anti-Semites supported the Dies Committee despite its occasional forays into their affairs.

Among others, the Committee's constituency included at one time or another George Sylvester Viereck, Father Charles Coughlin, William Dudley Pelley, Gerald L. K. Smith, and Gerald Winrod. The Dies Committee established a particularly close relationship with Joseph P. Kamp, director of the Constitutional Educational League and the subject of a far-reaching FBI investigation. Kamp organized mass mailing campaigns[8] to rally support for the often maligned Dies Committee and, according to Walter Winchell and others, had a secret agreement with Martin Dies granting him access to Committee files in return for information uncovered through the efforts of his own investigators. Hazel Hoffman, Kamp's private secretary, even worked for the Dies Committee for a short time as a special investigator.

THE INVESTIGATORS

Dies's priorities surprised few political observers. A conventional New Deal Democrat until 1937 and a protégé of future Vice-President John Nance Garner, Dies was first elected to the House in 1930 at the age of thirty. Garner, then Speaker of the House, arranged Dies's appointment to the prestigious Rules Committee, where the young Congressman offered a series of bills and resolutions to restrict immigration and curtail radicalism. As Chairman of the Special Committee to Investigate Un-American Activities, Dies abandoned his earlier efforts at law making. He viewed himself primarily as an educator, with the weighty responsibility of alerting the American public to the dangers of joining subversive organizations. "Primarily," Dies told President Roosevelt in 1940, "you educate innocent people so that they will get out."[9]

The beginnings of the Dies Committee were inauspicious. Dies's first act was to hire fellow Texan Robert Stripling as Committee secretary.[10] Stripling worked out of an office with a single desk and filing cabinet, assisted by a staff of two stenographers and four investigators—three of whom were quickly fired. The chief investigator, Edward F. Sullivan, was dismissed in September 1938 after the Senate Civil Liberties Committee revealed his record as a labor spy for the anti-Semitic Railway Audit and Inspection Company. Sullivan was then hired by the Ukrainian Nationalist Federation—a single interest pressure group intent upon annexing the Ukraine to the Third Reich. Sullivan, who had a long arrest record (he was arrested again in 1939 for impersonating an FBI agent), had once shared an office with James True, inventor of a head-busting billy club quaintly known as the Kike Killer. Dies explained Sullivan's dismissal by claiming the Committee lacked the funds to pay his salary.[11]

Even before he fired Sullivan, Dies was dissatisfied with the work of his investigative staff. Indeed, the House General Accounts Committee scaled down Dies's original request for a budget of $100,000 to $25,000 because it assumed the FBI would do much of the work for the new Committee. Dies solicited FBI assistance throughout the summer of 1938, confidently announcing that he would begin public hearings only when "G-men" and other "agents of the Committee" assembled adequate data. He eventually succeeded in arranging for at least one Army G-2 agent to take a leave of absence and join the staff as a free lance investigator, but had no success in securing the services of FBI agents. Hoover responded to Dies's request for assistance by advising Attorney General Cummings that the Bureau's resources were already overextended and, as a result, the Justice Department refused to "loan" a single Bureau agent to the Committee.[12]

Hoover did not advise Cummings of his decision to monitor the Dies Committee and to consider furnishing information to it on an informal basis. Dies Committee aide E. K. Gubin met in early July with FBI Assistant Director W. Richard Glavin, head of the Administrative Division, to inquire whether "it would be possible for Investigators of this Committee to secure advice from the various Field Offices of this Bureau." Glavin advised Gubin "that this would not be possible." "I believe, however," Glavin told FBI Associate Director Clyde Tolson later that same day, "that the Investigators of this Committee, if its personnel can be determined from Mr. Gubin, are such that it would be well worth while for the Bureau to communicate personally and confidentially with the various Special Agents in Charge [SACs] concerning the possible activities of the Committee." Glavin, in short, suggested that the Bureau cooperate with carefully selected Dies Committee personnel but not the temperamental Chairman. Hoover approved this proposal and another proposal that prohibited FBI supervisors at Bureau headquarters from talking with Gubin. Thereafter, interviews with this Dies Committee representative were handled only by senior FBI officials, namely Tolson, Glavin, and Edward A. Tamm.[13]

Martin Dies may not have received the assistance he wanted from the FBI. The Bureau, nonetheless, monitored Committee staff, and Dies Committee investigators kept in close contact with FBI headquarters and the various field offices. On one occasion, investigator Charles A. Randall had the FBI check a drinking glass, recently handled by a Committee witness, for latent fingerprints. Bureau officials also helped the Dies Committee avoid a repetition of the embarrassment it had endured during the Sullivan exposé. Working closely with two Committee members, Starnes and Jerry Voorhis (D., Cal.), when interviewing applicants for investigator positions in early 1939, FBI agents compiled reports on Randall, Peter J. Nolan,

Thomas J. Nash, James H. Steadman, George F. Hurley, and Robert B. Barker. All six applicants were quickly hired. Dies also hired Rhea Whitley after Starnes had first consulted with FBI Assistant Director Tamm. Whitley, a ten-year FBI veteran who had headed the New York City Field Office and had worked on the Dillinger case, was named Committee counsel. At least two other ex-FBI agents were hired as investigators. Whitley, in turn, received a modest research collection of published literature on bolshevism from his former superiors, was granted limited access to internal FBI documents, and arranged for Bureau personnel to make up a few charts for the Committee. When Whitley left the Dies Committee in 1940 following a dispute with the chairman, FBI officials Tamm and Nichols played an active, if behind-the-scenes and ultimately unsuccessful, role in choosing his successor.[14]

The appointment, on the recommendation of FBI confidant George Sokolsky, of J.B. Matthews, a former leftist, to replace the discredited Sullivan was the Committee's most significant personnel change. Though never a CPUSA member, Matthews had associated closely with Communists and other leftists before becoming America's foremost ex–fellow traveller. His memoir, *Odyssey of a Fellow Traveller*, became an anti-communist classic, a source of information for the lowliest blacklister on up to senior FBI officials. Among other extra-curricular activities, Matthews wrote *The Trojan Horse in America* "under Dies's by-line," spoke regularly before such organizations as American Patriots, Inc., and published in Father Coughlin's *Social Justice*. To Richard Rovere, all these activities made Matthews "a political psychopath."[15]

GATHERING INTELLIGENCE

Matthews's primary investigative technique was simple enough: it required only scissors. The Dies Committee's chief investigator and his staff spent hours indiscriminately clipping names from the Communist press, and they never questioned the veracity of lists compiled from the *Daily Worker* or *Masses and Mainstream*. When Matthews discovered that the *Daily*

Worker had erroneously listed him as one of five American representatives to the 1933 International Commission to Aid the Victims of German Fascism, he said he had never heard of this front and noted the standard Communist practice of listing people fraudulently to inflate the size of party fronts. Having unburdened himself, Matthews continued clipping names. After he named Shirley Temple as an unwitting Communist dupe, Secretary of the Interior Harold L. Ickes acidly warned, in a widely publicized speech, that Dies and Matthews were "leading a *posse comitatus* in a raid upon Shirley Temple's nursery."[16]

Ickes's reference to vigilantism was appropriate. Committee investigators, usually accompanied by local police, often entered CPUSA or other organizations' headquarters for the announced purpose of serving a subpoena *duces tecum*. Instead, Committee staff or their agents would seize all available records and cart them away—thereby gathering evidence even before the Committee held its first public hearings. On July 6, 1938, Dies Committee aide Gubin advised the FBI of his instructions to "certain of the Investigators to confiscate anything that they wanted in any business office to which they may be sent and . . . not worry particularly about legal procedure."[17]

The most publicized Dies Committee raids were carried out against the American League for Peace and Democracy. Between 1938 and 1941, Communist party records were also seized in Philadelphia, Los Angeles, Boston, Baltimore, Hoboken, and Montgomery, and homes of CPUSA leaders in Pittsburgh were searched. In one case, Pennsylvania State Police guarded Dies Committee witness James H. Dolsen's Pittsburgh home while Committee investigators and Secret Service agents searched it. (The Secret Service became involved after the Dies Committee discovered a Party membership book in Dolsen's possession made out to a "Franklin D. Roosevelt.") In Detroit, city police raided the apartment of a local committee to aid the Spanish Republic, confiscated financial records and correspondence, and turned the documents over to Dies. In New England, according to the FBI's report to the White House, Committee staff dug up a bundle of official CPUSA records, allegedly wrapped in oilskin and buried by Earl Browder, near the home of Fernanda W. Reed, one of the *Daily Worker*'s publishers. In Chicago, Communist officials slammed their safe shut as Deputy U.S. Marshals and members of the local red squad entered their offices. This raid, as well as a search of four other undesignated places, took place on the very day that U.S. Marshal J. Tobias and Chicago Police Lieutenant Make Mills appeared in executive session before Martin Dies who was holding one-man subcommittee hearings in the windy city.[18]

The courts finally condemned these crude investigative techniques in May 1940 following a spectacular foray in Philadelphia. Escorted by a squad of motorcycle police and eight detectives, Dies Committee investigators George Hurley and Chester Howe led a raid on the Philadelphia headquarters of the Communist party and the International Workers Order (IWO), filled a two-ton truck with files, books, pamphlets, membership lists, and financial records, and fled with their "big haul" across the Delaware Bridge into New Jersey. The CPUSA and IWO responded by calmly filing a petition that same day in U.S. District Court asking that their files be returned. The next day, Judge George A. Welsh requested Dies not to make use of the purloined documents until he had ruled on the complaint. He also ordered the arrest of Police Lieutenant Albert A. Granitz and Committee sleuths Hurley and Howe.

Dies had anticipated Judge Welsh's interference and timed the raid perfectly. The documents were seized late in the afternoon and rushed to a hideout in New Jersey. "I had a photostat machine set up," Dies recalled fourteen years later, "and we spent all night making copies of this stuff. The next morning the federal judge issued an injunction, and so I hid out in a blind office until we completed the photostating. Then I came out and announced we were going to honor and obey this injunction." Judge Welsh, nonetheless, ruled the Committee's raid illegal and in clear violation of the Fourth Amendment. Though Dies defended the raid on the grounds that he could not obtain documentation by any legal means, Welsh's decision tempered the Committee's ache for highway adventure. Old

45

habits, however, die hard. In August 1940, Committee staff raided the offices of four pro-Nazi German groups in New York City and on November 20, 1940, Dies claimed that in the past two days Committee agents had raided the headquarters of fifteen subversive groups in Chicago.[19]

Local and state police departments were less dramatic but more productive sources of information. The Dies Committee heard testimony from a variety of seasoned red-hunters, including Lieutenant Mills of the Chicago Police Department and Sergeants Harry Mikuliak and Leo Maciosek of the Detroit Police Department's Special Investigations Unit. A twenty-three-year veteran of the Chicago radical squad, Mills provided Committee staff with virtually unrestricted access to his files—a precedent that helped establish the symbiotic relationship which evolved between the Chicago Police and congressional investigating committees (notably HUAC and the Senate Internal Security Subcommittee) and lasted nearly thirty years. In Detroit, Mikuliak and Maciosek, known as "Mic" and "Mac" to local radicals, operated a formidable spy network. Mikuliak alone claimed to be running forty operatives in the local Communist branch.[20]

Some of the information received from local red squad officers was volunteered during testimony before the Committee or simply read into the record by officials such as Detroit Police Superintendent Fred W. Frahm, who inserted a series of police memorandums giving details of 147 sit-down and 40 walk-out strikes that took place in the city between November 1936 and October 1938.[21] The Committee received most of its information from police officers in confidence through the efforts of Stephen W. Birmingham and other Dies Committee investigators. Birmingham had been a first-grade detective in the New York Police Department's (NYPD) safe-and-loft squad from 1910 to 1920, and thereafter a private detective with an aggressive strike-breaking business. He had also served as chief investigator for the McCormack-Dickstein Committee and routinely called on and solicited information from local police. After Birmingham received NYPD reports on, for instance, actor Melvyn Douglas, writer Waldo Frank, and New York Municipal Judge Dorothy Kenyon, he then made these reports available to Westbrook Pegler on a confidential basis. Other Dies Committee sleuths, such as Robert B. Barker, had access to Pennsylvania State Police reports.[22]

Like the FBI and the Dies Committee, local red squads generally concentrated on Communists and other left-of-center dissidents but did not ignore the Right. When investigating the German-American Bund, the Dies Committee persuaded the Pennsylvania State Police to plant two undercover specialists, along with a Committee mole, in Bund camps in New Jersey. Similarly, the New Jersey State Police assisted the Committee during its probe of the Bund's Nordland camp in Andover Township. Surveillance of incoming automobiles and a check of their license plate numbers with the State Motor Vehicle Department in Trenton revealed the names of those attending Nordland. (New Jersey State Police, New York State Police, and the NYPD regularly ran license plate checks for the Committee.) Additional data, including social security numbers and places of employment, were received from the Social Security Board. As a final step, Dies turned over a list of 3,500 Bundists to the State Department. The State Department, in turn, forwarded the list to the FBI, who, at President Roosevelt's direction, sent the names of those working in any defense-connected industry to their employers.[23]

Information gathered by Dies Committee staff—during raids or from liaison with local red squads—was readily available to the FBI. By late 1941 Dies had worked out a formal system whereby Bureau agents had unrestricted access to Committee files. He appointed a clerk for the sole purpose of aiding the FBI, and Bureau officials, for their part, assigned a liaison agent to work on a daily basis at Committee offices. According to Dies, twelve to fifteen FBI agents consulted the files "almost every day," with additional inquiries being made at the Committee's Los Angeles, Chicago, Philadelphia, New York, and Detroit offices. Bureau investigators even reviewed Dies Committee files when checking applicants for the position of FBI special agent.[24]

Although these files contained documents seized illegally, they were no more than a supplement to the Bureau. By 1942,

FBI agents were engaged in extensive wiretapping and bugging of CPUSA members' homes and offices, in break-ins (to plant bugs or photograph documents), and in the furtive propagation of derogatory information either to expose Communists and their sympathizers or to alert management to potentially subversive employees.[25] FBI agents in the field also had sources of information in the communications industry that allowed them to monitor most long-distance messages. In February 1941, for example, Washington SAC Guy Hottel received from a "very confidential contact at Postal" copies of telegrams sent by the *New York World Telegram*'s city editor to his Washington correspondent. FBI interest in the *World Telegram* arose from the newspaper's claim than an unnamed FBI agent had provided it with information concerning the suicide of former Soviet intelligence officer Walter Krivitsky, once a Bureau informant and Dies Committee witness.[26]

THE WITNESSES

With a thirty-man investigative staff, directed by Matthews and Committee counsel Whitley and operating out of six branch offices, it was hardly surprising that the Dies Committee was prolific and sometimes reckless. Though the Committee's first published volume of hearings covered only eleven days in August 1938, it listed some 640 organizations and 438 newspapers as Communist controlled, and 284 labor organizers and perhaps a thousand other individuals as CPUSA members.[27]

The two most ambitious witnesses during the Dies Committee's initial hearings were Walter S. Steele and John P. Frey. Frey, who was head of the AFL's Metal Trades Department, named nearly 300 rival CIO organizers as Communists. The FBI immediately began to quote Frey in its own reports, and Dies sent the names of 238 exposed CIO organizers to the chiefs of every police department operating a subversive squad. William Green and other AFL officials attempted to have the Frey indictment printed as a separate volume that could be widely and quickly disseminated to non-CIO unions and state labor federations. This scheme failed because, in the absence of an anticommunist consensus and with the Committee's shortage of funds, limited demand could not justify printing Frey's testimony separately.[28]

Since the mid-1930s, at least, Frey's operatives had been infiltrating the CPUSA, obtaining photostats of membership cards and dues receipts, Young Communist League membership books, mailing lists of various left-wing organizations, and other "confidential Communist documents." Following his August 1938 testimony, Frey continued to send the Dies Committee "an immense amount of documentary evidence" and to put the services of his investigators at the Committee's disposal.[29] He performed similar services for other congressmen, including Senator Vandenberg. After Frey accused Dr. Louis Bloch of associating closely with Communists in San Francisco, Vandenberg requested Frey to undertake a more detailed investigation of Bloch's activities. The Michigan Senator already possessed a photostat of what purported to be Bloch's party membership card, but he wanted additional ammunition to block the appointment of the alleged red to the Maritime Labor Board during hearings before the Senate Commerce Committee.[30]

Even more spectacular charges were levelled by Frey's fellow witness, Walter S. Steele, editor of the far-right *National Republic* magazine and advisory board member of an anti-Semitic coterie, the Paul Reveres. Steele, who had close ties to Hoover and the FBI's Washington office,[31] was chairman of the National Security Committee of the American Coalition of Patriotic, Civic, and Fraternal Societies and described himself as the spokesman for twenty million patriots. When testifying, Steele named hundreds of individuals as CPUSA members and hundreds of organizations as Communist "infested." Like the FBI, the Committee was eager to exploit Steele's files— reputedly the most extensive private collection of information on subversive activities in the pre–Cold War era. The Committee devoted over 400 pages in its initial volume of hearings to Steele's revelations.[32]

During Steele's testimony, J. Parnell Thomas interrupted to announce that the Dies Committee had yet another source of information. Thomas said he had just been handed a confidential FBI report on CIO organizer Harry Bridges, which Dies cited "as evidence of the fact that they [FBI officials] desire to cooperate whenever possible." Thomas, abandoning his earlier complaint that the Bureau had been giving him "the run-around," affirmed that he had "received very fine cooperation from the F.B.I."[33]

Thomas, however, had made a mistake. He had been given not the Bridges file but the file on Paul Edwards, who was the Federal Arts Project Administrator in New York and yet another Dies Committee target. (This file was made available by Bureau officials after consultation with Assistant Attorney General Alexander Holtzoff, who later became Hoover's personal counsel and a fiercely anticommunist federal judge.) And even though Justice Department officials appeared to be aware of this leak to Thomas, the FBI purposely attempted to mislead them—except the reliable Holtzoff. When Gordon Dean, then a special assistant to the Attorney General in charge of public relations and later chairman of the Atomic Energy Commission, attempted to find out through Holtzoff's office the name of the Dies Committee member who received the file, an FBI agent advised Holtzoff's secretary "that I did not recall the name and I did not know how we could locate it." Though this response was intentionally misleading, the FBI Director commended it: "Right. We of course do not want to give publicity to such requests."[34]

GOING AFTER THE NEW DEAL

One reason for Hoover's reluctance to publicize such assistance was the Dies Committee's partisan effort to discredit the New Deal. Indeed, the Committee's interest in Bridges arose from chief investigator Sullivan's charge that a high-level Labor Department official was protecting the Australian-born and unnaturalized Bridges from being deported. (The government opened what was to become a marathon deportation case against the left-wing Bridges in the aftermath of the 1934 San Francisco general strike.) Dies and Thomas used Sullivan's report as the basis for a sweeping attack on the Secretary of Labor, Frances Perkins, accusing her of coddling Communists. In reality, President Roosevelt had suggested that the Labor Department harass alien Communists active in the labor movement. In an August 1935 memorandum to Perkins, the President inquired: "How does Sam Darcy [a West Coast Communist activist] get in and out of this country? . . . Also, how about Harry Bridges? Is he not another alien?" Roosevelt was convinced, Perkins learned, that "we can prove propaganda directed at the destruction of the Government" in the Bridges case.[35] Regardless of FDR's interest, Perkins had no power to evict Bridges because of a recent U.S. Court of Appeals ruling in the Strecker case, which held that CPUSA membership did not provide adequate grounds for deportation.

In an effort to lessen the political consequences of this ruling, Solicitor General Robert H. Jackson invited Dies to help prepare the government's appeal of the Strecker decision to the Supreme Court. Dies responded by sending Jackson a twenty-four page attack on Perkins. The affair, moreover, refused to fade away, with Thomas calling for Perkins's impeachment and with J. Edgar Hoover publicly entering the fray in December 1940 by declaring Bridges a card-carrying Communist. Then, in May 1941, J. B. Matthews read into the Dies Committee record what he said was an FBI report on labor organizer Ralph Dawson—who was described in the report as "Harry Bridges' right-hand man." The case dragged on until the Supreme Court finally overturned Bridges's deportation order in 1945.[36]

The Dies Committee's telescopic focus on New Deal personnel extended into the White House, with the First Lady a particularly alluring target for Dies and Thomas. Mrs. Roosevelt had actively supported a number of left-wing youth organizations, including the American Youth Congress (AYC), and was a good friend of Joseph P. Lash, then national secretary of the American Student Union.[37] In late November 1939, the Committee held hearings on these two youth groups and heard testimony from Lash and other national officers. Eleanor Roosevelt attended the hearings to provide moral support, declining Committee member Starnes's invitation to sit with the inquisitors and choosing instead to sit with the leaders of these youth groups. During a break in the hearings she took six of them to the White House for lunch. That evening, they were invited back to dine with Mrs. Roosevelt and her husband.

If tolerant of radicalism, Mrs. Roosevelt was not oblivious to the Communist front charges leveled against the AYC. Before the Dies Committee hearings opened, she requested an FBI file check on the Youth Congress. Though Hoover responded graciously ("it is indeed a pleasure for me to be able to make available to you the data contained in the memorandum"), the First Lady ridiculed the report in a private letter to the FBI Director: "I am glad . . . to have this information as it shows me the type of fact which has been used to substantiate the Roman Catholic attitude that this organization is Communist controlled." Regardless of her caustic assessment of the Bureau's work, in 1940 following the Dies Committee hearings, Mrs. Roosevelt asked for an FBI report on former AYC official Viola Ilma and solicited other FBI reports in 1942 and 1943 on an International Ladies Garment Workers Union officer, journalist Westbrook Pegler, and a Wichita, Kansas, businessman accused of making fascist speeches. The FBI cleared the Wichita man but noted his "decidedly anti-Administration attitude." Mrs. Roosevelt continued to solicit Bureau assistance after leaving the White House, though the no-longer-solicitous Hoover generally refused her requests—including an appeal of February 6, 1951, for information on the House Committee on Un-American Activities.[38]

FBI officials were perfectly willing to ingratiate themselves with the President's wife while covertly working to discredit her and the New Deal by leaking derogatory information about her to conservative publicists.[39] Mrs. Roosevelt, in any event, continued to support, albeit more discreetly, Joseph Lash and the AYC—despite the Youth Congress's ideological gymnastics in the wake of the Nazi-Soviet Pact. After September 1939 Youth Congress activists supported neutrality and opposed FDR's increasingly interventionist policies, which they feared would drag the United States into an "imperialist" war. The

AYC abruptly shifted its position in June 1941, following the German invasion of the Soviet Union, to call for American involvement in this "people's" war. By then, Lash was leery of so-called Communist fronts and Mrs. Roosevelt had broken with the Communist-dominated Youth Congress. She still continued to support Lash, however, and in 1942 interceded on his behalf (Lash was seeking a commission in Naval Intelligence) with the FBI and the Dies Committee. That same year, FBI agents burglarized the AYC's New York offices where they successfully completed their intelligence objective by photographing the First Lady's correspondence of 1940–1941 with Youth Congress leaders.[40]

Dies Committee efforts to discredit the New Deal were assisted as well by the private sector—as when Harper L. Knowles testified before the Committee in October 1938 and received front-page coverage in the *New York Times*. Though he introduced himself as the chairman of the Radical Research Committee of the American Legion, in reality Knowles was closely connected with a private vigilante organization, Associated Farmers, Inc. (Among other endeavors, Associated Farmers was sponsoring a campaign to ban John Steinbeck's *Grapes of Wrath* from California's public libraries.) In typed and bound testimony delivered to the press before he took the witness stand, Knowles accused California's Democratic nominees for Governor (Culbert Olson) and United States Senator (Sheridan Downey) of being Communist tools. Significantly, the Republican nominee for Downey's Senate seat, millionaire landowner Philip Bancroft, was a member of the board of Associated Farmers. The FBI later quoted selectively from Knowles's testimony when dispensing derogatory public source information to the press. With ex-FBI agent Nat Piper, Knowles went on to establish the Western Research Foundation, which fed information to the Dies Committee's successor and provided a political dossier service for West Coast companies.[41]

Knowles's testimony was not atypical. Shortly before the 1938 elections, six other Dies Committee witnesses smeared Minnesota Governor Elmer Benson and his Farmer-Labor party. This testimony, intended to support Republican gubernatorial candidate Harold Stassen, was coordinated by Mark Gehan, a former Republican mayor of Saint Paul who was then an attorney for yet another employers' association, the Committee on Industrial Relations. Gehan's brother served as Stassen's campaign manager and Gehan himself was able to exploit the Dies Committee forum only after receiving six blank subpoenas signed by Dies. "If I had more subpoenas," Gehan said, "we could have got him enough witnesses to keep this stuff going for several days." The FBI also reported in 1940 on the less successful efforts of Wick Fowler, a former member of the Austin, Texas, Police Department and head of the Dies Committee's regional office in the Southwest, to smear the associates of Arizona Democratic party gubernatorial nominee Sidney P. Osborn. According to the Bureau's informant, Fowler was working on behalf of Governor Bob Jones (recently defeated by Osborn for the Democratic nomination) or his "friends" and Arizona State Attorney General Joe Conway.[42]

J. B. MATTHEWS AND THE CONSUMER MOVEMENT

Perhaps the most explicit example of Martin Dies's ideological preference involved J. B. Matthews's investigation of Communist influence in the consumer movement, long a favorite target of the Committee's chief investigator. When Matthews had been a vice-president of Consumers Research in 1934, he and Consumers Research President Fred J. Schlink co-authored *Partners in Plunder*, a consumer-oriented indictment of profit-gouging manufacturers. But when Schlink's own employees formed a union and struck in August 1935, Matthews, siding with management, denounced the strike as a Communist conspiracy. The strikers then broke off and set up the rival Consumers Union. Four years later, Matthews compiled a detailed exposé of the consumers movement, charging Communist infiltration of every national consumer organization—excepting his former employer and his wife's current employer. With Dies's backing, Matthews released his report to the press.

54

The decision to release the report enraged Jerry Voorhis and other Committee members who were not even aware of its existence. Voorhis pointedly dismissed the report as the unsubstantiated opinion of a disgruntled ex–consumer activist and eventually forced Dies and Matthews to retreat. The full Committee membership overruled the Chairman, and Matthews's study of Communist influence in the consumer movement was never printed in the official Committee record.[43]

Contrary to Voorhis's charge, Matthews's report was not solely motivated by a personal quest for revenge. The release of the report and accompanying publicity were carefully arranged by various special interests in reaction to a Federal Trade Commission (FTC) decision of August 17, 1939, to cite Hearst's *Good Housekeeping* for fraudulent advertising practices. The FTC specifically challenged the magazine's "seal of approval," charging that "the use of Good Housekeeping seals is calculated to, and does, mislead and deceive a substantial part of the purchasing public." One manufacturer claimed a seal of approval could be obtained simply by advertising in *Good Housekeeping*. On the other hand, if manufacturers cancelled their ads, the seal was summarily withdrawn. Though the FTC acted because of pressure brought by retailers and manufacturers and not by Communists in the consumer movement or "communistic" New Dealers, the Hearst press responded by red-baiting its critics.

Under Hearst Corporation Executive Vice-President Richard E. Berlin's direction, Hearst launched a massive anti-communist advertising blitz. In a telegram to 2,000 business executives and 1,000 publishers and editors on the day the FTC cited *Good Housekeeping*, Berlin warned of a Communist-dominated consumer movement that "must now be publicly exposed." Furthermore, when the FTC hearings opened that same month, Dies threatened to investigate "Communist influences" in consumer groups. He specifically urged "business leadership" to begin a purge of those "demagogues and racketeers who are able to sway the emotions of an uninformed people and teach them the damnable doctrines of socialism and communism." Matthews, in turn, accused Donald Montgomery, a consumers' counsel in the Department of Agriculture, of aiding and abetting Communists in the consumer movement.[44]

This joint strategy of red-baiting consumer activists and their New Deal benefactors was further refined during a dinner hosted by NAM trouble-shooter George Sokolsky. Attending Sokolsky's dinner party were Matthews, George Gallup and Raymond Rubican of the public relations firm of Young and Rubicam, Bristol-Meyers president Henry P. Bristol, representatives from the Association of National Advertisers, and other conservative corporate opponents of the New Deal. Fred Schlink, Matthews's former boss and president of the pristine Consumers Research, also attended. Though all guests claimed the dinner was strictly a social gathering, a specific course of action had been agreed upon. Matthews's ill-fated report was released to the press six days later.

On December 9, 1939, the day before Dies approved the release, Berlin, in a memorandum to hundreds of advertisers and manufacturers, praised Matthews's study for setting "forth precisely the facts I had in mind" when previously calling for public exposure of the subversive consumer movement. Berlin even gained access to some of the stencils Committee staff had prepared for their own press release and thus was able to reproduce and mail numerous copies of Matthews's report. Berlin, in short, had read, approved and widely disseminated what was announced as an official Dies Committee report before most Committee members—perhaps all except Dies—had even seen it.[45]

THE PRESIDENT AND THE INVESTIGATOR

During the popular front era, New Deal agencies like the FTC and New Deal liberals who tolerated Communists were natural threats to men like Matthews, Dies, and Thomas, who considered "fascism," "Nazism," "bolshevism," and "New Dealism" to be "the four horsemen of autocracy."[46] They were concerned because too many of the young men and women who flocked to Washington to staff the new alphabet agencies demonstrated an unholy tolerance of radicalism. But there was a more fundamental reason for the Dies Committee's concern. Quite simply, many congressional conservatives were troubled by the growth of presidential power, what the Committee called the "creeping totalitarianism" of the executive's "effort to obliterate the Congress of the United States as a co-equal and independent branch of government."[47] Though clearly partisan, the Dies Committee was essentially anti-executive.

The Committee's attacks on Franklin Roosevelt and the Democratic party were not unprecedented. Conservatives had red-baited the New Deal from the day Roosevelt launched his Hundred Days reforms, but throughout most of the 1930s congressional investigating committees sympathetic to the New Deal were dominant—prompting many conservatives to support Dies because they saw his Committee as an effective counter to Wisconsin Senator Robert M. La Follette, Jr., and his Civil Liberties Committee.[48]

Predictably, then, the Roosevelt administration and the Democratic party (except for the conservative Southern wing) attempted to counter the Dies Committee. During the abortive investigation of the consumer movement, for instance, the President urged Secretary of Agriculture Henry A. Wallace and the First Lady to exploit the affair by publicizing Matthews's careless charges and the embarrassing dinner party hosted by Sokolsky.[49] FDR even collected the most scurrilous missives sent in to the White House by hard-boiled Dies-haters and showed them to House Democratic majority leader Sam Rayburn of Texas and Assistant Attorney General Thurman Arnold. Then, in the fall of 1938, Charles Michelson, director of publicity for the Democratic National Committee, arranged for reporter Paul Y. Anderson to deliver on NBC radio a highly critical, first-hand account of the Dies Committee's procedures. Shortly thereafter, Harold Ickes secured a certified statement revealing that Dies had paid no taxes on his home and lot in Texas for eight years. Ickes also accused Dies Committee witness Alice Jemison of being "closely connected with" and "probably" financed by "certain pro-Nazi groups in this country." Jemison had appeared before the Committee to denounce the Commissioner of Indian Affairs, John Collier, for

Communist sympathies—a charge picked up by a Nazi press anxious to compare U.S. policy toward American Indians with the Third Reich's action against Jews.[50]

In November 1940, furthermore, Attorney General Jackson passed on a rumor to Hoover that Dies's father had been pro-German during the last war and that former Bureau Director Bielaski "had a large dossier on him." Six months later, following Dies's unsuccessful bid for the United States Senate, Roosevelt ordered the FBI to investigate for election fraud. According to Lyndon B. Johnson, then the New Deal candidate for the contested Senate seat, the FBI probe showed that a large proportion of Dies's vote in his strong counties was shifted to the eventual victor, Texas Governor W. Lee ("Pappy") O'Daniel. On another occasion in April 1942 FDR specifically requested an FBI investigation of Dies's campaign finances. The President's directive was inspired by an anonymous memorandum, forwarded to the White House by Supreme Court Justice Felix Frankfurter, charging Dies's campaign manager with receiving a $20,000 payment from Dr. Gerhardt Westrick—a German national who had solicited closer trade relations between the United States and Hitler's Reich prior to America's entry into the European war. Frankfurter vouched for his source and Roosevelt promptly wrote Attorney General Biddle: "This is so important that I think it should be pursued by you immediately. It comes to me from someone in whom I have great confidence." Four days later Biddle advised FDR of the FBI's failure to link Westrick's money with Dies's campaign manager despite "a painstaking investigation."[51]

Roosevelt also directed the FBI, on occasion, to investigate the Dies Committee's constituency, and the White House received Bureau reports on the Committee's activities as well. Hoover even forwarded newspaper cartoons critical of Dies to Roosevelt's aides. And in 1943, when responding to the President's request for a dossier on the nation's most ambitious anti-Semite, Gerald L. K. Smith, Hoover outlined Smith's contacts with Henry Ford, Harry Bennett, Senators Robert Reynolds and Gerald Nye, and Congressman Martin Dies.[52] FBI officials, however, did not share the administration's sometimes uncompromising opposition to the Dies Committee, for they primarily opposed Dies's style and not his announced purposes. Thus, eager to acquire political capital, Hoover also forwarded to the White House information received from Committee informer Harry Riley, the AFL's Chicago chief, regarding a CIO strike at International Harvester. More significantly, Hoover reported regularly to the White House on the anti-Dies Committee activities of Communist and other left-wing organizations.[53]

Such FBI services may help explain Franklin Roosevelt's restrained public position on the Committee.[54] The President and House leader Rayburn felt they could best contain the Dies Committee not by public confrontation but by working behind the scenes to limit the Committee's appropriations. They also tried to enlarge Committee membership by packing it with New Dealers and to beef up the La Follette Committee. These strategies failed, though Roosevelt did work with Voorhis and Starnes in an attempt to moderate the Dies Committee's behavior while Dempsey cooperated with administration officials in an attempt to embarrass and discredit the Chairman. And in December 1940, when the House passed a bill calling for the registration of foreign agents (it contained an amendment proposed by Dies that specifically required CPUSA officers and members to file), Roosevelt, White House aide Marvin H. McIntyre, and Supreme Court Justice James F. Byrnes responded by carefully devising a strategy to defeat the Dies amendment. Neither Byrnes's role in initiating this plan nor the fact that the White House supported it were to be revealed.[55]

Yet another strategy to contain Dies was to have the Justice Department investigate the various organizations he had been attacking. This simple approach was conceived by Attorney General Frank Murphy, a staunch liberal who, according to Ickes, "had weakened under pressure from Hoover." Murphy reasoned that if a grand jury convened and handed down indictments for espionage or other activities prohibited by criminal statute, Congress would see that the administration was acting responsibly and conclude that there was no reason to renew the Dies Committee's appropriations. Unknown to

Ickes at the time, Hoover's pressure on Murphy to pursue this particular approach might not have been mere routine. Within a month after Murphy was named Attorney General in late December 1938, the FBI opened a secret file containing derogatory information about Murphy's personal life and kept this file open even after Murphy moved on to the Supreme Court.[56]

Although a grand jury was never convened, the Roosevelt administration began to implement Murphy's strategy in January 1939 following FDR's announcement at a press conference that the Justice Department would investigate Dies's charges and prosecute all violators. Murphy, in turn, said that the FBI was still too busy to assign agents to assist the Committee on a regular basis. The Department, nonetheless, would consider specific requests for assistance. Murphy then ordered the FBI to investigate Dies's charge of Communist influence in the New York branch of the Federal Writers' Project and allegations that various fascist organizations were engaged in espionage. Later that same year, Justice Department attorneys and FBI agents began consulting Dies Committee files in these and other cases.[57]

In addition, Roosevelt acceded to some of Dies's demands. When Ickes issued a permit in June 1939 to the Workers Alliance Congress (WAC) to use an auditorium in the Labor Building, FDR ordered this permit withdrawn because a confidential FBI report seemingly confirmed Dies's charge that the WAC was a Communist front. Acting on the advice of Voorhis and Murphy, Roosevelt also acceded in May 1939 to Dies's request that the Committee be permitted to inspect federal income tax returns. Noting that Dies did not intend a "blanket search," Voorhis advised FDR to grant the request for political reasons. Murphy agreed. The Treasury Department, he predicted, could prevent "such excursions afield as are feared."[58]

Once war broke out in Europe and, in particular, after the rapid German advance in early 1940, Roosevelt was even more tolerant of the Dies Committee (though he never stopped trying to discredit the Chairman), while other liberals began to champion the Committee's work as complementing the FBI's. "The Committee, not the FBI," said Voorhis, "had to tell the country the story of Un-American activities. But the FBI, not the Committee, had to discover the basic facts on which the story could be built." As Hitler's successes mounted, members of the House who had long opposed the Dies Committee as a threat to civil liberties concluded that there was a place for the Committee in the American polity. Maury Maverick (D., Tex.), for one, offered to cooperate with his fellow Texan, and James F. O'Connor (D., Mont.), who had originally opposed the Dies Committee because he felt that it interfered with the FBI, announced that he had "been recently informed that the F.B.I. is in favor of its continuation and that both are working together."[59]

THE ROOSEVELT LOYALTY PROGRAM

Despite these public overtures from the administration and liberal congressmen, Dies continued to assail the New Deal and its personnel. He claimed that, during the Committee's seven-year lifetime, he had compiled files on more than 5,000 suspect government employees "with questionable records" and submitted their names to the administration. Indeed, the Special Committee to Investigate Un-American Activities was only a few months old when Dies first pressured Roosevelt about the federal employment of alleged subversives. In December 1938 Dies presented to the State Department a list of subversive organizations (including the ACLU) and asked the department to treat their members as agents of foreign governments.[60] This strategy, of submitting "evidence" and then criticizing the executive for not acting on it, became standard practice during the later McCarthy era. Its implications were fully appreciated by the Roosevelt administration.

In late 1938, for instance, J. Parnell Thomas requested a list of Communists employed by federal agencies, but Hoover responded that the Bureau had no such list. Less than a year later, however, Dies claimed that the Justice Department was investigating 2,850 known Communists in government and that FDR had ordered a purge of these federal employees. According to the *Chicago Tribune*, this list had been prepared by the FBI. But Roosevelt ordered no such purge and the *Tribune* later reported that the list was suppressed and FBI Director Hoover rebuked by the President.[61] Similarly, Eleanor Roosevelt recalled "one occasion [where] my husband and I were given a confidential list of organizations which were considered communist or subversive or un-American, a list compiled by the FBI for the use of the Dies Committee." Secretary of War Henry L. Stimson, Secretary of the Navy Frank Knox, Mrs. James Roosevelt (FDR's mother), and other people close to the administration were listed as financial contributors to two or more of the suspect groups.[62]

By 1941 pressure brought by the Committee began to have an effect. In February Hoover forwarded information to the White House regarding Dies's plans to investigate government employees. In early summer Congress approved a rider adding $100,000 to the Justice Department appropriations bill to enable the FBI to investigate "employees of every department, agency and independent establishment of the Federal Government who are members of subversive organizations" and report its findings to Congress. This rider, together with provisions of the Hatch Act of 1939 (which prohibited federal employee "membership in any political party which advocates the overthrow of our constitutional form of government"), also inspired the creation of the first Attorney General's list of subversive organizations. At the beginning, in June 1941, only eight organizations were declared subversive. Then in September the FBI distributed the list to its local field offices, and by February 1942 the Bureau had investigated twenty-two additional groups and recommended inclusion as subversive to Attorney General Biddle. Though Biddle proceeded cautiously, by May the list had grown to twelve Communist or Communist-front groups, two American Fascist organizations, eight Nazi and four Italian Fascist groups, and twenty-one Japanese groups. Membership in any of the proscribed organizations was grounds for dismissal from federal employment.[63] Except for the CPUSA, the Silver Shirts, and the German-American Bund, the listed organizations were kept secret— though a copy of the list was somehow leaked to Dies.[64]

The Roosevelt administration's loyalty program, furthermore, remained relatively moderate. More than 1,300 job applicants were rejected, but fewer than 200 federal employees lost their jobs or were subjected to disciplinary action during the entire wartime loyalty program. Roosevelt clearly intended to limit abuses and requested that a former New Deal official, journalist John Franklin Carter, compile a confidential report on "'Blacklisting' Government Employees." Significantly, Carter's report contained information about the FBI practice of searching Dies Committee files for derogatory information on federal employees. On the other hand, there was a touch of irony about this report. Carter served as the President's personal "spook," working closely with the FBI and occasionally reporting on such prominent Republicans as Wendell Willkie and Thomas E. Dewey. Operating a unit closely connected with a reluctant State Department, Carter's "specialized investigative work" received hundreds of thousands of dollars from the President's Emergency Fund. By the end of 1941 Carter's unit employed a staff of eleven. Jealous of Carter's prerogatives, the FBI began to spy on Franklin Roosevelt's private spy—advising the Attorney General in January 1942 that Carter recently spent 350 taxpayer dollars on cocktails "for the upper crust in New York."[65]

Despite an affinity for political intelligence, Roosevelt's loyalty program was characterized by restraint and not excess. And this restraint frustrated Dies *and* Hoover, who hoped the new loyalty program would legitimize the Bureau's effort to gather "comprehensive information in this field . . . through a program of progressive intelligence and not through isolated investigations of overt acts." In an effort to undercut Dies's charges and "to prevent recurrences of situations like the Dies-Henderson controversy" (where Leon Henderson, FDR's choice to head the Office of Price Administration, was accused of membership in five CPUSA fronts),[66] Biddle asked the Chairman for information relating to federal employees' membership in subversive organizations.

The FBI, of course, had ample files on the subversive associations of federal employees and was quite willing to publicize information from these files if it could be done without "embarrassing the Bureau." At least one federal employee named by Dies as a subversive, for instance, was the subject of an FBI "blind" memorandum (that is, unsigned and containing no identifying letterhead) connecting him to the allegedly subversive Consumers Union. Bureau officials, however, were reluctant to provide Biddle with much of the information contained in their files because it had been obtained illegally by break-ins at the offices of the American Youth Congress, the National Lawyers Guild, the Washington Committee for Democratic Action, and, possibly, dozens of other left-wing organizations. While considering Biddle's request, Dies solicited the advice of Albert C. Mattei, president of the San Francisco–based Honolulu Oil Company, financial backer of Republican party candidates in northern California, and close friend of Herbert Hoover. Mattei, in turn, checked with another close friend, FBI official Louis Nichols, and then advised Dies to send his list of names to the Attorney General and the FBI. Dies responded promptly by forwarding a list of 1,124 allegedly subversive federal employees to Biddle and Hoover. According to Jerry Voorhis, Dies's list was compiled from membership and mailing lists of the Washington Committee to Aid China, the Washington Bookshop, and the Washington branch of the American League for Peace and Democracy—as well as lists from at least one FBI break-in target, the Washington Committee for Democratic Action.[67]

Biddle, in turn, directed the FBI to compile "all available information concerning the [accused] employee's participation in un-American activities." The FBI was also authorized to investigate complaints of un-American activities on the part of federal employees received from other sources. As of August 22, 1942, the Bureau had received complaints concerning 4,579 federal workers. Only 149 of the workers were placed in the vague un-American category; most of the others were accused of Communist associations. Of the nearly 5,000 workers whose names had been referred to the FBI, only 36 (including 2 people on Dies's original list of 1,124) had been discharged. Another 13 were subjected to disciplinary action.[68]

Dies's response was to charge a cover-up. In September he claimed to possess an FBI report revealing that the Attorney General had allowed the Bureau to investigate only a small fraction of the 1,124 persons on his list. Under procedures established by Biddle, the FBI was required to forward individual complaints to appropriate department heads. Only they could request an FBI probe of the accused employee. There were only 193 requests for follow-up FBI investigations during the first three months of the loyalty program, even though the Bureau had forwarded 1,579 complaints to department heads.

This lack of response and Dies's continual criticisms pressured Biddle into revising the original procedure. Thereafter, the FBI was authorized to investigate solely on the basis of complaints received. The results of its probes were then turned over to department heads for individual evaluations. The new standards pleased Dies, but the Roosevelt administration still refused to initiate a sweeping purge. By the end of 1942, the FBI had investigated 601 people on Dies's original list, forwarding unevaluated reports to the department heads where the suspect federal employees worked. In 101 cases, the FBI's reports were not even acknowledged. Only two more people on Dies's list were fired, bringing the total to four. Two other federal employees were disciplined.[69]

If the Roosevelt administration intended these FBI investigations to deprive the Committee of its most volatile issue and further demonstrate a responsible attitude toward the Communists-in-government problem, the immediate result was quite different. As Ickes noted in a letter to FDR, "a departmental report clearing the man and a decision not to fire him may simply serve to prove Dies' main point, that your Administration cherishes men who want to subvert the Government."[70] And if New Deal officials did not then have to pay a major political price for ignoring FBI loyalty reports, in the long run they would. Dies responded to the administration's condescending effort to investigate his cover-up charges by arguing that those department heads who had refused to purge their staffs were abetting communism. This position was supported wholeheartedly by the FBI.

In response to Dies's charges, FBI officials first obtained "access to confidential records" of forty-seven "subversive groups," then identified suspect federal employees by name, and finally submitted a detailed four-volume report to the Attorney General with a recommendation that it be made available to Congress. According to these Bureau officials, the President, on the other hand, "was primarily interested in having the Bureau's summary report discredit the Dies Committee." Thus after consulting with House Democratic Leader Rayburn, Biddle ordered a reluctant FBI to prepare for Congress only a brief twenty-page report, "anonymous in nature both as to names of the persons investigated and the organizations which had been declared subversive." In contrast to Biddle, Rayburn, and Roosevelt, Hoover and his top aides wanted to name each and every suspect federal employee and all forty-seven groups on the Attorney General's list of subversive organizations. Dies, for his part, was aware that the original report "had been sent back to the FBI to be 'toned down.'"[71]

THE KERR COMMITTEE

Martin Dies, however, did not allow the Communists-in-government issue to lapse. His March 1942 denouncement of thirty-five Board of Economic Warfare (BEW) employees prompted Vice-President Wallace to sneer that the effect of Dies's charges on government employees' morale "would be no less damaging if Mr. Dies were on the Hitler payroll." Wallace, nonetheless, promised that the FBI would investigate all thirty-five. Even when Dies inspired a libel lawsuit (he confused BEW worker David B. Vaughn with another David Vaughn), the House paid Dies's court costs and the Chairman continued to name names. He supplemented a list of nineteen suspect government employees from September 4, 1942, with the names of thirty-nine "irresponsible, unrepresentative, crackpot, radical bureaucrats" on February 1, 1943. After an abortive attempt to withhold the salary of one of these federal workers, the House set up a special committee chaired by John H. Kerr (D., N.C.) to investigate the charges.

The so-called Kerr Committee, described by Ickes as part of "a vicious political campaign" led by "a small group of men determined to smear . . . the Administration, irrespective of the cost to the war," ultimately investigated nine people. It cleared six of them but deemed the other three unfit for government service. Its findings were based primarily on evidence presented to the Civil Service Commission by the FBI, with the Dies Committee preparing detailed charges supported by its files. FBI officials closely monitored the Kerr Committee proceedings and furnished it with at least two "blind" memorandums. One blind memorandum involved the ACLU. Another concerned a film entitled *The Negro in America* and contained data submitted to the FBI by the State Department "in the strictest of confidence."[72]

Whether the FBI worked through Kerr Committee support staff or had direct contact with Kerr Committee members is not known. By 1945, however, Congressman Kerr was serving the FBI as a conduit. On one known occasion he called Hoover with a request for FBI "material 'to get some things over to the public.'" The Bureau responded by preparing a speech for Kerr that was read into the *Congressional Record* and reproduced in the *FBI Law Enforcement Bulletin*. Kerr, in turn, thanked FBI Associate Director Tolson for the "splendid statement . . . in reference to the work of the F.B.I."[73]

AT ODDS

Although the FBI covertly assisted the Kerr Committee in order to support Dies's charges, Dies and Hoover did not often work in harmony. Problems first arose during the summer of 1938, when Dies unsuccessfully attempted to borrow FBI agents for his Committee. Then, in January 1939, after the Philadelphia SAC, A. Bernard Leckie, had attended Dies's luncheon address at the Penn Athletic Club, Hoover issued a directive: "I think it is undesirable for our agents to attend such affairs. There can be placed misinterpretation upon such attendance to our embarrassment." Edward Tamm responded by rebuking the SAC, "*pointing out that Mr. Dies has been accusing the Department of investigating him* and . . . even alleging that the Bureau is being used by the White House to whitewash the purportedly astounding conditions that he has uncovered."[74]

These strained relations developed into a feud between Dies and Hoover in 1940 when Dies reportedly referred to the FBI's agents as "a bunch of boy scouts." He then labeled Bureau efforts to contain sabotage in defense plants inadequate and announced that the Special Committee on Un-American Activities could supplement the FBI's more orthodox methods by exposing prospective foreign agents. According to Dies, there were 5,000 potential saboteurs—Bundists, Communists, and aliens—in Detroit alone. In May 1940 Dies called for the establishment of a "Home Defense Council" to coordinate national defense matters. Hoover responded to this proposal by advising the White House that it was unnecessary. The President had already designated the FBI as the central coordinating agency and, further, the Bureau was spying on all groups espousing "un-American principles."[75]

Dies's concern over sabotage seemed well founded. In September 1940 the Hercules powder plant in New Jersey blew up, killing fifty-one people. Two months later, three other East Coast powder plants exploded within an hour of each other. Public concern was further heightened in November by the Vultee strike. Many suspected that this strike, led by United Automobile Workers Union organizers (whom John Frey had named as Communists before the Dies Committee), was a Communist-directed attempt to cripple America's aircraft industry. Then, after Committee investigators raided the headquarters of German and Italian organizations in New York and Chicago, Dies announced that a confessed Gestapo agent, Heinrich Peter Fassbender, had identified several official representatives of foreign governments in the United States as espionage agents. The November 20 release of a Committee "white paper" detailing these alleged espionage activities was considered premature and led directly to Justice Department criticism of the Dies Committee and a public rebuke from Hoover.[76]

The white paper consisted of staff reports on various Nazi organizations and individuals in the United States, supplemented by facsimiles of documents seized during the recent raids. (Much of the white paper concentrated on Manfred Zapp, director of the Transocean News service. Many of Zapp's personal letters, cablegrams, and telegrams revealed close ties with high-ranking German Nazis and showed that Transocean News was spreading Nazi propaganda in South and Central America.) Though the Committee exaggerated the extent of German espionage and propaganda activities in the United States, the press gave the white paper front-page publicity, thereby implying that the Dies Committee knew more about the espionage/sabotage problem than the FBI did.

The white paper did appear to catch the FBI off guard. Upon first learning in early October that Dies was investigating Zapp and Transocean, Hoover demanded to know why his agents "weren't . . . on top of this?" The affair also raised the prospect of criticism from a source normally supportive of both the Dies Committee and the FBI. Paul Mallon, an editor and columnist for the Hearst-owned King Features Syndicate, responded to Dies's revelations by sending a confidential letter critical of the Bureau to several (perhaps all) newpaper editors associated with Hearst's International News Service. Hoover countered by contacting Edmond D. Coblentz, publisher of the *San Francisco Call Bulletin* and supervisor of the editorial division for the entire Hearst conglomerate, for advice and assistance in "straighten[ing] Mallon out."[77]

Attorney General Jackson responded to the Zapp-Transocean episode by condemning the Committee's interference with an ongoing criminal investigation. (The Bureau had filed a confidential if rather belated report with the White House on Zapp's activities three weeks before the Committee released its report to the press but nearly four weeks after learning of Dies's interest in Transocean.)[78] Complaining on November 24 that premature publicity had effectively precluded the successful prosecution of Zapp and cohorts, Jackson again condemned the timing of the Dies Committee exposé. (The Attorney General, nonetheless, conceded the value of exposing subversive activities.) Ridiculing Dies's suggestion that the FBI was not doing its job, he dismissed the Chairman's chief witness, Fassbender, as a "professional and unreliable" informer who had been investigated twice for white slavery and was suspected of operating a confidence game. Then, to head off another promised Dies Committee probe, Jackson announced that there was no need for the Committee to look into the Vultee strike because the FBI had already concluded it was orchestrated by Communists.[79]

Hoover responded to Jackson's press release on November 23 by directing the heads of FBI field offices to distribute it "to all friendly newspaper contacts in your district to insure . . . the widest possible coverage." In New York, FBI Assistant Director Nichols worked with city editor Paul Schoenstein and reporter Frank L. Donoghue of the *New York Journal American*, arranging an exclusive interview with Hoover that was read into the *Congressional Record*, reproduced for distribution by the FBI, and syndicated in the Hearst press.[80] Bureau officials also worked closely with Homer Chaillaux of the American Legion's National Americanism Commission and ACLU attorney Morris Ernst, while escalating their surveillance of the Dies Committee. After approving a suggestion "that each and every employee of the Dies Committee be checked out," Hoover forwarded FBI reports on at least three Committee employees (Matthews, Mandel, and Birmingham) to Jackson. The rationale for these investigations was a "suspicion" that certain staff members were in reality CPUSA moles and, thus, that the Dies Committee was a Communist front with a mission to destroy the FBI. Hoover, for his part, concluded that "the Dies attack smells and there is certainly something in back of it other than that which appears on the surface."[81]

But Dies did not criticize the FBI when responding to Jackson. Instead, he complained of "technical limitations" imposed upon the Bureau, alluding to "many cases in which the Attorney General has failed to act, in spite of evidence furnished by the FBI." Dies offered as an example the dismissal of indictments against the Spanish Civil War veterans arrested *en masse* by the Bureau in February 1940 during predawn raids in Detroit, Milwaukee, and New York. Nor did Dies hesitate to redbait the Attorney General. He cited Jackson's support of such Communist fronts as the American League for Peace and Democracy (which sold anti–Dies Committee Christmas cards) and the League of American Writers.[82]

Dies also called for more assistance from the executive branch. This plea led President Roosevelt to send the Chairman a telegram at his home in Orange, Texas, that, though critical of the Committee's interference in ongoing criminal investigations, advised Dies that "as soon as this distinction [between un-American and criminal activities] is clearly recognized, there is no reason why there should not be complete harmony between your committee and the executive branch." Roosevelt, who had been receiving FBI reports on Dies's alleged criticisms of the FBI even before the Chairman had made them public, then met face to face with Dies (with a stenographer present) on November 29.

Despite FDR's refusal to initiate Dies's sweeping seven-point countersubversive program or even to provide the Chairman with a transcript of their conference, the President and Dies had nonetheless come to an agreement of sorts.[83] Conceding the need for "education . . . just so long as you don't hurt human lives," Roosevelt suggested that Dies "go to the Attorney General" and "work out a *modus operandi* . . . leaving in large part to the committee the very excellent and essential work which is arousing the country to the potential dangers that exist in our midst everywhere. That is perfectly all right, a perfectly proper thing for the committee to do." Dies, for his part, promised not to interfere with ongoing criminal investigations and pledged to cooperate fully with the FBI. He then went on a speaking tour, assigning Voorhis to reach a more formal agreement with the Justice Department.

An agreement was reached on December 10. In a letter to Voorhis, Jackson began by noting that efforts by the FBI and the Dies Committee should be complementary rather than competitive. He then promised to "comply" with requests "to furnish the committee information which . . . is not involved in probable prosecutive action." Thus, the Justice Department would secretly and "informally" forward FBI reports to the Dies Committee. Such a procedure, Jackson added, had already been implemented on an ad hoc basis. Committee members Voorhis, Starnes, Dempsey, "and perhaps others" had been given "specific information." "Any limitations that we have asked on publicity," Jackson concluded, "have in each instance been faithfully observed."[84]

Seven days after the Dies Committee and the Justice Department arrived at this understanding, the Department released a report that Hoover had originally submitted on November 28 (the day after Dies met with FDR). Hoover rebuked Dies for holding "the F.B.I. up to ridicule" by summarily dismissing his charges of widespread sabotage in defense industries, but nonetheless affirmed that there was a place for the Committee. Hoover's report branded Dies Committee adversary Harry Bridges a Communist and indirectly praised the Committee's Appendix I (a lengthy report also released on November 28 that sought to document the Party's advocacy of violent revolution) by declaring that the CPUSA sought to overthrow the U.S. government by force and violence. To bolster public confidence in the Bureau's investigative prowess, Hoover revealed the existence of a "defense index" of some 6,000 persons judged by the FBI to be "potential enemies of the nation."[85] Dies, for his part, had confided to Albert Mattei, the FBI confidant and Republican party politico, that his attack on the FBI was "unwarranted." According to Mattei's briefing of Bureau official Nichols, the repentant Dies "now wants to right himself and if anybody goes after the boss [Hoover], he in turn is going after him."[86]

A RED-HUNTER'S REWARD

Thereafter, the FBI occasionally supported the Dies Committee; its support, however, was cautious and limited. The Voorhis-Jackson agreement had little effect on the Committee's fortunes and did not change the FBI Director's opinion of Martin Dies as a rank amateur. (In February 1941, after J. B. Matthews revealed Committee plans for a round-up of Soviet agents, Hoover wrote: "Now that it is announced that the hunt is on I imagine the OPGU agents will sit and wait for Buck Dies and his merry men to arrive.")[87] The Dies Committee quietly expired in December 1944 at the end of the Seventy-Eighth Congress. Seven months earlier Dies, in the midst of a protracted battle with the CIO's National Citizens Political Action Committee, announced that he would not stand for reelection. He cited poor health and a desire to return to private business. Dies did not return to the House until 1953 and though he served as a representative-at-large until 1959, he remained too controversial for the new generation of red-hunters to accept.[88]

His own party refused to appoint him to HUAC, an affront which prompted Dies to unearth yet another list (of 100,000 subversives this time) and to threaten to "move independently" if the Committee failed to act. Senator McCarthy was one of the few congressional anticommunists to support Dies's efforts to get back into the game—though an Eisenhower aide suggested (perhaps facetiously) that the President appoint Dies to be his "personal representative in assembling information and data from all sources relative to Communist activities in government circles." In 1963, nine years before his death, Dies made his last public pronouncements ("lest I be asked on Judgment Day, 'Why did you sin by silence when you knew the truth?'") in his autobiography on the Communist threat. Filled with Christian revivalist rhetoric and gloomy predictions for the capitalist West, Dies's account of his life lends some credence to Walter Goodman's characterization of the Chairman. Goodman contended that Martin Dies

> represented . . . an aching nostalgia for pre–World War I America . . . for a style of life that was being shaken by industrial unions, by the Negro awakening, by revolutionary currents of every sort. He stood for fundamentalist enthusiasm against the radical enlightenment . . . for capitalism and the Constitution and God, and these were under attack from Pennsylvania Avenue and from New York City as much as from Moscow.[89]

Dies may or may not have longed for the good old days or resented his loss of status. Vice-President Garner's 1939 prediction, as recalled by Harry S. Truman, was probably closer to the mark. "The Dies Committee," said Garner, "is going to have more influence on the future of American politics than any other committee of Congress."[90] Under the direction of Dies's heirs, and with more systematic assistance from the FBI, the Committee nearly proved Garner right. Dies and his Committee refined many of the methods and techniques later identified with McCarthyism. They mined the Communists-in-government issue, strove to legitimize guilt by association, championed the veracity of ex-Communist witnesses, and worked diligently to open a direct pipeline to the FBI. Dies also named "more names in a single year," as Robert Griffith said, "than Joe McCarthy did in a lifetime."[91]

More importantly, Dies and his Committee became a symbol of anticommunism, as HUAC and McCarthy would after 1950—a rallying point for crusading ex-Communists, right-wing interest groups, and the conservative press. Nonetheless, when the Dies Committee expired at the end of 1944, anticommunism remained the peculiar prerogative of right-wingers and was summarily dismissed by most Americans as a conservative anti–New Deal politics. This political style matured only during the postwar period, obtaining a legitimacy that Dies had never been able to obtain. Then, the more respectable anticommunist interest groups that had made up the old Dies Committee constituency were joined by J. Edgar Hoover's FBI in a more formal, sustaining relationship. The Bureau, the Dies Committee's successor, and their journalist allies took up where Dies left off. Though the Dies Committee paved the way, the anticommunist political style triumphed only when the FBI provided the type of assistance to HUAC and to other anticommunist interests that Martin Dies had ached for.

CHAPTER **III**

Making the Cold War: Shaping Public Opinion

With the demise of the Dies Committee and the voluntary retirement of Martin Dies, the domestic Communist issue appeared to have run its course by the time the Seventy-Ninth Congress convened on January 3, 1945. When Rule Committee Chairman Adolph Sabath (D., Ill.) moved to adopt the rules of the previous Congress, however, John Rankin offered an amendment to make the old Dies Committee a permanent committee of the House and to increase its membership from seven to nine. This shrewd parliamentary maneuver, Rankin later boasted, caught Sabath and other Dies Committee opponents "flat-footed and flat-headed." Because the House had not yet organized itself, the resolution could not be referred to the Rules Committee. Rankin forced a roll call vote and won 207 to 186. The coalition that voted to establish a standing Committee on Un-American Activities included Republicans, conservative Southern Democrats, and, by default, cautious New Dealers like Lyndon B. Johnson (D., Tex.) and thirty-nine other congressmen who voted a neutral present.[1]

HUAC's initial membership included Democrats Rankin (Miss.), Herbert C. Bonner (N.C.), J. Hardin Peterson (Fla.), John R. Murdock (Ariz.), and J. W. Robinson (Utah), Republicans George W. Landis (Ind.), Karl E. Mundt (S.D.), and J. Parnell Thomas (N.J.), and chairman Edward J. Hart (D., N.J.), whose enthusiasm for the task quickly cooled. Only Rankin and Dies Committee alumni Mundt and Thomas played much of a role in the new Committee's deliberations.[2] Dominated throughout 1945 by Rankin, a primitive racist

75

adept at baiting Communists, blacks, and Jews (he once referred to Walter Winchell as "a little slimemongering kike"), the Committee proceeded slowly, if not cautiously.[3] HUAC issued no reports in 1945 and limited its investigations to three days of public hearings on the Office of Price Administration (OPA) in June and four days of hearings on the Communist party in late September and October. Thereafter, as the CPUSA jettisoned its wartime accommodation policy and the FBI poised to resume battle with the real enemy (J. Edgar Hoover even sent a report to the White House on Communist demonstrations in support of the OPA in the midst of the HUAC hearings), the Committee became very busy indeed.[4]

TOWARD AN INFORMED PUBLIC OPINION

The Committee's more effective activities, after its first bumpy year as a standing committee of the House, can be traced in part to a decision made by senior FBI officials to provide covert support to HUAC and the various anticommunist interest groups that coalesced around it. At an FBI executives' conference in February 1946, D. Milton Ladd proposed that the Bureau initiate a pervasive program to undermine Communist support among "labor unions," "persons prominent in religious circles," and "the Liberal elements." Going far beyond mere containment or surveillance of Communists and their alleged liberal benefactors, Ladd called for a domestic propaganda campaign to dramatize the seriousness of the threat posed to America's internal security by CPUSA radicals and those indigenous dissidents who defended their constitutional rights.

By compiling and disseminating "educational materials" through "available channels," Ladd reasoned, the FBI could and should mobilize its public relations machinery for the purpose of nurturing an anticommunist consensus. In contrast to the Bureau's last major effort to shape public opinion—the anticrime campaign of the gangster-ridden 1930s—the current campaign was intended to develop "an informed public opinion" about "the basically Russian nature of the Communist

Party in this country." To prepare for this new effort, Ladd further recommended a special training seminar for "Communist supervisors" from some twenty key FBI field offices. The FBI executives' conference approved all of Ladd's recommendations.[5]

At this time the party was already in decline (by the FBI's own estimate CPUSA membership peaked at about 80,000 in 1944), but the program proposed by Ladd and initiated by the Bureau in February 1946 did not represent a shift in FBI officials' perception of the seriousness of the internal Communist threat. The Bureau had instructed Americans on the red menace both before and during World War II, forwarding information to the Dies Committee and alerting management to potentially subversive employees. Prior to February 1946, these efforts were mostly informal, episodic, and ad hoc. Ladd's contribution was one of expansion rather than innovation. He called for the FBI to assume the ambitious task of shaping the emerging national debate on the domestic Communist issue.

Ladd's proposals were carried out enthusiastically by Hoover, who intensified his own extracurricular ventures. He appeared frequently as a speaker on the anticommunist circuit under the auspices of such patriotic societies as the Daughters of the American Revolution or the Veterans of Foreign Wars (VFW) and testified before HUAC in March 1947 as an expert witness on the menace.[6] HUAC members and other congressmen invariably read these speeches into the *Congressional Record*. Hoover's HUAC testimony, broadcast over a national radio network, was later reproduced and disseminated by the Committee and the FBI.

With dozens of FBI agents from the Crime Records Division (CRD) writing his speeches and arranging radio coverage and other forms of dissemination, Hoover emerged as one of the nation's most prolific authors. From February 1946 until his death in 1972, Hoover published nearly 400 major items—over 200 articles (including, in 1947, a front page *Newsweek* magazine story on the red menace), 37 speeches, interviews in nationally syndicated magazines (*U.S. News and World Report* was a particular favorite), reports, pamphlets—and many

77

lesser items in obscure dailies and periodicals. He also frequently wrote columns, under his own signature, for vacationing newspaper columnists. Both a scholar and a popularizer, Hoover assailed reds, "pseudo-liberals," and assorted other "rats" in the pages of *Popular Mechanics* and the *Harvard Business Review*. (He contributed some 60 articles to law reviews and professional journals.) His magnum opus, *Masters of Deceit* (1958), sold 250,000 copies in hardback and two million copies in paperback—with honorific book reviews written and planted by the CRD who also assumed responsibility for adequate distribution. Hoover's less earthy *A Study of Communism* (1962), written as a high school text, sold nearly 125,000 copies. Nearly everything Hoover and the CRD wrote publicized either the red menace, the FBI, or both.[7]

Though Hoover received all the credit (and virtually all the royalties) for everything written in his name, it was Louis Nichols who directed the CRD and was the chief architect of the FBI program to shape public opinion. A graduate of Kalamazoo College and the Washington University Law School, Nichols joined the Bureau in 1934 and participated in the manhunt for Alvin Karpis and other gangsters. By 1938 Nichols was in charge of the Research Division at Bureau headquarters, supervising such projects as the indexing of Dies Committee reports and hearings, the researching of FBI files for Courtney Ryley Cooper, and the cultivation of John D. Rockefeller and other powerful Americans.[8] In 1939, he was made Inspector and named his first child after J. Edgar Hoover. Three years later, he rose to the position of Assistant Director[9] and in 1951 was named one of two Assistants to the Director. According to Nichols, the other Assistant to the Director, Ladd, was responsible for the "investigative stuff" while he, Nichols, "handled policy and administrative matters, plus the outside contacts and, well, the grief for the Bureau."[10] "Well known at headquarters as a man who believed himself capable of selling anyone anything," Nichols was the only person inside the Bureau who could challenge Hoover or convince him to reverse decisions. When Nichols left the Bureau in 1957 at the age of fifty-one, he persuaded his new employer, Louis S. Rosenstiel of Schenley Industries, to establish and endow the J.

Edgar Hoover Foundation. Thereafter, and at a reported salary of $100,000 a year, Nichols served Schenley officially and the FBI unofficially as a lobbyist in Washington.[11]

The Press. As FBI Assistant Director in charge of Crime Records, Nichols's public relations responsibilities were not limited to supervising the writing of speeches, books, and articles for release under Hoover's signature or to distributing up to one-half million copies per year of the CRD promotional pamphlet, *The Story of the Federal Bureau of Investigation.*[12] To fulfill the policy objective agreed on at the February 1946 FBI executives' conference, Nichols cultivated national publicists (available channels) to whom he leaked, from the FBI's confidential files, derogatory information (educational materials) that seemed to confirm FBI officials' contention that Communists and other dissidents posed a serious threat to America's internal security.

To identify those publicists discreet enough to receive information from Bureau files without disclosing the source of their information, the CRD conducted extensive investigations and in the process developed a "not to contact list" of "individuals known to be hostile to the Bureau." And these publicists—including historian Henry Steele Commager, "personnel of CBS," and former Secretary of the Interior Ickes— were often themselves the subjects of FBI leaks. On January 4, 1950, Hoover ordered memorandums prepared for each name on the "not to contact list." If publicists were considered indiscreet but were nonetheless sufficiently anticommunist to attract Nichols's attention, the Crime Records Division "fed them raw meat" in the form of anonymous, blind memorandums mailed to their offices in unmarked envelopes. Discreet and reliable FBI contacts, in contrast, did not always need to be pointed in the right direction. Accordingly, the CRD occasionally forwarded information directly to these publicists but more often served as a source of corroboration—for instance, assuring anticommunist reporters that those they planned to name really were CPUSA members and, whenever possible, even supplying party card numbers.[13]

Publicists who could be counted on to publish Bureau stories in return for a promise of future favors by Nichols or his protégé, Cartha DeLoach, included nationally syndicated radio commentators and newspaper columnists: Walter Winchell; Drew Pearson; Jack Anderson; Victor Riesel; Paul Harvey; David Lawrence; George Sokolsky; Westbrook Pegler; and Fulton Lewis, Jr., and reporters: Karl Hess and Ralph de Toledano of *Newsweek*; Scripps-Howard's Frederick Woltman (who won a Pulitzer Prize in 1947 for a series of articles published the previous year on Communist infiltration); United Press Washington bureau chief Lyle Wilson; *New York Herald Tribune* Washington bureau chief Don Whitehead; *Chicago Tribune* Washington bureau chief Walter Trohan; *Chicago Tribune* staff writers Willard Edwards and Ronald Koziol; Hearst's Jim Bishop and David Sentner; Ed Montgomery of the *San Francisco Examiner*; Sandy Smith (later of *Time* and *Life* magazines); and Jeremiah O'Leary of the *Washington Evening Star*.[14] In the field, FBI Special Agents in Charge were encouraged to establish their own newspaper contacts. In 1946, for instance, the *Milwaukee Journal*'s crusade against Communists in the Milwaukee labor movement was based on material leaked by the local FBI office.[15]

Books, Films, Radio, and Television. The Bureau's practice of selectively distributing data gleaned from its classified files contrasted starkly with FBI Director Hoover's public posturing. "Should a given file be disclosed," he advised a Senate Foreign Relations Subcommittee in 1950,

> the issue would be a far broader one than concerns the subject of the investigation. Names of persons who by force of circumstance entered into the investigation might well be innocent of any wrong. To publicize their names without the explanation of the associations would be a grave injustice. Even though they were given an opportunity to later give their explanation, the fact remains that truth seldom, if ever, catches up with charges. I would not want to be a party to any action which would

"smear" innocent individuals for the rest of their lives. We cannot disregard the fundamental principles of common decency and the application of basic American rights of fair play. . . . [16]

Despite the civil libertarian ring to such rhetoric, Hoover was not interested in protecting the integrity of FBI files or buttressing President Harry S. Truman's claims of executive privilege.[17] Whereas Truman sought to prohibit congressional access—particularly by HUAC members and Senator McCarthy—to FBI reports and other loyalty data, Hoover intended only to set the terms of their access.[18] Hoover's policy objectives, in striking contrast to Truman's, required the FBI to provide conservative congressmen and other anticommunist interests with limited access to Bureau files. Accordingly, FBI officials, and not the President, unilaterally and secretly decided who would and who would not gain access to the educational materials locked in FBI files. "All requests of this type," as an FBI executives' conference of October 1953 put it, "are individually considered and information is furnished where the best interests of the Bureau would be served." In all other cases FBI officials relied on their "standard claim that the files of the FBI are confidential" and referred the requests to the Attorney General.[19]

While pursuing this dissemination strategy, FBI officials worked simultaneously to enhance the Bureau's image as a disinterested, nonpartisan, fact-gathering investigative agency. Indeed, Hoover's testimony to the Senate Foreign Relations Subcommittee was widely publicized by Don Whitehead in *The FBI Story*, a work based upon Whitehead's privileged access to Bureau files. Grounded in documents "spoon-fed" by Nichols, Whitehead's manuscript was promoted by the FBI Recreation Association, which purchased copies to boost sales and distribution, and by the CRD, which wrote and planted book reviews. *The FBI Story* eventually became a best-seller, inspiring a film version starring James Stewart.[20]

Whitehead was only one of many authors who promised both to champion the FBI's apolitical image and to publicize FBI officials' conviction that CPUSA members were dangerous. Thus, when writing *The FBI's Most Famous Cases*

81

Andrew Tully had access to Bureau files, and Harry and Bonaro Overstreet were assisted with *The FBI in Our Open Society*. Again, the FBI Recreation Association distributed thousands of copies of these books.[21]

FBI officials' efforts to enhance their own image and to dramatize the red menace extended beyond the print media. The Bureau provided script material, content editing expertise, production consultation, and sometimes even special agents as actors to radio producers for such serials as *This Is Your FBI* (1945-1952);[22] to television producers for the ABC series *The FBI* (1965-1974);[23] and to movie producers for at least eight films between 1945 and 1959, including *Notorious* (1946) and *Street with No Name* (1948). *Big Jim McClain* (1952), written by William Wheeler and Richard English and based on HUAC investigator Wheeler's experiences searching for Communists in Hawaii, starred John Wayne—whose moves around the set were duly noted by local Bureau agents in reports to Hoover.[24]

Even these successes could not satisfy the insatiable Nichols. When reporting to Clyde Tolson on the efforts of American Civil Liberties Union counsel Morris Ernst to persuade Sam Goldwyn to make a film on the Bureau, Nichols noted the desirability of keeping "a picture in the process of development at all times" to insure "the release of a feature picture approximately every two years." The only problem, Nichols added, was the inevitable drain on Bureau resources. Though two FBI films were produced in 1948, Hoover, for the time being, rejected Nichols's proposal. "*Our whole* public relations," he said, "has been in the doldrums for the last nine months. We must get the *essential* things working properly before embarking on such a project as this."[25] Nichols soon straightened things out to the FBI Director's satisfaction. Between 1951 and 1959 the Bureau helped produce four feature films, thereby meeting Nichols's goal of at least one film every two years.

Anticommunist Liberals. Ernst's role as intermediary between the Bureau and Goldwyn suggests that Nichols sometimes enlisted the support of discreet anticommunist liberals. FBI officials worked closely with Ernst and with G. Bromley

Oxnam, Methodist Bishop of Washington and a president of the World Council of Churches. In April 1947 Oxnam asked Hoover to meet with a group of Methodist bishops to discuss the emerging Communist issue. Though he declined this invitation, the FBI Director forwarded a copy of his recent HUAC testimony and said he would send Nichols, a fellow Methodist, to see him. Thereafter, Oxnam occasionally provided confidential information to Nichols and helped him contain criticisms of the Bureau emanating from radical Methodist clergy. Nichols, in turn, granted Oxnam access to FBI files, whether by delivering a particular file for the bishop's perusal or forwarding summaries of derogatory information.

In January 1951, for instance, Oxnam requested information on the Reverend Edward D. McGowan of the Bronx because "he has not been particularly effective as a Negro" and was rumored to be a member of the American Labor party (ALP). Nichols responded by sending "public source data" on McGowan and the ALP. Two years earlier, Nichols had shown Oxnam the FBI file on the Reverend Jack R. McMichael, executive secretary of the Methodist Federation for Social Action. Oxnam later confronted McMichael with the charge of CPUSA membership, but refused to reveal the source of his information. McMichael denied the charge. He claimed it could be traced to a series of biased press stories by Frederick Woltman that, in turn, had inspired Hoover's article, "God or Chaos," in the February 1949 issue of *Redbook*. Once again Oxnam checked with Nichols who assured him that the Bureau did indeed have evidence on McMichael.[26]

McMichael, of course, had it wrong. Hoover's articles were not based on information uncovered by Woltman. The Crime Records Division had instead leaked information not only to Oxnam but to Woltman on alleged Communist infiltration of the Protestant clergy in an effort to implement the Bureau's policy objective, as outlined at the February 1946 executives' conference, of undermining support for and tolerance of Communists by "persons prominent in religious circles." Accordingly, Hoover directed a propaganda drive to highlight Communist infiltration of the clergy—advising HUAC in March 1947 of his "real apprehension so long as Communists are able to secure ministers of the Gospel to promote their evil work."

The Committee, for its part, cooperated with this FBI effort, concentrating on Communist infiltration of the National Council of Churches. First named as a CPUSA front by a Naval Intelligence officer in 1935, the National Council was singled out for its alleged modernist and socialist influence by such far-right preachers as Carl McIntyre and Billy James Hargis. HUAC regularly disseminated derogatory information on the Council to virtually anyone who requested it. McIntyre in particular worked closely with HUAC, providing a list of one hundred fellow-travelling Protestant clergymen to the Committee in 1948. One of those named by McIntyre, the Reverend Charles Hill of Detroit, was later lectured by HUAC member Donald L. Jackson:

> Men who have the high calling of the ministry, men who are dedicated to God and to His works are today rotting in prison cells in every country in the Communist orbit. Their Bibles are rotting beside them. . . . For a minister, for a man of the cloth, to aid or comfort or endorse or lend his assistance to the Communist Party, is to compound the offense by including God Almighty in his treason.[27]

As this statement suggests, at least some HUAC members shared the fundamentalist intolerance of men like McIntyre and Hargis. And if McIntyre's extremism led the FBI to investigate his activities, the Bureau kept anticommunist clergymen like Oxnam under surveillance as well and may have arranged (without Oxnam's knowledge or consent) his later testimony before HUAC. A bona fide fellow traveller during the 1930s, Oxnam had a hefty FBI file, which was summarized at Hoover's request in June 1948. Five years later, following McIntyre's publication of a pamphlet entitled *Bishop Oxnam, Prophet of Marx* and J. B. Matthews's notorious *American Mercury* article on Communist infiltration of the Protestant clergy, HUAC Chairman Harold Velde (R., Ill.) launched an investigation of his own by subpoenaing Oxnam and his nemesis, Jack McMichael. A prolific critic of HUAC, Oxnam exploited his public appearance both to rail against the

Committee's methods and to highlight his own anticommunist credentials, which had been chronicled by the FBI since 1943.

The FBI was not a disinterested party as these events unfolded. HUAC's charges against Oxnam closely paralleled the bill of particulars that FBI officials had drawn up for Hoover's use five years earlier. And despite the concomitant embarrassment caused by Matthews's *American Mercury* article and its controversial thesis ("the largest single group supporting the Communist apparatus in the United States today is composed of Protestant clergymen"), Hoover tactfully supported Matthews. He advised Senator Harry F. Byrd (D., Va.) that the CPUSA was using unwitting Protestant ministers and conferred, according to I.F. Stone, with the junior Senator from Wisconsin on the choice of a replacement for the discredited Matthews. (Matthew's embarrassing article had led President Eisenhower and Vice-President Nixon to pressure McCarthy to fire Matthews from his post as executive director of McCarthy's Permanent Subcommittee on Investigations.) McCarthy, in turn, quickly hired Frank P. Carr, a former supervisor in the FBI's New York Field Office.[28]

Thereafter, the once tolerant Oxnam refused to become involved with any group suspected of radical taint without first checking with higher authorities. On one occasion after the Southern Conference Educational Fund (SCEF) solicited his support, Oxnam wrote to Attorney General William P. Rogers asking if SCEF was listed either on the Attorney General's list of subversive organizations or on any list compiled by the Un-American Activities Committee.[29] The FBI, moreover, continued to publicize Communist infiltration of organized religion despite a temporary setback in October 1961 when an FBI Assistant Director, William C. Sullivan, assured an audience at the Highland Park Methodist Church in Dallas that there had never been "extensive or substantial infiltration of the American clergy." Sullivan's contention was immediately challenged by the Church League of America and the United Klans of America—and was privately rebuffed by FBI Director Hoover. Thus, when senior FBI officials noticed a seemingly insignificant detail in a Detroit field office report the next year regarding anti-HUAC activist Frank Wilkinson's claim that he had been elected vice chairman of his church's board of directors in Los Angeles while imprisoned for contempt of Congress, they responded promptly. FBI officials ordered the Los Angeles Field Office to investigate Wilkinson's contention and, if it was "determined to be accurate," to forward the details "to all continental offices" under the caption "Communism and Religion."[30]

The Blacklisters. Though such organizations as the Church League of America and the Ku Klux Klan were generally too extremist for the FBI to support, Bureau officials did seek to exploit the conservative interest groups that made up HUAC's constituency in pursuit of their February 1946 policy objective. And most of the major private-sector blacklisting organizations of the Cold War era had close ties to the FBI, to HUAC, or to both. One organization, the Church League of America, was born in 1937 when a Chicago advertiser, George Washington Robnett, envisioned a profitable political dossier service, aimed primarily at the National Council of Churches, and began collecting names from the Fish Committee's hearings on communism. Robnett later added published HUAC hearings and reports and established a close liaison with HUAC member Mundt. By the 1960s, Church League files included the papers of its research director, J. B. Matthews; of *Counterattack* founder and ex-FBI man John B. Keenan; and of the Wackenhut Corporation, the nation's third largest private detective firm, which was founded in 1951 by one-time FBI agent George Wackenhut and managed by such anticommunist stalwarts as General Mark W. Clark and former FBI Assistant Director Stanley J. Tracy. (Wackenhut's files were said to contain complete dossiers on every name in HUAC's files. This collection of political intelligence helped make George Wackenhut a multimillionaire with a yacht named the *Security Review*.) By 1968, two years after Matthews's death, the Church League's files, containing over seven million index cards, were housed in the new J. B. Matthews Memorial Library in Wheaton, Illinois.[31]

Another blacklisting organization, the American Security Council (ASC), was founded in 1955 as the Mid-America

Research Library. The Chicago-based ASC, whose political intelligence collection included the files of Harry Jung's anti-Semitic Vigilante Intelligence Foundation, serviced the needs of such corporate clients as General Electric, Honeywell, Stewart-Warner, Motorola, Lockheed, U.S. Steel, and nearly 3,000 other corporations. Former Bureau agents filled most of the key positions on ASC staff, including operating director Jack E. Ison, research director William K. Lambie, Jr., and field director W. Cleon Skousen, author of *The Naked Communist*. HUAC staff members also developed close rapport with the Security Council. When the Committee's successor came under increasing attack in the late 1960s and 1970s as a Cold War aberration, the ASC masterminded the "terrorism" strategy designed to make the Committee more relevant by redirecting the hunt away from potential subversives and Communists and toward potential terrorists. The Committee's last Chairman, Richard Ichord, had extremely close ties with ASC officials and sometimes covertly disseminated their propaganda. Similarly, the FBI secretly ordered and distributed 6,000 copies of an ASC pamphlet on the New Left, *The Anarcho-Communist Coalition*.[32]

The FBI had even closer ties with yet another powerful member of the HUAC constituency, the American Legion. Always anticommunist (at the end of World War I the Detroit post alone boasted "one thousand Bolshevik Bouncers"), the Legion had refined its red-hunting techniques by the mid-1940s. In part, the new Legion image was a result of the FBI's American Legion Contact Program of 1940–1966. It arose from a proposal by Legion officials to Attorney General Frank Murphy in 1939 that called for local Legion posts to investigate and report all indications of subversive activity to the Bureau. Murphy rejected this proposal, but FBI officials proposed an alternative plan to use Legionnaires as "confidential sources." Approved by Murphy's successor in November 1940, the Contact Program ultimately involved over 100,000 Legionnaires and their agents who collected information and submitted reports, with copies to the Bureau. Terminated in November 1945, FBI officials pledged continued "support and active cooperation" with the Legion and all "other civic

87

organizations" formerly associated with the Bureau under formal "contact programs" (among others, the American Bar Association, B'nai B'rith, the Boy Scouts, the United States Chamber of Commerce, the Daughters of the American Revolution, Kiwanis International, Knights of Columbus, Optimists International, Rotary International, and the Veterans of Foreign Wars). In July 1950, following the outbreak of the Korean war and in response as well to current FBI "public relations" needs, Bureau officials unilaterally reinstated the Legion contact program.[33]

Lee Pennington, the first FBI liaison agent with the Legion, went on to chair the Legion Americanism Commission in 1953, less than one week after he quit the Bureau, and to help establish the American Security Council. Among other duties, Pennington was responsible for the tone and content of the Legion's *Firing Line*, which also received confidential HUAC files in its efforts to police the various blacklists. With a membership of over three million during the early Cold War years, the Legion was blessed with virtually unlimited funds and pursued a sophisticated, FBI-assisted anticommunist politics—utilizing mass mailing techniques, the production of elaborate booklets, legislative lobbying in Washington and in various state capitals, and speaking tours by the National Commander and other representatives. The Legion also produced its own films, established close relations with Hollywood film producers, and published its own newspaper and magazine.[34] To set the tone for the Legion campaign, FBI Director Hoover appeared in September 1946 before its national convention in San Francisco to speak on the menace.[35]

When Pennington left the Bureau in 1953, Nichols's protégé, Cartha DeLoach, joined the Legion at Hoover's request to insure that its anticommunist activities continued to supplement the FBI's. And DeLoach was even more successful than Pennington. By 1958 he was in a position to run for National Commander, but Hoover vetoed this as "too political." Instead, DeLoach assumed the chairmanship of the Legion's National Public Relations Commission. Assisted by other Crime Records Division officials, including Donald G. Hanning, who served as the Commander's representative to the National

Americanism Commission, DeLoach ran the FBI operation so smoothly that by the early 1960s, Hoover's close friend Walter Trohan, Washington bureau chief of the *Chicago Tribune*, was struck by the totality of the Bureau's domination. In a letter to Hoover, Trohan wrote:

> It was a most refreshing experience for me to attend The American Legion Convention, and find people cheering the country and its traditions and saluting the flag instead of cheering the ADA [Americans for Democratic Action] and calling for conciliation of Communists. . . . It was also an invaluable experience, because I find The American Legion is an adjunct of the FBI with FBI men writing speeches for prominent orators, drafting resolutions and sparking the show generally.

The Legion, in some ways, was exactly as Trohan described it. DeLoach arranged for Trohan to receive the Legion's coveted Fourth Estate Award and drafted the address he presented to the Legion Convention audience of 12,000.[36] The Legion (and the VFW, as well) also printed and distributed under its own name Bureau-authored pamphlets on the menace.[37]

Additional outlets for the dissemination of information from FBI files were the publications of American Business Consultants (ABC), particularly the newsletter *Counterattack* and the booklet *Red Channels*. The ABC blacklisting service originated in 1946 when Alfred Kohlberg, an importer and head of the so-called China lobby, decided to finance an anticommunist publication, after meeting with HUAC research director Benjamin Mandel and ex-FBI agents Kenneth Bierly, Theodore Kirkpatrick, and John Keenan. They were brought together by a Catholic priest, John F. Cronin, who was one of FBI Assistant Director Nichols's available channels. Kohlberg financed a publication and research service, selecting Isaac Don Levine to edit the publication, later named *Plain Talk*, and placing Bierly, Kirkpatrick, and Keenan in charge of the research service. He described this service as "a sort of Un-American Activities Committee or FBI file system for the use of the magazine and for others interested."

In the spring of 1947 the ex-FBI men broke off from *Plain Talk* to provide a slick blacklisting service for the entertainment industry, anticommunist unions, industrial manufacturers, small businessmen, and others. Working out of an old Madison Avenue office accessible only by freight elevator, American Business Consultants patterned its filing system on the FBI's and regularly consulted with Bureau personnel to verify information. A former co-editor of *Counterattack*, Karl Hess, described the Madison Avenue enterprise as "practically a branch office" of the FBI—a portrait of J. Edgar Hoover hung in ABC's offices. *Counterattack* editor Francis J. McNamara, moreover, later served as HUAC's staff director and Committee liaison with the Crime Records Division.[38]

Hoover's warning before HUAC in March 1947 that the Communist party "has departed from depending upon the printed word as its medium of propaganda and has taken to the air" (quoted on page one of *Red Channels*), along with the Committee's search for subversives in Hollywood, were cues for American Business Consultants to concentrate on the entertainment industry. Indeed, the entertainment industry blacklists not only attracted ABC businessmen, HUAC members, and FBI officials, but almost every other anticommunist interest group. The Legion hired J. B. Matthews to study communism in Hollywood, while former *Counterattack* editor McNamara worked for the VFW American Sovereignty Campaign before joining HUAC's staff in 1958. In addition, Kenneth Bierly left *Counterattack* to work for Columbia Pictures as a liaison with veterans' groups.[39]

HUAC's interest in uncovering Hollywood reds dated from August 1938 when Dies Committee investigator Edward Sullivan named nearly forty film personalities—including Paul Muni, James Cagney, and Joan Crawford—as financial contributors to Communist causes. Sullivan based his information on privileged access to Los Angeles Police Department reports. Two years later, a preliminary Dies Committee staff report on communism in Hollywood was somehow leaked to several motion picture moguls. By early 1941 the Committee, with the assistance of several Hearst investigators, had compiled an estimated thirty volumes of reports on the subject.[40]

These thirty volumes of reports were never made public and the Committee labored, for the time being, without the benefit of FBI assistance. Instead, the Bureau carefully monitored the maneuverings of Dies and his successors in Hollywood, with Cecil B. DeMille and other "sources" reporting on a confidential basis to Nichols and Richard B. Hood, head of the Los Angeles Field Office. Hood, for instance, learned in August 1945 that HUAC investigator Louis Russell was trying to contact Gary Cooper, Clark Gable, and Ginger Rogers.[41] At that time Hoover remained leery of the Committee; the Bureau's relationship with HUAC continued to be affected by the FBI Director's feud with Martin Dies nearly five years earlier. FBI interest in working with the Committee to establish a blacklist (whether of the motion picture industry or any other industry) was for the time being of secondary importance. The Bureau was more interested in developing information which could be used to discredit Dies and the Los Angeles office was specifically directed, in 1941, to collect "any information . . . with respect to testimony furnished before the Dies Committee which caused undue hardships on private citizens. . . . "[42]

With the coming of the Cold War things changed. In March 1947 John Rankin called for a cleansing of the film industry and in May of that year Robert Stripling, John McDowell, and HUAC's new Republican Chairman, J. Parnell Thomas, arrived in Los Angeles to hold a series of preliminary hearings in closed session. After listening to several witnesses, Thomas telephoned Hood on May 12 to advise him of the Committee's plans and to request him to testify before the subcommittee. The HUAC Chairman wanted to know, as Hood put it, "what we [the FBI] were doing with respect to the Communist picture in the movie industry." When Hood advised Hoover of his meeting with Thomas, McDowell, and Stripling, the FBI Director, troubled by "Hollywood and its dank air of Communism," ordered him to cancel all travel plans (including a scheduled trip to Washington, D.C., for the Bureau's "special Communist conference on Monday") and to tell Thomas that the FBI was anxious "to cooperate." Another meeting with Thomas, McDowell, and Stripling was immediately arranged and held at the Biltmore Hotel.

Thomas promptly "indicated that they [the HUAC subcommittee] were severely handicapped by lack of any infor-

91

mation," citing as an example an alleged Hollywood red who
testified earlier that day and admitted attending one Communist party meeting. Thomas and Stripling then gave the
name of this witness and nine other names to Hood, requesting
"any information we [the FBI] had" and "any data we can
furnish on Communist infiltration of the motion picture
industry." When advised of this request, FBI Assistant Director
Nichols approved the preparation of blind memorandums on
the ten names and in addition told Hood to prepare a summary
memorandum on Communism in Hollywood, including "the
names of known anti-Communists" and data on various
Communist front groups and their officers. Ratifying Nichols's
decision, Hoover approved the dissemination of virtually
anything "provided . . . that the disclosure of such data will
not in any way embarrass the Bureau." He ordered Bureau
agents to "expedite" the preparation of these blind memorandums and specifically directed "Hood to extend *every* assistance to this Committee."[43]

On May 13 Hood "personally delivered" the requested
information "to Robert Stripling . . . after personal discussion with Congressman Thomas" and "with the understanding
that under no circumstances will the source of this material ever
be disclosed." One blind memorandum given to Stripling
contained the names of and background information on dozens
of prospective witnesses in both the "hostile . . . uncooperative" and "cooperative . . . friendly" categories—including
the president of the Screen Actors Guild, Ronald Reagan.[44]

Thereafter, HUAC members began preparing in earnest for
a public exposure of the red menace in Hollywood. Working
closely with the FBI, Louis Russell and two other ex-FBI agents
on the Committee's staff, A. Bernard Leckie and H. A. Smith,
conducted most of the research for the Hollywood hearings
which began in October. They managed, for instance, to obtain
photostatic copies of the CPUSA membership cards issued
years earlier to the so-called Hollywood Ten. They also
contacted the heads of most of the major studios to inform
them, as in the case of M-G-M's Louis B. Mayer, "that the
Committee meant business . . . and that if necessary, Mr.
MAYER would be subpoenaed." Smith later gave Hood

the names of fifty-six "possible friendly witnesses" and eighty-nine "possible unfriendly witnesses" and a preliminary itinerary for the hearings. More importantly, the Bureau assisted HUAC's investigation of the subpoenaed witnesses. Documents in the FBI's individual case files on Larry Parks and Bertolt Brecht reveal this assistance—with Parks's FBI file containing a list of questions prepared by the FBI for Thomas's use during the scheduled hearings. (Neither Parks nor Brecht were members of the Hollywood Ten. Though Parks later named names for HUAC, he did not testify in 1947. Brecht left the country immediately after his appearance.)[45]

While the current and ex-FBI agents were doing the necessary spade work for the public hearings, the FBI, in response to a request from the White House, compiled yet another report on Communist activities in Hollywood. (This FBI report highlighted the efforts of "known Hollywood Communists" to finance Henry Wallace's radio addresses, which were critical of President Truman's containment policies.) And after the Hollywood Ten refused to cooperate with HUAC on First Amendment grounds (a tactic which led to their indictment and imprisonment for contempt of Congress), FBI Director Hoover reported to the Attorney General and to presidential aide Harry Vaughan on their defense strategy.[46]

From September 1946, when Bureau officials identified "Communist penetration of the motion picture industry" as an investigative priority, until the 1960s, the FBI had a stake in the entertainment industry blacklist—complete with a COMPIC (Communist picture) file and SECURITY MATTER-C (Communist) individual case files on such alleged reds as Lucille Ball. (And if once a CPUSA member or sympathizer it was nearly impossible to convince the FBI of a change of heart. Even the testimony of the Hollywood actors and writers who cooperated with HUAC in the early 1950s was sometimes dismissed by Hoover as "self serving and solely for [the] purpose of getting a Committee 'whitewash.'") Throughout the 1950s William Wheeler, formerly a Secret Service agent assigned to FDR's bodyguard detail and then HUAC's West Coast investigator, worked closely with Marcus M. Bright, Andrew J. Decker, Jr., and other FBI agents to pursue

Hollywood reds. The Los Angeles Field Office routinely provided Wheeler with the addresses of and employment data on hundreds of persons "connected with radio, cartoonists, music, or acting industry in Hollywood" even in cases where Wheeler admitted that he did "*not have specific evidence* [of Communist associations] *against them.*" In this particular instance Wheeler brought twenty-nine names to the Bureau and expressed his hope, as the Los Angeles SAC put it, that subpoenas would lead "one or more of them . . . [to] contact him prior to the hearings" and thus "supply [the] evidence he does not now have." Later, in April 1960, when the blacklist began to crack and a member of the Hollywood Ten signed a film script contract, FBI officials carefully monitored this development and considered various strategies to insure the continued success of their efforts to contain the "hard-core CP in Hollywood."[47]

In contrast, the efforts of anticommunist congressmen to insure the success of the blacklists were less discreet. When Leon R. Yankwich, a federal judge in California, ruled in favor of blacklisted screenwriter Lester Cole's suit against M-G-M in 1952, former HUAC member Richard B. Vail (R., Ill.) called for a congressional investigation of Yankwich's fitness for the bench.[48]

Anticommunist Congressmen. FBI efforts to insure the creation and maintenance of an anticommunist consensus were not limited to supplying information to "cooperative and reliable" newspaper reporters or to providing support to various private-sector blacklisters. Nichols and the Crime Records Division cultivated, as well, those congressmen who shared their conservative world view. Conversely, the CRD identified its enemies and potential enemies in the Congress: placing Congressmen Vito Marcantonio (American Labor, N.Y.) and Robert L. Condon (D., Cal.) and Senator Paul Douglas (D., Ill.) on the Security Index; reviewing Dies Committee and HUAC reports to connect Marcantonio with various Communist fronts and disseminating the charge that Marcantonio "maintains a secret apartment on 16th Street in New York for 'inner circle' Party meetings and for his blonde sweetie"; and investigating incumbent congressmen and non-incumbent candidates for congressional office. By February 1972 the Bureau held 883 files on Senators and 722 files on Representatives.[49]

Recipients of information leaked from FBI files and beneficiaries of other FBI favors included Congressmen Louis C. Rabaut (D., Mich.), John J. Rooney (D., N.Y.), Richard M. Nixon (R., Cal.), Karl E. Mundt (R., S.D.), Gerald Ford (R., Mich.), H. R. Gross (R., Iowa), J. Parnell Thomas (R., N.J.), Howard Smith (D., Va.), and Edward Cox (D., Geo.), and Senators Joseph R. McCarthy (R., Wis.), Homer Ferguson (R., Mich.), Thomas J. Dodd (D., Conn.), Strom Thurmond (R., S.C.), Pat McCarran (D., Nev.), Barry Goldwater (R., Ariz.), Bourke Hickenlooper (R., Iowa), and James Eastland (D., Miss.). The FBI cultivated these and other congressmen by assisting them with research problems that could not be solved by their own staffs or by the Library of Congress staff; by drafting letters and speeches (in one case the FBI leaked derogatory information regarding Communist party efforts to subvert Lyndon B. Johnson's Vietnam policy to a conservative congressman, then wrote a speech for him and disseminated it to private corporations and the presidents of several universities); by providing the services of FBI Assistant Director Sullivan for private lectures on the menace in House and Senate office buildings; and by helping answer constituent inquiries. In return, these and other select congressmen championed the FBI's position on various political issues. Senator Mundt, for one, read into the *Congressional Record* at the FBI's request newspaper and magazine articles written by Don Whitehead, Edward J. Mowery, Lyle Wilson, David Lawrence, and Miriam Ottenberg.[50]

Congressional committees, notably HUAC and the Senate Internal Security Subcommittee (SISS), also benefited from close liaison with the Crime Records Division.[51] Set up in January 1951 to rival the Un-American Activities Committee, SISS was chaired during the 1950s by Pat McCarran, William Jenner, and James Eastland, and included among its membership Mundt, Ferguson, and Dodd. The FBI routinely provided the Subcommittee with Bureau-prepared monographs, formed a "McCarran special squad" for the apparent purpose of aiding the investigation of the Institute of Pacific Relations, and alerted SISS to such alleged reds as Stanley Levison, adviser to Martin Luther King, Jr., and New York Attorney General Jacob Javits. In return for these favors, SISS publicized the red menace in a manner compatible with Bureau objectives and defended the Bureau's apolitical image. After disgruntled ex-FBI agent Jack Levine broadcast a series of radio interviews for the Pacifica Foundation in late 1962, SISS Chairman Eastland subpoenaed seven Foundation officials.[52]

The FBI's relationship with the Senate Internal Security Subcommittee was unique and evolved from a March 15, 1951, meeting between Hoover, McCarran, and Attorney General J. Howard McGrath. "Our cooperation was being solicited," as Nichols later summarized, "to help the committee [SISS] whittle out the chaff, provide the committee with leads and to prevent the committee from needless effort, as well as provide the committee those matters which we had already investigated, which would not be necessary for them to cover." The FBI Assistant Director went on to describe the "arrangement" as "very satisfactory" and "to the mutual benefit of both the Department and the Bureau, as well as Congress and the general public."

It is not known why McGrath approved this arrangement or whether he was acting with the consent and knowledge of President Truman. The arrangement may have been a trade off, a case of an overzealous Truman appointee attempting to steer the Senate Subcommittee away from the Communists-in-government issue: the only FBI data formally denied SISS involved federal employee loyalty cases. In any event, the Bureau forwarded hundreds (perhaps thousands) of blind memorandums to SISS with copies "to the Attorney General, per his request." McCarran and his assistant, Jay Sourwine, even received executive session testimony given before the Un-American Activities Committee which the Bureau had received from ex-FBI agents Raphael Nixon, Louis Russell, and other "confidential [HUAC] sources." The "program of cooperation" with the Senate Subcommittee, moreover, was continued by the Eisenhower Administration and Attorney

General Herbert Brownell, Jr. When former CIA agent and newly appointed SISS chief counsel Robert Morris contacted Nichols in February 1953 to inquire about the continuation of the program, he was referred to Brownell. Nichols, however, considered Morris "a bulldog" on the Communists-in-government issue and "told . . . [him] that he could be certain that we would maintain our friendly relationship and if we could be of service to him personally . . . we would do so."[53]

In some cases (for example, the Hollywood Ten hearings), the Un-American Activities Committee received even more enthusiastic assistance from the FBI; but this relationship was rockier, to say the least. The Hoover-Dies feud of 1940 was only the first of several conflicts which plagued the Bureau's relationship with the Committee. In February 1953 Hoover advised HUAC's new Republican Chairman, Harold Velde, that past problems prevented "as close a coordination . . . as I believed there should have been." "Certain public source information would be [made] available," Velde learned, and the Bureau would "be as cooperative as it could be when the same goal was being sought by a Congressional Committee and the FBI." Despite the intermittent feuding and the problem of what Nichols described as the "different personalities" in the House which made it difficult to duplicate the FBI-SISS arrangement, the Bureau provided Committee members and staff with oral briefings, summaries of reports, letterhead memorandums, blind memorandums, reports from other investigative agencies, and current addresses and employment data on hundreds of prospective witnesses. In 1952, for instance, the FBI furnished blind memorandums on at least seven witnesses to HUAC investigator William Jones in connection with the Committee's scheduled hearings in Chicago. The next year, HUAC sleuths Donald Connors and Edward R. Duffy received "information" regarding the United Electrical, Radio and Machine Workers of America in the Pittsburgh area. Quite simply, as one Committee investigator, an ex-FBI agent, put it in 1957: "We wouldn't be able to stay in business overnight if it weren't for the Bureau."[54]

The Bureau maintained particularly close relations with the ex-FBI agents on HUAC's sizeable staff and these men reported regularly to their former colleagues on the Committee's planned activities. From a modest ten employees in early 1947, the Committee's staff mushroomed to forty-seven by 1948. By the mid-1960s HUAC was paying $109,707.65 in staff salaries for each elected representative serving on the Committee—over sixty percent more than its closest competitor, the House Government Operations Committee. This formidable bureaucracy allowed the FBI to work through the staff with little danger of compromising its activities and to exercise close control over its make-up. Dating at least from mid-1945, the FBI recommended specific individuals for investigator positions and investigated all staff members and applicants, compiling unofficial loyalty files for HUAC's use. As Mundt advised a prospective employee in May 1945, "your application will be on file and the FBI report will be in their files down there available at any time we should decide to call it up." In September 1946, moreover, Hoover urged William Conway, a Chicago attorney, to accept the position of Committee counsel for the purpose of making "a real affirmative contribution to the welfare of the country."[55]

Given the close ties between FBI officials and certain HUAC members and staff, it was hardly surprising that the Committee launched an anticommunist program of its own shortly after the February 1946 FBI executives' conference. As early as January 12, 1945, Mundt was gathering the names and addresses of virtually every well-known publicist in the country "in connection with some Committee work I am doing." By June 1946 he was forwarding confidential data from HUAC's files to anyone who said he wanted to fight the menace. In one instance, Tom Finan, Jr., editor of *Today's World*, requested dossiers on officers of the CIO's National Citizens Political Action Committee. "We are going after them with a complete exposure—and pictures, if obtainable," Finan advised:

Help us with . . . names, if you can, please . . . We are going to name as many of the critics of your Committee as we can—including the *Daily Worker*, *PM*, the *New Masses* and the *St. Louis Post-Dispatch*; also any you want to suggest who are indulging in this hue and cry against you. We are going to print NAMES, Congressman Mundt, and let them take us to court if they want to.

Mundt responded by commending Finan's mission, sending the requested data, and suggesting that each issue of *Today's World* expose two or three organizations promoting the Communist party line.[56]

By the end of 1946 the Committee was ready to launch a formal educational campaign. Shortly after the November elections, Chairman-designate J. Parnell Thomas announced an eight-point program to draw the attention of the American people to the specter of Communist influence in every area of American life. Thomas's program included the publication of a directory of subversive organizations, the production of regular HUAC reports on various aspects of the menace, and the development of a sophisticated, well-funded distribution system. (Although the FBI's role in this particular effort is not clear, Thomas boasted of secret meetings in hotel rooms with Hoover and other FBI officials, and recently declassified FBI files reveal that the Bureau routinely disseminated published HUAC hearings and reports.)

The Committee program began in mid-1948 with the publication of *100 Things You Should Know About Communism in the U.S.A.*, the first of six pamphlets in a series which ultimately had two million copies in circulation. Over half the copies were distributed free, with Committee staff mailing the first pamphlet to every newspaper editor in the United States. Nearly seven million copies of additional Committee hearings and reports, published between 1948 and 1960, were distributed free of charge by HUAC or sold by the government printing office.[57] In addition to these formal publications, which totaled over 93,000 pages, between June 20, 1946 and December 22, 1948, the Committee compiled informal reports on 25,591 individuals and 1,786 organizations at the request of members of Congress, including Senators McCarthy, Eastland, Thurmond, and Alexander Wiley (R., Wis.). Additional reports were compiled at the request, for example, of blacklister George Washington Robnett; the president of a Sioux Falls,

South Dakota, steel company; columnist Westbrook Pegler; and the National Conference of Bar Examiners. Not everyone, however, was treated equally. When longtime Dies Committee critic Ellis Patterson (D., Cal.) approached HUAC in late 1945 to inquire about the activities of Committee investigators in Hollywood, he was refused any information. Shortly afterward, the requested information appeared in Gerald L. K. Smith's magazine, *The Cross and the Flag.*[58]

Other Available Channels. After laying the groundwork in the period 1946 to 1948, Bureau efforts to inform public opinion were not limited to leaking derogatory information. In addition, the FBI cooperated closely with HUAC's and later SISS's series of spectacular hearings launched in 1947 to expose Communist influence in the entertainment industry; in labor unions; in federal, state, and local government; and in the nation's schools and universities. Both committees relied indirectly (and sometimes directly) on FBI investigative reports and, beginning in 1950, almost exclusively on the testimony of paid FBI informers. FBI officials also publicized information in their files as a result of Smith Act prosecutions and the Truman administration's loyalty program. Similarly, the requirements of the Internal Security Act of 1950 and the Communist Control Act of 1954 (that all Communist, Communist-front, and Communist-action organizations register with the Subversive Activities Control Board [SACB] and declare their publications Communist propaganda) provided additional opportunities for public dissemination of material in Bureau files. Smith Act prosecutions, Loyalty Review Board deliberations, and SACB hearings, like HUAC proceedings, relied predominantly on FBI reports and the testimony of FBI informers.

CHAPTER **IV**

Making the Cold War: Influencing National Politics

After the February 1946 FBI executives' conference, FBI officials were in the forefront of the domestic Communist issue. But they were not the only ones sowing the seeds of what became known as McCarthyism. President Harry S. Truman also sought to encourage antiradical fears to ensure bipartisan support for his anticommunist foreign policies.[1] Though FBI officials sometimes worked with the Justice Department and the President to publicize the internal Communist threat, the Bureau more often acted and reacted according to its own political priorities. FBI officials viewed the domestic Communist threat as far more serious than did the Truman administration. In effect, they viewed the administration itself as "subversive" and sought to document Truman's alleged "softness" on communism. This posture is illustrated not only by Louis Nichols's attempts to cultivate HUAC and its constituency, but by the FBI's ability to influence, if not direct, the emerging congressional debate on the Communists-in-government issue from February 1946 to February 1950, when Senator McCarthy vaulted into national prominence.

CONGRESS AND THE COMMUNISTS-IN-GOVERNMENT ISSUE

Prior to the Cold War, the anticommunist political style was generally dismissed as the particular prerogative of either right-wing crackpots or conservative anti–New Deal politicos as diverse as Martin Dies and Thomas E. Dewey. During the

Cold War, in contrast, anticommunism on the home front gained new force and legitimacy. It did so not only because the emerging global confrontation between the two superpowers provided the context, but because the FBI decided, in effect, to underwrite those who saw the red menace primarily as an internal security issue.

The McCarthyite or anticommunist political style began to gain this new legitimacy in 1945–1946 when a group of conservative congressmen challenged the loyalty of federal employees and, in particular, security procedures in the State Department.[2] Their concern had been aroused and seemingly confirmed by the FBI raid in June 1945 on the offices of *Amerasia*, an obscure left-wing periodical on Far Eastern politics. Its staff had surreptitiously obtained classified Navy, State Department, and OSS documents. Then, on June 27, 1946, a Canadian Royal Commission report detailed the meanderings of a Soviet wartime espionage ring in Canada. By July 6, the House Civil Service Committee had responded to these disclosures by appointing a special subcommittee to investigate the loyalty of federal employees. And the Senate approved conservative Democratic Senator Pat McCarran's rider to a State Department appropriations bill, which granted the Secretary of State summary dismissal authority "in his absolute discretion."

The congressional assault on State Department personnel and loyalty procedures—led by Senators McCarran, Eastland, and Kenneth Wherry (R., Neb.) and Congressmen Rankin, Cox, Rabaut, George Dondero (R., Mich.), Edward Rees (R., Kans.), and Richard Wigglesworth (R., Mass.)—was based not on the Royal Commission's disclosure, however, but on information leaked directly or indirectly from FBI files. The FBI had received most of its information from Elizabeth Bentley, a self-styled Soviet espionage agent turned informer who allegedly first approached the Bureau in August 1945. With her story as their basis, in December 1945 and early 1946 FBI officials flooded the White House with reports on Soviet espionage cells in the government. Truman aide Stephen Spingarn estimated that up to eighty percent of all material received was strictly "Bentley's stuff." Attorney General Tom

Clark, in turn, asked the FBI Director whether the reports he was circulating contained enough evidence to justify prosecuting the people named therein. Hoover refused to make this recommendation.[3]

Then, in March 1946, Hoover, Clark, and Secretary of State James F. Byrnes worked to force Alger Hiss, then director of the Office of Special Political Affairs, from State Department employ by leaking details of his alleged Communist associations "to certain key men in the House and Senate." Such a strategy, Clark and Hoover reasoned, would divert potential criticism of the Bureau and the State Department and insure that Hiss would not be alerted to the FBI's ongoing investigation. At Hoover's suggestion, several legislators were contacted and Byrnes later advised Hiss on March 20 that "two separate committees 'on the Hill'" were questioning his loyalty. When Byrnes refused to fire Hiss summarily (at that time the Secretary of State did not have such authority, and the FBI Director himself opposed a mandatory Civil Service hearing because "the material against Hiss was confidential"), Hoover began his own campaign of leaks to members of Congress and the press. Some six weeks before the Senate approved the McCarran rider, McCarran attempted to persuade Hoover to appear before the Senate Appropriations Committee and to bring along "the Bureau files relating to Alger Hiss."[4]

At the same time, the FBI Director was acting unilaterally to pressure the Secretary of State. This action is obliquely confirmed by Byrnes's claim, in his memoirs, that he had no idea the FBI was investigating Hiss until February 1946, when he was so informed by Senator Eastland.[5] More significant was the FBI's assistance in late 1945 and 1946 to Father John Cronin, an assistant director in the Social Action Department of the National Catholic Welfare Conference. Relying on material provided secretly by the FBI and Benjamin Mandel, who was then serving a brief stint with the State Department before returning to his post as HUAC research director, Cronin prepared a report on communism in the United States. Released for private circulation among Catholic bishops, this report named suspected CPUSA members in government (including Alger Hiss, Lee Pressman, and John Abt) and was intended to enlist the church in "a positive program" to "counter . . . Communist propaganda."[6]

Not content with the report's limited impact, Cronin sought to reach a wider audience—apparently, with the support of the FBI. (Hoover was convinced that there was a leftist attitude in the lower echelons of the State Department.) In a speech on March 10, 1946, to the annual communion breakfast of the St. Thomas More Holy Name Society in Arlington, Virginia, Cronin claimed that 130 Communists held key government positions from which they could influence departmental policies. Though refusing to name names or divulge his sources, Cronin specifically called for an immediate investigation of the State Department. Such a probe, he said, "would shake the country." The next day, Edward Rees, ranking Republican member of the House Civil Service Committee, demanded a congressional investigation of these charges. The conservative assault on State Department personnel was on, culminating in the McCarran rider and the special subcommittee probe. Conservative Republican congressmen, moreover, continued to press the domestic Communist issue throughout 1946. B. Carroll Reece, chairman of the Republican National Committee, called the November elections a choice between "Communism and Republicanism" and a young Californian named Richard Nixon accused his opponent, former Dies Committee member Jerry Voorhis, of following "the Moscow-PAC [CIO Political Action Committee]-Henry Wallace line." And when the Republicans captured the House, the new majority leader, Joseph W. Martin of Massachusetts, promised to "remove the Red menace from America" and to cooperate fully with HUAC.[7]

Cronin's services as publicist for the FBI were further exercised when Emerson Schmidt, an official of the U.S. Chamber of Commerce Committee on Socialism and Communism, hired him to ghost-write three pamphlets on the menace. Released under Chamber of Commerce executive Francis P. Matthews's signature at intervals beginning in late 1946, these pamphlets again named no names but had a considerable impact. Over 200,000 copies of the first pamphlet were distributed by the end of October. During November, the Chamber received orders for 25,000 to 30,000 copies a day.[8]

The Chamber rushed to publish its second pamphlet, *Communists Within the Government*, both to prevent a "whitewash" by Truman's recently established Temporary Commission on Employee Loyalty, and to protect FBI appropriations. According to syndicated radio commentator and FBI confidant Walter Winchell, the Bureau of the Budget, one of the allegedly Communist-infiltrated departments Cronin mentioned in his Arlington speech, had recently recommended an $8 million cut in the FBI's budget. Then, on January 17, 1947, FBI Assistant Director Ladd appeared before the Temporary Commission and cited the Chamber pamphlet as independent corroboration of the FBI's demand for a sweeping loyalty program. Two months later, Emerson Schmidt testified before HUAC, and the Committee read all three Chamber pamphlets into its record, insuring even greater distribution. Thereafter, the FBI's media allies used the Chamber estimate of 400 Communists in government as a yardstick by which to judge the effectiveness of the Truman Administration's loyalty program. In May, for instance, Lyle Wilson complained that Truman had not yet purged "a single Communist, Fascist or other subversive character."[9]

When the Communists in government issue once more dominated congressional politics in the summer of 1948, culminating in the so-called congressional spy hearings, the FBI again played a key role. For more than a year a federal grand jury in New York had listened to the testimony of Elizabeth Bentley, Louis Budenz, and scores of present and past government employees accused by these FBI informers of membership in Soviet-controlled cells. When it became clear that the grand jury would hand down no indictments, FBI officials decided to act independently. And they were supported by Senator Homer Ferguson and other congressional red-hunters who worked to make "the public understand and realize the difference between the FBI and the Attorney General."[10]

According to columnist Drew Pearson, Louis Nichols took the Bureau file on Bentley to Senator Ferguson sometime in 1948. This allegation, however, was never widely publicized because the *Washington Post* excised all critical comments regarding the FBI Assistant Director from Pearson's "Merry-Go-Round" column. At the time, Attorney General Clark also suspected Nichols of leaking "Communist stuff" to Ferguson, concluding that "he was getting reports before I got them" through "a direct pipeline to the F.B.I."[11] As a result, when Senator Ferguson's Investigations Subcommittee of the Committee on Expenditures in the Executive Departments opened the spy hearings on July 30, Subcommittee members and staff were armed with hard questions regarding William W. Remington, a Commerce Department employee identified as a Soviet agent by Bentley. (Pearson also claimed that Nichols, rather than leaving the Bentley file with Ferguson, "prepared a brief digest from which Ferguson could ask questions.") Thus, the Subcommittee was aware that Remington, prior to being hired by the Commerce Department, had been discharged from the Naval Reserve after the FBI briefed the Office of Naval Intelligence, even though there was no indication of this briefing on Remington's official service record.[12]

Though Remington was later indicted for perjury and imprisoned (not for denying Bentley's allegations but for denying CPUSA membership), Ferguson's competitors on the Un-American Activities Committee heard even more spectacular testimony from Bentley on July 31 and from Whittaker Chambers in early August. After a minor jurisdictional dispute over the rights to Bentley's revelations, HUAC agreed (by a vote of 3 to 2) to leave the Remington case to the Senate Subcommittee.[13] Committee members, and in particular freshman Congressman Nixon, chose instead to concentrate on Alger Hiss, then president of the Carnegie Endowment for International Peace, whom Chambers had accused of belonging to a Communist cell that sought to infiltrate the New Deal and influence policy. Again, as in 1946, Father Cronin assumed a prominent role as FBI liaison.

Even Richard Nixon's critics have noted the dogged determination and quiet self-confidence with which he pursued the seemingly impossible task of undermining the credibility of Alger Hiss, a New Dealer of impeccable credentials. According to former FBI Assistant Director Sullivan, however, the FBI helped build Nixon's reputation as "the great anti-Communist congressman" by forwarding information to him on the Hiss case. Similarly, Father Cronin revealed during an interview with Garry Wills that FBI agent Ed Hummer regularly briefed Cronin on the Hiss case and that he in turn forwarded this information to Nixon. Nixon lamely confirms this account in his memoirs by conceding "some informal contacts with a lower-level agent."[14]

Recently declassified FBI files are more revealing than either Cronin's or Nixon's memory. According to one document, Nixon boasted on December 9, 1948, to former FBI agent Patrick Coyne, that he had an ongoing relationship with the Bureau and not simply with a lower-level agent. Coyne relayed Nixon's boast to FBI headquarters: "Nixon had nothing but praise for the Director and the Bureau. He voluntarily stated during the course of the evening that he had worked very close with the Bureau and with Mr. Nichols *during the past year* on this matter" (emphasis added).[15]

Was this simply the boast of an ambitious freshman congressman, or did Nixon really work with Nichols long before the spy hearings opened on July 30, 1948? Although the available evidence is limited and some of it is clearly contradictory,[16] Nixon seemed aware of at least the broad outline of the Chambers-Bentley story as early as February 5, 1948, when he questioned Attorney General Clark, then testifying before HUAC on proposed legislation to curb domestic Communists. Later, when Bentley first appeared before HUAC on July 31 and Nixon suggested calling Hoover to corroborate her story, J. Parnell Thomas responded: "The closest relationship exists between this committee and the FBI. . . . I think there is a good understanding between us. It is something, however, that we cannot talk too much about." (This assessment is again confirmed by Coyne; in October 1947, when still working for the Bureau, Coyne noted matter-of-factly in a memorandum to Ladd the "close relationship" between "Mr. Parnell Thomas" and "Mr. Nichols."[17]) And on December 1, after returning from Whittaker Chambers's farm, Nixon telephoned Nichols in the middle of the night to apprise him that HUAC would soon come into possession of documentary evidence against Hiss, the so-called Pumpkin papers (developed and undeveloped microfilm of confidential government documents, some of which Hiss had allegedly passed to Chambers). Nichols's memorandum on this phone call again suggests that Nixon's relationship with the Bureau was not simply an informal, backdoor affair with a freelance agent. The seemingly audacious advice of a freshman congressman—"that the Bureau not look for the documents themselves" and "not tell the Attorney General that we [the FBI] were told of this information"—inspired Hoover to direct Nichols: "Do so and let me know result."[18]

FBI attempts to exploit if not inspire the so-called spy hearings went beyond leaks to Nixon and Senator Ferguson. Staff members Louis Russell and Robert Stripling and Committee members Nixon and Mundt briefed the Bureau on the Committee's progress, and in late July and August 1948 FBI officials also forwarded information to Mundt, David Lawrence, and Fulton Lewis's assistant, Russell Turner. Nichols "told Turner that in connection with the Washington underground that we, of course, were fully cognizant of the deficiencies of the law, the difficulties of presenting evidence and corroborating evidence which we had and which we believed to be true." Hoover intended, Turner also learned, to seek indictments of those named before the grand jury by Chambers and Bentley. If indictments were not handed down (and they were not—at least until Chambers produced the Pumpkin papers), Hoover favored a public grand jury report to protect the FBI's image and to alert the American people to the ubiquitous Soviet espionage ring that operated in Washington, D.C.

When the grand jury decided not to publicize its report, thereby leaving the burden of exposure in HUAC's lap, both Lawrence and Lewis attacked the Committee's critics as "left wingers" and "parlor pinks" and defended its ability, as Lawrence wrote, "to reach persons who otherwise can escape punishment through technicalities." Similarly, when Nichols spotted "a snotty remark . . . regarding the Bureau" in John Kramer's August 6 column in the *Washington News*, he outlined the Bureau's role in the spy hearings for Kramer's "personal and confidential information." "I told him," Nichols later advised Clyde Tolson, "while we did not want him to do anything on this at the present time, we did want him to have the facts."[19]

Bureau officials were also involved in the partisan conflict that was brewing during the spy hearings. And their involvement did not escape the attention of the Truman administration. At a cabinet luncheon on August 30, Truman and Clark Clifford, special counsel to the President, discussed Senator Ferguson's request to have Hoover testify before his Subcommittee regarding the Remington case. Both agreed that Hoover might be able to defuse the politically explosive issue of Communists-in-government, but decided not to allow the FBI Director to testify, having concluded that he could not be trusted. According to an account of this meeting by White House aide Eben Ayers: "the President said the trouble was that Hoover was concerned with his own future, if he thought the Democrats would win the election in November, he would [answer proper questions and refuse to answer improper ones] but if he thought the Republicans would win he would probably answer all questions." Instead, the White House pursued a strategy intended both to minimize the HUAC spy hearings and to publicize "the successful operation of the President's Employee Loyalty Program." Truman did try to enlist Hoover's assistance in this strategy, directing Attorney General Clark to "get a statement of facts from the FBI about the meddling of the House Un-American Activities Committee and how they dried up sources of information which would have been accessible in the prosecution of spies and communists."[20]

FBI officials refused to issue such a statement. After Clark called Bureau headquarters in an attempt to coax a statement from Ladd, the FBI Assistant Director advised Hoover: "I very carefully made no commitment or acknowledgment . . . so that [my] statement could not be attributed to me or the Bureau as being critical of the Committee." Then, after hearing of Mundt's claim that he was receiving information from the FBI "under the table," Clark again called Ladd and read him the riot act: "Any S.O.B. that gives Congressman Mundt any information gets his ass kicked out of this building. . . . I want you to get the word around that anyone giving information to the Committee is out—O-U-T."[21]

The Bureau's refusal to cooperate with the administration was not dictated by a lofty commitment to nonpartisanship.

The spy hearings were timed, according to Thomas, "to put the heat on Truman." And the FBI actually aided New York Governor Thomas E. Dewey's 1948 presidential campaign by drafting position papers, issued as Republican campaign literature, and trying to help Dewey "create the impression that Truman was too ignorant to deal with the emerging Communist threat." (The Democratic National Committee countered Dewey's FBI-assisted strategy by raising the specter of communism in New York state, pointing out that over seventy percent of CPUSA members resided in the Governor's home state and asking why the American people should expect Dewey to do a better job cleaning the reds out of Washington.)[22] The FBI continued its partisan activities during the 1952 campaign. They leaked a summary report on Soviet espionage in the United States (which served as the basis of a HUAC report entitled *The Shameful Years*) and alerted Republican vice-presidential nominee Nixon to Clark's promise to fire any FBI agent who aided HUAC's effort to expose Alger Hiss. Noting that "nothing would please the Kremlin more" than a victory by Adlai Stevenson in the upcoming elections, Nixon used this information about Clark to bolster his claim that Hiss "would still be free and active today" if Truman had "had his way."[23]

The FBI's assistance to Nixon both before and after Hiss's conviction in January 1950 was not atypical. Hiss's conviction "confirmed" the contention of FBI officials, conservative journalists, and McCarthyites that America faced a serious internal security menace. Accordingly, the FBI and HUAC, in spite of the enigmatic nature of evidence, defended the integrity of the second Hiss perjury trial (the first trial ended in a hung jury) by dismissing as Communists or Communist dupes those who questioned Hiss's guilt. And regardless of his guilt or first-hand knowledge of the murky world of Soviet espionage described by Whittaker Chambers, Alger Hiss did not receive a fair trial.

As documented by Hiss's unsuccessful *coram nobis* petition (rejected by a Federal court in 1982, the petition requested the court to declare an error in his earlier trial—specifically, that he had been denied his right to counsel under the Sixth Amendment and his right to due process under the Fifth Amendment), FBI officials and Justice Department prosecutors committed "a multitude of improprieties" of "constitutional dimensions" in their attempt to impeach Hiss's integrity and thus insure his conviction. The FBI's "technical surveillance" of Hiss, for instance, included wiretaps, mail openings, stakeouts at his home and office, interviews with unnamed informers, and physical surveillance. Nor were these abuses limited to technical surveillance excesses:

> Thus, the prosecution maintained an informer in the legal councils of the defense for several critical months before the trial; pre-trial statements, given by Chambers to the FBI and prosecution, were concealed and the very existence of these statements was falsely denied; critical facts concerning the typewriter on which, the government claimed, the stolen documents were copied or extracted were kept from the defense, the court and the jury; and the prosecution suffered perjury to be committed by its witnesses without protest.[24]

In addition, Nixon and Mundt and HUAC research director Mandel compiled dossiers on defense witnesses and others (possibly including the jury foreman) and the FBI monitored Senator McCarran's attempt to intimidate the judge in the first trial. According to the Bureau's informant, "McCarran told Judge [Samuel H.] Kaufman that he hoped it would not be necessary for the Senate Judiciary Committee to make inquiry as to how the judge functions in the Hiss-Chambers case."

The FBI's stake in the outcome of the Hiss case is further highlighted by the Bureau's voluminous files on Alger Hiss and his friends and supporters after his January 1950 conviction. The FBI kept contributors to the Hiss Defense Fund under surveillance and monitored the efforts of HUAC and Senator McCarthy to publicize the names of contributors to the fund. In 1951 they forwarded "derogatory" information to the Truman White House about Harvard Dean Erwin N. Griswold's allegedly close association with Hiss. According to the FBI, at the first Hiss trial Griswold conferred during an intermission with Alger and Priscilla Hiss, with one of Hiss's attorneys, and with another unidentified individual. One contributor to the Hiss Defense Fund, CIA analyst William Bundy, was also the subject of an FBI leak in 1953 to Senator McCarthy. Bundy, who was Dean Acheson's son-in-law and a former member of the same law firm as Hiss's brother, managed, with Allen Dulles's help, to avoid an appearance before HUAC or the Senate Permanent Subcommittee on Investigations.

Shortly after Hiss's conviction, the Bureau assisted Win Brooks with an *American Weekly* article on "How the FBI Trapped Hiss" and began helping Whittaker Chambers with his memoirs. Chambers submitted his unpublished manuscript and, later, the galleys of *Witness* to the FBI for approval. Nichols also considered helping journalist Bert Andrews, who had worked closely with Nixon on the Hiss case, with his book. He advised Tolson that "we will have to find some way whereby we can get across to Andrews in an informal manner, of course, our side in order that we can insure against unfavorable comment." Whether Nichols found an appropriate way to assist Andrews is not known. The Bureau did help former HUAC member Mundt in his effort to counter Alger Hiss's book, *In the Court of Public Opinion*, providing research assistance to Mundt for his review for the United Press. Hoover also sent a copy of the Bureau's own analysis of the Hiss book to the Eisenhower White House.[25]

THE BUREAU, THE COMMITTEE, AND PRESIDENTIAL POLITICS

The search for Communists in government inspired, at least in part, President Truman's internal security program. For example, Truman reportedly told Federal Communications Commission member Clifford Durr that he created the Temporary Commission on Employee Loyalty "to take the ball away from Parnell Thomas." At the time, Truman was also troubled by the FBI's influence in Congress, predicting in May 1947 that Congress would support the Bureau's demand that it be granted exclusive power to investigate federal employees: "J. Edgar Hoover will in all probability get this backward looking Congress to give him what he wants. It's dangerous."[26]

In any event, Truman was hardly a helpless civil libertarian. His own efforts to mobilize public and congressional opinion for his containment policies (the Truman Doctrine and the Marshall Plan) led him to tolerate the FBI's and the Justice Department's active support of HUAC from 1946 to 1948. But FBI officials' attempts to influence the President were not limited to supporting Truman's conservative congressional critics. They also sought to influence presidential politics by working through the Attorney General and by keeping Truman up-to-date on the activities of Communists and other administration critics.

When attempting to dramatize the seriousness of the Communist threat, the Truman administration, in effect, worked the same side of the street as the FBI and HUAC. By March 13, 1947, the day after the President delivered the Truman Doctrine speech to a joint session of Congress, administration officials were categorically dismissing critics of the new containment policy as "clearly inspired" by Soviet apologists. And the FBI fully briefed the White House on potential critics of the President's foreign policy, forwarding a memorandum to Harry Vaughan on March 18 that detailed the reaction of CPUSA leaders and select "Congressional leaders and their associates" to the President's call for passage of his Greece-Turkey aid bill. Not surprisingly, the White House also received reports on the alleged Communist and other left-wing associations of Senators Claude Pepper (D., Fla.), Glen Taylor (D., Idaho), Joseph Guffey (D., Pa.), and Harvey Kilgore (D., W.Va.), and Congressmen Adolph Sabath (D., Ill.), Hugh DeLacy (D., Wash.), William Green (D., Pa.), Vito Marcantonio (American Labor, N.Y.), Adam Clayton Powell, Jr. (D., N.Y.), Ellis Patterson (D., Cal.), and George Sadowski (D., Mich.).[27]

It is difficult to ascertain the precise influence on Truman's internal security policies of the hundreds of FBI reports forwarded to the White House—reports that invariably characterized the President's foreign policy critics as Soviet dupes or worse. Truman did attempt to build a bipartisan and anticommunist foreign policy consensus. FBI officials and their kindred soul in the Justice Department, Attorney General

Clark, did exploit Truman's anticommunist efforts in pursuit of the similar policy objective outlined at the February 1946 FBI executives' conference.

One example of this overlap involved the red-white-and-blue Freedom Train that toured the country from September 1947 to December 1948 under the highly visible sponsorship of Clark and the Heritage Foundation and the less visible sponsorship of Hoover and Truman. A travelling museum of Americana, displaying the original drafts of the Declaration of Independence, the Emancipation Proclamation, and other historic documents, the Freedom Train was in reality "a high pressure" campaign using "the method of open salesmanship" to "reawaken in our people enthusiasm for the American way of life." Clark, who received regular reports from Hoover regarding the activities of Communist and other critics of the privately funded Freedom Train, described its purpose in even more explicit terms:

> I am disturbed, also, by the impact of alien ideologies. These always thrive on dissension. Particularly during a period of economic stress do they hold forth promise to the hungry or the gullible. It is our responsibility to create safeguards against such eventualities—through the constant scrutiny of subversive elements—and through affirmative programs in democracy.

"Indoctrination," the Attorney General added, was the "essential catalytic agent needed to blend our varying groups into one American family," to fulfill the goal of instilling "in the hearts and minds of our countrymen a pride in our achievements and a loyalty to our institutions."[28]

Anticommunism was the unifying force in Clark's plans to indoctrinate Americans; hence his efforts intersected with President Truman's efforts to "sell" his containment policies and the FBI's self-described educational program. Nor did Clark hesitate to exploit Hoover's impeccable anticommunist credentials. Shortly before HUAC announced its own educational program in January 1947, Committee Chairman Thomas invited the FBI Director to testify. Although he was eager to appear and rail against the Communist party, Hoover nonetheless sent a memorandum to Clark requesting that "steps be taken to make it unnecessary for me to testify on the subject of Communism." "The discussion of legislation" to "curb or outlaw Communism," Clark also learned, was only an "excuse" for Thomas to extend an invitation. The HUAC hearing, "in reality," would "be a full-dress denunciation of Communism" for the purpose of "spotlighting and focusing public attention upon Communism."[29]

Hoover did not advise the Attorney General, however, of Nichols's recent meeting with Thomas. The HUAC Chairman, remembering the Dies-Hoover feud of November and December 1940, saw the FBI Director's appearance before the Committee as a way to make peace with the Bureau. (Hoover also remembered the feud and as late as June 1946 declined Mundt's invitation to attend a Committee-sponsored off-the-record conference with officials of the American Legion and other anticommunist groups: "I am not putting on any bally-hoo for anyone.") Thomas told Nichols "that he of course knew that the Director had been under wraps for years, that the [Truman] Administration favored Communists." To rectify this perceived problem, Thomas offered Hoover the "use" of "the Committee as a sounding board" and promised to provide "a grand opportunity for the Director to say anything he wanted to say."

The HUAC Chairman then "harped on the matter of cooperation and pointed out that his Committee . . . would be very happy to work with the Bureau in every possible way but that cooperation is a two-way vehicle." He specifically requested as a sign of good faith FBI files on five persons employed by the Atomic Energy Commission (AEC) in Oak Ridge, Tennessee. Nichols wanted to know "how he meant us to furnish the information—namely, on a personal and confidential basis or whether it would be necessary to furnish the information to him officially." When Nichols explained that any information "furnished officially" would have to be cleared by the Attorney General, Thomas "stated he did not want to do that." Nichols then took the list of names, promising to "see if there was anything we could furnish him" and recommending to FBI Associate Director Tolson that the leaks be approved "on a personal and confidential basis."[30]

The FBI immediately began preparing blind memorandums on the five Oak Ridge employees and received another request from Thomas for FBI material on CPUSA General Secretary Eugene Dennis. Nichols again wanted to know "what type of information he wanted on Dennis" and when the HUAC Chairman persisted in his demand to "see the main file," the FBI Director referred the request to Clark. Dennis, like Hoover, was scheduled to testify before HUAC regarding two bills to outlaw the Communist party. On March 25, the same day this request was forwarded to Clark, the FBI Director ordered "a summary [memorandum] . . . prepared on Dennis at once" and directed Nichols to make final arrangements for his appearance before the Un-American Activities Committee. "I want to go on this week," Hoover wrote: "Advise [HUAC investigator Louis] Russell to fix it for Wednesday."[31]

It is not clear why Hoover issued this sudden order. It appears possible, however, that he was attempting to pressure the Attorney General. Concerned with maintaining the FBI's apolitical image, Hoover, as late as March 24, urged Clark to contact Thomas once again and "see what he could do."[32] As far as Clark knew, Hoover did not want to testify. But when the Attorney General appeared willing to back Hoover's apparent position, the FBI Director decided to act. In any event, Clark allowed Hoover to testify and apparently authorized the FBI to supply HUAC with a list of organizations classified as subversive. He also appeared before the Committee eleven months later. "Our strategic objective," Clark told HUAC members when outlining the Justice Department's anticommunist program, "must be to isolate subversive movements in this country from effective interference with the body politic." Through surveillance, prosecution, and "the vaccine of public exposure," Clark hoped to alert the public to the true nature of Communists and "fellow travellers [who] corrupt American life."[33]

However, the Attorney General only pursued this strategy of prosecuting CPUSA leaders under the Smith Act of 1940 through the influence of FBI officials in pursuit of "a broad but immediate objective of the Bureau." After receiving a letter from Thomas in April 1947 urging prosecution of the CPUSA "for being an agent of Russia," Clark consulted Hoover. The FBI Director recommended that the Criminal Division "bring up to date its material on the illegal status of the Communist Party" and the "antiquated" list of subversive organizations compiled by former Attorney General Francis Biddle, "as otherwise these groups would claim that their civil liberties were being infringed upon." Clark told Hoover "that he would have this done," and the Justice Department immediately began revising the Attorney General's list of subversive organizations.

Prosecution of Communists was a more difficult matter and Clark initially refused to make this commitment. Nearly a year later, on February 5, 1948 (one month before the public release of the Attorney General's list), Clark told HUAC that advocacy prosecutions of Communists who conspired to violate the Smith Act by teaching or advocating the violent overthrow of the United States government, would not be feasible. The very next day, and in response to an earlier request of the Attorney General to prepare "an investigative brief . . . with the idea of predicating an action against the Party," the FBI delivered a 1300-page brief with 546 exhibits to Clark urging "prosecution of important officials and functionaries of the Communist Party." (Thomas and other HUAC members also continued to pressure Clark; indeed, since 1940 the Committee had advocated Smith Act prosecutions and published a 650,000-word report, described by Stripling as a "textbook" for federal prosecutors, detailing the CPUSA's advocacy of force and violence. Shortly after the Attorney General testified, Hoover "instructed that this report be indexed completely.") In contrast to Clark, FBI officials viewed the Smith Act as a vehicle for publicly demonstrating "that the patriotism of Communists is not directed towards the United States but towards the Soviet Union and World Communism." They astutely concluded that the Justice Department might be persuaded to exploit the Smith Act as "a campaign of education directed to the proposition that Communism is dangerous."[34]

The Bureau's interest did not subside after the initial Smith Act indictments. "In view of the extreme importance of this case to further investigations of Communist Party matters, as

117

well as its inherent significance from a public viewpoint," the FBI monitored Judge Simon Rifkind's statements during pretrial hearings. Hoover alerted Clark to at least one statement by the judge that "might prejudice or . . . impair . . . the Government's case." (Clark privately, and rather lamely, termed such direct Bureau involvement "unprecedented.") Hoover also reported to the White House on Communist party strategy "to combat the prosecution of its leadership." Federal employees who criticized the Smith Act prosecutions were investigated by the FBI. In contrast, government prosecutor John F. X. McGohey was appointed a federal judge by Truman the day after the Foley Square Smith Act trial ended. By 1956 more than one hundred people had been convicted under the Smith Act, leading the FBI to note approvingly, in a classified report, that these prosecutions had "convinced the American people that the Communist Party, USA, is not an orthodox political party . . . but . . . an integral part of an international conspiracy."[35]

Clark also sought to publicize the true nature of Communists and "fellow travellers [who] corrupt American life" by cooperating with the Un-American Activities Committee. After Carl A. Marzani lost his job with the State Department under the McCarran rider, Clark forwarded to HUAC Chairman Thomas certain derogatory political information on Marzani that the FBI had compiled. This leak occurred in January 1947, four months before Marzani was convicted in federal court on eleven counts of perjury—including the charge that he had falsely concealed CPUSA membership in order to keep his job at the State Department.[36] Then, in early 1947, the Justice Department launched a series of prosecutions against uncooperative HUAC witnesses—notably officials of the National Council of American-Soviet Friendship (NCASF) and the Joint Anti-Fascist Refugee Committee (JAFRC) and suspected Communist agents Leon Josephson and Gerhart Eisler.

All had been cited and indicted for contempt of Congress for refusing to comply with Committee subpoenas that demanded, in the case of NCASF, "all books, records, papers, and documents showing receipts and disbursements of money by the said National Council . . . and its affiliated organizations, and all letters, memoranda and communications from, or with any persons outside and within the United States."[37] Highly politicized, these prosecutions were intended to dramatize the seriousness of the domestic Communist threat and to highlight the Truman administration's determination to confront it. Both NCASF and JAFRC were critical of the President's emerging containment policies and, consequently, were the subjects of FBI surveillance and regular reports to the White House.

HUAC's interest in JAFRC, a relief organization founded in 1942 to assist Spanish Civil War refugees, dated from late 1945 when HUAC counsel Ernie Adamson first asked the War Relief Board to revoke the group's license and then subpoenaed its confidential records. JAFRC officials decided not to comply— a decision supported by at least two members of the House, Ellis Patterson (D., Cal.) and Charles R. Savage (D., Wash.), whose efforts on behalf of the Communist-infiltrated JAFRC were the subject of an FBI report to the White House.[38] In addition to the constitutional issues involved, particularly the Fourth Amendment provision against unreasonable search and seizure, HUAC's interest threatened to reveal both the identities of the group's 30,000 American supporters and, given J. Parnell Thomas's close ties to the Franco government, the identities of many underground Republican activists still in Spain.

To frustrate the Committee, the JAFRC devised a "musical chairs" strategy. Chairman Edward K. Barsky, a prominent New York City surgeon who had directed the International Medical Service in Republican Spain, appeared in executive session on February 13, 1946, to advise HUAC members that he had no authority to produce the subpoenaed documents. Such authority, he said, rested in the group's executive board. The fifteen other executive board members were promptly subpoenaed. They claimed to have transferred their authority to executive board secretary Helen R. Bryan. Ultimately, these JAFRC officials were cited for contempt of Congress and, on March 31, 1947, indicted by a Washington grand jury.[39]

Shortly before these indictments were handed down, HUAC summoned Leon Josephson and Gerhart Eisler, the reputed

Communist International agent. Both refused to testify and were promptly cited and indicted for contempt of Congress. The Justice Department, in turn, actively supported the Committee in these and other contempt cases. When Thomas requested that Eisler be placed under twenty-four-hour surveillance by the FBI, Attorney General Clark ordered U.S. Marshals to arrest Eisler and detain him at Ellis Island. Two days later, on February 6, the Immigration Service delivered Eisler to HUAC. On February 18 Richard Nixon, delivering his maiden speech in the House, asked for a contempt citation. On February 27 the Justice Department obtained an indictment. Then, on the eve of Clark's own appearance before HUAC nearly a year later, the Attorney General had Eisler arrested again. "I ordered Mr. Eisler picked up for deportation," Clark advised the Committee, "because he had been making speeches over the country that were derogatory to our form of government and our way of life, and we had a case down here against him also."

Significantly, the Committee had "broken" the Eisler case with help from two of the FBI's "reliable and cooperative" newspaper reporters, Frederick Woltman and Howard Rushmore. Furthermore, HUAC's chief investigator, Robert Stripling, had received an FBI report on Eisler. The Committee also possessed copies of checks issued to Eisler by the JAFRC and the FBI Director's statement, dated October 16, 1946, exposing Eisler as a Communist agent, recommending that he be deported, and pointing out falsifications in his earlier statements to Immigration authorities.[40]

A. Devitt Vanech, an assistant attorney general and chairman of the President's Temporary Commission on Employee Loyalty, also advised the FBI that "the Attorney General desires that . . . summaries *be prepared immediately*" on two individuals (probably Leon Josephson and Samuel Liptzen) connected with the Eisler investigation for Stripling's use. Hoover responded by directing FBI Assistant Director Tamm to "tell Vanech we will of course prepare summaries but . . . I am absolutely opposed to such practices being adopted and it will open 'flood gates' to *all* committees and set a precedent long to be regretted . . . we simply haven't manpower to be stopping our regular work and preparing summaries." The FBI Director then wrote Clark to complain in greater detail about the danger of any congressional committee establishing a "pipe-line" to the Bureau. When Clark finally agreed, Vanech again contacted Tamm to advise that the original order had been cancelled and Tamm told Vanech that the summary memorandums would not be prepared. Hoover, for his part, did not object to furnishing the Committee information. He did object to the intrusion of the Attorney General. Once the matter was settled, he requested "memorandums on both" the individuals connected with the Eisler case "so I can see where we stand."[41]

Eisler was ultimately convicted of contempt of Congress and by May 1949 also faced five years in prison for illegal entry and deportation after that. He responded by fleeing the country aboard the Polish ship *Batory* after buying a twenty-five-cent visitor's pass. JAFRC officials, in contrast, chose to remain and face tax audits and imprisonment until their organization finally expired in 1955 during yet another legislative investigation—this time by the New York Joint Legislative Committee on Charitable and Philanthropic Agencies and Organizations. At the time, the Subversive Activities Control Board was also looking into JAFRC affairs.[42]

The effects of these and other cases that arose from the contempt citations of 1947 were widespread. Because the Truman administration also hoped to exploit these prosecutions, the FBI kept the White House posted on the activities of those who questioned the propriety of the Committee's conduct in the Eisler and JAFRC cases. Hoover reported to presidential aide Harry Vaughan on former Assistant Attorney General O. John Rogge's criticisms of HUAC; on JAFRC plans to present an executive clemency petition to the President (signed by "prominent people who are 'liberal' and whom the President 'thinks a lot of'"); and on various aspects of JAFRC defense strategy. The FBI Director also warned the White House to expect a Communist party propaganda blitz claiming "that the Federal Bureau of Investigation has been directing [HUAC's] action, particularly in view of the 'technical charges' which have been brought against Gerhart Eisler."[43]

If the Truman administration hoped its attentiveness to the contempt prosecutions would demonstrate its appreciation of the seriousness of the domestic Communist threat and thereby enhance the prospects of the President's containment program, the administration got more than it bargained for.[44] Upholding the contempt indictments prosecuted by the Justice Department in 1947, the courts handed down decisions that, for all practical purposes, unleashed the Un-American Activities Committee. According to a student of the contempt process, the political scientist Carl Beck, these decisions included a number of important points of law:

It was held that the existence of a quorum of the committee could only be challenged during the hearing, not upon trial; it was held that testimony taken during investigations was admissible in the trial even though it was to be used to incriminate the witness; it was held that a trial jury may be composed of government employees even though their freedom of decision may be restricted by government loyalty oaths and security programs; it was held that the committee could subpoena documents particularly where there existed some evidence of subversive activities; it was held that a member of a board of directors of an organization was responsible for corporate decisions; it was held that the witness cannot decide what is pertinent and not pertinent because he might well challenge all questions; it was held that freedom of speech was not unduly impinged by an investigation into political associations; and finally it was held that the resolution establishing the Committee on Un-American Activities and the subpoenas issued by the committee did not suffer from the vice of vagueness.[45]

Though this was still a few years before the era of the Fifth Amendment Communist, the writing was on the wall. Hereafter, as District Court Judge Alexander Holtzoff wrote in *U.S. v. Barsky,* "a person who declines to cooperate with a direction of the Committee on the basis of a claim that the Resolution creating it is invalid, or that the Committee is exceeding its jurisdiction, acts as his own peril."[46] It was fitting that Judge Holtzoff, who also sentenced Eisler to a year in jail and a $1,000 fine in June 1947, played such a prominent part in determining the scope of HUAC's authority. Born in Riga, Russia, in 1886, Holtzoff served as a special assistant to the Attorney General from 1924 until his appointment in 1945 to the U.S. District Court for the District of Columbia. As an Assistant Attorney General, Holtzoff had served as a legal adviser to the FBI (which led Eisler to petition, unsuccessfully, for his removal as a biased judge)[47] and counseled Bureau officials in their dealings with the Dies Committee. Holtzoff falsely denied Hoover's involvement in the notorious Palmer raids in his well-publicized correspondence with historian Mary Beard.[48]

The Truman administration's attempts to exploit HUAC's publicity activities ended when the Committee and the administration clashed over the alleged subversiveness of federal employees Edward U. Condon, director of the National Bureau of Standards, nuclear physicist J. Robert Oppenheimer, and, of course, former State Department official Alger Hiss. In all these cases, the Committee's charges were partly based on information in FBI files.

Condon was the subject of several FBI reports to the Truman White House between 1945 and 1949, and in March 1948 J. Parnell Thomas labeled him "one of the weakest links in our atomic security." This charge was the culmination of Thomas's year-long attack on Condon. In mid-1947 the HUAC Chairman had leaked information that led to three front-page articles in the *Washington Times-Herald* and had also referred to Condon's subversiveness in articles written for *Liberty* and *American* magazines. Thomas said an unnamed former security officer in the Manhattan Project had suggested he review Condon's FBI file. And in September 1947 a Committee investigator, William Wheeler, was permitted to look at Condon's Commerce Department loyalty file, which included a copy of a letter of May 15, 1947, from Hoover to Secretary of Commerce W. Averell Harriman. But before Wheeler could finish copying the letter he was stopped.

What Wheeler had managed to copy was included in the Committee's report on Condon and seemed to link him to Nathan Gregory Silvermaster, the government economist whom Elizabeth Bentley had named as a Soviet master spy. HUAC's report, however, excluded a key sentence contained in the Hoover letter: "There is no evidence to show that contacts between this individual [Silvermaster] and Dr. Condon were related to this individual's espionage activities." After the Committee leveled charges, both HUAC and Condon demanded that the full text of Hoover's letter be made public. When the Committee subpoenaed the document, Truman cited what became known as executive privilege. He took physical possession of the letter in the White House and told his staff, "now let them [HUAC] come and get it."[49] To the Committee, it seemed a cover-up.

Whether the FBI was actually leaking information to HUAC regarding Condon is not known. The Committee, in any event, had wide-ranging sources of information; Condon even thought Committee staff were intercepting his mail.[50] The case of J. Robert Oppenheimer, moreover, suggests that HUAC may have received some of its information from the FBI. In December 1947, President Truman appointed Oppenheimer, known to some as the "father of the atomic bomb," to the nine-man General Advisory Committee to the Atomic Energy Commission despite a series of FBI reports to the White House questioning his loyalty. In January 1948, the other Advisory Committee members elected him chairman.

Such credentials, combined with Oppenheimer's radical past, made him a likely quarry for the FBI and HUAC. In March 1947 Hoover urged AEC chairman David Lilienthal to review Oppenheimer's loyalty file, and to pay particular attention to the "Chevalier incident." And in October 1947 ex-FBI agent Louis Russell, a HUAC staff member, appeared before the Committee in executive session, outlining the incident that had so intrigued the FBI Director. (The Chevalier incident involved the efforts of Haakon Chevalier, a professor of French at the University of California, to solicit atomic secrets from Oppenheimer.) The Associated Press reported that the FBI had approved Russell's testimony. In fact, recently declassified FBI files confirm that Hoover had met with J. Parnell Thomas shortly before this testimony was presented. Hoover then wrote Attorney General Clark, advising him of HUAC's plans and claiming that Thomas's detailed knowledge of Oppenheimer's past was the result of leaks from General Leslie Groves, the former head of the Manhattan Project.

Hoover was not being candid with Clark. As early as February 1947, FBI agents prepared a blind memorandum at Hoover's request for an unspecified party. Then on July 12, 1947, James Walter wrote a front-page story on Oppenheimer for the *Washington Times-Herald* based on access to or at least familiarity with the contents of the FBI's Oppenheimer file. Walter, indeed, discussed the case two days later with FBI Assistant Director Nichols. Whether or not the FBI furnished information to Thomas and Walter on Oppenheimer he was kept under surveillance. (On one occasion in June 1953, Hoover and Nichols advised Senator McCarthy and McCarthy aide Roy Cohn on "the Oppenheimer situation.") Finally, Oppenheimer's security clearance was revoked in 1954, though President Eisenhower privately conceded that his FBI file contained "no evidence that implies disloyalty." "However," Eisenhower added, "this does not mean that he might not be a security risk."[51]

If the FBI was not forwarding information to HUAC members and others regarding Condon and Oppenheimer, why did Hoover order a blind memorandum and not a letterhead on Oppenheimer's activities? (FBI policy required blind memorandums to be "used in those instances where the Bureau's identity must not be revealed as the source.")[52] And why had FBI officials lamented the paucity of available "public source" information and noted the near impossibility of documenting Oppenheimer's subversiveness without utilizing the more detailed information picked up through "technical surveillance" (that is, wiretaps)?[53] It does not seem unreasonable to conclude that the FBI was covertly supporting the Committee in its efforts to "get the reds out of Washington." And it was HUAC's pursuit of New Deal and Fair Deal personnel, and not the Committee's pursuit of the other items on its anticommunist agenda, that finally led Truman to call for HUAC's abolition.

But by December 1948, when Truman directed Tom Clark to prepare a memorandum that he hoped House Democratic leaders would use to abolish HUAC, the political climate had changed.[54] The dramatic developments of late November and December in the Alger Hiss case seemed to legitimize what the Committee had been saying all along—namely, that Communists had infiltrated the Democratic administrations of Franklin D. Roosevelt and Harry S Truman. (Hiss, after all, had attended the Yalta conference in 1945 as an assistant to Secretary of State Edward Stettinius. And had not Truman called the Hiss case a "red herring"?) Truman responded by abandoning his plan to call for HUAC's abolition in his forthcoming State of the Union address—perhaps, in part, because of FBI reports emphasizing the Communist associations of the Committee's critics and CPUSA efforts to enlist the White House in the abolition campaign.[55] He continued, nevertheless, to criticize the Un-American Activities Committee. To congressional red-hunters, these criticisms seemed hollow and, as in the Condon case, again suggested that Truman's attentiveness to the Communists-in-government problem left much to be desired.

THE LIMITS OF THE EVIDENCE

Thirteen months later, in February 1950, Senator Joseph R. McCarthy claimed to have a list of 205 known Communists in the State Department. The spectacular nature of McCarthy's charges—following hard on the heels of Alger Hiss's perjury conviction, the "loss" of China to Mao's red army, and the Soviet's successful detonation of an atomic bomb—help explain McCarthy's success. Nevertheless, the junior Senator from Wisconsin, much like the pre-McCarthyites of 1946–1950, relied on the FBI for guidance and information. (With the approval of Hoover and his top aides, McCarthy and his Permanent Subcommittee on Investigations routinely received "information" from the FBI "up until the late Summer" of 1953.)[56] But if FBI bureaucrats effected the development of McCarthyism (whether by leaking educational material through available channels or by attempting to direct the search for subversives in the Roosevelt and Truman administrations), the existing documentary record minimizes both the magnitude and effect of the FBI's political activities. Under careful guidance of Hoover and Nichols, detailed filing procedures were devised to preclude discovery of the Bureau's political activism. On the most basic level, access to domestic intelligence files was carefully controlled and denied even to congressional oversight committees and officials in the Justice Department. More importantly, documents on FBI assistance to congressmen and other available channels were very often recorded in such a way as to permit their safe and non-discoverable destruction.

Hoover's Official and Confidential file on Alger Hiss contains three documents of March 1946 regarding the FBI Director's suggestion that Secretary of State Byrnes leak derogatory (and unsubstantiated) information to conservative congressmen to force Hiss's resignation from the State Department. As all three of Hoover's memorandums are captioned "This Memorandum is for Administrative Purposes to be Destroyed After Action is Taken and Not Sent to Files," they might not constitute all of the so-called Do Not File documents in this particular Bureau case.[57] These three documents were released in response to Freedom of Information Act requests for the FBI's files on Alger Hiss only because in December 1948 the FBI Director had ordered their transfer from the non-retrievable "personal files" of FBI Associate Director Tolson, where they had been stored since March 1946, to Hoover's Official and Confidential files (which were incorporated and then serialized in the FBI's central files after Hoover's death in May 1972). No other FBI documents recording congressional action on Hoover's March 1946 proposal have been released.

Files on other important Cold War political cases, including the investigations of Oppenheimer, Remington, and the National Lawyers Guild also contain evidence that further confirms the Bureau practice of destroying documents on sensitive contacts with conservative congressmen and newspaper reporters and on connivance in congressional conservatives' attempts to embarrass the Truman administration. In addition, other Do Not File documents have been found in the FBI's headquarters file on HUAC and in the unserialized Official and Confidential files of the FBI's chief leaker, Louis Nichols.[58]

Document destruction procedures were relatively fool-proof,[59] but certain situations required specific refinements.

One such situation involved written requests from conservative congressmen for privileged access to the FBI's confidential internal security files. To establish their apolitical role and their commitment to the confidentiality of Bureau files, FBI officials created a paper record indicating that such requests were routinely denied. In practice, however, when an FBI agent hand-delivered Hoover's letter denying access, he also brought along the specified file and was prepared to answer questions about information in the file.[60] Similarly, when Senator Mundt publicly compromised Bureau leaking practices in 1953–1954, FBI officials worked with the unwitting congressman to contain the resultant embarrassing publicity.

During a November 1953 informal address before the Bonneville, Utah, Knife and Fork Club, the former HUAC member and then ranking McCarthy committee member inadvertently disclosed the FBI practice of "tipping off" congressional committees in cases involving Communist infiltration where there was not enough evidence to justify an indictment. Mundt's remark, reported in an approving *Salt Lake Tribune* editorial, came to the attention of J. D. Williams, a University of Utah political scientist. Concerned about "F.B.I. connivance in substituting Congressional Committees for the courts," Williams wrote, ironically, to Walter Winchell and, more significantly, to Senator J. William Fulbright (D., Ark.) to complain about this practice. In March 1954 Fulbright widely publicized Mundt's "tipping off" remark.

At Nichols's direction, FBI agents interviewed Williams, advising him that Mundt had denied making the controversial statement. Mundt also wrote Williams to this effect and, at Hoover's suggestion, sent a copy of this letter to Fulbright. (The *Salt Lake Tribune* editorial writer, nonetheless, affirmed the accuracy of his original report.) Hoover privately advised Mundt that these letters "should once and for all lay to rest the canard which has been so widely disseminated," while he publicly dismissed charges of FBI assistance to conservative congressmen as "an absolute lie." Citing Winchell as an example, Hoover claimed that the FBI did not "play favorites" with any member of the press. Attorney General Herbert Brownell, Jr., and Senator McCarthy also sought to refute this contention. Affirming his dedication "to keeping inviolate the confidential nature of the F.B.I. files," Brownell stated that during his tenure as Attorney General no information had been given to the McCarthy committee or to HUAC. Although the frequent recipient of FBI leaks, McCarthy brazenly accused Fulbright of a "most irresponsible and most vicious" assault on the Bureau.[61]

CHAPTER V

Bureau Enemies:
The National Lawyers Guild
and Max Lowenthal

While carrying out their self-appointed task of nurturing an anticommunist consensus, FBI officials also worked tirelessly to discredit those who challenged their Cold War ethos. A public assault, however, could adversely affect the Bureau's influence, which was based on political neutrality, and belie its carefully cultivated image. Hoover's FBI, of course, was a well-harnessed political beast and the Director was a political activist, though often a decidedly non-visible one. But at the time, the Bureau's involvement was not so readily apparent, despite such blunders as Senator Mundt's revealing Salt Lake City remark. It was the Bureau's image of impartiality and nonpartisanship that led many Americans to distinguish between the FBI Director's "colorful" rhetoric and the "irresponsible" rantings of such red-hunters as McCarthy, Velde, Jenner, and McCarran.

This FBI image, and the political clout that backed it, also led conservative journalists and congressmen to accept as gospel carefully selected information from Louis Nichols. Though Hoover and his top aides rarely hesitated to denounce Communists, Communist dupes, and other liberal critics of the FBI, their principal mode of operation was less overt. The attack on the National Lawyers Guild (NLG) offers an explicit example of this dual strategy, for the Lawyers Guild not only criticized the Bureau but threatened to provoke an investigation of the FBI at a time when it was especially vulnerable.

130

THE LAWYERS GUILD AND AN EMERGENT McCARTHYISM

The left-wing attorneys who flocked to the National Lawyers Guild during the New Deal years had long troubled the FBI and the Dies Committee. CPUSA members and other far-left radicals were well represented in the Guild, but its membership also included prominent liberals (Thomas I. Emerson, O. John Rogge, Arthur Garfield Hays, Thurgood Marshall, and Clifford Durr), several United States senators and representatives (among others, Pennsylvania Democrat and future HUAC Chairman Francis Walter), two state governors, and many attorneys working in New Deal executive agencies and departments. Though the proportion of Communists was never very high (approximately one hundred of the nearly three to four thousand Guild members in the late 1930s), the NLG tolerated Communist party members and rejected proposals for anticommunist oath requirements in 1939 and again in 1940. That same year, FBI Director Hoover sent a memorandum to the Justice Department asking whether Guild members who were government employees should be considered security risks if the United States became involved in the European war. Although the Justice Department rejected Hoover's implicit suggestion, in the spring of 1940 Attorney General Robert Jackson, Judge Ferdinand Pecora, Assistant Secretary of State Adolf A. Berle, Jr., and other prominent New Dealers publicly denounced the Guild as Communist dominated. Criticism from such respectable liberals caused NLG membership to drop dramatically, perhaps by as much as seventy-five percent.[1]

Despite a general thinning of the ranks, the National Lawyers Guild continued to function. After the FBI was severely criticized in 1940 by, among others, Senators Wheeler and Norris, Professor Franz Boas, the *Milwaukee Journal*, the *New Republic*, and even Westbrook Pegler for predawn arrests of Spanish Loyalist sympathizers in Detroit and Milwaukee, the NLG worked to keep the issue of political surveillance before the public.[2] The Guild publicized the extraconstitutional exploits of FBI agents throughout 1940, and passed a resolution the next year condemning "the Gestapo activities of the

Federal Bureau of Investigation." Guild members then called on Congress to reduce the FBI's budget and President Roosevelt to fire Hoover. The Dies Committee, which had reasons for opposing the Lawyers Guild, duly noted these criticisms and formally labeled the NLG a Communist front in its notorious Appendix IX—a voluminous, carelessly compiled report entitled *Communist Front Organizations.* On February 1, 1943, Martin Dies read an excerpt from a Guild pamphlet, circulated to every member of the House, charging the Committee with being "the secret weapon with which Adolf Hitler hopes to soften up our Nation for military conquest."[3]

Later, when President Truman and Tom Clark decided to compile and publicly release the Attorney General's list of subversive organizations, Hoover immediately nominated the NLG. In August 1947, nineteen FBI field offices were directed to investigate Guild activities in their areas. In November, FBI agents tapped the telephone in the NLG's Washington, D.C., office. A few months later, Washington Field Office agents burglarized this Guild office and photographed membership records. When Clark decided not to include the National Lawyers Guild on his list of pariah groups, the FBI drew up its own "thumbnail sketch"—citing the Dies Committee's Appendix IX and Adolf Berle's accusations in lieu of the Attorney General's list.[4]

Clark's failure to include the Lawyers Guild as a subversive organization did not stop the FBI from reporting NLG activities to the White House. In December 1948, Hoover advised Harry Vaughan that the NLG planned to arrange a conference with Truman through the intercession of Bartley C. Crum, a corporate lawyer and a Republican but also the subject of an FBI wiretap and an attorney for several unfriendly witnesses during HUAC's investigation of communism in Hollywood. Crum and the NLG delegation, Hoover reported, would try "to persuade the President to intervene with Democratic leaders to take steps to abolish the House Committee on Un-American Activities." Included in the proposed delegation were Clifford Durr, identified by Hoover as a critic of the President's loyalty program, and Paul O'Dwyer, well-known activist and brother of the mayor of New York

City. Quoting *Counterattack*, Hoover described O'Dwyer as a "party liner" and "a backer of Communist fronts."[5]

THE COPLON FLAP

The Bureau's running feud with the National Lawyers Guild exploded in June 1949 during the espionage trial of Judith Coplon. An employee in the Justice Department's alien registration section, Coplon was arrested on March 4, 1949, as she was allegedly about to pass twenty-eight FBI documents to a Soviet national, Valentin Gubitchev, in New York City. Indicted and tried in both Washington, D.C. (for unauthorized possession of government documents) and New York City (for intent to transmit them to a foreign agent), Coplon requested that the complete texts of all twenty-eight documents found in her handbag be introduced as evidence. Judge Albert Reeves overruled the prosecution's objections to this motion on the theory that the court could not judge the government's contention that the stolen documents were vital to the national security while, at the same time, refusing to reveal their contents on national security grounds. Hoover later complained to Attorney General J. Howard McGrath that his predecessor, Tom Clark, had given in too easily. The Justice Department, Hoover maintained, should have "flatly refuse[d]" to produce the documents.[6]

The twenty-eight documents revealed no state secrets. They did reveal the FBI's pervasive political surveillance and intrusive investigative techniques. Information for fifteen of the twenty-eight reports had been acquired through wiretaps. The Coplon documents further exposed the Bureau's penchant for spying on prominent New Deal liberals (Edward U. Condon and David Niles), Hollywood personalities (Fredric March and Edward G. Robinson), financial supporters of Henry Wallace's 1948 presidential campaign, HUAC's opponents, and even the author of a master's thesis on the New Deal in New Zealand. After these revelations, the Coplon defense asked the government if the Bureau had tapped their client's phone as well. Judge Reeves denied this motion.

133

Sylvester Ryan, the presiding judge in Coplon's second trial, was more amenable to the motion for a pretrial hearing. And it was during this hearing that defense counsel learned of the FBI's extensive wiretapping—at Coplon's office and apartment and at her parents' Brooklyn home. These taps continued for two months after her arrest, which enabled the FBI to intercept privileged attorney-client conversations. At least one FBI agent had given false testimony when he claimed during the early stages of the pretrial hearing that he had "no previous knowledge" of wiretapping in the Coplon case. This agent later admitted that he had destroyed "quite a number" of the tapes recording Coplon's telephone conversations—not "as a routine matter" as earlier attested, but in response to a directive from FBI headquarters ordering the action "in view of the imminence of her [Coplon's] trial."[7]

Though HUAC members (principally Nixon and Velde), conservative reporters (among others, David Lawrence, Rex Collier, and Constantine Brown), and even some liberals (led by columnist Marquis Childs and Methodist Bishop G. Bromley Oxnam) supported the FBI during its ordeal, the press publicized the Coplon trial revelations and the Bureau was thoroughly "embarrassed."[8] Attorney General Clark came to the Bureau's aid on March 31, 1949, by announcing that FBI wiretaps were applied selectively and only "with the express approval in each individual instance of the Attorney General." Clark and his successor, J. Howard McGrath, also announced (falsely in Clark's case; perhaps ignorantly in McGrath's) that the Justice Department's current wiretap policy simply continued the policy established by Franklin D. Roosevelt.[9]

The FBI responded covertly to the Coplon affair. First, on June 29, 1949, Hoover authorized a new filing classification system, code named "June mail." FBI agents in the field were thenceforth required to submit all information acquired through "sources illegal in nature" (including wiretaps and microphones) or from "extremely sensitive" sources ("such as Governors, secretaries to high officials") under the June caption. These reports were then filed under "lock and key" in "separate confidential files of the Bureau and by the SACs in the field." Beginning in July 1950, moreover, all future instructions from senior FBI officials regarding "June matters" were "transmitted orally."

One week after the June procedure was initiated, Hoover issued Bureau Bulletin No. 34, which required FBI agents to exclude all "facts and information which are considered of a nature not expedient to disseminate or would cause embarrassment to the Bureau, if distributed," from the body of FBI reports and to note them only on the appended "administrative" page. Because administrative pages were not serialized in the Bureau's central records system, this procedure enabled FBI officials to circumvent court-ordered disclosures. The FBI could release formal FBI reports to the courts but withhold the unserialized administrative page, insuring technical compliance with discovery orders without arousing either defense counsel suspicions or revealing embarrassing surveillance.[10]

Bureau Bulletin No. 34 and the June mail filing system promised to prevent a recurrence of the Coplon debacle, where FBI reports were made available, as Hoover lamented, "to shyster and subversive lawyers."[11] FBI officials also acted to contain the ongoing Coplon revelations, which were widely publicized by civil liberties groups. From the Bureau's perspective, potentially the most damaging threat came from the National Lawyers Guild.

In a letter of June 20, 1949, NLG president Clifford Durr brought the Coplon affair to Harry Truman's attention and suggested the appointment of a blue-ribbon presidential commission "of outstanding citizens, including representatives of the national bar associations and civil liberties organizations, to undertake a comprehensive investigation into the operations and methods of the Federal Bureau of Investigation." Truman's evasive response to Durr's demand satisfied neither NLG activists nor FBI officials. That same month, FBI Assistant Director Nichols worked closely with United Press Washington bureau chief Lyle Wilson and Associated Press Washington bureau chief Merrimam Smith to elicit a firm assurance from the President's press secretary, Charles Ross, that Truman had no intention of authorizing an investigation of the FBI. Even after "Lyle and Merrimam Smith . . . really pinned this thing down," Nichols "checked with" still other media contacts to insure proper press coverage of Ross's assurance. He then drafted a letter for release over Hoover's signature thanking Wilson for his "recent assistance."[12]

Since the President was understandably reluctant to investigate FBI surveillance practices, the NLG launched its own probe. By November 1949 the Guild had compiled a rough draft of a report on the Bureau's domestic political intelligence activities, prompting Hoover to order FBI agents to compile an up-to-date report on the Guild. A 300-page study was prepared that sought to document the NLG's Communist-front credentials by highlighting its opposition to HUAC. The FBI also secured (probably through a break-in at the Guild's Washington office) a copy of the NLG's not-yet-published critique. Then the Bureau leaked information based on the minutes of a recent NLG executive board meeting to Lyle Wilson. Two days after Wilson's United Press story appeared, the Bureau sent its own report, together with other political intelligence on the NLG, to Attorney General McGrath.

In a letter prepared by FBI officials, McGrath warned Truman to expect the NLG report to be a left-wing, Communist-inspired diatribe demanding a thorough investigation of the FBI. Truman also learned that the Guild was planning a national publicity campaign to highlight the report's conclusions and that they intended to arrange a meeting with him. Hoover again briefed Harry Vaughan, and McGrath sent Truman an FBI memorandum, described by Hoover as "a summary of all pertinent information appearing in the files of this Bureau concerning the Guild. It will be noted that much of these data were obtained either from public sources or incidental to other investigations conducted by the Bureau." Whether or not Truman and McGrath were thus misled regarding the nature of the FBI probe (which included wiretaps and break-ins), the President responded by complaining of "crackpots" in the NLG "who like very much to stir up trouble." Because he concluded that there was no "way to stop the [NLG] report," Truman advised McGrath to "handle it in the best possible manner when it comes out."[13]

With the National Lawyers Guild set to release its report on

January 23, 1950, the Bureau continued its intensive scrutiny of the group. After intercepting a telephone conversation between journalist I. F. Stone and Guild officers Durr and Robert Silberstein (discussing ways to maximize press coverage of the NLG report on the Bureau), FBI officials forwarded this intelligence to the White House, the Department of Justice, and possibly HUAC member Nixon. On January 22, 1950, the day before the Guild's planned press conference, Nixon phoned three national wire services to read his letter to Chairman John Wood, asking for a HUAC investigation of the Lawyers Guild. (The Bureau had previously been alerted to the contemplated investigation either by Nixon or one of its other sources on the Un-American Activities Committee.)[14]

The FBI-HUAC alliance in this instance was predictable. The Committee, for instance, used FBI documents unearthed in the Coplon trial not to embarrass the Bureau but to highlight the Communist associations of two government employees, Philip and Mary Jane Keeney. And Committee research director Benjamin Mandel kept an extensive "file on activities against the FBI" which included at least "two reports of the Central Intelligence Agency."[15] Among its many accusations, the Lawyers Guild charged that an ongoing and rather seamy relationship existed between the Bureau and the Committee— a charge highlighted by Judith Coplon's revelation that FBI officials monitored the Committee and sent confidential memorandums to the Justice Department regarding its activities. Other prominent liberals who supported the Guild effort to investigate the FBI, such as Joseph L. Rauh, Jr., national executive committee chairman of Americans for Democratic Action, also noted HUAC's pipeline into the FBI. In a well-publicized speech on February 24, Rauh launched a scathing attack on the FBI, concentrating particularly on its role in the Coplon trial, its wiretapping practices, and its infiltration of the Wallace movement. Rauh further complained of an FBI informer surfacing before HUAC and regaling the Committee with tales of Communist machinations in the Wallace movement only two days before the Progressive party national convention convened.[16]

Given this potential problem, the FBI investigation con-

137

tinued after the NLG released its report. In early February, Hoover advised the Senate Appropriations Committee of a Communist-inspired, NLG-led plot to discredit the FBI. Lyle Wilson duly highlighted Hoover's testimony after it was publicly released, claiming that the CPUSA considered Hoover "a dangerous enemy, second only to the Catholic Church."[17] The next month, after the FBI's Springfield Field Office learned of Guild plans to have its report reviewed by a state bar association, the Bureau forwarded its thumbnail sketch of the NLG to the Illinois Bar Association's Civil Liberties Committee.[18] The Bureau also leaked correspondence it had microfilmed regarding the Guild's affiliation with the International Association of Democratic Lawyers (IADL).[19] One letter suggested a pro-Soviet attitude on the part of NLG officer Robert Silberstein, who had attended the 1949 IADL convention in Rome. (Silberstein supported the majority decision to expel the Yugoslav delegation and failed to mention this episode in his later report to the Guild.) The FBI's Washington Field Office concluded "that considerable dissension in the ranks of the Lawyers Guild could occur if this matter became public." Perhaps unaware of the source, Murray Kempton publicized this information in his *New York Post* column just two weeks prior to the Guild's May 1950 convention in New York City. Similarly, when an FBI agent discovered a letter from a prominent French Communist in Silberstein's trash the Bureau promptly forwarded this information to HUAC member Velde, and the ex-FBI agent alerted Fulton Lewis, Jr.[20]

Then, in the spring of 1950, the Bureau disseminated portions of a classified report on the NLG to HUAC, which released the information under its own name in September.[21] Three months later, another HUAC report accused the NLG of financing the National Committee to Defeat the Mundt Bill. HUAC's report on this "Communist lobby" contained intelligence derived from the FBI tap on the Guild's telephone.[22] These leaks were not exceptional as senior FBI officials worked closely with certain HUAC members and staff throughout 1950. Committee members Nixon and Burr Harrison (D., Va.) and research director Mandel briefed Nichols on the progress of their report on the NLG and, presumably, their report on the

Committee to Defeat the Mundt Bill as well. On July 12 Nichols, in turn, briefed FBI Associate Director Clyde Tolson, lamenting that HUAC's study of the NLG "got snarled up in Committee." A week later, after hearing from Nixon, an apologetic Nichols advised Tolson that the reason for the Committee's hesitancy was Francis Walter's past membership in the Guild.

When briefing Nichols, Nixon also relayed Harrison's request "to get a list of the names of all members of the Lawyers Guild released with the report." Though Nichols told Nixon "he did not know where an accurate up-to-date list could be secured," someone connected with HUAC, or so Nichols said, later furnished the FBI with a list of NLG members "who are presumably still in government." HUAC's apparent source was Edward Nellor, a reporter and a contact of Nichols who was later an employee of one of the FBI's most prolific publicists, Fulton Lewis, Jr. Apprised of these developments, the FBI Director ordered: "If and when Committee report is issued we should call A.G.'s [Attorney General's] attention to it and to our previous memos re Lawyers Guild and suggest consideration again for declaring it subversive." HUAC member Harrison also wrote McGrath (Mandel drafted his letter) in a similar effort to pressure him into including the Guild on the next installment of the Attorney General's list of subversive organizations. Mandel forwarded a copy of Harrison's letter to Guy Hottel, the Special Agent in Charge of the FBI's Washington Field Office.[23]

Though McGrath did not accept the Harrison-Mandel and FBI recommendations, FBI officials continued to use HUAC's report as independent corroboration of their contention that the National Lawyers Guild was indeed subversive and worthy of a spot on the Attorney General's list. More importantly, the Committee's report allowed the Bureau to update its thumbnail sketch. For example, FBI reports, letterhead memorandums, and blind memorandums on Erwin Griswold of the Harvard Law School noted such facts as his refusal to disband the Guild's Harvard chapter and then identified the NLG as subversive by citing the Dies Committee's Appendix IX and HUAC's more recent characterization.[24] For the next two

139

decades the FBI relied on HUAC's description of the National Lawyers Guild as "the foremost legal bulwark of the Communist Party" when disseminating derogatory information on the group, its members, and its ex-members.

While HUAC members were preparing their FBI-assisted reports on the National Lawyers Guild and the National Committee to Defeat the Mundt Bill, yet another NLG-related problem was unfolding. In the summer of 1950, Max Lowenthal, a former civil servant and onetime NLG member, was preparing a carefully researched, if tendentious, history of the FBI. A personal friend of President Truman, Lowenthal had received some arcane research assistance from Truman's White House staff and sent a copy of his manuscript to the President. Truman responded on June 17, commending Lowenthal's "wonderful service to the country." He wrote to Lowenthal again on June 22 with similar praise. The President "got a great kick out of reading . . . [the] manuscript and making notes on the margin," and on July 25 sent Lowenthal a letter that he had received from FBI Director Hoover regarding the manuscript. Truman thought Lowenthal would "get a kick out of it."

At least one senior member of Truman's staff did not share the President's opinion of Lowenthal's "wonderful service to the country." George Elsey was "deeply disturbed" by a "grossly biased" manuscript containing "absolutely nothing favorable to the FBI" and smacking of a methodology "strikingly similar to Senator McCarthy's." Convinced that Truman did not share Lowenthal's opinion of Hoover and the Bureau, Elsey recommended a staff conference to "consider how we can best keep the President and the White House from being in any way publicly associated with Lowenthal's production." Later, at a press conference, Truman declined to comment on the book on the grounds that he had not read it.[25]

Elsey's suggestion was the politically expedient one. HUAC assisted the Bureau in late August and again in September, when Committee staff members paid several visits to the

Lowenthal home (late at night when his wife was home alone and undressed) and to the offices of his publisher, William Sloane Associates, and eventually subpoenaed Lowenthal. Lowenthal secured the services of former Senator Wheeler to serve as counsel during his scheduled HUAC appearance. Wheeler's son Ed told Lowenthal that Wheeler had been approached by "a man who has close relations with the Committee's staff, with the suggestion that the Senator not represent me." "It seems that they really used police state methods to prevent the publication of this book," President Truman wrote Lowenthal when apprised of HUAC's efforts, "but I am glad you are going through with it." Lowenthal did, appearing before the Committee in executive session on September 15, where he was questioned about his past membership in the National Lawyers Guild. Two months later, on the day before his publisher released the book, *The Federal Bureau of Investigation*, HUAC publicly released Lowenthal's testimony.[26]

The FBI's media allies (led by Trohan, Winchell, Lewis, Sokolsky, and Woltman) and supporters in the academic community (including Father Walsh of Georgetown University) defended the Bureau and attacked Lowenthal and his publisher as procommunist. The FBI Crime Records Division, after carefully reviewing Lowenthal's HUAC testimony, wrote and planted critical book reviews, assembled and disseminated derogatory information on Lowenthal and his publisher, and launched a crude attempt to suppress the book. FBI agents visited hundreds of bookstores, attempting to persuade the owners not to stock the book. Hoover even wrote a "Dear Comrade" letter to his close friend Trohan thanking him for his scathing review of Lowenthal's study. "The whole thing," Hoover mused, "makes neither rhyme nor reason and it would certainly be interesting if we had the full facts behind, not only the author's motive, but that of the publisher." This is not to say that the Bureau made no attempt to discover the full facts. Six years later Trohan was still discussing Lowenthal with Nichols and keeping fellow publicist Westbrook Pegler up-to-date.[27]

Ironically, the most convincing rebuttal to Lowenthal's book came from an NLG founder and American Civil Liberties

Union official, who had come to favor the "responsible" red-baiting techniques championed by those Cold War liberals who flocked to the "vital center." Morris Ernst applauded the FBI's "magnificent record of respect for individual freedom" in a December 1950 *Reader's Digest* article entitled "Why I No Longer Fear the FBI." After reprinting Ernst's article, the FBI and the Society of Former Special Agents of the FBI distributed it "by the thousands." Society president Robert W. Dick even sent Harry Truman a copy of this "most interesting" article. The Society chose Ernst's piece, Dick told Truman, because "the charge of prejudice could always be levelled at us," but not a civil libertarian of Ernst's stature. It was "mere coincidence," Dick added, "that it [the *Reader's Digest* article] appeared in print about the time of the publication of the [Lowenthal] book."[28]

In a sense, Dick was right about the timing of Ernst's article. The *Reader's Digest* piece had originally been conceived to counter an earlier article by former Federal Communications Commission chairman James L. Fly on FBI wiretapping, which had appeared in the September 27, 1949, issue of *Look* magazine. The Fly article, written in the wake of the Coplon trial revelations, had been approved for publication while the editor of *Look*, Gardner Cowles, Jr., was vacationing in Europe. Upon his return Cowles advised staff writer Edward Nellor of the need to counter the Fly story. Nellor and *Look* consultant Leo Rosten then contacted Nichols, who suggested they approach Morris Ernst or, if Ernst was not acceptable, "some great Constitutional lawyer." Hoover concurred, selecting Ernst as his first choice to put Fly (whom he referred to as "a stinker and a liar"), in his place and "some outstanding lawyer or dean of some law school" as his second choice. FBI Assistant Directors Nichols and Hugh Clegg then suggested candidates—including former Supreme Court Justice James Byrnes, Father Walsh of Georgetown, Charles S. Collier of George Washington University, and New Jersey Supreme Court Justice Arthur Vanderbilt. FBI officials, however, lobbied successfully for Ernst and thus were able to assist him not only with the *Reader's Digest* article but also with a July 1950 *Look* article. *Look* consultant Rosten was also granted priviledged access to FBI files for yet another article in September 1950.[29]

Ernst's eventual *Reader's Digest* article was originally conceived in a similar fashion by Nichols and Fulton Oursler, then a senior editor at *Reader's Digest*. Hoover initially contacted Ernst, suggesting that he stop by and talk to "Nick [Nichols]." Thereafter, and closely following Hoover's directive to "give every help possible," the FBI Crime Records Division became deeply involved in "the Ernst projects" (in addition to the *Reader's Digest* and *Look* pieces, there was a response to a critical *American Scholar* article on the federal employee loyalty program and a luncheon engagement with news commentator Edward R. Murrow) by providing research and editorial assistance and by forwarding material from FBI files to Ernst and Oursler.[30]

Nor was this the first time the Bureau cooperated with Ernst. In August 1943, after two anonymous articles (possibly written by Lowenthal) critical of the FBI's conduct in loyalty investigations appeared in *The Nation*, Hoover promptly contacted Ernst. The FBI Director was concerned because *The Nation*'s audience not only included "the so-called Communist front boys and girls" but "many persons of perfectly serious liberal views and intentions . . . [who] may absorb some of this venomous poisin [sic] which The Nation is disseminating about the FBI." Upon receipt of Hoover's letter, Ernst visited Clyde Tolson at Bureau headquarters and soon after defended the Bureau in a public letter to *Nation* editor Freda Kirchwey. In December 1949, Hoover alerted Ernst to the National Lawyers Guild's proposed criticisms of the FBI and thanked him for "endeavoring to keep people in the middle of the road." When Fly and other ACLU officials criticized Hoover, based upon documented FBI abuse of power as revealed in the Coplon espionage trial, Ernst advised ACLU official George E. Rundquist to stop "sniping at the FBI," to be thankful that such an impartial, nonpolitical patriarch as Hoover was heading the Bureau—and not "the New York Chief of Police, or a Tom Dewey type." Before mailing this letter to Rundquist, Ernst discussed its contents with Nichols and allowed the FBI Assistant Director to photocopy it. (Ernst also assisted the

Bureau effort to develop derogatory information on Sylvester Ryan, the trial judge in the Coplon case, and relayed to Nichols the substance of his conversation with Appellate Court Justice Jerome Frank regarding Coplon's appeal.) And in September 1950, Ernst contacted Nichols to offer his services to HUAC as a friendly witness willing "to tell the story" on the National Lawyers Guild. Because the Bureau was not then "on too intimate terms with the Committee," Nichols declined Ernst's offer. Nevertheless, he promised to "keep them [HUAC] in mind should the opportunity ever present itself."[31]

THE ONLY GOOD INDIAN

A further opportunity to neutralize Lowenthal and the National Lawyers Guild arose in late November 1950 when the NLG called a press conference to publicize Yale Law Professor Thomas I. Emerson's rebuttal to HUAC's recent character-ization of the Guild as subversive.[32] At this press conference, Nichols arranged for a trio of "protagonists"—Scripps-Howard reporter Tony Smith, *Washington Times-Herald* reporter James Walter, and United Press reporter James Donovan—to give "the boys" a hard time. When Emerson dismissed the HUAC report as too one-sided, Nichols reported to Tolson, "Tony Smith told them that he had read the Lawyers Guild report on the FBI some months ago and had also read the Max Lowenthal book and weren't they just as one-sided." Emerson was also asked to explain "the significance of the Lawyers Guild press conference following on the heels of the Lowenthal book," and whether "it wasn't a fact that the FBI was making it hot for the Communists." All in all, Nichols concluded, "some of the good people around town just about broke up the Lawyers Guild Press Conference this morning."[33]

Not content with crippling the NLG, the FBI continued its investigation in the 1950s—working closely in 1951, for instance, with Austin Canfield, chairman of the American Bar Association's (ABA) Special Committee to Study Communist Tactics, Strategy, and Objectives. The FBI supplied Canfield with four blind memorandums on Guild officers after he had contacted the Bureau, and Nichols, who later became a member of Canfield's committee, apparently supplied him with a classified FBI report regarding a recent NLG convention. Canfield's special committee also maintained a close relationship with HUAC and the American Legion, regularly exploiting their lists to inspire disbarment proceedings against attorneys who took the Fifth Amendment before congressional investigating committees.[34]

The FBI, furthermore, continued to work closely with HUAC in its effort to immobilize the NLG's insurgent attorneys. When the Guild's West Coast chapter announced its intention in November 1951 to mail excerpts from the forthcoming California Smith Act trial proceedings to thousands of state attorneys, the local FBI field office promptly notified Bureau headquarters. Within two weeks, HUAC began preparations for hearings on Communist infiltration of the legal profession in California and in January 1952 heard the testimony of five cooperative witnesses who identified thirty-two California lawyers as Lawyers Guild members. Ben Margolis and other Smith Act counsel were described as active Communists. (These hearings continued on and off throughout the year, with the ABA sending a representative to Los Angeles for the specific purpose of gathering information "designed to encourage the passage of laws by . . . state legislative bodies for the disbarment of . . . attorneys identified as active in the CP movement.") The source for at least some of HUAC's information, not surprisingly, was the FBI. In October 1950, an ex-Guild member approached the Bureau with a list of names and tales of Communist intrigue in the NLG. The list of radical attorneys that this informer provided the FBI was nearly identical to the list disseminated by HUAC during its public hearings. Morris Ernst again came to the Bureau's assistance, providing the FBI with information on fellow ACLU official Fly's attempt to organize opposition to HUAC's proposed probe of California attorneys.[35]

FBI officials further assisted the efforts of HUAC members and others to cleanse the legal profession by providing loyalty check services to the ABA and various state bar associations regarding applicants to the bar and disbarment proceedings against radical attorneys. Bureau officials continued this practice even after the National Conference of Bar Examiners inadvertently "abus[ed] our confidence by advising that we have been furnishing information." After this abuse of confidence in October 1953, the FBI restricted its leaking practices in disbarment cases to those instances, as in "the case of Emanuel Bloch," attorney for the recently executed Rosenbergs who accused President Eisenhower, Attorney General Brownell, and FBI Director Hoover of "murder," where "it is to the public interest that the Bureau furnish as much information as is possible."[36]

Yet another attempt to unleash HUAC on the National Lawyers Guild occurred in 1953 when the FBI sought to have Thomas Emerson appear before a congressional investigating committee. In a memorandum to Tolson, Ladd, and Alan H. Belmont, Hoover lamented:

> it has been impossible up to the present time to have Emerson called before any Committee of Congress because of the intercession on his behalf of Senator [Robert] Taft [R., Ohio], who is on the Board of Trustees at Yale University. I indicated to the Attorney General that the House Committee on Un-American Activities had contemplated calling Emerson but had refrained from doing so because of the intercession of Senator Taft and that the same incident happened to the Jenner Committee.

When Emerson finally appeared before the Senate Internal Security Subcommittee in executive session on June 16, 1953, the FBI received a transcript of his "secret" testimony and a report from SISS counsel Robert Morris—who bemoaned Emerson's deftness in parrying the Subcommittee's questions. When another SISS source advised Nichols that the Subcommittee would subpoena Emerson again if he could be linked to "some international group of Communist lawyers," the Bureau tried to oblige.[37]

HUAC's September 1950 report on the National Lawyers Guild had sparked a wave of resignations. The FBI's continued attempts to neutralize the NLG virtually destroyed the organization. By 1958, five of nine local chapters had collapsed, draining the Guild of four-fifths of its membership.[38] But even with the Lawyers Guild reeling, the Bureau maintained its initiative. In May 1958, Crime Records Division official Gordon A. Nease forwarded to SISS counsel Jay Sourwine individually prepared blind memorandums highlighting "pertinent subversive activities" of seventy attorneys who had defended Communists in court or before congressional committees. Significantly, the FBI, and not Sourwine, selected all seventy targets through a review of every attorney listed on the Security Index. The intent of this massive leak—to provide SISS with "lead material"—was underscored by the inclusion of an FBI-prepared memorandum entitled "Use of Lawyers and Courts to Further Communist Propaganda" and photostats of five other documents, including the 1950 edition of the NLG's *Lawyers Referral Directory.* These documents, FBI Assistant Director Belmont noted, "could be used to help establish the necessity for [SISS] hearings in this connection." Nine months later, HUAC published a report of its own on "Communist Legal Subversion" and in December 1960 the NLG's New York City office was the subject of a formal FBI counterintelligence operation.[39]

With the cooperation of ABA leaders, HUAC and the FBI had scored a resounding victory in their struggle to discipline the legal profession and help silence critics of Cold War politics and priorities. The FBI's assumed task of alerting the public to the allegedly subversive Lawyers Guild was not a visceral attempt by FBI bureaucrats to discredit their critics or to assuage the piqued feelings of the FBI Director. Rather, the Bureau investigated the dissident attorneys who coalesced around the National Lawyers Guild because they challenged Cold War values and threatened the FBI's ability to function without fear of restraint. HUAC's principal charge against the Guild centered on the NLG's record of having filed *amicus curiae* briefs on behalf of leading Communists and other dissidents during some of the McCarthy era's major political trials—including those of HUAC witnesses Gerhart Eisler, Leon Josephson, John Howard Lawson, Dalton Trumbo, Eugene Dennis, Richard Morford, George Marshall, and Edward K. Barsky, former State Department employee Carl

Marzani, and the Foley Square Smith Act defendants. HUAC's report on the NLG, moreover, listed the names and addresses of Guild attorneys who had represented witnesses before the Un-American Activities Committee.[40]

Like FBI officials, NLG attorneys were in the education business. According to Guild activists, however, the principal threat to the Constitution came not from Joseph Stalin's palsied revolutionaries but from FBI Director Hoover's lawless agents. As Hoover well knew, had the Guild succeeded in inspiring an executive or congressional investigation of the FBI in 1949, the domestic Communist issue might have collapsed. It was simply a reflection of the FBI's political muscle that Congress responded, through HUAC, as it did—by investigating the National Lawyers Guild but not the FBI.

CHAPTER VI

Cold War Justice:
The Trials of William Walter Remington

Not every challenge to the hardening Cold War *Zeitgeist* came from such eager combatants as the National Lawyers Guild's attorneys. Others, like William Walter Remington, joined the battle reluctantly, more from a sense of desperation than a commitment to civil liberties. But Remington, no less than the NLG's spirited activists, posed a serious threat to the Bureau when challenging the truthfulness of a key FBI informer, Elizabeth Bentley. And for a time things were indeed rough for Bentley and those who had invested so heavily in her credibility, from senior FBI officials down to the lowliest HUAC investigator.

From the first day she appeared as a public witness in July 1948 until June 8, 1950, when Remington was indicted for perjury by a federal grand jury in New York City, Bentley's tales of Soviet espionage cells in the United States government had been seriously challenged, and she had been dubbed, by A. J. Liebling, a "nutmeg Mata Hari." Not a single person she named had been prosecuted. And after she repeated her charges against Remington without the protection of congressional privilege on *Meet the Press* in September 1948, the exposed Commerce Department official sued. Remington's $100,000 slander suit against Bentley, the NBC network, and the program's sponsor, General Foods, was settled out of court in March 1950 for $9,000.

Bentley was not a party to the settlement and made no retraction. In February 1949, moreover, the Loyalty Review Board cleared Remington (reversing an earlier decision of a regional loyalty board) and ordered him reinstated—only after it failed to persuade Bentley to appear and testify. Others who had built careers on the Communists-in-government issue privately called upon the FBI to persuade Bentley to oblige the government loyalty panel. D. Milton Ladd, however, advised one of these, Father Cronin (whose own efforts had failed), that the Bureau could not perform such a service. Hoover ratified this decision: "Right. We cannot become involved in it."[1]

Contrary to Hoover's and Ladd's apolitical pronouncements, the FBI had invested heavily in Bentley's integrity. When an opportunity to vindicate the so-called Spy Queen arose, Bureau officials launched a massive investigation of William Remington, declaring that the case "must receive continuous attention looking towards successful prosecution." This investigation, handled as a "special" and followed closely by Hoover and his top aides, ultimately involved forty-four FBI field offices and agents in seven foreign countries.[2]

If the Alger Hiss case suggests that the FBI and its allies in the Justice Department were relatively indifferent to the processes of justice, the Remington case demonstrates the pervasive impact of the Cold War on the American polity. As in all political trials, only the final verdict mattered, and Remington—though vulnerable and perhaps even culpable—lost because of the array of groups interested in vindicating the premise of Bentley's charge. Bentley, after all, was not only a star HUAC witness but the FBI's prize informer. The Bureau relied upon her revelations even more than those of Whittaker Chambers to document the maneuvers of Soviet espionage agents, CPUSA members, and fellow travellers in New Deal executive agencies and departments.

ENTER HUAC

Like Alger Hiss, William Remington had impeccable credentials. Born on October 25, 1917, in New York City, Remington grew up in Ridgewood, New Jersey, where he served as a choir boy at Saint Elizabeth's Protestant Episcopal

150

Church. In 1939 Remington graduated with a Phi Beta Kappa key and a degree in public administration from Dartmouth and the following year received a master's degree in economics from Columbia. He became an assistant at the National Resources Planning Board and later worked at the Office of Price Administration and the War Production Board. In April 1944 he joined the Navy as an ensign in Naval Intelligence and later was assigned to the Office of War Mobilization and Reconversion, where he remained until March 1947. The next year the Commerce Department hired Remington to manage the section that cleared export licenses for companies trading with Soviet bloc nations. In response to Bentley's charges, the Commerce Department suspended him in August 1948, pending a full-field loyalty investigation by the FBI.[3]

The Loyalty Review Board decision of February 1949 to reinstate Remington in the Commerce Department perplexed HUAC investigators Donald Appell and Courtney Owens. When they began to sift through the Remington case once again, both were struck by Remington's tendency to minimize the nine months he had spent in Tennessee in the mid-1930s. Following leads furnished by Paul Crouch, an ex-Communist and current FBI informer, Appell called at the Bureau's Knoxville Field Office on October 10, 1949, to advise them that HUAC was reopening the case.[4]

When he was eighteen years old, Remington interrupted his studies at Dartmouth to work in Knoxville as a Tennessee Valley Authority (TVA) messenger from September 1936 to May 10, 1937, returning to Dartmouth the following fall. For at least part of the time he lived in Knoxville, Remington's address was Post Office Box 1692—the same address used by a local Communist party branch, according to Crouch, who had briefly served as a CPUSA organizer in Tennessee during the late 1930s. Later, HUAC subpoenaed the original application for this post office box and turned over a photostat to the FBI. More importantly, Appell identified several people who might have known Remington as a Communist in Knoxville, and another HUAC employee located yet another prospective witness through ex-FBI agent and *Counterattack* founder Ted Kirkpatrick.[5]

151

HUAC's efforts to reopen the Remington case prompted the FBI to carefully monitor the Committee's activities while they received tips from Father Cronin and various newspaper reporters. On February 6, 1950, Hoover also ordered FBI agents to reactivate Remington's espionage case file. Two months later, on April 5, the Bureau geared up for another full-scale (if less precise) loyalty investigation after a "newspaper source" advised Louis Nichols of HUAC's plans "to throw the Remington case out into the open in a couple of weeks." Eight days later, Hoover notified the chairman of the Loyalty Review Board, Seth W. Richardson, of the FBI's ongoing "supplemental" investigation.[6]

HUAC provided the impetus for this flurry of activity. Appell's trip to Knoxville and investigation of Post Office Box 1692 led him to a pair of ex-Communists: Kenneth McConnell, a poultry farmer from Weaverville, North Carolina, and Howard Bridgman, an economics professor at Tufts College. When contacted by Appell, both agreed to appear before HUAC and to swear that Remington was a CPUSA member during the nine months he worked for the TVA. When one of the Bureau's sources at the Committee, ex-FBI man Louis Russell, "confidentially advised" the FBI's Washington Field Office of HUAC's plans to hear McConnell and Bridgman in executive session, Hoover sent an "urgent" teletype ordering his agents to interview these prospective witnesses. These interviews took place on April 19 at the Wardman Park Hotel in Washington.

McConnell, however, "was extremely reluctant to furnish information" because he felt he had a "contractual obligation" to HUAC. The FBI agents conducting the interview finally persuaded him to talk by implying that their own investigation would complement HUAC's. The Committee later advised McConnell that he had made the right decision in being completely candid with the FBI. Both McConnell and Bridgman (who "had not been located by the Committee," according to FBI Assistant Director Ladd, at the time of his first Bureau interview) told the FBI the same story they later told HUAC. They readily identified Remington as a CPUSA member in Knoxville during the mid-1930s. But neither could supply evidence to support their assertions, and McConnell was described by sympathetic FBI agents as an "alcoholic" who "ordered two bourbon highballs" during the interview. Such "negative information," including the reference to McConnell's contractual obligation" to HUAC, was included only on the unserialized administrative page of the FBI report recording this interview.[7]

When McConnell testified before HUAC in executive session on April 20 (with Bridgman scheduled to appear in executive session nine days later), FBI Assistant Director Alan H. Belmont recommended telephone calls to four field offices to expedite the Bureau's investigation and to insure that FBI informer Crouch's role would be highlighted. Hoover scribbled his authorization on Belmont's memorandum: "Yes we must get this done immediately." Then, when the Committee subpoenaed Remington to appear at public hearings on May 4 and May 5 and Elizabeth Bentley for executive session testimony on May 6, the FBI Director penned yet another order: "Make certain we are keeping abreast and if possible ahead of all developments in Remington case and giving top priority to all investigative leads."[8]

At first glance, it appears that the Committee had caught the Bureau flatfooted and that the FBI was scrambling to avoid the embarrassment of being scooped by a lone pair of HUAC investigators. The FBI, however, had no trouble in keeping abreast and, if possible, ahead of the Committee. Six days before McConnell testified, Guy Hottel of the Washington Field Office advised Hoover of Louis Russell's agreement to keep the Bureau fully posted and to provide transcripts of all executive session testimony. In addition to the Bridgman, McConnell, and Bentley executive session testimony, the Committee was scheduled to hear Merwin Scott Todd on April 21, Solomon Adler on April 25, and William and Margaret Hinckley on June 8.[9] Though the full Committee did not decide until later to release the testimony of all these witnesses, the Bureau gained immediate access and put this confidential information to use in an effort to persuade the Loyalty Review Board to dismiss Remington.

The FBI, of course, was not in the habit of directly

disseminating secret congressional testimony. All executive session testimony received was duly noted on the fail-safe administrative page of the FBI's reports.[10] To circumvent this dissemination problem and to protect their informer at HUAC, as well, senior FBI officials recommended a circuitous strategy. Thus, when a HUAC source (probably Russell) alerted the Bureau to Committee Chairman John Wood's plans to send a letter on Remington to Loyalty Review Board Chairman Richardson, the FBI decided that it would be most beneficial for Richardson to see the one executive session transcript already in the Bureau's possession and additional transcripts later. Assistant Director Belmont suggested that an FBI representative contact Wood for permission to distribute all pertinent transcripts but to alert Russell first. Belmont also cautioned any agent who might approach the HUAC Chairman not to "disclose that we already have the one transcript [of McConnell's executive session testimony]."[11]

Whether Committee Chairman Wood was contacted and misled is not known, but on May 3, the day before Remington appeared before HUAC, FBI Director Hoover wrote Deputy Attorney General Peyton Ford in an effort to have the Justice Department formally request HUAC to forward its executive session transcripts to the Loyalty Review Board. The FBI Director also suggested that the Department contact Senator Homer Ferguson and request the release of the August 1948 testimony of Robbins Barstow, Jr. (Barstow knew Remington at Dartmouth and had appeared before Ferguson's Investigations Subcommittee.) Hoover, moreover, was less than candid with Ford. The Bureau, he said, had learned of Wood's letter to Richardson from "the public press" and, further, the FBI had no idea whether the Loyalty Review Board desired to consider "testimony which might have been given before the House Committee on Un-American Activities." Again, it is not known if the Department followed Hoover's advice. The issue quickly became moot, as HUAC apparently agreed to the Bureau strategy and released all of its executive session testimony. The Committee also made arrangements with Senator Ferguson to publish Barstow's testimony.[12]

Neither the Committee nor the Bureau was content merely to

pressure the Loyalty Review Board or to rely on Secretary of
Commerce Charles Sawyer's unilateral action when Remington once again became an embarrassment both to the Loyalty
Review Board and the Truman administration. The President's
aides were only able to come up with a rather puerile
suggestion for dealing with the problem. Stephen Spingarn
suggested that the President respond to a probable press conference question regarding HUAC's reopening of the Remington affair by emphasizing the Republican complexion of the
Loyalty Review Board that had recently cleared him. Not
surprisingly, then, Sawyer asked for Remington's resignation
privately on May 26 and publicly on May 27, chiefly on grounds
of inefficiency. Remington, Sawyer said, was wasting taxpayers' money because he was frequently absent from his job
when testifying before grand juries, congressional committees,
and loyalty boards. Remington resigned on June 9.[13]

THE PURSUIT OF JUSTICE

On May 3 Hoover wrote yet another letter to Peyton Ford to
advise him of Remington's scheduled appearance the next day
before HUAC and Bentley's forthcoming appearance on May
6. The FBI Director also alerted Ford to the Committee's plans
to issue a report later that month pointing out the possible basis
for a perjury prosecution against Remington. FBI officials had
learned of the Justice Department's interest in Remington from
Thomas Donegan, a government prosecutor and former FBI
agent, who soon presented evidence to the federal grand jury
that indicted Remington and later helped prosecute him for
perjury. Donegan had a vested interest in the case. He
represented Bentley as her attorney (obtaining over $7,000 for
her in one legal action) during the interim between his resignation from the FBI and his return to government service.[14]

Remington himself took a roundabout route to Donegan's
grand jury. The HUAC hearings created quite a stir, and
Remington was promptly summoned by a Washington, D.C.,
grand jury. After this grand jury refused to hand down an
indictment, a new grand jury was convened in New York, and

Remington was subpoenaed. Despite Donegan's efforts, this grand jury was also reluctant to indict—but only at first. Like Donegan, the grand jury foreman, John Brunini, had close ties to Elizabeth Bentley. Brunini and Bentley had a contract whereby Brunini would help Bentley prepare her memoirs for the Devin-Adair publishing company. Bentley began negotiating with Devin-Adair in the spring of 1950 and a contract was drawn up that identified Brunini by name and specified his financial interest, according to a former employee of the publishing company who was subpoenaed as a defense witness at Remington's subsequent perjury trial. This contract, however, was destroyed and a new one was drawn up a few days before Remington's indictment in June 1950. Though Donegan was aware of this questionable relationship, the FBI was apparently kept in the dark until Bentley contacted the New York Field Office in October to discuss this potential problem. The local Special Agent in Charge, who waited four days before alerting FBI headquarters, was admonished by senior FBI officials for not notifying the Bureau immediately. At that time, the FBI Director was primarily concerned over the possibility that the Bentley-Brunini connection might become "known to the general public."[15]

It was hardly surprising, then, that Brunini and Donegan, when interrogating Remington's ex-wife Ann and other witnesses, let nothing deter their search for evidence. Donegan stood silently by as Brunini falsely advised Ann Remington that she had no privilege to refuse to testify against her ex-husband. In a dissenting opinion following Remington's conviction, Judge Learned Hand quoted selectively from the grand jury minutes (which still have not been released) to describe the crude third-degree treatment that led Ann to change her testimony:

> Pages on pages of lecturing repeatedly preceded a question; statements of what the prosecution already knew, and of how idle it was for the witness to hold back what she could contribute; occasional reminders that she could be punished for perjury; all were scattered throughout. Still she withstood the examiners, until, being much tired and worn, she said: "I am getting fuzzy. I haven't eaten since a long time ago and I don't think I

am going to be very coherent from now on. I would like to post-
pone the hearings. . . . I want to consult my lawyers and see
how deep I am getting in." This was denied, and the questioning
kept on until she finally refused to answer, excusing herself
because she was "tired" and "would like to get something to
eat. . . . Is this the third degree, waiting until I get hungry,
now?" Still the examiners persisted, disregarding this further
protest: "I would like to get something to eat. But couldn't we
continue another day? Or do I have to come back?"

One final harangue, characterized by Judge Hand as the coup
de grâce, finally "broke" Mrs. Remington. Brunini pointedly
warned her

> that we have been very kind and considerate. We haven't raised
> our voices and we haven't shown our teeth, have we? Maybe
> you don't know about our teeth. A witness before a Grand Jury
> hasn't the privilege of refusing to answer a question. You see, we
> haven't told you that, so far. You have been asked a question.
> You must answer it. If a witness doesn't answer a question, the
> Grand Jury has rather unusual powers along that line. We are, to
> a certain extent, what you might call a judicial body. We
> can't act, ourselves. Our procedure is, when we get a witness
> who is contemptuous, who refuses to answer questions, to take
> them before a Judge. Now, at that point there will be a private
> proceeding. He will instruct the witness to answer the question.
> Then we come back here and put the question again. If the
> witness refuses to answer the question, we take him back to
> court and the judge will find him in contempt to [sic] Court and
> sentence him to jail until he has purged himself. . . . I don't
> want at this time to—I said "showing teeth." I don't want them
> to bite you.[16]

Following Ann Remington's testimony, she was interviewed
by agents of the FBI's Washington Field Office. (Seventeen
pages of the nineteen-page report summarizing this interview
were included on the administrative page.) The FBI then
drafted a statement for her to sign, but she refused to do so,
reportedly advising the Bureau on June 1 "that her signing
would contribute little to the Government's case and would be
of doubtful benefit to her." On the same day, Donegan called

FBI Assistant Director Ladd with a complaint of his own. The government, Donegan lamented, had not been able to develop a "strong case" against Remington because Mrs. Remington had steadfastly refused to sign a statement. Despite her continued insistence that she wanted to "avoid" testifying "before any Court, Committee or Loyalty Hearing Board" against her ex-husband and "would definitely not willingly testify concerning any other person," Remington was indicted on June 8 for one count of perjury—denying CPUSA membership to the grand jury.[17]

Though Ann Remington clearly did not want to testify, her collapse under duress before the grand jury effectively prevented her from claiming a husband-wife privilege during the subsequent trials. On the other hand, there was no love lost between William and Ann Remington. After years of marital problems, Ann hired private detectives to shadow her husband to gather evidence in support of her successful attempt to divorce him. Moreover, Ann's testimony was vitally important to the government's case. The allegations of HUAC witnesses McConnell and Bridgman might have reopened the case, but Mrs. Remington was the only one who could corroborate Elizabeth Bentley's characterization of Remington as an espionage agent.

But other corroborative problems remained. From his public exposure in 1948 to his indictment in 1950, Remington's testimony dovetailed with Bentley's on one key point— namely, that when they met in Washington in 1942 and 1943, they met alone. Remington thought, or so he said, that he was simply giving information to a *PM* researcher, while Bentley said that their dozen or so meetings were secret rendezvous where confidential information changed hands en route to the Soviets. Both agreed that no third party had been present. The government now presented, in the words of Fred J. Cook, Mrs. Remington as "the invisible woman" who "had been there all the time." Bentley adjusted her testimony accordingly.[18]

THE FIRST TRIAL

Such testimony was not out of character with the tone of Remington's first trial in New York Federal Court. Remington hired as counsel the liberal activist Joseph L. Rauh, Jr., and William C. Chanler of the Wall Street law firm in which Henry L. Stimson had once been a partner. The government prosecution team was headed by Irving S. Saypol, later described by *Time* magazine as "the nation's number one legal hunter of top Communists" for his role in the second Alger Hiss trial, the Foley Square Smith Act trial, and the Julius and Ethel Rosenberg atomic espionage trial. Assisting Saypol were Donegan, Roy Cohn, and dozens of FBI agents, not always working quietly behind the scenes. On the bench, Judge Gregory F. Noonan promptly established his own bias. When responding to Chanler's initial motion that the indictment be dismissed because the government was accusing his client of CPUSA membership while refusing to define "what constitutes that status," Judge Noonan implied that Remington knew what constituted party membership better than the court or the government. Noonan ruled that it was "not incumbent on the Government in a perjury trial to define terms relating to Communism." With such an array of Justice Department attorneys and an anticommunist judge who admonished Chanler that "the double-talk that goes on in Communism defies definition," Remington faced nearly insurmountable odds.[19] And the FBI and the Committee were poised to see that nothing was left to chance.

Among other techniques to insure a successful prosecution, the government kept a special grand jury in session during Remington's trial for the sole purpose, or so it seemed to Chanler, of subpoenaing potential witnesses for the defense. Chanler recalled one instance where he located several ex-Communists who promised to refute Mrs. Remington's contention that her husband had been a party member during his student days at Dartmouth. Chanler told them to remain in New Hampshire until he needed them. "Then," Chanler later surmised,

> I suppose, I made a mistake. I telephoned them from my office, using my regular phone, and told them to come to New York. The next morning when they arrived, two FBI agents were waiting on the station platform with subpoenas for them to appear before the grand jury. They were so frightened that they notified us they would claim their constitutional privilege and

refuse to testify. And so we had to let them go back to New Hampshire, unheard.[20]

Whether or not the FBI wiretapped Chanler's telephone, this was not an isolated instance of Bureau interference in the councils of the defense. The FBI placed an informal surveillance on the defense before and during the first trial, with the Boston SAC reporting to FBI headquarters in October 1950 on Remington's and attorney James Rosenman's visit to Dartmouth College. According to the FBI's "confidential source" at Dartmouth (who had earlier reported to the FBI on HUAC investigator Alvin Stote's research at the college library), Remington and Rosenman requested and received permission from the head librarian at Baker Memorial Library to review the school newspaper and other campus publications for the years Remington had been enrolled at Dartmouth. This confidential source responded to the Bureau's keen interest by promising to "furnish this office [Boston Field Office] with complete list of all articles requested by Remington or his attorney." The FBI's New York Field Office, in turn, alerted U.S. Attorney Donegan, who ordered his staff to review the relevant back copies of the Dartmouth newspaper and yearbook so that the government would not be caught off guard.[21]

Two months later, according to the New York SAC, the Justice Department ordered FBI investigations of prospective defense witnesses. The New York Field Office responded on December 26, in an "urgent" teletype to the Boston Field Office, by specifically requesting the SAC to expedite the probe of Dartmouth President Emeritus Ernest M. Hopkins— an investigation that "should be conducted as discreetly as possible and confined, at present time, to confidential informants and sources and known reliable contacts." The New York SAC then directed the Boston office to submit its findings by cover letter and "blind memo." Two TVA officials, general manager George Gant and chairman Gordon R. Clapp, were also selected, with the New York Field Office requesting the Washington office to forward "all personal derogatory information concerning" Clapp. The Washington SAC responded, in part, by ordering a search of HUAC files. These FBI investigations, however, had barely enough time to begin. On December 27 the New York SAC told the Washington and Boston offices to disregard prior instructions. Hereafter, investigations of defense witnesses were to be limited exclusively to an indices check of FBI files.[22]

Other potential defense witnesses, including Henry C. Hart of Madison, Wisconsin, were co-opted by the ubiquitous FBI. The Milwaukee Field Office's contact with Hart, who had roomed with Remington in Knoxville nearly fifteen years earlier, was not recorded in a formal FBI report but in a "separate letter because it deals with the relationship and recent exchange of communications between HENRY C. HART and JOSEPH L. RAUH, JR., attorney for REMINGTON." On May 4, 1950, the day Remington testified before HUAC, Rauh wired Hart to inquire if he had ever known Remington to have been a Communist or if he knew HUAC witnesses McConnell and Bridgman. Hart answered by night letter the same day, but early the next morning contacted Western Union to cancel it. Relying on rough draft notes, he advised the Milwaukee Field Office of his original reply:

> I roomed with William Remington at 920 Temple St. in Knoxville from October 1936 to May 1937. I worked as a messenger with him in TVA and spent much additional time with him. I got no indication whatever that he was a member of the Communist Party. As his roommate I would have had every opportunity to know it if he was.

Hart's night letter also claimed that he had never heard of McConnell and though he knew Bridgman "and shared a house with him during the summer of 1937 . . . [he] did not indicate to me in any way that Remington was a member of the Communist Party." Instead of sending the night letter, Hart called Rauh the next morning to tell him he did not know whether Remington had been a CPUSA member. He also made Rauh's telegram available to the FBI.

According to the Milwaukee Field Office agent who interviewed him, Hart later reversed his statement completely and became convinced—largely because of the recently released

161

executive session testimony of HUAC witness Bridgman—that Remington had been a party member while living in Knoxville. Accordingly, on September 20, 1950, Hart again wrote Rauh (this letter was also copied by the Bureau) that he now believed his client guilty, though "I know no facts which prove that Remington was a party member." The Milwaukee SAC's "informal" report to Bureau headquarters concluded by noting Hart's reluctance to appear as a witness "in view of his previously friendly relationship with REMINGTON and because it will revive again the publicity attendant upon every public revelation of HART'S former membership in the Communist Party." Instead, Hart intended "to protect his position as a potential government witness" and, if contacted by Rauh, would not mention anything that "might possibly form part of the government's case." Leaving nothing to chance, Donegan issued a subpoena for Hart to appear before the federal grand jury in New York. He specifically requested the Bureau to advise Hart "that he is to be served with this subpoena so that he will not be embarrassed or antagonized by this service."[23]

Burton J. Zien, another potential defense witness, would have risked even more if he had chosen to assist the Remington defense. Given the FBI's advantage in resources and personnel, it was hardly surprising that the Bureau reached Zien before Rauh did. And when Rauh finally contacted Zien in Milwaukee, he suspected the FBI had intimidated his prospective witness. In a memorandum to private investigator Frank Bielaski, Rauh claimed FBI agents had questioned Zien "for 8 solid days" and threatened him with a perjury indictment "at a moment's notice." Zien, who resigned his position as a field examiner with the National Labor Relations Board in Knoxville on May 24, 1950, was vulnerable because he had previously denied CPUSA membership under oath. The Justice Department then advised the FBI, in effect, that it would not even consider proceeding against Zien until he had testified in the Remington trial and various "other cases arising out of the Loyalty Program." Thus, Zien immediately reported to the FBI after he talked to Rauh. According to the Bureau, he "furnished absoutely no information to RAUH nor did he advise RAUH as to what information he had furnished to the Government." The Milwaukee Field

Office then sent its detailed account of Rauh's dismal interview to FBI headquarters "for the information of the Bureau and for the information of the prosecution in New York City."

Though Rauh did not have access to the relevant FBI and Justice Department documents, the implication was clear. He attempted once again to interview Zien through private detective Bielaski, who directed two ex-FBI agents on his staff to interview Zien on Remington's behalf. The former FBI agents, however, flatly refused to conduct "an investigation which is on its face in direct opposition to the work of the Federal Bureau of Investigation." Instead, they turned a copy of Rauh's November 10 memorandum to Bielaski over to the Bureau—prompting Hoover to send them a thank-you letter and to forward Rauh's memorandum to the prosecution.[24]

The FBI was able to surmise the defense strategy regarding yet another prospective witness through the efforts of David Lawrence, publisher of *U.S. News and World Report*. One of Lawrence's employees, Bernard Redmont, was of vital importance both to the Remington defense and, it would seem, to the prosecution. But the FBI and government prosecutors were not much interested in Redmont until they learned, through Lawrence, of Remington's plans to subpoena him. The prosecution's reluctance to place Redmont, a former government employee whose real name was Bernard Rosenberg, on the witness stand was clear. Elizabeth Bentley claimed that Remington had volunteered Redmont's name during the spring of 1943 (she later changed the date to the summer of 1942) as a source who might be able to furnish information for the Soviet Union. Thereafter, Bentley added, Redmont supplied "considerable information," which was transmitted to the Russians. Similarly, Ann Remington told the FBI that Redmont and his wife were the only people, except herself and former *New Masses* editor Joe North, who had knowledge of her husband's relationship with Bentley. Remington himself identified his friend Redmont as a probable Communist during an interview with the FBI and, later, in executive session testimony on July 30, 1948, before Senator Ferguson's Subcommittee on Investigations. (When HUAC publicly released this executive session testimony in June 1950, Redmont's name was deleted.) During

163

the first perjury trial, however, Remington claimed the FBI had "bamboozled" him into identifying Redmont as a Communist.[25]

Remington and Redmont drifted apart in 1946 when Redmont first went to South America and, later, to Paris as a regional editor for *U.S. News and World Report*. Confident that Redmont would corroborate their client's story and not Bentley's, Remington's attorneys contacted Redmont's employer to advise him of their interest. David Lawrence responded on October 21 by warning Louis Nichols. A week later, Lawrence contacted Nichols again to advise "the Bureau in confidence that defense counsel has requested him to 'alert' Redmont to the fact that he might be needed as a witness." Lawrence lamented that he could not object to one of his employees being subpoenaed, but had no intention of cooperating with the Remington defense even to the extent of informing Redmont that he would be subpoenaed. Instead, FBI officials directed the New York Field Office to brief the prosecution and to make the Bureau's entire file on Redmont available to Donegan and Saypol "in order that they will be fully prepared to explore Redmont's alleged Espionage and Communist Party activities during cross-examination."

Lawrence continued to keep Nichols posted on the Remington defense strategy regarding Redmont, who eventually testified (and denied CPUSA membership) in January 1951. And the FBI continued to forward information received from Lawrence to the prosecution—including the contents of Remington's recent correspondence with Redmont, who had wanted to keep his employer posted on developments. (Lawrence apparently relayed everything Redmont told him to Nichols on a "strictly confidential basis.") According to the FBI Assistant Director, Lawrence "reiterated that his identity should never be revealed as a source of the information." He also relayed advice to the prosecution through Nichols and advised the FBI Assistant Director of his personal belief "that both Remington and Redmont were hoping to evade proof of Communist Party membership by the fact that they probably were not members of any official cell and did not have cards."

Lawrence, indeed, fired Redmont prior to his appearance as a defense witness. When radio commentator Walter Winchell suggested that the dismissal resulted from his scheduled appearance as a defense witness in the Remington case, Lawrence again briefed Nichols, claiming the termination resulted from Redmont's failure to gain accreditation from military authorities. The *U.S. News and World Report* publisher then told Nichols to alert United States Attorney Saypol to the possibility "that the defense might seize upon this incident and by distortion of the facts charge intimidation of witnesses." On January 22, Hoover relayed Lawrence's suggestion in an "urgent" teletype to the New York SAC.[26]

THE SECOND TRIAL

The results of the FBI's massive effort were hardly surprising. On February 7, 1951, after deliberating a mere four hours and twenty-five minutes at the end of a six-week trial, the jury convicted Remington of perjury. Six months later, a unanimous Circuit Court of Appeals reversed the decision, citing principally Judge Noonan's failure to specify to the jury what constituted CPUSA membership and the government's refusal to provide Ann Remington's grand jury testimony to the defense. Although the Court of Appeals did not quash the indictment, the government chose not to cover the same ground again. Instead, a new grand jury was convened and a five-count perjury indictment was obtained on October 25, 1951, based on Remington's trial testimony in his own defense. Then, the government coolly moved to dismiss the original Brunini-Donegan indictment.

The FBI, for its part, continued to monitor the Remington case. A month after Remington's initial conviction in February 1951, the Bureau's New York Field Office finally learned that Remington had financed his defense through the Robert Marshall Civil Liberties Foundation. Then, on October 27, two days after Remington was indicted for a second time, Hoover brought to Assistant Attorney General James McInerney's attention a speech made ten days earlier by HUAC member Harold Velde. The Committee, Velde said, had been examining Marshall Foundation disbursements and "discovered" two payments of $10,000 each to Joseph L. Rauh, Jr., who had signed these checks over to Chanler's Wall Street law firm of Winthrop, Stimson, Putnam and Roberts. On January 22, 1953, five days before the second Remington trial concluded, Hoover informed the Justice Department of yet another $10,000 payment to Rauh. He quoted from a Dies Committee report of March 19, 1944, to describe the Robert Marshall Foundation as "one of the principal sources for the money with which to finance the Communist Party's front."[27]

Remington's second trial was short (January 13–27, 1953) and, in some ways, perfunctory. Found guilty on two counts of perjury, he began serving a three-year prison sentence on April 15 at the federal prison in Lewisburg, Pennsylvania. In November, the Circuit Court of Appeals affirmed his conviction by a two to one majority, with Learned Hand dissenting. A year later, on the morning of November 22, 1954, Remington was beaten by two or three fellow inmates wielding a brick wrapped in cloth. The FBI and prison officials said Remington's assailants had been looting his cell and that he had tried to stop them. Later that same day, at the age of thirty-seven, Remington, his skull fractured in several places, died on an operating table in a prison hospital. Four months later, the Washington Field Office SAC briefed senior FBI officials on efforts to investigate one aspect of this tragedy. An agent had just returned from the Bureau of Prisons at the Department of Justice, the SAC said, and had copied the names of individuals who had written to chastise prison officials for not adequately protecting Remington. The names of these letter writers were then disseminated to various FBI field offices "for any use deemed appropriate."[28]

Whether or not his wartime association with Elizabeth Bentley was part of the world of secret agents and confidential government documents, Remington had clearly converted to the anticommunist persuasion by the time of the Truman loyalty program. A moderate in economic policy whose anti-Soviet sentiments sometimes had to be toned down by senior Commerce Department officials, Remington volunteered in June 1947 to serve as a quasi-informer for the FBI in the

American Veterans Committee.[29] Even if Remington was simply trying to ingratiate himself with the Bureau, he was no longer a security threat—if, indeed, he had ever been one.[30] The Remington case, even more than the Alger Hiss affair, was a Cold War horror story, with the FBI, HUAC, Catholic activist John Cronin, and anticommunist journalist David Lawrence all scrambling to vindicate Elizabeth Bentley's murky tales of espionage. The lesson to be learned from Remington's sad fate—a lesson not lost on the potential defense witnesses Chanler and Rauh approached—was one of vulnerability and power. William Walter Remington and a whole generation of liberals who had tolerated radicals or who had espoused a Marxian materialism during the more tolerant 1930s were surely vulnerable, for those who sat in judgment during the Cold War were truly committed to the anticommunist politics nurtured by HUAC and Hoover's FBI.

CHAPTER VII

The FBI, HUAC,
and Cold War Liberalism

When the FBI executives' conference approved an informal yet sweeping program in February 1946 to develop an informed public opinion about "the basically Russian nature of the Communist Party in this country," Bureau officials had an immediate purpose. In the event of a "national emergency," they intended to counteract the anticipated "flood of propaganda from Leftist and so-called Liberal sources" that might accompany the mass arrest of dissidents on the Bureau's top secret Security Index. This would be difficult but nonetheless was imperative, it seemed to D. Milton Ladd, because liberals generally tolerated Communists, defended their constitutional rights, and were more interested in bread and butter issues than ideology. "To a large extent," Ladd concluded when proposing this Bureau program in February 1946, "the power and influence of the Communist Party in this country, which is out of all proportion to the actual size of the Party, derives from the support which the Party receives from 'Liberal' sources and from its connections in the labor unions. The Party earns its support by championing individual causes which are also sponsored by the Liberal elements."

Thus began the FBI's tireless campaign to eliminate CPUSA influence in labor unions and to undermine liberal support for and tolerance of domestic radicals, Communists and others. In the broadest sense, the FBI's efforts were intended to develop an anticommunist consensus. On the one hand, this consensus could be realized by "neutralizing" those who challenged it (the National Lawyers Guild or William Walter Remington, for

168

example) and by buttressing already reliable right-wing anti-communist interests, such as HUAC, conservative journalists, and other public opinion leaders. On the other hand, by compiling and disseminating educational materials through available channels, FBI officials hoped to persuade liberals "that, in truth, Communism is the most reactionary, intolerant and bigoted force in existence."[1]

The FBI cannot be blamed for the Cold War or even the attendant evisceration of traditional liberal values. The Bureau campaign was given a boost by Soviet adventurism abroad and by the Truman administration's consistant attempt to portray that adventurism as a sinister plot to gain world domination. And the "God that failed" genre of Arthur Koestler and others certainly had a greater impact on liberals than the cruder literary efforts of Hoover, Nichols, and the FBI Crime Records Division. Cold War liberals, nevertheless, conceded the terms of the anticommunist debate on the home front. This debate, of course, was not over the need to investigate law-abiding dissidents (Soviet apologists and those who defended CPUSA members' constitutional rights) but rather over who should investigate—the executive (the FBI) or the Congress (HUAC and other McCarthyites who were covertly assisted by the FBI). Because Cold War liberals accepted the restrictive terms of the debate, they made an almost blind commitment to the FBI and its public posturing as a disinterested, fact-gathering, apolitical investigative agency. This commitment helps explain how the FBI was able to underwrite the charges raised by HUAC members and how its investigators were able to operate in a political vacuum for nearly three decades.

It was not an inevitable or necessary outgrowth of the Cold War that mistrust of the Soviets abroad would be projected onto native Communists and other dissidents at home or that traditional liberal tolerance of radicalism would dissipate. It was in this area that the Bureau did influence national politics and public opinion. FBI officials can be held responsible not for causing the Cold War, but for nurturing that piece of Cold War baggage known inappropriately as McCarthyism.

If, as many argued at the time, the Cold War could have been waged more effectively without McCarthyism, it was not. And many liberals and labor leaders, while condemning the McCarthyite style, particularly as practiced by HUAC, nonetheless embraced a politics of anticommunism. By the late 1940s their faith in the efficacy of "responsible" red-baiting confirmed the erosion of liberal tolerance. Fratricidal red-baiting of fellow travellers qualified Cold War liberals' self-righteous and increasingly timid criticisms of HUAC and others, thereby strengthening the intolerant climate that so pleased the Committee. Even when Cold War liberals appeared to respond effectively to HUAC and, later, to Senator McCarthy, their response actually strengthened the FBI's unilateral role of final arbitrator for material selectively leaked from its classified domestic intelligence files. Mainstream liberals defended expansive executive privilege claims to prevent an irresponsible Congress, led by McCarthy and HUAC, from indiscriminately browsing through FBI loyalty files. Only the highly professional, non-political FBI could be trusted as custodian of such sensitive information. Many Cold War liberals, in short, championed the FBI as a responsible alternative to the implacable HUAC and the incorrigible junior Senator from Wisconsin, thereby unwittingly permitting the Bureau to pursue its own brand of McCarthyism.

CHANGING VALUES

In February 1946, FBI officials assumed no less a task than to shape the liberal response to the domestic Communist issue. They must have been pleased with the shift in liberal values that had occurred by 1950. Many liberals had abandoned what Arthur M. Schlesinger, Jr., called the "tendermindedness" of the Popular Front era in favor of a new "tough-minded" liberalism, free from any delusions about the intent (or rights) of American Communists. Emotionally identifying with what they deemed the responsible anticommunism of the Truman administration and dismissing critics of the pax Americana as Stalinist stooges, the new Cold War liberals rejected traditional tenets (a belief in progress, popular democracy, and man's inherent goodness and perfectibility) in favor of a new creed that stressed man's corruptibility, the inevitability of conflict among nations, and the dangers of democratic rule.[2]

This altered world view had not characterized liberal politics in the years immediately after World War II when the FBI had just begun its educational campaign. As late as 1948, many liberals defended the civil liberties of native Communists and dismissed anticommunist charges as masking a reactionary politics intended to discredit the New Deal and the Fair Deal. By 1950, however, their position had so shifted on at least one key point—the necessity of insuring absolute security—as to be virtually indistinguishable from Cold War conservatives. Intellectual political activists in the American Civil Liberties Union, the American Committee for Cultural Freedom (ACCF), and other groups argued among themselves over just how anticommunist one should be and just how dangerous and naive were those few civil libertarians who claimed American Communists were entitled to constitutional protections.[3] Though some liberals refused to abandon the Left for the "vital center," their stance was distinctly unrepresentative of postwar liberalism. In this new climate, mainstream liberalism abandoned a tolerant set of beliefs for an ideology that denied traditional First Amendment rights to Communists and, to a lesser extent, fellow travellers.

Cold War liberals no longer defended the Popular Front era's antifascist concerns or attendant tolerance of American Communists as they had during the heyday of the Dies Committee. Instead, the majority chose an alternative, indeed contrary, response. Red-baiting of maverick liberals, in short, was not peculiar to conservative politicians and intellectuals; the logic of conservative red-baiting did not differ substantially from the tenets that Cold War liberals applied to condemn fellow travellers. For liberals did not object to red-baiting, only to indiscriminate and irresponsible red-baiting—and mostly to confusing liberals with Communists.[4]

The vulnerability of liberals who refused to surrender to the new anticommunist politics was enhanced by the elastic definition of Stalinism offered by some Cold War liberals. "There are," Diana Trilling calculated, out and out Stalinists, party members. There are out and out non-party members. There are Stalinoids and pseudo-Stalinists and proto-Stalinists and crypto-Stalinists. There are conscious fellow-travellers and unconscious fellow-travellers. There are Communist liberals, both conscious and unconscious. There are even ex-Communist Communist liberals.

By 1947 Robert M. LaFollette, Jr., whose Senate Civil Liberties Committee had been praised in the 1930s by liberals as an effective counterpoint to the Dies Committee, called—in language Martin Dies and J. Edgar Hoover could understand—for "the spotlight of publicity . . . to shine" on Communists and fellow travellers. To counter conservative attacks on the New Deal and the Fair Deal, Richard Rovere facetiously suggested that liberals red-bait Republicans. After all, Rovere noted, Vito Marcantonio first went to Congress as a Republican. Rovere further characterized I.F. Stone's "wholly dishonest" study of the Korean War as a piece of Soviet propaganda. "It is scarcely news," Rovere said, "that semi-demi-hemi-Stalinists like Izzy [Stone] make asses of themselves, tell lies." And Arthur M. Schlesinger, Jr., championed "factual exposure," providing hints for identifying "Communists and fellow travellers who pose as ordinary liberals."[5]

RESPONSIBLE RED-BAITING

Some of the nation's most prestigious liberal organizations emulated HUAC's tactics in even greater detail. To neutralize conservative critics who accused the National Association for the Advancement of Colored People of abetting communism, regional and local NAACP officials organized a not-very-efficient intelligence network and began to compile dossiers on individual CPUSA activists. Beginning in 1947, these dossiers were used to screen NAACP applicants and others. On one occasion in late 1949, William L. Patterson, a Civil Rights Congress (CRC) official and well-known CPUSA functionary, wrote acting NAACP secretary Roy Wilkins to request that the CRC be allowed to participate in a NAACP-sponsored National Civil Rights Mobilization. When denying Patterson's request, Wilkins red-baited him and other CRC officials in a

letter reprinted by the fiercely anticommunist *New Leader.*
Wilkins then sent a copy of his letter to Clark Clifford as part of
the NAACP effort to persuade President Truman to address
the Mobilization. The FBI, which had some 150 informers and
confidential sources operating in and around the NAACP, also
briefed the White House on alleged CPUSA plans to infiltrate
the NAACP-sponsored event.

This experience partially inspired the NAACP to compile
and disseminate a list of Communist fronts to local NAACP
units. The effort escalated in 1950 when the NAACP's national
convention approved a resolution granting the national office
authority to expel any local affiliate that, "in the judgment of
the Board of Directors," was Communist-controlled. Though
never used, this resolution has been described by the NAACP's
historian as "a public gesture to protect the organization's good
name, a warning to the Stalinists to keep hands off, and an
educational device for its own members.[6]

If the NAACP was reluctant to purge its local affiliates, other
liberal organizations were not. The once tolerant CIO brought
charges against all its left-wing member unions and in November 1950, following executive board trials patterned after
loyalty hearings and HUAC investigations, expelled them all.
The CIO was in part responding to government pressure. From
the days of the Dies Committee's Appendix IX until the early
1950s, HUAC had been, for all practical purposes, at war with
the CIO. Between 1948 and 1952, the House Committee on
Education and Labor, the Senate Committee on Labor and
Public Welfare, and two subcommittees of the Senate Judiciary Committee also investigated left-wing CIO unions.

The CIO, however, was not simply caving in to these
pressures; some CIO leaders were sympathetic to the anticommunist world view. One such official was United Automobile Workers (UAW) president Walter Reuther, who became a
CIO vice-president in 1952.[7] Reuther exploited the Communist
issue to strengthen his own position in the UAW and regularly
capitalized on situations created by HUAC. One opportunity
arose in March 1947 when Michigan's Republican Governor,
Kim Sigler, fortified with state police red-squad files, testified
before the Un-American Activities Committee.[8] He named
Reuther's UAW opposition—including R. J. Thomas, George

Addes, and Richard Leonard—"Communist captives." (The
FBI had also labeled Addes a subversive in a leak to *New York
Herald Tribune* reporter Frederick Woltman.) Reuther's major
victory over the "Stalinist" faction came on the heels of
Woltman's FBI leak and Sigler's HUAC testimony. Addes, a
devout Catholic with a history of denouncing the CPUSA at
public meetings and firing union organizers who had been
labeled Communist, was defeated in his bid for reelection as
UAW secretary-treasurer.[9]

Even after Reuther secured control of the UAW national
office, he still faced the problem of Local 600, an anti-Reuther
local that represented auto workers at the Ford Motor Company's River Rouge complex. In 1950 a UAW "trial committee"
had failed to convict five Local 600 members on charges of
subservience to the CPUSA line. Two years later a new
opportunity arose when HUAC scheduled hearings in Detroit.
Reuther supporters circulated rumors that their opponents
would receive subpoenas and reportedly supplied the Committee with several "friendly" witnesses. Before the hearings
began, the FBI obliged Reuther (though he was not one of the
Bureau's favorites)[10] by interviewing left-wing union members
and supplying HUAC with recently surfaced informers. HUAC
investigators also contacted the 1950 UAW trial committee.

Following the HUAC hearings in March 1952, the UAW
International Executive Board (IEB) held its own hearings. The
IEB concluded, as had HUAC, that Local 600's "policies,
programs, and publications" were being subverted by a
"disciplined communist minority" for "their own ends and
against the best interests of Union membership." When the IEB
imposed an administratorship on the local, the last substantive
vestiges of "Stalinism" were removed from the UAW.[11]

Reuther and the CIO had become active participants in an
anticommunist politics, marking a departure from the CIO's
role during the 1930s and the early and mid-1940s. At that time,
AFL officials John Frey, William Green, Matthew Woll, and
George Meany sought to smear the rival CIO as Communist
dominated by testifying before the Dies Committee or confidentially furnishing derogatory information on CIO organizers
to HUAC.[12] During the Cold War years the CIO embraced the

anticommunist politics of its rival. Whether the CIO did so to further specific policy objectives or because it simply succumbed to Cold War pressures (an unlikely contention because CIO officials launched their purge in November 1946), the role of the FBI in the evisceration of the American labor movement cannot be ignored. The extent and impact of FBI efforts to influence trade union policy through leaks to congressional committees like HUAC and newspaper reporters like Woltman, however, cannot be determined without access to all of the FBI's files on Communists in labor unions.

TRUMAN, THE ADA, AND THE ANTICOMMUNIST STYLE

Liberal intellectuals, the NAACP, and the CIO were not the only new converts to the anticommunist political style. During the Cold War years, Democratic party politicians and liberal pressure groups also employed the very tactics they had unequivocally condemned when used by Martin Dies. By the late 1940s, they were more discriminating. W. Averell Harriman red-baited Ohio's Republican stalwart, Robert Taft, who was also attacked on the state level by the Ohio Democratic party. In 1950 the North Carolina Democratic primary was enlivened by Willis Smith's charge that his opponent, Frank P. Graham, had belonged to eighteen groups cited by HUAC as Communist fronts. Graham lost the primary. Helen Gahagan Douglas had better luck in the California Democratic primary, where her opponent accused her of consistently voting with Vito Marcantonio.[13]

The red-baiting resorted to by liberal political activists, if more tactful than HUAC's more indiscriminate brand, was often orchestrated by the White House. President Truman exploited anticommunism as purposefully as Committee members or FBI officials, labeling, for instance, Republican opponents of his foreign policy "Kremlin assets" who might just as well be shooting "our soldiers in the backs in a hot war."[14] Truman's use of the Communist issue, moreover, was not limited to foreign policy issues. And if Truman was concerned in 1948 with Progressive party candidate Henry Wallace's

175

attempt to forge a cohesive political force out of liberal and radical opposition to the Truman Doctrine, he was also concerned with his own reelection prospects.

In a memorandum of November 1947 "based solely on an appraisal of the politically advantageous course to follow," Clark Clifford, the President's principal campaign adviser, proposed a dual strategy to insure liberal support for Truman in the coming election. First, Clifford noted the administration's vulnerability to leftist charges that too many of its members had Wall Street connections. To counter this, he suggested the President should thereafter appoint noted liberals to administration posts. Second, if Wallace chose to run on a third party ticket, he should be redbaited and isolated by persuading "prominent liberals and progressives—*and no one else*—to move publicly into the fray. They must point out that the core of the Wallace backing is made up of Communists and the fellow-travellers."[15]

Wasting little time and fortified by a steady stream of FBI reports forwarded to the White House, Truman criticized "Wallace and his Communists" in a Saint Patrick's Day address in New York City. Though the President's blunt remarks surprised some lower-level White House staff members, Truman aide Matthew Connelly had worked on the red-baiting portions of the speech for "some time" and consulted with Democratic party leaders "in many states." Truman even tipped off the press to expect a bombshell. Later, he joked about this leak because it had come from the highest levels of government.[16]

The nation's most prominent coalition of liberals, Americans for Democratic Action (ADA), clearly took Clifford's stratagems to heart. While ADA had only recently abandoned its "dump Truman" effort and its curious draft of the conservative Dwight D. Eisenhower, the language favored by ADA was indistinguishable from Truman Doctrine globalism: "Because the interests of the United States are the interests of free men everywhere, America must furnish political and economic support to democratic and freedom-loving peoples the world over." The day after Truman's Saint Patrick's Day address, the ADA executive committee directed "the National Office

. . . [to] get out a pamphlet on Henry Wallace, send periodic fact sheets to the Chapters, and prepare a plan of action for an offensive against Wallace."[17]

Even HUAC admired the ADA offensive, a model of fratricidal red-baiting that effectively tarred as Soviet-inspired all left-wing opposition to Harry Truman's pax Americana abroad and national security state at home. Because CPUSA members played such a prominent role in the Progressive party, Wallace was especially vulnerable to this strategy. Among other operations, ADA collected and prepared literature linking Wallace's Progressive party with Stalin's Communist party. This literature was then mailed to local ADA affiliates, newspapers and periodicals, AFL and CIO leaders, Democratic party officials, and nearly every Democratic candidate facing a Progressive party challenger. The ADA even distributed clippings from Isaac Don Levine's *Plain Talk*, a far-right magazine more suited to the temperament of the FBI Crime Records Division. ADA officials were especially proud of their pamphlet, *Henry Wallace, the First Three Months*, which the executive committee called the "best thing ADA has done so far." Francis Biddle affirmed this assessment in 1950 when, as ADA national board chairman, testifying before the House Select Committee on Lobbying, he said: "I think the best job on the Wallace movement was done by ADA. . . . They did a pamphlet . . . that show[ed] the Commie tie-up right down the line."[18]

ADA liberals further imitated HUAC's tactics by exposing the "Communist associations" of Progressive party financial supporters. ADA paid for advertisements in major urban newspapers listing the names of Progressive party contributors and the organizations on the Attorney General's list with which they were or had been associated. Inspired by this maneuver, HUAC member Karl Mundt selected twelve large contributors from the ADA list and ordered Committee staff to compile individual dossiers. In an uneasy if self-serving alliance of sorts, Mundt and HUAC "corroborated" the ADA charges by announcing that certain Wallace backers had "records of Communist support and sympathy if not outright membership in the party."[19]

Progressive party activists rightly concluded that the greatest damage to their cause was done not by Mundt and HUAC, but by ADA.[20] Such blatant anticommunism, however, was of recent vintage, even though FBI officials and others had long been circulating rumors about Wallace's alleged Communist sympathies.[21] ADA's forerunner, the Union for Democratic Action (UDA), had also been anticommunist but (usually) in a more responsible way. UDA evoked Dies Committee ire in the early 1940s for, among other things, aiding and abetting a "creeping totalitarianism" (that is, supporting the expansion of executive power). As late as 1945, the UDA and the *New Republic* co-sponsored a testimonial dinner for Wallace. Summing up the eulogies offered at this dinner, the UDA monthly newsletter described Wallace as "the chief spokesman of the New Deal, the liberal conscience of the Administration, the living symbol of its enduring values." Two years later, ADA publicly condemned the Truman loyalty program as repressive and unfair and opposed the enactment of internal security legislation as unnecessary and unconstitutional.[22]

By early 1948 things had changed. The few lingering doubts of ADA activists regarding the wisdom of containment were swept aside by the Czech coup of February 1948. Thereafter, ADA began a sustained campaign to strengthen its anticommunist credentials in order to facilitate its own policy objectives and to insure its own invulnerability to HUAC-inspired charges of being soft on communism. Nor were ADA efforts limited to Henry Wallace and the Progressive party. In July 1950 ADA helped arrange for a coalition candidate to oppose Vito Marcantonio's bid for reelection to the House. An ADA press release dismissed Marcantonio, the only member of the House who never wavered in his opposition to the Dies Committee and HUAC, as "another Communist hero . . . the party-line member of Congress from New York City." And if ADA had deemed Truman's original loyalty program repressive, it did not publicly criticize the April 1951 order amending the federal standard of dismissal from "reasonable grounds" to "reasonable doubt as to the loyalty of the individual involved." Instead, ADA officials sought a private meeting with the President to express their concern over the inevitable injustices resulting from adoption of such sweeping standards.[23]

In 1950 ADA advocated HUAC's abolition, calling the Committee "a threat to freedom of political opinion." But not until 1959 did an ADA platform again call for the Committee's demise, and then only in a toned-down resolution. Similarly, in the wake of the Supreme Court decision upholding the Foley Square Smith Act convictions of Eugene Dennis and other top CPUSA leaders, the ADA national board refused to issue a statement drafted by Joseph L. Rauh, Jr., and James Wechsler condemning the decision. Because "the Dennis case was tried with great fairness and patience," Francis Biddle advised national board members, the proposed statement "would do the A.D.A. infinite harm." Biddle found the Rauh-Wechsler position insufficiently anticommunist, "calculated chiefly to afford us the luxury of expressing a theoretic 'liberalism' which has little relation to the facts."[24]

SOME LIBERALS AND HUAC'S METHODS

In substance although not in degree, the rhetoric and tactics of ADA activists and other Cold War liberals did not differ from those of Martin Dies, J. Parnell Thomas, and Joseph McCarthy. For Carey McWilliams and other non-Communist unreconstructed radicals, liberal ADA activists like Arthur M. Schlesinger, Jr., simply spoke "the language of McCarthy with a Harvard accent." Nor could these liberal anticommunists "much longer escape the noose they have been trying to tighten around the necks of others." And they did not escape; the FBI classified Schlesinger and others bona fide enemies. HUAC, McCarthy, and other conservative anticommunists were unwilling, as Diana Trilling lamented, "to make the difficult necessary discriminations between protecting democracy and weakening it." Trilling objected not to HUAC and McCarthy per se, but to the fact that "the wrong people" were running the congressional investigating committees. Similarly, Sidney Hook praised the "educational" accomplishments of these committees while chastising liberal congressmen for not assuming "a more prominent part in" the "deliberations" of HUAC and its imitators.[25]

Inevitably, then, Cold War liberals' criticisms of HUAC and

McCarthy were confined to their "methods." Schlesinger condemned the Dies Committee and HUAC for their "reckless accusations and appalling procedures," "promiscuous and unprincipled attack on radicalism," their failure "to distinguish anti-Communist liberals from fellow-travellers." HUAC's film industry probe of 1947 led Schlesinger to bemoan Hollywood's "particularly favorable climate for the spread of communism" and the one-time presence of "fellow-travelling, ex-proletarian . . . film hacks" who "refused to own up to their political beliefs before a committee of Congress." And the UAW, fresh from its HUAC- and FBI-assisted house cleaning, criticized the Committee's return to Detroit in 1954 "to smear genuinely non-Communist liberal and independent organizations . . . and individuals." Before offering this qualified criticism, the UAW press release highlighted the union's own anticommunist activities, conceded the existence of "an organized Communist conspiracy" that "should and must be exposed and stamped out," and endorsed the Committee's "professed purposes."[26]

Other liberals were even more tolerant of the Committee's methods. The Dies Committee, Morris Ernst announced, functioned as "a kind of national Huey Long," eagerly supported by that "unwitting aid," the press. Yet Ernst also urged the government to "smoke out all underground cowardly movements. Make them stand up and be counted. Then we can defend them under our Bill of Rights." Privately, Ernst urged presidential adviser Harry Hopkins and FBI Director Hoover to use the Bureau of Internal Revenue to harass "propaganda organizations." Over twenty years later, Richard Rovere, in his foreword to Walter Goodman's study of HUAC, still championed a politics of exposure. "With few exceptions," Rovere noted, "the investigators and the investigated have seemed richly to deserve each other—though, of course, poetic justice is never to be equated with that of the blindfolded goddess with the true scales." Rovere then commended Goodman for, on the one hand, "his own liberal and humanistic intelligence, his commitment to democratic values—a commitment shared neither by the Committee nor by most of its victims"—and, on the other hand, for being "no less anti-Communist than Martin Dies or any of Dies's successors." Goodman, in short, refused to "accept the view that the Communists whom the Committee harassed—along, of course, with many non-Communists— were undeserving of any form of investigation or political censure."[27]

The great majority of Cold War liberals remained consistent if cautious critics of HUAC and McCarthy. Yet by advocating surveillance and exposure of anyone who unwittingly aided Communist causes, Cold War liberals undermined their own critique of the wild-swinging red-baiting favored by HUAC and McCarthy. More importantly, Cold War liberals often demanded the surveillance of dissidents by apolitical FBI agents but not partisan congressmen. From the Dies Committee's formation in 1938 to the early 1970s, many liberals viewed the FBI as a libertarian alternative to HUAC, championing an impartial executive intelligence instead of the inefficient partisanship of congressional investigating committees. On the Right, the FBI and HUAC had the same constituency. But on the Left the FBI could count many liberals among its most loyal supporters. Even Alan Barth, in his caustic and much-heralded critique, "How Good is an FBI Report?", concluded that the Bureau's formidable collection of political intelligence—including, as the FBI Director himself readily admitted, in- nuendo, allegation, gossip, and outright lies—would be "a terrible instrument of oppression . . . in the hands of a police chief less scrupulous than Mr. Hoover."[28]

To contain HUAC and McCarthy, then, Cold War liberals supported expansive executive privilege claims designed to deny irresponsible, red-hunting congressmen access to FBI files. By doing so, they staked much on the integrity of Presidents Truman and Eisenhower and FBI Director Hoover. This blind trust was not only unwarranted but threatening to a constitutional system of government. The response of several national officials of the American Civil Liberties Union to what they perceived as a serious internal security threat offers the starkest example of how liberal values were thus perverted.

Since the Dies Committee labeled the ACLU a Communist

front in 1939, the organization had grown increasingly anti-communist.[29] Because this charge was soon retracted and, coincidentally, because ACLU then dropped its plan to bring a broad First Amendment lawsuit challenging the Committee's investigative authority, ACLU board member Corliss Lamont and others thought the ACLU leadership might have "reached an understanding" with Martin Dies. Dies's retraction came after a "cocktail conference" attended by himself, Committee member Jerry Voorhis, and ACLU counsels Morris Ernst and Arthur Garfield Hays. Jerome Frank and Assistant Secretary of State Adolf A. Berle, Jr., also attended, representing the Roosevelt administration. According to Dies, this meeting was called "to explore the possibility of a united action on the part of liberals and conservatives to investigate and expose Communists in the United States." Working together, Dies reasoned, "we could destroy the Communist apparatus." As an incentive, Dies promised to allow the ACLU to "share in the credit." Ernst and Hays rejected these overtures. Ernst, however, began to work closely with the Dies Committee after this meeting. On one occasion in 1940, Dies asked Ernst to "look over" his seven-point countersubversive program before presenting it to President Roosevelt. Ernst then served as an intermediary between Attorney General Robert Jackson's office and the Dies Committee.[30]

Whether a deal had been struck (an unlikely contention) or the ACLU leadership was reacting to the recently signed Nazi-Soviet Pact, the American Civil Liberties Union soon began to act in a manner that legitimized guilt by association, public censure of people advocating unpopular ideas, and other techniques pioneered by Martin Dies. ACLU officials not only abandoned their planned First Amendment suit against the Committee, but in February 1940 began to purge their own board of directors. Targets included Communists, such as CPUSA official Elizabeth Gurley Flynn, and fellow travellers, such as ACLU national board chairman Harry F. Ward. A Methodist minister and professor of Christian ethics at Union Theological Seminary, Ward resigned to head the Civil Rights Congress. The ACLU board of directors asked Flynn to resign and "tried" her when she refused. An open Communist party member who had been reelected unanimously to the board prior to the signing of the Nazi-Soviet Pact, Flynn was found guilty on three counts of misconduct and expelled. Two of the counts were based on her public criticisms of the ACLU. The third centered on her party membership. When testifying before HUAC eight years later, Arthur Garfield Hays explained the ACLU's motives to Richard Nixon. "We thought," Hays said, "people who were on the board should have the same ideas we had."[31]

Thereafter, the ACLU continued to move steadily toward the center. In a letter to J. Parnell Thomas in 1947, ACLU officials criticized HUAC's "continued violence [sic] of fair procedure," but noted, "we hold no brief for the Communist Party . . . [and] its anti-democratic aspects." By 1949 the ACLU included similar disclaimers in all its briefs where communism might be an issue and sometimes tried to avoid defending CPUSA members and those accused of Communist associations. One case involved Corliss Lamont, a member of the ACLU national board since 1931, and his planned challenge to Senator McCarthy's authority to probe political activity. After he received a subpoena from the McCarthy Committee in 1953, his name was removed from a list of nominees for the board of directors, and the board turned down a proposal to support him against McCarthy. A few days later, however, this decision was reversed. Lamont denied Communist party membership before the McCarthy Committee—prompting the FBI to launch a "perjury" investigation even though Lamont had never been a party member and the Bureau knew it.[32] The national office also tried to purge its general membership, though local ACLU affiliates refused to embrace the national office's anticommunist politics. Nineteen of twenty-three ACLU corporate affiliates voted against a referendum that would have sanctioned an ideologically pure ACLU by refusing membership to Communists or others mesmerized by "totalitarian doctrines."[33]

Perhaps the ACLU's greatest failure of nerve arose from the controversy surrounding Merle Miller's *The Judges and the Judged.* Published in 1952, Miller's study culminated a five-month ACLU investigation of blacklisting, concentrating on

American Business Consultants and its 213-page booklet, *Red Channels*, and newsletter, *Counterattack*. Initially, the ACLU found Miller's evidence compelling enough to file a complaint with the Federal Communications Commission (FCC) and timed it to coincide with the pubic release of *The Judges and the Judged*. Although the ACLU looked forward to "the beginning of a long educational program" aimed at blacklisting, its ambitious plans quickly ground to a halt.

The first substantive criticism of Miller's work did not come from HUAC or the ex-FBI agents who ran American Business Consultants. Instead, Merlyn S. Pitzele, an ACLU board member and a *Business Week* labor editor, emerged as Miller's chief critic. Primarily upset because *The Judges and the Judged* presented McCarthyism, rather than the CPUSA, as the principal threat to civil liberties in the United States, Pitzele publicly voiced his objections in the *New Leader*. He objected to factual errors and to Miller's heavy reliance on anonymous sources, a tactic favored by the authors of *Red Channels* and *Counterattack* and their secret FBI and not-so-secret HUAC benefactors. The controversy quickly degenerated as each protagonist claimed to be the more sophisticated anticommunist. When Miller trotted out his credentials, Pitzele dismissed him as an unregenerate romantic, "one of those fellows who believe that the guilt of Alger Hiss is still unproven." The ACLU appointed a special committee to investigate Pitzele's charges and acknowledged certain factual errors in Miller's study. More importantly, the ACLU abandoned its FCC suit, and its ambitious antiblacklisting program faded away.[34]

FBI MEN IN THE ACLU

Some ACLU officials were not content to toughen their rhetoric or quietly shelve civil liberties programs that threatened the vested interests of the blacklisters. One such ACLU official, Irving Ferman, director of the organization's influential Washington, D.C., office, served as an FBI informer. Throughout the 1950s, Ferman supplied information on the ACLU and the activities of some of its members to the FBI

Crime Records Division. After the release in 1977 of the FBI's files on the ACLU under the Freedom of Information Act, Ferman defended his earlier assistance to the Bureau. He intended to keep HUAC and the American Legion from attacking the American Civil Liberties Union. Ferman, then professor of law at Howard University, said his services to the FBI allowed the ACLU to devote its time to protecting civil liberties. There was a real possibility of the ACLU's becoming absorbed in a protracted effort to defend itself against irresponsible charges of Communist influence by HUAC and the American Legion. With FBI assistance, Ferman added, he helped to suppress a potentially crippling HUAC staff report on the ACLU.[35] Indeed, the Bureau's second- and third-ranking officials, Clyde Tolson and Louis Nichols, carefully monitored this never-released HUAC report.

When first apprised of the Committee's report on the ACLU in July 1955, Ferman alerted Lee Pennington, the former FBI Inspector and then director of the Legion's National Americanism Commission. Pennington promptly contacted FBI official Cartha DeLoach. Nichols also received information second-hand from HUAC staff member Karl Baarslag, a former Legion employee and McCarthy aide "who is known to the Bureau." After telephoning the assistant director of the Legion's legislative division, Baarslag warned that the one-hundred-page research study was already in page proof but that several HUAC members, led by former FBI agent Harold Velde, were demanding that it be suppressed. Velde objected because "he is viciously against the Chief Clerk of the Committee, Tom Beal, [on] whom the Bureau has rather extensive information in its files." Later, Nichols learned, the Committee voted to suppress the report. Velde and HUAC Chairman Walter, nonetheless, gave a copy to Ferman and invited him to file a confidential analysis. Ferman submitted a copy of his response to the FBI. Either Baarslag or Ferman then turned over a copy of the HUAC report on the ACLU to the Bureau, where it was forwarded to the Domestic Intelligence Division and incorporated into the files for "informational purposes."[36]

Had the Bureau really helped Ferman keep HUAC and the

Legion from immobilizing the ACLU? Or was Ferman being less than candid when explaining his motives twenty years later? The incompleteness of FBI files released thus far under the Freedom of Information Act makes these questions difficult to answer conclusively. But there is some evidence that suggests tentative answers.

At the Legion's national convention in October 1955, DeLoach was appointed a member of the Americanism Commission and assigned to serve on a subcommittee responsible for Legion resolutions. This same Legion convention approved a resolution demanding the distribution of the HUAC report on the ACLU to the general public. Whether or not DeLoach helped draft this particular resolution, his influence in the Legion and the close working relationship between Legion officials and FBI bureaucrats suggest that the FBI possessed enough clout to suppress any resolution unfavorable to Bureau interests. In addition to DeLoach, three other FBI agents were working behind the scenes during this convention. All three later received letters of commendation from Hoover for arranging "favorable publicity" for the FBI. And the entire Bureau effort at the Legion convention was supervised by FBI Assistant Director Nichols.[37]

Ferman's services as an informer, in addition, were not nearly as discriminating as he later claimed. He had close ties not only with Nichols and DeLoach, but also with the Legion's ex-FBI man, Lee Pennington, and former HUAC staff member Benjamin Mandel. Nor did Ferman limit himself to reporting on the activities of his ACLU colleagues. He worked closely with Nichols and Pennington in 1954 to insure that the ACLU distributed Hoover's "question and answer" article on communism published in the March issue of an American Legion publication. Three years later, when Ferman learned of anti-HUAC activist Frank Wilkinson's attempt to solicit ACLU support, Ferman wrote Nichols to advise him of Wilkinson's efforts and forwarded a copy of his letter to Mandel. The next year, Ferman advised the Bureau that Congressman James Roosevelt's (D., Cal.) secretary was a friend of Wilkinson.[38]

Ferman was not alone in servicing the FBI and, indirectly, HUAC. Another ACLU official, Morris Ernst, regularly forwarded to the FBI the names of people he deemed suspicious, including four individuals who might have been associated with William Remington. Since the early 1940s, Ernst, at Franklin Roosevelt's suggestion, had "worked with" Hoover on various countersubversive operations. He volunteered in December 1941, for instance, "to be of assistance" in counteracting articles critical of the FBI in *The Nation* and the *New York Daily News*. Thereafter, Ernst regularly championed issues on the Bureau's behalf. In late 1945 he tried to persuade Harry Truman to unleash the FBI, warning the President that one of the "top men at your Labor Management Conference is not a free agent . . . [but] acting on orders of the Communist Party." For more details, Ernst referred Truman to Hoover. He also appeared before HUAC in 1948, defending the FBI's carefully cultivated image and dismissing Henry Wallace as a CPUSA "nightshirt." Ernst routinely sent Nichols blind copies of his personal correspondence and once, in March 1952, relayed the proposed defense strategy of counsel for the Newhouse newspapers. At the time, these attorneys were defending the *Syracuse Star* against a libel suit brought by Senator McCarthy.[39]

The FBI, in turn, assisted Ernst's anticommunist activities. In February 1952, Special Agent William C. Sullivan (later an FBI Assistant Director) reviewed a draft copy of Ernst's book-length manuscript (published as *Report on the American Communist*), held a lengthy interview with Ernst and Nichols at Bureau headquarters, and suggested numerous changes in the manuscript. Nichols also arranged, "on an informal basis," to have five FBI field offices assist Ernst with his research.[40]

Four years later, Nichols suggested contacting Ernst to handle a problem for the Bureau. This particular case involved Communist party plans to have the ACLU publicize the FBI program of harassing Communists by interviewing them. (The FBI learned of these plans when intercepting a conversation of CPUSA leader Claude Lightfoot.) Though concerned, Nichols was pleased to note the party's assessment of the "interview" program. Because Communists viewed it as a "harassment," the FBI had positive "proof of its effectiveness." To counter efforts by Communists and by "some of the left wingers on the

American Civil Liberties Union board" to "embellish what we are doing," Nichols next contacted ACLU Executive Director Patrick Malin. Nichols was confident enough to be honest when briefing Malin. "I can inquire when Pat will be in Washington," he advised Tolson, "and just sit down and have a frank talk with him about the program. I have no doubt as to being able to justify this program [deleted]. . . . This is one case where the truth will not hurt, and we might avert some unfavorable publicity."[41]

Though FBI-ACLU relations were generally one-sided, ACLU officials sometimes tried to exploit the FBI. Like Ferman, Ernst attempted to use his Bureau contacts to keep HUAC at bay. After learning of Committee plans to subpoena a woman active in the Newspaper Guild's anticommunist purge, Ernst gave her name to Nichols and suggested an interview. "I think her story can be of some slight value to you," Ernst said, "and that possibly with propriety you can agree that no social good would result from her testimony before the House Committee." Responding for Nichols, Hoover wrote Ernst to thank him for this suggestion and to advise him of Bureau plans to interview the woman. More often, however, Ernst served as an FBI emissary within the ACLU. In February 1952 he forwarded to Nichols the minutes of a January 21 ACLU executive board meeting. These minutes, which Ernst fleshed out in a conversation with Nichols, updated the Bureau on the ACLU's proposed program on blacklisting and intent to file a complaint with the Federal Communications Commission. The Bureau was interested in this project, and when ACLU board chairman Ernest Angell first briefed the FBI Director in November 1950, Hoover—in an unserialized Do Not File memorandum—immediately alerted his top aides.[42]

Ernst also aided FBI officials regarding another matter discussed at the ACLU's executive board meeting. James L. Fly had criticized the FBI's alleged practice of including special sections labeled "derogatory information" in all loyalty reports. As an example, Fly cited the FBI practice of highlighting instances where attorneys served as defense counsel in political cases. Ernst defended the Bureau during the meeting, arguing that the FBI must report everything and yet evaluate nothing. Fly countered by noting that FBI agents were highly selective when questioning suspect federal employees and presenting evidence to government loyalty boards. ACLU Executive Director Malin promised to look into the matter.

To contain Malin's possible inquiry, Nichols directed the Domestic Intelligence Division to "make an immediate survey of the situation and get material together so that we can furnish the information to Mr. Ernst and be in a position to answer Malin should he write to us." After the Domestic Intelligence Division completed its survey, Hoover outlined the Bureau's position in a letter to Ernst. The FBI did not prepare a special derogatory information section in its loyalty reports. If technically correct, Hoover's denial was largely an exercise in semantics. FBI loyalty investigations were, in toto, purposeful attempts to uncover derogatory information—particularly if the suspect was the subject of a HUAC investigation. And FBI files were routinely searched for derogatory information, which could be forwarded to the press or used to identify discreet newspapermen and public opinion leaders. Thus, when J. Addington Wagner of Battle Creek, Michigan, was elected national commander at the American Legion convention in 1955, FBI files were searched immediately, but Nichols reported: "No derogatory information found [on Wagner] in Bureau files."[43]

THE RETURN OF THE ACLU

The FBI's relationship with Ernst, Ferman, and other national ACLU officials helped contain the American Civil Liberties Union during the 1950s. FBI officials, nonetheless, did not share Ferman's and Ernst's opinions regarding the ACLU's responsible anticommunism. Nichols found Ferman, Ernst, Malin, and Herbert Monte Levy to be trustworthy, but was leery of Fly and most other national officials. Local ACLU affiliates caused even greater problems for the FBI. Bureau officials were particularly concerned because these local affiliates, in contrast to the national office, were active in the campaign to abolish HUAC. National ACLU officials not only failed to encourage the abolition campaign, but Malin sent a memorandum to all affiliates urging them not to support a national abolition petition. It was indicative of the ACLU leadership's limited goals that Malin instead advised local affiliates to "devise means to curb the House Committee." Malin's memorandum, furthermore, was somehow made available to *Counterattack*. This leak convinced Malin that HUAC had access to the ACLU's internal communiqués and had forwarded them to *Counterattack*.[44]

Whether or not the FBI leaked this particular document to *Counterattack* (or to HUAC), Bureau officials were principally concerned with the ACLU's Seattle chapter, which demanded an investigation of the FBI's domestic intelligence operations, and with the Los Angeles chapter, which circulated a petition calling for HUAC's abolition. Thus, when the FBI received an inquiry asking whether the Bureau had ever characterized the ACLU as subversive, Hoover declined to answer. He specifically advised the correspondent not to "infer from my inability to be of assistance that we do or do not have in our files the information you desire." A note on the bottom of the Bureau copy of Hoover's letter explained the FBI Director's reasoning: "If we advise the correspondent we have not investigated the ACLU, it may possibly be construed as a clearance of the organization by the FBI. In view of the activities of [the Los Angeles and Seattle] chapters . . . on the west coast and the correspondent's desire to obtain material to be used in writing to the newspapers, it is believed the above reply will best serve the interests of the Bureau."[45]

FBI officials, on the one hand, did not want it known that they were investigating the ACLU. On the other hand, they wanted an authoritative body to issue an official declaration that certain ACLU affiliates were subversive. Many of the FBI's voluminous files on the ACLU and its affiliates begin with the Bureau's solemn announcement that it never conducted an investigation of the group. Yet the FBI amassed some 13,000 pages of intelligence on it. Because this information was not gathered under a formal investigative heading, the FBI could claim never to have investigated the ACLU. Bureau files recording FBI officials interest in having the organization's Los

Angeles chapter declared a Communist front challenge this denial.

One such FBI memorandum of May 1955, captioned DOCU-MENTATION OF L.A. CHAPTER OF AMERICAN CIVIL LIBERTIES UNION, recorded the FBI's interest in having the California State Senate Fact-Finding Committee on Un-American Activities declare the Los Angeles chapter subversive. The California committee had previously cited the chapter as subversive and the committee's chief counsel, Richard Combs, advised Bureau agents that this characterization would not change in an updated and soon-to-be released report. Combs also stated that his committee had reluctantly abandoned its plan to probe ACLU activities in greater detail because the Los Angeles affiliate had supported a suit brought against the committee by a group of discharged Pacific Gas and Electric Company employees. Although this suit had been dismissed, the discharged employees filed an appeal. Combs, as a result, refused to jeopardize the committee's favorable position with the courts. National ACLU officials were also concerned about the California committee. An ACLU representative visited Combs's offices that same year in an unsuccessful attempt to persuade the committee to withdraw its Communist-front charge. As a sign of good faith, the national ACLU official noted the recent purge of two Los Angeles chapter members accused of Communist sympathies.[46]

By late 1959 the FBI's problems with ACLU affiliates had spread. In September, Lawrence Speiser of San Francisco, a counsel for the Northern California ACLU affiliate from 1952 to 1957, was named to succeed Irving Ferman as director of the powerful Washington, D.C., office. When briefing Speiser, Ferman introduced him to the new head of the FBI's Crime Records Division, Cartha DeLoach. As a "first impression," DeLoach found Speiser "extremely idealistic," advising Clyde Tolson of the need to check Bureau files—presumably, for derogatory information. FBI Director Hoover, in a hand-written note at the bottom of DeLoach's memorandum to Tolson, specifically directed the CRD to "be most circumspect in dealing with Speiser."

Hoover's order was based on the Bureau's extensive investigation of Speiser, an investigation begun the same day the Bureau learned of his appointment to succeed Ferman. The FBI file check revealed the type of derogatory information Fly had earlier cited. Office of Naval Intelligence reports submitted to the Bureau noted Speiser's penchant for providing legal advice to "various individuals with subversive backgrounds." Another reported that Speiser, while studying at the University of California, had signed a request to have Henry Wallace address the student body. All in all, according to San Francisco SAC William Whalen, Speiser and the Northern California ACLU affiliate had "represented Communists and procommunists [before HUAC and other tribunals] almost exclusively," thereby "interfering with [FBI] Security subjects in numerous investigations."

One event that particularly upset Whalen involved the FBI's harassment of Communists through interviews. In late 1953 and early 1954, Speiser became involved in the FBI's investigation of Security Index subject Nelson Tucker. Apparently, Tucker told Speiser that local FBI agents requested him to appear for an interview at the Bureau's Oakland resident agency, that four or five agents participated in this interview, and that one of these agents referred to the ACLU as a Communist front. Speiser then wrote to the FBI's San Francisco Field Office to determine whether the alleged smear of the ACLU actually took place. At the direction of senior FBI officials, SAC Whalen obtained a signed statement from Tucker refuting this allegation.

Even if Speiser's specific charges were incorrect, the FBI remained vulnerable because of its harassment of people like Tucker. Nor were senior FBI officials satisfied with Whalen's contention that his office had "set [Speiser] straight." Hoover ordered Nichols to bring the affair to the attention of national ACLU officials in New York City "as another instance of San Francisco ACLU misstatements." Nichols promptly telephoned ACLU general counsel Herbert Monte Levy, who "appreciated having the information and said he would be on the alert for any inclination on the part of Speiser to exaggerate in which event he would jump him rather severely."

This episode did not endear Speiser to the FBI. And Bureau

officials wasted little time enjoining their allies. After reading the CRD background synopsis, FBI Associate Director Tolson scribbled a note: "Suggest House Committee be alerted to Speiser's designation." Hoover concurred. That same day, DeLoach's office "called Dick Arens [HUAC staff director Richard Arens] . . . and gave him a rundown [deleted]." Arens remembered Speiser as "a 'smart aleck,'" "appreciated being alerted," and said the Committee would "be on guard."[47]

The replacement of the anticommunist ACLU leadership in the late 1950s and 1960s with Speiser and younger, more tolerant activists marked a serious erosion of the anticommunist consensus. And though the ascendance during the McCarthy era of the anticommunist political style within the ACLU, the CIO, the NAACP, and the ADA cannot be explained by the actions and programs of FBI officials, it nevertheless offers, in part, a chilling testament to the FBI's long campaign to shape the response of the "Liberal elements," as D. Milton Ladd proposed at the February 1946 FBI executives' conference, to American dissidence. This is not to suggest that the FBI "created" Cold War liberalism. The actions of Joseph Stalin and his disciples, whether in Czechoslovakia in February 1948 or within the American labor movement during and immediately after World War II, clearly had a greater impact on liberal intellectuals and trade unionists than anything the Crime Records Division could dream up. The response of Cold War liberals nevertheless legitimized a red-hunting politics and helped to define McCarthyism. Their contribution was mostly a failure of nerve, a headlong rush to embrace what Arthur M. Schlesinger, Jr., called "the best professional counterespionage agency we can get to protect our national security."[48] By siding with the FBI and thus attempting to influence the nature of the red hunt, mainstream liberals abandoned the difficult task of maintaining both a principled anti-Stalinism and a principled anti-McCarthyism.

CHAPTER VIII

Counterintelligence

While ACLU officials Morris Ernst and Irving Ferman were busy collaborating with the FBI, the United States Senate condemned Joseph R. McCarthy for conduct unbecoming a United States Senator. The condemnation did not, however, terminate McCarthyism as a political phenomenon. In some ways, McCarthy's demise ushered in a more pervasive McCarthyism. The House Committee on Un-American Activities and the Senate Internal Security Subcommittee continued to promote the menace, while FBI officials' priorities remained unchanged. In 1959, two years after McCarthy's death, over 400 agents in the FBI's New York Field Office were assigned to "communism" and only four to organized crime.[1] FBI assistance to the congressional internal security committees also escalated dramatically in response to a new program launched by the FBI in 1956—the first of the COINTELPROs. Never content merely to spy and gather intelligence, FBI officials had always intended to use the information gathered during their investigations to discredit dissident political activities. Hereafter, they pursued these objectives on a truly grand scale.

McCARTHYISM AT BAY

This apparent paradox—the escalation of McCarthyism at the very time the junior Senator from Wisconsin was fading into oblivion—can be explained in part by the anticommunist politics favored by the Eisenhower administration. Less than two weeks after his inauguration, President Eisenhower directed his congressional liaison, General Wilton B. Persons, and Vice-President Nixon to work with HUAC and the various congressional investigating committees searching for Communists in government. Nixon and Persons hoped to direct the congressional red-hunters by identifying "what ought to be investigated," thereby confining the ongoing search for subversives to New Deal and Fair Deal personnel while precluding "investigations of the present Administration." Justice Department officials, moreover, felt that the Republicans' electoral success had led to "changed conditions" and thus the FBI should now extend "as much cooperation as possible" to HUAC and other red-hunting committees.[2]

Secretary of State John Foster Dulles hired former FBI agent R. W. Scott McLeod to run the State Department security office. McLeod, in turn, cooperated with Senator McCarthy, SISS Chairman William E. Jenner, and HUAC Chairman Harold Velde. In early 1953 Nixon organized a luncheon meeting with FBI Assistant Director Nichols; Persons and his assistant Jerry Morgan, a former employee of the Un-American Activities Committee; Velde, Kearney, and Jackson of HUAC; and Jenner and Robert Morris of the Senate Subcommittee to establish another delimitations agreement for the planned congressional investigations on Communist infiltration of schools and universities. According to Eisenhower's top aide, Sherman Adams, the purpose of this meeting was "to effect coordination of investigations of educational institutions so as to avoid duplications." Tacitly supporting this behind the scenes effort and ignoring what Persons described as "strong pressure" to speak out against the committees' move into the educational field, the President publicly questioned whether CPUSA members should be allowed to teach. Even when teaching mathematics, Eisenhower mused, party propagandists could substitute political symbols for apples and oranges. J. Edgar Hoover also supported the HUAC-SISS investigations. In March he ordered twenty-four field offices to compile reports on "subversive persons" employed at fifty-six universities and colleges. A month later, the FBI Director warned the House and Senate Appropriations Subcommittees of Communist infiltration in education at all levels.[3]

The administration's support for the anticommunist politics of HUAC and FBI officials was further reflected in the decision to create a new loyalty-security program. Established by executive order in April 1953, the Eisenhower loyalty-security program made it easier to fire not only potential security risks and those few Communists who had infiltrated the government, but New Deal holdovers as well. (In June 1954 Attorney General Herbert Brownell, Jr., told the Cabinet that there were "some 500 Government employees on an FBI 'pick-up list' in case of an emergency.")[4] Then, at HUAC's recommendation, the President amended the loyalty-security program by authorizing loyalty review boards to take into consideration whether a federal employee had ever taken the Fifth Amendment before a congressional investigating committee. Led by Attorney General Brownell, the administration also lobbied for an immunity bill and on August 20, 1954, Congress passed the Compulsory Testimony Act. President Eisenhower commended the virtues of this new law three days later:

> Investigation and prosecution of crimes involving national security have been seriously hampered by witnesses who have invoked the Constitutional privilege against self-incrimination embodied in the Fifth Amendment. This Act provides a new means of breaking through the secrecy which is characteristic of traitors, spies and saboteurs.[5]

Although this act empowered congressional committees to request the District Court for the District of Columbia to grant immunity to recalcitrant witnesses, neither HUAC nor any of the other red-hunting committees made much use of it. The Un-American Activities Committee was quite content to fire twenty or more questions at unfriendly witnesses and receive the same answer each time: "I refuse to answer on the grounds that it may incriminate me." In addition, the Supreme Court had recently decided, in *Hoffman* v. *U.S.*, that Fifth Amendment protections extended to questions about other individuals and could further be invoked in response to any question that tended to incriminate, whether it was incriminatory or not. In *Rogers* v. *U.S.* the Court had ruled that a witness who testified regarding his or her own Communist affiliations thereby waived all constitutional rights and must answer questions regarding other persons as well. In these circumstances, those summoned by the Velde, Jenner, and McCarthy committees had few choices. They could take the Fifth, become a Committee informer, or refuse to testify on other grounds—in which case they risked indictment for contempt of Congress and, ultimately, jail. (The FBI even kept Justice Department prosecutors posted on the strategy that members of allegedly subversive groups intended to pursue when called to testify.) Witnesses who took the Fifth also risked losing their jobs and were routinely investigated by the FBI for inclusion on the Security Index. The Bureau held a dossier on everyone who took the Fifth Amendment before a congressional investigating committee.[6]

The condemnation of Senator McCarthy might have signalled a thaw in the domestic Cold War, but the anticommunist politics favored by the Eisenhower administration, HUAC, and FBI officials remained unchallenged. A series of Supreme Court rulings in 1956 and 1957, however, did impose substantive restrictions on FBI officials' attempts to exploit antiradical fears and the administration's concomitant attempt to devise a "total program [that] will have the effect of outlawing the Communist Party without becoming involved in the constitutional complications of actual outlawry."[7] These decisions limited the scope of permissible testimony by FBI informers and granted defense counsel greater access to pretrial statements that government witnesses had made to the FBI; challenged the procedures of congressional committees investigating subversive activities; and questioned the constitutionality of Smith Act prosecutions, Subversive Activities Control Board hearings, and certain aspects of the Eisenhower administration's loyalty-security program.[8]

The Supreme Court's rulings did not reflect a change in congressional temperament. HUAC member Donald Jackson was not alone when he charged that the Court's decision to invalidate a contempt of Congress citation against John T. Watkins for refusing to answer Committee questions was "a victory greater than any achieved by the Soviet on the battlefield since World War II." During the Eighty-Fifth Congress, 101 anti-Court and anti–civil liberties bills were introduced. Led by Louis Nichols, the FBI lobbied extensively for new legislation to undo the effects of the recent rulings, particularly the *Jencks* decision, which granted defendants greater access to FBI reports. In 1959, two years after he left the Bureau, Nichols wrote an influential American Bar Association report that inspired in part yet another attempt by anticommunist congressmen to shore up the nation's internal security machinery.[9]

THE ESCALATION OF McCARTHYISM

The FBI's response to the Supreme Court decisions of 1956 and 1957 was not so narrowly limited. Realizing that it would no longer be feasible to prosecute Communists, in August 1956 Bureau officials decided to augment their earlier political activities. They launched the first of a series of formal counter-intelligence programs (COINTELPROs) designed "to expose, disrupt, misdirect, discredit or otherwise neutralize" groups and individuals whom FBI officials had categorized as opposed to the national interest. The FBI's counterintelligence program was initiated unilaterally without the knowledge or authorization of the Attorney General or the President, at a time when Communist party membership was declining spectacularly, and when even FBI officials no longer considered the CPUSA an espionage threat. Thus began a massive campaign to bring Communists "into disrepute before the American public."

Once institutionalized within the Domestic Intelligence Division (headed from 1961 to 1971 by William C. Sullivan), this COINTELPRO–Communist party expanded to include indigenous radicals and nonradicals. In March 1960 another Bureau program, COMINFIL, sought to prevent Communist infiltration of "legitimate mass organizations" ranging from the Boy Scouts to the NAACP. Under COMINFIL, the FBI began to investigate those whom FBI officials considered as being possibly under Communist influence. In time, the Bureau expanded its structured counterintelligence activities to include such diverse groups and amorphous movements (and their sympathizers) as the Socialist Workers party (1961), "White Hate Groups" (1964), "Black Nationalist Hate Groups" (1967), and the "New Left" (1968).[10]

Counterintelligence operations (some of which violated criminal statutes relating to mail fraud, incited violence, and involved sending obscene material through the mail and extortion) were not intended merely to invoke sanctions against dissidents.[11] They also had an explicitly educational purpose—developing logically, if not inevitably, from the earlier and less formal program of February 1946. Under the counterintelligence programs, FBI officials were more concerned with dramatizing the Communist threat than neutralizing the Communist party. When the CPUSA began to disintegrate in the late 1950s, FBI officials felt compelled to serve as cheerleaders for their archfoe. Accordingly, the collapse of the party newspaper in 1958 prompted FBI officials to draft a "statement which the Director may desire to use as an official publicity release explaining the discontinuance of the 'Daily Worker' for the American people." Hoover rejected this suggestion and instead ordered the Crime Records Division to give the FBI-authored statement to Hearst columnist George Sokolsky.[12]

This leak to Sokolsky was not atypical. The FBI's attempts to shape public opinion accelerated between 1956 and 1971, the years the Bureau operated the various COINTELPROs. The most frequently used techniques, however, had long been employed by FBI Assistant Director Nichols. These included anonymous mailings (whether reprints of published articles or FBI-authored pamphlets, news stories, or poison-pen letters); leaks to friendly journalists, congressmen, and other public opinion leaders; and efforts to prevent radicals from speaking, meeting, teaching, writing, and publishing.

Following Nichols's retirement from the Bureau in late 1957, Cartha DeLoach carried on these activities. Starting out as an agent assigned to investigate Communists in Toledo and Akron, Ohio, DeLoach moved to Washington D.C., after World War II and was assigned to the Crime Records Division. Appointed

FBI Assistant Director for Crime Records in 1959, he directed all FBI investigative activities six years later. Cultivating newsmen, congressmen, and even President Lyndon B. Johnson, DeLoach, like Nichols before him, was Hoover's troubleshooter.[13] Less concerned than Nichols with the possibility that his activities would become publicly compromised, DeLoach not only furnished information to newspaper reporters and other publicists but supervised the production and distribution on college campuses of a newspaper, the *Rational Observer,* billed as the work of "a small group of students." After leaving the Bureau in mid-1970 to work for Richard Nixon's friend Donald Kendall, chairman of the board of Pepsico, Inc., DeLoach became the recipient of FBI leaks—with the External Affairs Division (successor to Crime Records) doing name checks for him in connection with his work at Pepsico.[14]

As part of his counterintelligence responsibilities, DeLoach developed a "Mass Media Program" that included over 300 newspaper reporters, columnists, radio commentators, and television news investigators. Under DeLoach's supervision on the local level, FBI field offices cultivated their own media contacts. The Chicago Field Office, for instance, had one or more sources at various newspapers *(Chicago Tribune, Chicago American, Chicago Daily News, Chicago Sun-Times, Chicago Defender, Joliet Herald, Rockford Register Republic, Rockford Morning Star,* and *Waukegan News Star),* television stations (ABC, NBC, and CBS local affiliates), radio stations (WGN), and news organizations (City News Bureau and Field Communications Corporation). These sources could be counted on to publicize the FBI's position on virtually any issue and to discredit not only the CPUSA but "the liberal press and the bleeding hearts."[15]

COUNTERINTELLIGENCE AND THE COMMITTEE

As part of the counterintelligence program, DeLoach and other FBI officials also worked closely with the House Committee on Un-American Activities—whether by directing

Committee staff to FBI informers or public source information, servicing HUAC requests for specific files, providing Committee members and staff with FBI reports, or assisting the Committee's efforts to compile charts detailing the "structure and organization" of the CPUSA.[16] The FBI, in return, routinely exploited HUAC's public hearings to expose the Communist associations of Security Index subjects, including a person active in a Harlem tenants' association and a vice-president of the Cleveland chapter of the Women's International League for Peace and Freedom.[17] On another occasion, the FBI's Boston Field Office mailed an anonymous letter to three Communist party functionaries falsely charging that one of their comrades made a deal with HUAC.[18]

Other targets were selected under COINTELPRO through regular reviews of the seemingly endless lists of names of people whom FBI informers had identified as Communist during testimony before the Committee. (Even though the counterintelligence program was launched in August 1956, FBI field offices had been instructed to monitor all HUAC hearings and to prepare a memorandum for each person named before the Committee.)[19] Those exposed before the Un-American Activities Committee sometimes received poison-pen letters mailed by the FBI in "commercially purchased envelopes," and their employers or associates were alerted to their "subversive" background through such techniques as pretext telephone calls (where an agent would falsely identify himself as a CPUSA member or a friend of the target), anonymous letters, and leaks to newspaper reporters.[20]

The FBI occasionally forwarded derogatory information directly to HUAC to insure that those named would lose their jobs. In 1964, as Buffalo Field Office agents were preparing for HUAC's arrival to probe the local Communist party and the Progressive Labor Movement, senior FBI officials approved a leak to the Committee for the sole purpose of influencing the State University of New York (SUNY) at Buffalo to fire English teacher Paul Sporn. Described by the Buffalo office as its "most celebrated security figure," Sporn was subpoenaed to testify publicly before the Committee because of his perceived vulnerability. The so-called Feinberg Law required all SUNY

faculty to sign a certificate denying current CPUSA membership. Former Communists were required to confer with the
president of SUNY before signing or accepting employment.
The FBI first arranged for an informer to identify Sporn as
having attended two special meetings of the Erie County
Communist party in 1961. FBI Assistant Director DeLoach
then "discreetly" advised HUAC staff director Francis J.
McNamara that Sporn had indeed signed the Feinberg certificate. Although FBI officials knew that Sporn would refuse to
answer any of HUAC's questions, they intended to "make it
difficult for New York State authorities not to try some
affirmative action to remove him from the State University
where he is now teaching." Sporn was fired.

Later, the local Special Agent in Charge advised FBI
headquarters of the "tangible results" of this and other
counterintelligence operations (notably a series of leaks to the
Buffalo Evening News and the *Buffalo Courier Express*)
carried out in conjunction with the HUAC hearing. The SAC
noted "an awakening of citizen curiosity . . . concerning subversive groups" and a call by Republican Congressman John R.
Pillion for the Governor to launch a probe of Communist infiltration in the state university system. This joint FBI-HUAC
operation not only cost Sporn his job at SUNY-Buffalo, but "virtually destroyed" the local branch of the Progressive Labor
Movement; forced many Communists and Progressive
Laborites to leave town; caused a graduate student to lose a
fellowship; possibly contributed to five other lost jobs; and
raised the possibility that a public school teacher who had
attended the Buffalo hearings as a spectator would not have her
contract renewed.[21]

Though the Buffalo operation was not atypical, the FBI's
most frequently used counterintelligence technique involving
the Committee was the distribution of its published hearings
and reports to, among others, "reliable and established news
media sources who may be relied upon to protect this Bureau's
interest."[22] The last time the Committee had visited Buffalo, in
1959, the Bureau attempted to force the dismissal of three
public school teachers who had invoked the Fifth Amendment
by forwarding their HUAC testimony to a newspaper reporter

for an exposé article. Similarly, the FBI's Newark Field Office worked closely with American Legion officials who were appearing regularly before civic organizations to read testimony from HUAC hearings—a tactic that led to the dismissal of an officer of the Ringwood, N.J., Library Association. DeLoach also sent "pertinent HCUA[23] testimony" to the Detroit Field Office for release to an American Legion official and local newspaper contacts in an effort to discredit *Labor Today*, a magazine allegedly financed by the Communist party. Later, when *Labor Today* published an article by James Hoffa, FBI officials again approved the dissemination of Committee publications in an effort to discourage Teamsters Union support.

Other HUAC material was sent anonymously to Hearst's *Baltimore News-Post*, an NAACP official in Hartford, a YMCA official in Los Angeles, Boy Scout executives in Detroit, and the parents of student activists. The leak to the YMCA official was accompanied by a pretext telephone call from a "father" who was concerned that his son would come under the influence of an employee who in 1954 had been identified as a Communist by an FBI informer before HUAC. A follow-up pretext telephone call revealed that a special YMCA committee fired the allegedly subversive employee—without apprising him why he was being dismissed "on the advice of counsel since this might have led to a prolonged legal battle."[24]

The Bureau's dissemination of published HUAC hearings and reports did not begin with the new counterintelligence program. It dated from January 1939[25] and escalated under the Truman loyalty program. Because Truman's program required FBI and Civil Service Commission investigators to search HUAC files for information bearing on the loyalty of incumbent or applicant federal employees, two FBI agents were assigned permanently to the Committee file room. (Prior to March 25, 1947, when Truman established the loyalty program by issuing Executive Order 9835, Committee staff searched the files; after that date agency investigators did their own searching because file room staff could not keep pace.)[26] When President Eisenhower expanded the loyalty program in 1953 but did not specifically mention the Committee's files,

Hoover announced that the FBI continued to check the data accumulated by Martin Dies and HUAC in all federal employee security investigations.[27]

More importantly, six days after Truman issued Executive Order 9835, HUAC Chairman J. Parnell Thomas named John McDowell (R., Penn.), Richard Vail (R., Ill.), and John Wood (D., Ga.) to a three-man subcommittee that was to draw up a master list of subversive organizations. The first installment, scheduled to be completed and presented within a few days to Attorney General Tom Clark, was to serve as a guide for loyalty investigators. HUAC demanded the immediate dismissal of any federal employee who had been or remained a member of any proscribed organization. This list, and subsequent installments, had an immediate impact. The FBI treated the Attorney General's list of subversive organizations as only one list among many lists—and a rather limited one at that. If a federal employee was a member of a group listed by HUAC but not by the Attorney General, the FBI reported that fact to the Justice Department and to the appropriate loyalty board.[28]

The FBI also relied on the Dies Committee's Appendix IX, published in 1944 and aptly entitled *Communist Front Organizations*. Prepared when the Dies Committee's future was very much in doubt by a subcommittee headed by John M. Costello (D., Cal.), Appendix IX was a hastily compiled, rather careless cross-section of the Committee's files. When finished, it totaled seven volumes and just under 2,000 pages. Some 250 groups were labeled Communist fronts and the seventh volume consisted of a 22,000 name index. Although 7,000 sets were published at a cost of $20,000, the full Committee membership deemed Appendix IX irresponsible, expunged it from the record, and ordered the existing copies destroyed. Appendix IX was immediately removed from the Library of Congress and government document rooms. A few sets, however, had already been sold to private subscribers and government agencies. The FBI immediately cross-indexed its copy.[29]

When political scientist Robert Carr interviewed Richard Nixon and John Wood regarding the continued use of Appendix IX, both claimed to be unaware of its contents and the facts surrounding its controversial publication. In March 1950, however, Committee Chairman Wood announced that HUAC staff were updating Appendix IX to make it "a bible of subversive activities in the United States."[30] Appendix IX, of course, was already a bible of sorts and not only for intelligence and security officers. A Republican club in Chicago used it to redbait Senator Paul H. Douglas, and Senator McCarthy relied heavily on it because it was more extensive than the Attorney General's list. For example, of the twenty-eight alleged CPUSA fronts that McCarthy listed after New York City Municipal Court Judge Dorothy Kenyon's name, only four were cited by the Attorney General. According to ex-FBI agent Kenneth Bierly of *Counterattack*, "everybody has a copy"—including, among others, the staff of the American Legion's *Firing Line*, blacklister Allen Zoll of the National Council of American Education, and Richard E. Combs, counsel to the California Fact-Finding Committee on Un-American Activities. Appendix IX was so popular that a private organization reportedly reproduced it in 1954 to meet the needs of the blacklisters.[31]

The FBI and private-sector blacklisters also relied on another HUAC publication, the *Guide to Subversive Organizations and Publications*. Actively promoted by FBI agent Lee Pennington even before it was first published as a handbook in December 1948, the *Guide* declared 563 organizations and 190 publications subversive and was updated and expanded in 1951, 1957, and 1961. J. Edgar Hoover, for his part, furnished each field office with at least two copies and referred concerned citizens to the Committee's "convenient" report so they might "spot" fronts and "not be fooled into giving them . . . support."[32]

The FBI not only helped HUAC compile the various editions of its *Guide* (whether by directly leaking information to the Committee or through publicity given by the Committee to the testimony of FBI informers). FBI officials, in addition, monitored the various editions of the *Guide*, occasionally gleaning information previously unknown to the Bureau.[33] FBI officials and agents were most likely to use the *Guide* when preparing "characterizations" or "thumb-nail" sketches for dissemination outside the Bureau both to other government agencies and to friendly journalists.³⁴ Local FBI field offices were instructed to compile these sketches on five-by-eight cards and to review them periodically. These characterizations were not to be disseminated until they could be laundered (that is, until all of the sources or documentation cited were "public source" in nature). Confidential "T" symbols (to protect the identity of informants and sources such as break-ins, taps, bugs, trash and mail covers) were to be used only in the most unusual cases and, whenever used, were recorded not in the sketch but separately at the end. "T" symbols were to be replaced with "public source documentation" as quickly as possible.

The HUAC *Guide*, with over 100,000 copies in circulation, ranked as an authoritative public source second only to the Attorney General's list. In effect, the Committee's descriptions of the subversive organizations and publications listed in the *Guide* (excepting those also listed by the Attorney General) automatically became official FBI thumb-nail sketches and were quoted in full or in part whenever FBI reports characterized subversive organizations or publications. (The still-classified *Agents' Handbook*, dated February 1959, sec.49B 2m, p.66, spelled out the FBI's procedure for use of the HUAC's guide.)³⁵

The Bureau had long been in the intelligence laundry business—using HUAC as conduit for the furtive dissemination of political intelligence from its classified files. The so-called COINTELPROs, then, did not represent a change in FBI officials' anticommunist *Weltanschauung*. The counterintelligence programs of 1956 to 1971 differed from earlier FBI activities principally in that a complete paper record was created of FBI actions, a record that was maintained in both the central COINTELPRO file at Bureau headquarters and in the field office counterintelligence files. (In 1975 the former COINTELPRO–New Left supervisor claimed that the COINTELPRO caption was, in some ways, simply an "administrative device to channel the mail to" FBI headquarters.)³⁶ Under the various counterintelligence programs, field office proposals for disruptive or educational action, authorizations from senior FBI officials, and periodic summary reports recording tangible results were recorded in writing.

Prior to 1956 FBI officials had been reluctant to risk creating such a paper record of their political efforts. This reluctance stemmed not from a greater sensitivity to civil liberties but from a concern that formal record keeping practices could increase the FBI's vulnerability. Accordingly, written records of the Bureau's earlier assistance to HUAC and conservative newspaper reporters were destroyed under "Do Not File" procedures, falsified, or filed under the Bureau's individual case captions—making it difficult to ascertain the scope of the FBI's political activities without total access to the headquarters and field office files. In contrast, during the lifetime of the formal COINTELPROs, exactly 3,247 disruptive actions were proposed, of which 2,370 were carried out. This is not to say that the FBI's less formal activities ceased when COINTELPRO began. As Internal Security Section chief Alan H. Belmont noted in an August 1959 memorandum to Hoover, "the Counterintelligence Program is *one of the special programs* that we have devised to disorganize and disrupt the Communist Party" (emphasis added).[37]

One such program involved the dissemination of blind memorandums regarding subversive activities to local and state police officials. Another more formal program, begun in February 1951, authorized "the dissemination of information to appropriate authorities on a strictly confidential basis concerning Communist or subversive elements in public utilities or public or semi-public organizations." This so-called Responsibilities Program (Responsibilities of the FBI in the Internal Security Field) was launched on February 17 following Hoover's meeting with a group of state governors representing the executive committee of the 1951 Governors' Conference. All information volunteered by the FBI was oral and recipients included a "large number of state and local officials." The Bureau's role was not to be compromised; otherwise, as senior FBI officials noted, "our standard claim that the files of the FBI are confidential" would be threatened.[38] Participants in the Responsibilities Program included Chicago Police Commissioner Timothy J. O'Connor, who received derogatory information on social worker Milton Cohen, and Cincinnati city manager Wilbur R. Kellogg. One of the few participants to compromise the FBI during the life of this program, Kellogg received a briefing on a city employee and subsequently told "the press under political pressure that the Bureau was the source of his information."[39] Ohio Governor Frank Lausche was yet another participant. In 1951 Lausche requested and received FBI information on folk singer Pete Seeger and the Weavers—whose appearance at the Ohio State Fair was abruptly cancelled.[40]

As the episode with the Weavers suggests, the underlying purpose of the FBI's Responsibilities Program was to impose economic sanction (preferably unemployment) on individual dissidents. Teachers, both on the public school and the university levels, were especially vulnerable to these tactics. The FBI, for instance, alerted Harvard University officials to the one-time Communist affiliations of historian Sigmund Diamond and graduate student Robert Bellah and ran an indices check in early 1953 on every member of the faculty and staff at both Harvard University and the Massachusetts Institute of Technology after learning that HUAC and the McCarthy Committee would soon hold hearings on Communist infiltration of educational institutions in the Boston area. To assist HUAC's investigation, the local FBI office furnished Committee staff with the addresses of seventeen individuals whom the Committee intended to subpoena, including Harvard Law students Jonathan and David Lubell and five members of the Harvard faculty.[41]

That same year, after another Responsibilities Program leak in Philadelphia, Dr. George A. Bennett, dean of the Jefferson Medical College, told the local FBI office that three doctors on the Medical College faculty would be interviewed individually and "asked . . . to give full cooperation by divulging names of persons known in the past . . . as CP members." In the event they refused to cooperate, the three doctors would be subpoenaed by HUAC (preliminary arrangements had already been made through the Pennsylvania State Police and HUAC counsel Robert L. Kunzig). If they refused to answer all of the Committee's questions, they would be dismissed "as undesirable employees."[42]

The Un-American Activities Committee was in Philadelphia to investigate Communist infiltration of the teaching profession. HUAC originally intended to concentrate on "the Professional Section of the CP" and to expose college professors exclusively, but apparently abandoned this objective after Earl Fuoss, the ex-FBI agent directing the probe, learned of Milton Eisenhower's concern. (Milton Eisenhower, President Eisenhower's brother, was then president of Pennsylvania State College.) Fuoss also had difficulty obtaining "definite information regarding the Professional Section" of the CPUSA or specific college professors—besides the three "pinks" at the Jefferson Medical College and Temple University philosophy professor Barrows Dunham, who lost his job with Temple following his encounter with the Committee. Stymied in this approach, HUAC redirected its probe toward public school teachers after the Pennsylvania Attorney General's Office "offered the [Committee] all information in the files of the Pennsylvania State Police regarding Communist infiltration of the Philadelphia School System." Arrangements for this cooperation were made by Kunzig, a former assistant deputy attorney general for the state of Pennsylvania. The FBI (which had already forwarded "the results" of name checks on twenty-three Philadelphia teachers to SISS) aided HUAC's probe by directing Committee staff to unspecified "Confidential Sources" and by locating several prospective witnesses.[43]

Ultimately, HUAC subpoenaed over forty teachers. Twenty-six were discharged in early 1954 for "incompetence" following hearings before the Board of Education.[44] At least eight of the fired teachers had twenty or more years seniority in the Philadelphia school system. One teacher, Samuel M. Kaplan, eventually secured an office job in private business but even this job was not secure. FBI agents kept coming around to interview him and one of the agents who regularly pestered Kaplan was the very FBI man who had sought him out shortly before HUAC issued its subpoena. Wilbur Lee Mahaney, another teacher with over twenty years seniority, spoke freely about himself before the Committee but refused to discuss others. When the School Board imposed its suspension and the Committee added a contempt of Congress citation, however, Mahaney appealed to HUAC. After he identified sixteen associates as having been CPUSA members, the Committee assured him that it "would seek no further punitive action."[45]

The role of the FBI and its Responsibilities Program during this purge is clear. The Pennsylvania State Police received derogatory information on every subpoenaed Philadelphia school teacher. It should also be noted that the FBI routinely brought the names of public school teachers and college professors "identified [before HUAC] as communists by friendly witnesses" to the attention of "appropriate officials . . . in accordance with the . . . Responsibility [sic] Program"—and the Bureau defined "appropriate officials" broadly enough to include anticommunist school board members and university administrators.[46]

The Responsibilities Program clearly indicates that the launching of the first COINTELPRO in August 1956 did not represent a shift in Bureau policy. Nor can COINTELPRO be considered simply as a skeleton in the FBI's closet. Only a small number of the FBI counterintelligence actions conducted between 1956 and 1971 were carried out as formal COINTELPRO operations. The vast majority were thus not recorded in the central COINTELPRO file but were under other program files or individual case captions. For example, of the FBI's twenty leaks to the Un-American Activities Committee about the National Committee to Abolish HUAC only one was implemented as part of a formal counterintelligence operation.[47] Similarly, FBI Assistant Director DeLoach frequently disseminated "public source material" to the media as part of the FBI's "policy of continually analyzing the employment and activities of Security Index subjects"; the State Department Passport Office received "alert lists" of names and Bureau reports captioned "Passport Sanction," which quoted from HUAC's public record; FBI field office reports on the Black Panther party were distributed to several congressional committees; and Martin Luther King, Jr., was

210

subjected to extra-COINTELPRO harassment. Hoover approved one such operation after King's assassination, authorizing DeLoach to brief select HUAC members on King's allegedly subversive background so they could keep a bill to declare his birthday a national holiday bottled up in committee.[48] Earlier, when Joseph L. Rauh, Jr., criticized the Bureau for its lethargic enforcement of civil rights laws in a well-publicized speech before the National Students Association, the Crime Records Division distributed background data on the FBI's civil rights record to a number of friendly journalists—among others, Paul Harvey, Fulton Lewis, Jr., Miriam Ottenberg, Bob Allen, Ray Cromley, Edward J. Mowery, Ed O'Brien, Warren Rogers, and Ray McHugh.[49]

The FBI also selected for extra-COINTELPRO attention officials and associates of the Fund for the Republic, a non-profit educational corporation established by the Ford Foundation in 1952, and headed by such noted liberals as Paul G. Hoffman, Chester Bowles, Erwin N. Griswold, and W. H. Ferry. Fund priorities included the distribution of books, pamphlets, and films, and the awarding of outright grants to individuals and organizations committed to fighting racism and McCarthyism.[50] Given these priorities and the civil libertarian commitment of Fund leaders who believed that the FBI and HUAC, and not Stalinists, threatened American values, it was hardly surprising that the FBI attempted to "neutralize" the Fund or that FBI Assistant Director Nichols instigated the attack. The Fund, which is now known as the Center for the Study of Democratic Institutions and is no longer a politically adventuresome foundation, became a priority target in 1955 when it hired liberal Catholic activist John Cogley, previously of the Catholic Worker movement and *Commonweal*, to write a report on entertainment industry blacklisting. More importantly, the Fund had financed Richard Rovere's article on Harvey Matusow, an FBI informer who recanted, and had recently awarded a $25,000 grant to the Stanford Law School to study the testimony of four ex-Communist government witnesses—FBI informers Elizabeth Bentley, Whittaker Chambers, John Lautner, and Louis F. Budenz.

HUAC responded immediately by launching a preliminary staff investigation of the Fund for the Republic, while Fulton Lewis, Jr., began a series of radio broadcasts demanding a public probe by the Committee and that the Internal Revenue Service revoke the Fund's tax exemption. Lewis also denounced the Fund on television (he appeared on fifty TV stations) and in his syndicated column in the Hearst press. Supplied with information by the FBI and HUAC, Lewis was aware of confidential Fund projects and received copies of the organization's correspondence, which had been subpoenaed by Committee Chairman Francis Walter. Other media confreres with access to FBI files joined the assault. They included George Sokolsky, Westbrook Pegler, David Lawrence, Walter Trohan, Paul Harvey, and Frederick Woltman. FBI Director Hoover even sent Herbert Hoover, then a Stanford University trustee, a seventeen-page blind memorandum itemizing the alleged subversiveness of the Fund and its officers. Several eastern universities, including Georgetown, had already turned down the $25,000 Fund grant, and the former President convinced his fellow trustees to "examine" the award. However, the grant project was completed under Stanford law professor Herbert L. Packer's direction and published in 1962 under the title *Ex-Communist Witnesses*.[51]

Anticommunist liberals (notably Sidney Hook, Sol Stein, and Dwight Macdonald) also questioned the Fund's motives— while ACLU official Irving Ferman briefed Nichols on his contacts with Fund officer W.H. Ferry.[52] Cogley, for his part, received a HUAC subpoena three days after his report on blacklisting appeared. "We called you," Chairman Walter said, "for the purpose of ascertaining what your sources were in order to determine whether or not your conclusions were the conclusions that we would have reached had we embarked on this sort of project." HUAC and the FBI, moreover, endorsed Lewis's call for an IRS investigation, with Walter complaining that the foundation's "lack of objectivity" (its focus on congressional investigation of Communists, government security procedures, loyalty oaths, and regulation of immigration) clearly demonstrated that it was not "a bona fide educational . . . organization."[53]

The FBI-HUAC-Lewis effort to inspire an Internal Revenue Service investigation was not exceptional. It would later become a standard COINTELPRO technique, with the Bureau and the Committee establishing a particularly close liaison with the IRS "red squad"—the Special Service Staff (SSS).[54] Starting from at least the mid-1940s, the Committee consistently lobbied the IRS to investigate and revoke the tax exemptions of dissident political groups. The FBI at times endorsed these efforts, which were later legitimized in part by the public release of the Attorney General's list of subversive organizations.[55] In one instance in mid-1947, Karl Mundt worked with fellow Committee member John Rankin, Chicago attorney Thomas Creigh, and Hearst columnist Westbrook Pegler in an unsuccessful attempt to have the IRS revoke the tax exemption of the Friends of Democracy (FOD). This organization specialized in criticizing well-known personalities of the Right and was headed by L. M. Birkhead, a Columbia graduate and former Methodist minister who had advised Sinclair Lewis when he wrote *Elmer Gantry* and Clarence Darrow before he cross-examined William Jennings Bryan at the Scopes's "monkey trial." At the time, FOD's chief investigator was Avedis Derounian—an old enemy of Martin Dies and author, under the pseudonym John Roy Carlson, of the muckraking best-seller *Under Cover: My Four Years in the Nazi Underworld of America.* Much to Hoover's chagrin, Carlson, as he was generally known, billed himself as a former FBI undercover operative. Thus, on April 26, 1947, Hoover advised Pegler that Carlson had been utilized as a Bureau informer only because of a request by an Assistant Attorney General. His "services were . . . dispensed with [in October 1943]," Hoover added, "as he was contributing little of value." In his "Fair Enough" column three weeks later, Pegler dismissed Carlson as a "professional snoop" and "not a regular F.B.I. man," and demanded an Internal Revenue Service probe of the FOD's tax exemption.[56]

FBI interest in using the IRS to neutralize dissidents increased in 1950 when Congress passed the Internal Security Act. Among other provisions, this legislation prohibited tax exemptions for any organization deemed by the Subversive

Activities Control Board to be "Communist-action, Communist-front, or Communist-infiltrated." Accordingly, in May 1952, the House established a Special Committee to Investigate Tax-Exempt Foundations. Chaired by Edward Cox (D., Ga.) and after his death by B. Carroll Reece (R., Tenn.), this committee produced a detailed report in December 1954—a report based on privileged access to FBI files and compiled with the assistance of FBI personnel and ex-agents hired as staff investigators at the recommendation of FBI Assistant Director Nichols. The so-called Reece Committee determined that opposition to HUAC confirmed lack of objectivity. On this premise it claimed that Committee opponents such as Edward H. Levi, then a University of Chicago Law School dean, were biased and, therefore, should be denied grants by all right-thinking foundations.[57] Thereafter, the Bureau and the IRS worked closely to harry dissident activists and adventuresome foundations. Indeed, the counterintelligence program was only a few months old when the FBI forwarded the names of 336 carefully selected Communists to the Internal Revenue Service.[58]

THE CASE OF THE ROSENBERG-SOBELL COMMITTEE

Informal and formal counterintelligence operations to immobilize left-wing dissidents document the vested interest of FBI officials in the anticommunist politics of the Cold War era. Always eager to make radicals pay an economic price for their "heresy," FBI bureaucrats nonetheless went well beyond mere sanction. They promoted McCarthyism and defended its personnel (HUAC members and American Legionnaires) and machinery (the FBI informer system) against all critics—whether Communists, liberal congressmen, or private-sector civil libertarians from such organizations as the Fund for the Republic. The best illustration of FBI officials' priorities was their response to the lingering political debate over the Julius and Ethel Rosenberg atomic espionage case. Because this case seemingly confirmed the willingness of CPUSA members to spy on behalf of the Soviet Union,[59] FBI Assistant Directors

Nichols and DeLoach worked closely with the Un-American Activities Committee and the federal judge who had sentenced the Rosenbergs to death in an effort to discredit those who questioned their guilt.

The FBI concentrated on the National Committee to Secure Justice for the Rosenbergs and Morton Sobell (NCSJRMS). (Sobell, the Rosenbergs' co-defendant, had received a thirty-year prison sentence.) Bureau agents gathered intelligence through technical surveillances, anonymous sources, and trash and mail covers and used it in a series of pre-COINTELPRO, extra-COINTELPRO, and formal counterintelligence operations.

In April 1956, for instance, Nichols briefed Bill Hillman, a former Hearst reporter then helping Harry S. Truman write his memoirs, about the Saint Louis Committee to Secure Justice for Morton Sobell and its plans to approach the former President through a third party. Apprised of Nichols's warning, Truman told Hillman to relay his thanks and, further, "that Bill should tell the Director not to worry that if anybody approached him on the Rosenberg or Sobell matter he wouldn't even listen to them but will 'kick their ——' right out of the office."[60] On another occasion in May 1955, DeLoach directed the New York City SAC to assist George Williams, a HUAC investigator and ex-FBI agent, during his preliminary investigation of the NCSJRMS, and Williams was confidentially advised by the FBI that the IRS had recently audited the organization's books. Williams and other HUAC staff members continued to work closely with the Bureau before, during, and after the Committee's public hearings (which featured the testimony of FBI informers James W. Glatis and Herman E. Thomas). On August 6, 1955, the day after HUAC ended its hearings, President Eisenhower issued an executive order granting it access to IRS files to aid its effort to examine NCSJRMS fund raising activities in greater detail. A year later, the Committee released a detailed report entitled *Trial by Treason* that the FBI described as an "excellent 134-page summary . . . which sets forth the communist aspects of the Rosenberg case."[61]

Three years later, when a clemency petition signed by 282

clergymen urging President Eisenhower to free Sobell was given some publicity, DeLoach again assisted HUAC. The Committee, however, declined to implement the Bureau's plan to counter the petition by mailing *Trial by Treason* to 267 of the signers (whose addresses had been obtained by FBI agents from twenty-three field offices) "because of possibility of embarrassment and criticism." Accordingly, when another "clergy appeal" appeared in 1960, senior FBI officials instead "worked up background information . . . and . . . made it available to Crime Records Division for prompt exploitation in the mass media field." Hoover further ordered DeLoach to "bear down on this." Having arranged extensive publicity, DeLoach reported within a week:

> I have discussed this matter entirely with Fulton Lewis. He has all details. Our name, of course, will not be used. Lewis has hired an additional clerk in his office and is contacting by letter all clergymen whose names appear in the "Clergy Appeal" petition. He will give this matter considerable attention and plans to let us know the results prior to releasing the information publicly.
>
> After Fulton Lewis obtains the results of this matter and uses it on his radio program, we will then have Dave Sentner write an article regarding the same information. Sentner's article will be carried in the entire Hearst newspapers.[62]

FBI officials' relationship with Irving Kaufman, the federal judge who sentenced the Rosenbergs to die in the electric chair at Sing Sing, was far more disturbing. (When sentencing the Rosenbergs, Kaufman had implied they were responsible for the slaughter of thousands of American boys in Korea.) From at least May 1954, when at Kaufman's suggestion Nichols authorized the New York City SAC to furnish derogatory information on the Rosenberg-Sobell Committee to New York State Senator Bernard Tompkins and ex-FBI agent Nathan Frankel, the Crime Records Divison had worked with the judge to defend the Rosenberg trial and death sentence.[63] Following Nichols's retirement from the Bureau in late 1957, Kaufman became concerned that the FBI Assistant Director's successors were falling down on the job. Kaufman was particularly upset because Hearst reporter Jim Bishop, who had been working on a book about the Rosenberg case with Nichols's assistance, was not "making any progress." Advised by the New York SAC of Judge Kaufman's "impression that the Bureau had dropped out of the picture," DeLoach directed the SAC to "inform Judge KAUFMAN of the fact that officials at the Bureau had been working with BISHOP concerning the story . . . had been providing him with every possible assistance," and had "been steadily supplying him with information." "However," De-Loach lamented, ". . . there is no way that the Bureau can bring any pressure to bear on BISHOP to devote additional time to the story."[64]

EXPOSING THE BUREAU

As DeLoach's and Kaufman's complaints about Bishop's tardiness attest, the FBI was not omnipotent.[65] But if the emotional obsession with the Communist menace waned during the late 1950s, McCarthyism remained a prominent part of the American polity. In this sense, the FBI's efforts to sustain the myths of the Cold War while discrediting those who questioned their anticommunist ethos had a substantive effect. One need only recall the smearing of Martin Luther King, Jr., in the mid-1960s or the Johnson and Nixon administrations' fruitless attempts during the later 1960s and early 1970s to link indigenous protest at home with international communism abroad. Moreover, the responses of key congressmen and Nixon administration officials when the existence of an FBI counterintelligence program was first publicly compromised in 1971 confirms how pervasively the FBI had altered traditional American values.

On March 8, 1971, members of the self-styled Citizens' Commisson to Investigate the FBI broke into the Bureau's resident agency in Media, Pennsylvania, and stole approximately 1,000 FBI documents. Recording FBI practices in detail, these documents both compromised certain surveillance methods and highlighted the FBI's preoccupation with student antiwar groups and black activists. The Citizens' Commission then selectively and carefully released Xerox copies of these documents in batches to the press (the *New York Times, Washington Post*, and *Boston Globe*), sympathetic congressmen (George McGovern [D., S.D.] and Parren Mitchell [D., Md.]), organizations identified in the documents as targets, and individuals labeled therein as informants. One of these so-called Media papers, a September 16, 1970, memorandum captioned COINTELPRO–New Left, recommended that FBI agents exploit all opportunities to interview dissidents because it "will enhance the paranoia endemic in these [New Left] circles and will further serve to get the point across that there is an FBI agent behind every mailbox."

Other Media records, which the Commission periodically released to insure ongoing publicity, threatened the secrecy that surrounded the Bureau's domestic intelligence activities. Because it compromised the COINTELPROs, this burglary was directly responsible for FBI Director Hoover's April decision to terminate all formal counterintelligence programs for "security reasons." Influential newspapers, including the *New York Times* and *Washington Post*, demanded a congressional investigation, and the adverse publicity was further magnified by the details of the Bureau's bizarre attempt to solve the burglary (code named MEDBURG). In the midst of this probe, Hoover ordered a Bureau-wide switch to IBM machines because he thought the Xerox corporation had not been fully cooperative in assisting the FBI to identify the machine used to duplicate the Media papers.[66] More importantly, the Media papers inspired a series of scholarly critiques and conferences that concentrated on FBI surveillance practices, with the additional prospect that the Bureau's domestic intelligence investigations might become an issue in the 1972 presidential elections.[67]

From the FBI's perspective, the timing of the Media burglary could hardly have been worse. On February 23, 1971, under Sam J. Ervin's (D., N.C.) leadership, the Senate Subcommittee on Constitutional Rights began hearings on the impact of technology on the Bill of Rights, focusing that month on the massive U.S. Army intelligence network aimed at civilians—including Senator Adlai Stevenson III (D., Ill.) and Representative Abner Mikva (D., Ill.). (Under this program the Army occasionally employed COINTELPRO-type techniques on an ad hoc basis.) Then, on March 1, 1971, Senator McGovern released an anonymous letter, purportedly from ten FBI agents, alleging that FBI conviction statistics were padded and, further, that an inordinate amount of Bureau resources were devoted to polishing the FBI Director's image. (The Crime Records Division countered by circulating an anonymous memorandum dismissing McGovern's letter as a KGB concoction.) FBI agent Jack Shaw's seemingly arbitrary dismissal for mildly criticizing Hoover (actually for refusing a transfer to Butte, Montana) further reinforced McGovern's charges. When the Senate Subcommittee on Administrative Practice and Procedure attempted to explore Shaw's discharge, Hoover informed Subcommittee member Edward M. Kennedy (D., Mass.) that it "would not be appropriate" to comment because Shaw had filed suit. The FBI Director, however, had already outlined the FBI's position (the day before Shaw filed) in a letter to the *Atlanta Constitution*. Finally, Senator Edmund Muskie (D., Me.) secured an FBI document detailing FBI surveillance of congressmen and others attending an "Earth Day" environmental rally.[68]

Charges first made by Senator Joseph M. Montoya (D., N.M.) on March 19 and then expanded by House Democratic Majority Leader Hale Boggs (La.) in April received the most extensive newspaper coverage. Demanding Hoover's resignation, Boggs claimed that the FBI wiretapped the telephones of congressmen (he incorrectly claimed his own phone was tapped), spied on college campuses, and generally engaged in police state surveillance practices. Supported by the pilfered Media papers, Boggs's assertions should have precipitated a congressional probe or a Justice Department review of FBI domestic surveillance practices. Several members of Congress—including Representative Bella Abzug (D., N.Y.) and Senators Gaylord Nelson (D., Wis.) and McGovern—introduced resolutions calling for an investigation of allegations by Boggs and others. California Democrat Charles H. Wilson also introduced a bill limiting the FBI Director's tenure to ten years and setting mandatory retirement at age sixty-five. But all bills aimed at reforming Bureau procedures or initiating oversight hearings died in committee.[69]

Nixon administration officials immediately rallied to Hoo-

ver's defense. Attorney General John Mitchell claimed that the
Democratic majority leader was suffering from "Tappanoia"
(hinting at Boggs's heavy drinking at the time) while Deputy
Attorney General Richard G. Kleindienst wondered whether
he was "either sick or not in possession of his faculties." Charac-
teristically, the Bureau countered by disseminating in a blind
memorandum derogatory information about Boggs's drinking
habits. The Crime Records Division also drafted a speech,
delivered on April 30 by Congressman William Bray (R., Ind.),
that smeared the Bureau's critics en masse.[70]

Simultaneously, the Nixon administration sought to contain
the dissemination of the Media papers. Warning that publication could endanger national security and the lives of federal
agents, Mitchell announced that the stolen documents had been
carefully screened to create the false impression that the
Bureau was preoccupied with legal domestic dissent. Other
administration officials released documents implicating former President Johnson and several of his staff and cabinet
members, including Ramsey Clark and Joseph A. Califano, Jr.,
in domestic intelligence gathering activities. White House press
secretary Ronald Ziegler further attempted to minimize the
impact of the Media papers, Boggs's charges, and Muskie's
complaint of Earth Day surveillance by labeling these criticisms "blatantly political." (Earth Day spying was blatantly
political—a Nixon aide had specifically requested an FBI
report on the affair.)[71]

The events of March and April 1971 produced a backlash of
public and congressional support. A Gallup poll published in
May revealed that seventy percent of those interviewed rated
Hoover's performance either "excellent" or "good." And many
House members praised him on his forty-seventh anniversary
as FBI Director, challenging Boggs and other critics to produce
evidence to support their charges. House Republican leader
Gerald Ford (Mich.) summarily declared that the FBI had
never tapped the telephone of a congressman during those
forty-seven years. And Senate Democratic Majority Leader
Mike Mansfield (Mont.) called on "those who have legitimate
complaints . . . [to] present the evidence to the appropriate
congressional committees." Mansfield placed the burden of

proof on the FBI's critics, opposed a full-scale congressional investigation, praised Hoover, and claimed that the recent attacks on the FBI were "more noise than substance." In a crude attempt to politicize the issue, Senator William B. Saxbe (R., Ohio) warned that a Democratic victory in the 1972 presidential election would deprive the nation of Hoover's services. (Having concluded that the controversial FBI Director was overly cautious, in 1971 Nixon considered removing him—abandoning this plan only after concluding that it posed too great a threat to his own reelection prospects.)[72]

FBI officials categorically dismissed most allegations, but refused to document their denials or allow congressmen access to FBI records. Bureau officials declined to turn over documents to Congressman Henry S. Reuss (D., Wis.) after the Media burglary disclosed that his daughter, a Swarthmore College senior, was under FBI surveillance. More importantly, the Justice Department refused Senator Ervin's frequent requests for documents relating to any assistance the FBI might have provided to the Army's spying efforts. Ervin, in turn, refused to press for access to FBI files. Such an investigation was unnecessary, he announced, as his Subcommittee had uncovered no evidence of questionable Bureau activities.[73] For influential congressmen, such as Senator Ervin, the FBI's domestic political surveillance (in contrast to that of the Army) was legitimate. Ironically, the Ervin Subcommittee's insistence that Army officials provide certain sensitive documents resulted in the uncovering of the scope of the Army's domestic surveillance operation.

Although the FBI's noncooperative stance effectively precluded a meaningful congressional investigation of the FBI, it is also true that in March 1971 Congress did not demand access to the Bureau's relevent COINTELPRO files. The Media burglary might have terminated the FBI's *formal* counterintelligence operations; at the same time, the Bureau's symbiotic relationship with key congressmen successfully averted external congressional supervision. This success, however, did not end the matter, as public criticism of FBI activities mounted. In September 1971, in the midst of embarrassing publicity, Hoover fired FBI Assistant Director Sullivan, a man personally

responsible for many COINTELPRO techniques and initiatives. (Sullivan had publicly challenged Hoover's judgment.)
At the same time, as a group of distinguished scholars,
journalists, and former government officials were preparing
for a conference on the FBI at Princeton University, Bureau
officials launched a new and more ambitious offensive to
counter their critics.

The idea for a scholarly conference on the FBI was originally
proposed in February 1971 by H. H. Wilson of Princeton's
Politics Department and was quickly embraced by the recently
formed Committee for Public Justice (CPJ) and several
independent scholars—including Norman Dorsen of the New
York University Law School; former Attorney General Ramsey
Clark; Duane Lockard, chairman of Princeton's Politics Department; Burke Marshall, deputy dean of the Yale Law
School; Blair Clark, future editor of *The Nation*; and play-
wright Lillian Hellman. Held on October 29 and 30 and jointly
sponsored by the CPJ and the Woodrow Wilson School of
Public and International Affairs, the Princeton conference
attracted some fifty writers, panelists, and participants.[74]

With Robert Sherrill, Vern Countryman, Fred J. Cook,
Aryeh Neier, Thomas I. Emerson, Victor Navasky, Frank
Donner, and others scheduled to present papers, the FBI
decided, in the words of its Director, to "handle" this "group of
anti-FBI bigots."[75] On April 30, Hoover sent "thumbnails" of
ten CPJ activists to the Attorney General. Then, on May 5, one
week after Hoover terminated the counterintelligence programs (but not, "in exceptional circumstances," COINTEL-
PRO-type activity), Inspector Bowers of the Crime Records
Division briefed House Internal Security Committee Chairman Richard Ichord on the "subversive affiliations" of several
CPJ members. More detailed information was later furnished
to HISC's chief counsel, former FBI agent Donald Sanders, and
Ichord pledged to be alert for "an appropriate occasion
. . . whereby he or some other member of the Committee
could make use of it."[76]

Two occasions arose on October 28 and November 19 when
Ichord described Lillian Hellman's association with "about 100
different" Communist fronts, Frank Donner's "convenient"

reliance "on the fifth amendment when questioned about his connection with the Communist Party," and Telford Taylor's history of representing "Communist Party members before congressional committees." The HISC chairman went on to complain about "a whole gaggle of the beautiful people [who] have flocked to the Committee for Public Justice"—specifically, Jules Feiffer, Shirley MacLain, Candice Bergen, Mike Nichols, and Arthur M. Schlesinger, Jr.—and the likelihood of "extensive coverage from the practitioners of the new journalism, the east coast version."[77]

The FBI escalated its efforts during the month preceding the conference. After receiving two CPJ letters in confidence from William O. Bittman, a former Justice Department attorney who had been invited to attend the Princeton conference, the Crime Records Division began "preparing a detailed brochure-type memorandum concerning this conference which will include summary memoranda on 39 individuals mentioned in Bittman's two letters plus the members of the [CPJ] executive committee." Hoover ordered the CRD to "expedite" this project and, when it was completed, authorized the following actions: (1) the dissemination of FBI-authored "speeches to some of our good friends on the Hill," (2) a discreet suggestion to Ichord that he should "release appropriate material" on CPJ members, (3) oral briefings for "some of our good friends in the news media such as Victor Riesel, Bob Allen, Ed O'Brien, Ray McHugh, etc.," and (4) the cultivation of "Bittman so that we will be immediately advised of any further developments." Bittman was given "a detailed briefing regarding the individuals involved."[78]

All of these proposals were subsequently "handled." After contacting Ray McHugh of the Copley News Service, for instance, CRD chief Thomas E. Bishop reported to FBI Assistant Director W. Mark Felt: "I asked McHugh if he would be so kind to write a column on this matter which would clearly reflect the biased nature of [the CPJ]. Enclosed herewith is a copy of a column by McHugh which appeared in . . . the [October 24, 1971] . . . issue of all newspapers in the Copley chain. . . . Steps are being taken to have a copy of this column placed in The Congressional Record."[79]

The Bureau arranged to place the McHugh column in the *Congressional Record* by handing it, together with "background information," to Jack Cox, administrative assistant to Congressman Barry Goldwater, Jr. (R., Cal.), on November 1, two days after the Princeton conference closed. (Hoover also sent a thank-you letter to Congressman Floyd D. Spence, a Republican from South Carolina whose name graced the FBI's "Special Correspondents List," for his "thoughtfulness" in placing William F. Buckley, Jr.'s column on the CPJ in the *Congressional Record*.) The next day, Goldwater made a short speech on the Committee for Public Justice.[80]

Also on November 2, Republican Congressman John E. Hunt, a former New Jersey state policeman, contacted FBI Inspector Bowers. Bowers, who had already discussed the Princeton conference with Hunt and "furnished copies of the columns by William Buckley, Robert Allen, and Alice Widener," then met in Hunt's office with Hunt and his assistant, Ken Bellis; Ed Turner, an aide to Congressman Dan Daniel (D., Va.); Ronald Dear, an aide to Congressman Bill Archer (R., Tex.); Jerry James, an aide to Congressman Spence; Sid Hoyt, an aide to Congressman Samuel L. Devine (R., Ohio); Don Joy, an aide to Congressman Edward Derwinski (R., Ill.); Congressman Larry Hogan (R., Md.); and Jay Parker of the Friends of the FBI. The strategy concocted by this group called for Hunt to "take a 'special order' of one hour for himself and other Members to make remarks concerning the conference." Following the meeting, Hunt requested and received from the FBI "public source information concerning various individuals participating in the conference." He then assumed responsibility for dissemination "to the appropriate people without the FBI's being identified with it."[81]

On November 9, the day designated for Hunt "and several other congressmen" to "blast" the CPJ, brief speeches were given by Hunt, Spence, Hogan, Joe D. Waggonner, Jr. (D., La.), William M. Colmer (D., Miss.), William L. Dickinson (R., Ala.), and Jerry L. Pettis (R., Cal.). (Other congressmen had made commitments to "join in" and were apparently prevented from doing so only because the first seven speakers used up Hunt's hour.) Collectively, their remarks defended the

FBI's apolitical image, criticized the various papers presented at the Princeton conference (with Congressman Colmer blandly dismissing Robert Sherrill's paper on the Bureau's public relations machinery), and smeared the participants by linking them to some type of liberal-subversive plot. Hunt noted that Professor Lockard "had his two daughters go to Cuba" while Sherrill was simply described "as the Washington editor of the *Nation*"—as if no more need be said. Others (Vern Country-man and I. F. Stone) were "accused" of being active in the campaign to abolish the House Committee on Un-American Activities and its successor.[82]

The Crime Records Division, however, appeared to be fighting a losing battle as revelations of the FBI's sweeping domestic intelligence activities continued to mount. Writing in the January 27, 1972, edition of the *New York Review of Books*, former FBI agent Robert Wall made further damaging accusations, outlining in the process several counterintelligence strategies. FBI officials became increasingly apprehensive about these and other allegations and following Hoover's death on May 2, 1972, anticipated "congressional intervention."[83]

These fears proved warranted. Beginning in March 1973, Watergate-related revelations embarrassed Acting FBI Director L. Patrick Gray III and convinced many traditional Bureau supporters that something was wrong with the post-Hoover FBI. A more serious problem stemmed from a suit filed by NBC reporter Carl Stern under the Freedom of Information Act of 1966. On March 20, 1972, Stern requested "any documents which (i) authorized the establishment and maintenance of COINTELPRO-New Left; (ii) terminated such program and (iii) ordered or authorized any change in the purpose, scope or nature of such program." Following eight months of litigation and after in camera inspection, District Court Judge Barrington Parker ordered the release of the requested documents. Justice Department attorneys filed but later withdrew an appeal and then released COINTELPRO documents to Stern in December and again in March, exposing all formal counterintelligence programs excepting, inexplicably, COIN-TELPRO-Communist party.[84]

Simultaneous with the release of the first batch of COIN-

TELPRO memorandums to Stern, Acting Attorney General Robert Bork and Attorney General–designate William Saxbe initiated a departmental investigation. Composed of Justice Department attorneys and FBI agents, the so-called Petersen Committee, chaired by Assistant Attorney General Henry E. Petersen, did not actually examine the Bureau's intelligence files. Instead, FBI agents prepared summaries of these files that Justice Department representatives allegedly cross-checked for accuracy. Petersen later conceded that he had been conducting a "survey" rather than an "investigation," and "reasoned that if the Federal Bureau of Investigation were part of [the COINTELPRO probe] . . . it would tend to guarantee the integrity of the inquiry." FBI participation, instead, effectively neutralized what could have been a vigorous probe. The summaries prepared by FBI agents were bland and often patently misleading.

The disclosures contained in the partial report of the Petersen Committee's findings released on November 18, 1974, despite attempts by the FBI and Justice Department to sanitize the report, incensed key public and congressional leaders. Convening hearings on the COINTELPRO report on November 20, the House Subcommittee on Civil and Constitutional Rights heard testimony from Kelly and Saxbe. Chaired by Don Edwards (D., Cal.), one of over seventy former agents to serve in the House between 1950 and 1970, the Subcommittee sharply criticized past FBI practices and FBI Director Clarence Kelly's aggressive justification. While the Bureau's External Affairs Division quietly circulated (on plain white paper) its rationalization to supporters in the media, Kelly maintained that "for the FBI to have done less under the circumstances would have been an abdication of its responsibilities to the American people." Saxbe similarly contended that "most of the activities conducted . . . were legitimate . . . [and] in response to numerous public and even Congressional demands for stronger action by the Federal Government." In this same vein, the Petersen report concluded that "the overwhelming bulk of the activities carried out were legitimate and proper intelligence and investigative practices and techniques."[85]

The House Subcommittee's hearings on the Petersen report

could not uncover the true nature of the FBI's political activities. The Subcommittee was denied access to FBI files and thus could not adequately investigate the Bureau's surveillance practices. Congress's abdication of its oversight (supervisory) responsibilities or, at the least, its reluctance to mount a serious challenge to the FBI's refusal to allow Congress to review its files cannot be attributed to a lack of evidence. Attorney General Saxbe later claimed that he could not interest Congress in the Petersen Committee report and further that Senators Ervin, Byrd, Eastland, and Roman Hruska (R., Neb.) had "decided that no good purpose would be served by further ventilation."[86] As later congressional investigations documented, the accusations voiced in 1971 by Boggs, McGovern, and Muskie were not unwarranted. Perhaps fittingly, only one congressional committee responded in 1974 to allegations against the FBI (coincidentally initiating detailed staff reports and hearings concurrent with the Petersen investigation). And that committee was HUAC's successor—the House Internal Security Committee.

Few independent observers expected the Committee's investigation of the FBI to be either impartial or conclusive, and the inquiry certainly was not an adversary proceeding. HISC members were principally interested in ascertaining "the adequacy of the FBI's investigation of subversive activities in view of the creation of a so-called 'Plumbers Unit' in the White House, which suggested that in some ways the established investigative agencies . . . are not adequately serving their purpose." Blaming "an inept [Nixon] Administration" for the new problems that the FBI and other internal security agencies were encountering, the Committee was worried about the continuing breakdown in the Cold War domestic security consensus. "It is very difficult," John Ashbrook (R., Ohio) complained, "to even talk about internal and national security. People think you are talking about bugging the Democratic headquarters or breaking into [Daniel] Ellsberg's doctor's office." Dedicated to insuring that the FBI and other intelligence agencies would not be obstructed or inhibited "in the performance of their vital intelligence functions," Committee members hoped through public hearings to "facilitat[e] and, if possible, improv[e] that work." HISC Chairman Ichord particularly criticized the possibility of "severe restrictions placed upon the FBI."[87]

Scheduled to begin on November 8 with Deputy Attorney General William D. Ruckelshaus as the first witness, HISC's hearings were delayed by Ruckelshaus's resignation during Watergate's "Saturday Night Massacre." Ruckelshaus's replacement, Deputy Assistant Attorney General Kevin T. Maroney, was seemingly qualified to answer questions regarding the FBI's domestic intelligence operations. Maroney had helped organize the Justice Department's Interdivisional Intelligence Unit (IDIU) in 1967 and in 1974 was assisting the Petersen Committee's COINTELPRO probe. According to Richard Cotter, a twenty-six-year Bureau veteran and former chief of the Intelligence Division's research section, Maroney was "probably the most knowledgeable individual on the Department's staff regarding FBI security operations." Yet Maroney's testimony of April 8, 1974, unintentionally revealed the Justice Department's cavalier attitude toward COINTELPRO. Even though counterintelligence program documents had already been released to Carl Stern describing four separate COINTELPROs dating from 1961, Maroney erroneously asserted that the "so-called Cointel program . . . operated for about 3 years and discontinued in 1971."[88]

The Department of Justice's peculiar position partially explains Maroney's apparent unconcern (in minimizing both the constitutional issues raised by the counterintelligence programs and the policy issues of FBI insubordination and Department supervisory responsibilities). Justice Department obligations include the defense of executive agents against criminal charges and civil suits brought by the public. During the 1960s and 1970s, the Department also had a direct interest in safeguarding both the domestic intelligence gathering process (the IDIU) and techniques strikingly similar to COINTELPRO operations (such as its political use of federal grand juries). Equally important, the Department was either ignorant of FBI procedures and programs or, if not entirely uninformed (or misinformed), willingly ignored questions of legality and constitutionality and deferred to the FBI.[89]

HISC's objective during these hearings, in any event, had not been to uncover past FBI abuses and prevent their recurrence but to expand the Bureau's authority to investigate subversive activities—and, also, as HISC counsel Alfred M. Nittle put it, "the potential of subversive activities." Ichord indirectly commended the White Hate Group counterintelligence program, praising the Bureau's "creditable job" against the Ku Klux Klan and Minutemen: "You have destroyed them as viable organizations." Moreover, much of Maroney's testimony, and that of FBI Assistant Director W. Raymond Wannall, was devoted to lengthy expositions of the FBI's claimed authority (whether delegated by vague executive orders or criminal statutes) to conduct domestic intelligence investigations. For Nittle and Ichord, a further purpose of the hearings was to provide the FBI with a public forum. "There have been . . . many extreme and perhaps unfounded charges that the FBI is intruding into improper areas," Nittle announced, and ". . . they ought to have the opportunity to indicate that they were not doing so."[90]

The House Internal Security Committee might have intentionally avoided probing the FBI's COINTELPRO and other educational activities; another congressional committee soon conducted this inquiry. Holding well-publicized hearings in 1975 under the direction of Senator Frank Church (D., Ida.) and issuing spectacular and heavily documented reports in 1976, the Church Committee also highlighted the evisceration of Congress's supervisory role. But while the Church Committee seemed unclear as to whether its findings demonstrated the success or bankruptcy of a constitutional system based on separation of powers, there was scarcely a word about direct congressional participation in some of the FBI's most questionable activities. Through HUAC, after all, Congress had actively participated for nearly forty years in the political abuses that so outraged the Church Committee in 1975-1976. This contempt for the law characterized the activities not only of FBI bureaucrats J. Edgar Hoover, Louis Nichols, and Cartha DeLoach, but of two generations of red-hunting congressmen.

CHAPTER IX

Friendly Witnesses

From the Chambers-Bentley hearings of 1948 until the mid-1960s, FBI informers were the lifeblood of the House Committee on Un-American Activities. Although many FBI operatives who appeared before HUAC had already revealed their status as informants, under the COINTELPROs and other less formal programs Bureau officials frequently directed the Committee to potential witnesses or pressured those who were ready to be "surfaced" to appear before HUAC. In those cases where informers flatly refused to testify publicly, arrangements were sometimes made for them to confer with HUAC in executive session. This service provided the Committee with investigative leads and countless names that could be selectively released—as in 1953 when HUAC counsel Robert L. Kunzig interrupted his interrogation of an uncooperative witness to quote from FBI informer Bertha Grover's executive session testimony. By doing so, Kunzig was able to insert forty-three names in HUAC's public record. And for every person named before the Committee, whether by an FBI informer or another source, the reward was an FBI investigation. Bureau field offices were directed to "review . . . files, check . . . indices, . . . contact . . . informants . . . [and] ascertain if investigations should be instituted . . . on those persons who have not been separately investigated before."[1]

Most informants (Elmer Davis called them "seven-shot repeating witness[es]") needed no prodding from the FBI or HUAC to appear in public.[2] They were professionals in the strictest sense, receiving stipends when working undercover for the Bureau and later for their services as expert witnesses for the Justice Department in Smith Act prosecutions, Taft-Hartley Act hearings, and deportation and denaturalization proceedings. When no longer marketable as expert witnesses on the menace—whether because of the restrictive Supreme Court decisions of 1956–1957 or because they had testified too often before too many official government bodies against too many individuals and organizations—they often continued their professional anticommunist activities under the sponsorship of less prestigious benefactors. The most articulate informers were much in demand as authors and lecturers and as consultants to private blacklisters or to state and local government bodies investigating "un-American" activities.

FBI informers were most effective when testifying before HUAC, especially in the hometowns of the people they named as Communists or Communist dupes. And with HUAC convening in Chicago, Los Angeles, Portland, Seattle, New York, Pittsburgh, Charlotte, Philadelphia, San Francisco, Boston, Detroit, Milwaukee, and anywhere else Communist influence could be perceived, they had ample opportunity to do so until the mid-1960s, when the Committee begrudgingly halted its practice of touring the country.[3] Thereafter, HUAC chose to remain in the more familiar capital. In those cases where the Committee could not or would not (for fear of embarrassing protests) travel to the hometown of a particular dissident, HUAC relied on an alternative strategy. Encouraged by the Committee, and often by the FBI Crime Records Division as well, local newspapers inevitably (and often spectacularly) publicized charges of CPUSA membership made by an FBI informant and legitimized by a congressional investigation.

THE FBI INFORMER SYSTEM

Until late 1939, when President Roosevelt approved a radical expansion in FBI intelligence operations, Bureau use of informers had been minimal. When appearing before the House Appropriations Committee on November 30, 1939, to ask for a supplemental appropriation of $1.5 million for the "intelligence work which has been initiated this year," the FBI Director requested $100,000 for the "confidential fund" to pay informers.[4] By June 1940, the White House learned that Bureau informers had penetrated every "principal radical organization," "all groups of pronounced nationalistic tendencies," and "other groups of un-American principles." As of July 18, 1942, an additional 20,718 "confidential sources" were deployed in some 4,000 industries producing war materials.[5] From 1940 to the mid-1970s, the Bureau employed 29,166 "security" informants and 7,839 "extremist" informants.[6] Between 1966 and 1976 the FBI disbursed $2,476,485 to over 5,000 informers and other confidential sources in Chicago alone. During a sixteen-year period beginning in 1960, the FBI employed some 1,300 informers at an estimated cost of $26 million to infiltrate or monitor the Socialist Workers party.[7]

Most security and extremist informers were either recruited by FBI agents and then placed within an activist group, or were already members of the group who were "turned."[8] Others, such as Herbert Philbrick, simply volunteered. Philbrick, who later became a regular witness before HUAC, claimed to have been so inspired by FBI Director Hoover's speech in 1940 attacking foreign "isms" before the American Legion National Convention in Boston that he immediately volunteered his services as an informer. Later, in 1953, the Crime Records Division helped Philbrick write his memoirs.[9] Disillusioned Communists who had not yet broken with the party were perhaps the most heavily recruited. When James Kendall, a member of West Coast Local 90, Masters, Mates and Pilots Union, decided to leave, he simultaneously wrote Communist party officials in New York and the local FBI office to advise them of his decision. FBI agents promptly contacted Kendall and attempted to intercept his letter to Communist head-quarters in an unsuccessful attempt to turn him into an undercover operative. When this mail intercept failed, Kendall instead appeared in 1953 before HUAC.[10]

FBI agent-recruiters also resorted to intimidation. CPUSA members were often given the choice of informing on their comrades or facing criminal prosecution under the Smith Act. Aliens were threatened with the prospect of deportation. The threat of a phone call to an employer might also force a vulnerable radical to cooperate. Other dissidents were given the choice of assisting the FBI or receiving a HUAC subpoena. Those who rejected Bureau advice were often lectured by the Committee during their later testimony. "As a matter of fact," Harold Velde asked one witness in Portland, "didn't an FBI agent come to your door and you slammed the door in his face when he attempted to ask you . . . about your previous Communist record?" (FBI field offices were required to submit reports "reflecting the up-to-date activities" of prospective witnesses for HUAC and other congressional investigating committees and to interview these witnesses, when possible, *before* they were subpoenaed—advising the Senate Internal Security Subcommittee in 1953 that a random sampling of thirty-five witnesses who had invoked the Fifth Amendment before a congressional committee revealed that twenty-six had been previously interviewed by Bureau agents; the remaining nine were approached after testifying.) If coercion or appeals to patriotism and greed did not work, the FBI sometimes offered other inducements. Former FBI agent William Turner has claimed that draft deferments were used to attract student informers during the Vietnam War era.[11]

The practice of granting draft deferments to FBI informers was fairly widespread even prior to American involvement in Vietnam. One such deferment involved Charles Benson Childs, a student at the University of North Carolina who served as a paid FBI informant ($100 per month plus expenses) from October 1950 until he surfaced in April 1955 to testify against Smith Act defendant Junius Scales. During his testimony, Childs graphically described how an instructor at a CPUSA school taught him to kill a person with a pencil. Later, in March 1956, Childs appeared as a witness before HUAC in Charlotte. Then, in 1958, he testified at Scales's second trial in Greensboro and appeared as a government witness at the trial of John Hellman in Butte, Montana. FBI officials deemed Childs's services so important that in 1951 they arranged his deferment. For a time, even Childs did not know why his local draft board classified him 4-F. But when Smith Act defendant Scales attempted to find out, Justice Department prosecutors were "advised of . . . the extreme concern of Selective Service

Headquarters over the possibility that the Selective Service file on CHILDS would be produced in court." After considering the objections offered by the prosecution, the trial judge reviewed Childs's Selective Service file and ruled that it would not have to be produced.[12]

Informants who infiltrated specific groups—whether local CPUSA branches or suspected Communist fronts—were so highly regarded by the FBI because they could provide membership lists, correspondence, and financial records without FBI agents having to conduct "black bag jobs." FBI informer Angela Calomiris, who served as financial secretary for the CPUSA West Midtown Branch in New York City, conceded this advantage: "I had access to internal documents that the F.B.I. agents could have secured only by subpoena for specific purpose." Nor was Calomiris unique. She became an FBI operative in 1942, at the request of FBI agent and later *Counterattack* founder Kenneth Bierly, and testified against the top CPUSA leaders at the Foley Square Smith Act trial. Later, she published her memoirs, dedicated them to Bierly, and appeared before HUAC. Presumably, Committee members also had access to documents provided by Calomiris—and not only those made public during the Foley Square Smith Act trial. HUAC regularly subpoenaed the files and correspondence of organizations that had already been rifled by FBI informers. For instance, HUAC's 1,300-page appendix detailing the "un-American" character of the American Committee for the Protection of the Foreign Born (ACPFB) was based not only on ACPFB records subpoenaed by Chairman Francis Walter but on files supplied by a former Bureau operative, Marion Miller, who had masqueraded as a member of the organization's Los Angeles chapter.[13]

These were not isolated instances. When Matthew Cvetic unveiled himself as an undercover FBI man before HUAC in 1950, he claimed to have in his possession voluminous files taken from the Pittsburgh office of the American Slav Congress. These files, Cvetic said, would implicate several congressmen in the international Communist conspiracy. But when preparing to deliver his cache to the FBI, Cvetic announced that he had "lost" the most sensitive documents—

specifically, those linking unnamed congressmen to the CPUSA. George Dietze, a fellow FBI informer and HUAC witness, had better luck. Dietze was German born but became a naturalized citizen in 1929 and an FBI informer in 1940. He allowed local CPUSA members to use his Pittsburgh engraving shop as a meeting place. Dietze never attended party meetings, but "a hidden microphone in the shop picked up practically every word spoken at approximately 550 Communist sessions held there during the past several years." It is not known whether Dietze was running the operation himself or was acting under instruction from the Bureau, but he did turn the tapes over to the FBI.

Dietze's and Cvetic's documents and tape-recorded conversations inspired HUAC to resort to an old method of gathering evidence. On March 10, 1950, reportedly at the direction of the Committee's chief investigator, Louis Russell, a squad of Pittsburgh policemen raided American Slav Congress headquarters. The police confiscated thirty boxes of name cards, metal addressograph plates, and mailing lists, and four boxes of three-by-five cards containing résumé-type information on Slav Congress members and prospective members. According to the *Pittsburgh Post-Gazette*, the police promptly turned these files over to HUAC. Five months later, Pennsylvania State Judge Michael Angelo Musmanno led the vigilante group Americans Battling Communism on yet another raid on CPUSA offices in the Bakewell Building. The choicest documents were again made available to HUAC by way of FBI informer Cvetic—inspiring the Committee to subpoena Cvetic for additional testimony and to place several of the seized documents in its public record.[14]

The Committee's style did not change much over the years. In 1967, agents of the Chicago Police Department red squad burglarized the offices of the National Conference for New Politics and turned some of the intercepted intelligence over to HUAC. Nine years later, Jerome Ducote, a former deputy sheriff in Santa Clara County, ex-Birch Society official, and one-time member of the California State Republican Central Committee, admitted to committing seventeen burglaries of leftist offices in the late 1960s and early 1970s. After Ducote broke into the office of *Ramparts* magazine (which had just published an article detailing CIA ties to the National Students Association) in 1967, wealthy California grower Stephen D'Arrigo arranged for him to take his cache to Washington where it was shown to the CIA, Congressman Charles Gubser (R., Cal.), and HUAC's general counsel and chief investigator. Upon returning to California, Ducote allowed another CIA agent to review the stolen documents.[15]

THE MATUSOW FLAP

For a while during the 1950s, FBI informers were promoted as national heroes and a few emerged as minor celebrities. Matthew Cvetic, for one, appeared before HUAC four times and received $12,500 for movie rights to his career and $6,500 for a magazine serial. When the film version of Cvetic's life, *I Was a Communist for the FBI*, premiered at Pittsburgh's Stanley Theater, the mayor declared April 19, 1951, Matt Cvetic Day and held a special luncheon for him at the William Penn Hotel. *I Was A Communist for the FBI* was also produced as a successful radio serial—with FBI assistance in production of both the radio show and the film.[16] In contrast to Cvetic, Louis Francis Budenz never became an FBI operative while a CPUSA member. After his defection and 1946 testimony before HUAC, however, Budenz claimed he spent some 3,000 hours consulting with Bureau agents. Until health problems forced him into semiretirement in 1957, Budenz earned some $61,000 ($20,000 from magazine articles, $17,000 from book royalties, and $24,000 from lectures) as a professional anticommunist in addition to his regular salary as a professor at Notre Dame and Fordham Universities.[17]

By the mid-1950s the credibility of Cvetic, Budenz, and other FBI informers was seriously challenged. Suffering from "depressive reaction" and "alcohol addiction," Cvetic checked into the psychiatric ward at St. Elizabeth's Hospital in March 1955 to receive electric shock treatments. Budenz took the Fifth Amendment twenty-three times when cross-examined in a deportation proceeding against an alleged Communist—even though he had earlier advised the Senate Subcommittee on Immigration and Naturalization of the need to expel all Communists, subversives, and members of party fronts from the United States. Another FBI informer and HUAC witness, Paul Crouch, was declared a "tainted" witness by the United States Supreme Court, and Manning Johnson's career as FBI confidant and on-call Committee witness ended in 1954 when he accused Ralph Bunche of being a Communist. When testifying before the Subversive Activities Control Board, Johnson was asked if would "lie under oath in a court of law rather than run counter to your instructions from the FBI." Johnson said he would, "if the interests of my government are at stake. In the face of enemies, at home and abroad, if maintaining the secrecy of the techniques of methods of operation of the FBI who have responsibility for the protection of our people, I say I will do it a thousand times." Eventually, the Justice Department, which had paid Johnson over $9,000 as a consultant, initiated a half-hearted perjury investigation. Johnson, in turn, later became an insurance salesman and, before he died in 1959, an early member of the John Birch Society.[18]

The most serious threat to the informer system involved Harvey Matusow, an ex-FBI operative who, unlike Cvetic, Budenz, Crouch, and Johnson, recanted. Matusow joined the Communist party in 1947 on his own initiative. Quickly disillusioned, he volunteered his services to the government in 1950, serving as a full-fledged FBI spy for $70 a month until the CPUSA expelled him in January 1951 as an "enemy agent." Matusow then joined the Air Force and wrote a letter to HUAC denouncing lax military security standards. As evidence, he cited his own presence in the Air Force. After HUAC launched Matusow's public career in November 1951, chief investigator Donald T. Appell helped him secure a position as a consultant to the Ohio Un-American Activities Commission. From there, Matusow was available for a fee to SISS, the SACB, Smith Act prosecutors, the McCarthy Committee, and several congressmen (he was an effective campaign speaker). The *New York Times*, the Hearst press, the American Legion, and the New York City Board of Education also contracted for his services, but his most lucrative sideline was peddling subscriptions to *Counterattack.* He received a $9 commission on each subscription.[19]

In early 1954 Matusow began to reconsider his vocation, confessing his perjuries as a professional witness to Methodist Bishop G. Bromley Oxnam.[20] When Oxnam publicly announced the recantation, however, Matusow assured HUAC that the bishop was lying. Nevertheless, in March 1954 Matusow signed an affidavit admitting he had lied under oath when testifying before the Senate Internal Security Subcommittee. By the end of the year President Eisenhower himself was deeply troubled by Matusow's conversion, and Justice Department officials moved quickly to contain the controversy.

The Justice Department maintained that Matusow had invariably told the truth when testifying as an ex-Communist and that his more recent assertions as an ex-ex-Communist, in contrast, were part of a sinister plot to discredit the entire FBI informer system. There was just enough circumstantial evidence to make this story seem credible. In February 1955, two CPUSA attorneys for Clinton E. Jencks, an official for the Mine, Mill and Smelter Workers Union, approached the repentant informer. They were interested in Matusow's earlier testimony, which had led to Jencks's conviction for falsely executing a Taft-Hartley Act anticommunist affidavit. After consulting with Matusow, one of these attorneys, Nathan Witt, contacted publisher Albert E. Kahn. Kahn contracted with Matusow to publish a complete exposé of his testimony in the Jencks's case as well as his entire career as a professional informer.

Matusow's book, *False Witness,* spurred the Justice Department, HUAC, SISS, and the FBI into action. Attorney General Brownell convened a grand jury to investigate the affair and Matusow was promptly indicted for perjury. Then, in an April 1955 effort to document HUAC Chairman Walter's charge that the CPUSA had planted Matusow as a government witness, Cartha DeLoach authorized the FBI's New York Field Office to assist HUAC investigator George Williams in locating individuals whom the Committee wanted to interrogate re-

238

garding the Matusow matter. According to Brownell, Matusow was spearheading "a concerted drive to discredit government witnesses, the security program, and ultimately our sense of justice."[21] Matusow was eventually convicted and received a five-year sentence in September 1956 for lying under oath when he had stated earlier that he lied under oath.

Other vested interests also joined the fray. J. Edgar Hoover searched the Old Testament for quotes to justify the use of informers; the Senate Internal Security Subcommittee subpoenaed Matusow, Witt, and Kahn, recommended that Matusow be cited for three counts of contempt of Congress, and then released a 120-page report buttressed by 1,300 pages of testimony detailing the alleged Communist machinations behind *False Witness*; and HUAC member Donald L. Jackson suggested that Richard Rovere be subpoenaed as he might be able to aid the Committee's ongoing investigation. Rovere had just published a caustic account of the affair ("The Kept Witness") in *Harper's*—a general assault on the informer racket that nonetheless conceded a "distinctly Stalinist air about" Matusow's recantation. President Eisenhower also celebrated Matusow's conviction, concluding that it would strengthen the administration's loyalty-security program. In private, Eisenhower professed little faith in the honesty of ex-Communists. He confided to Brownell in 1953 his belief that "they are such liars and cheats that even when they apparently recant and later testify against someone . . . my first reaction is to believe that the accused person must be a patriot." Matusow, for his part, served his time and then launched a new career as a professional computer-hater with the International Society for the Abolition of Data Processing Machines.[22]

THE HUAC CONNECTION

When responding to the Matusow scandal, Brownell and Hoover also argued that the affair demonstrated the need for FBI informants to remain anonymous in all loyalty proceedings. Anonymity would guarantee the confidentiality of FBI files, prevent the accused from cross-examining informants or presenting witnesses in his own behalf, and circumvent court-ordered discovery in FBI files. As one adverse (to the FBI) reaction to Matusow's recantation, the Supreme Court reviewed the Jencks case in 1957 and ruled that defense attorneys must be granted greater access to pretrial statements made by government witnesses to the FBI. FBI efforts to protect the identity of informants, of course, had long been established practice. Since 1949, Bureau reports identified informers by name or by category (and used the term "informant" to mask such investigative techniques as break-ins, wiretaps, microphone surveillance, and mail openings) only on their administrative page. Within the body of FBI investigative reports, informants were identified by informant symbols (for example, "confidential informant T-2"). These procedures enabled the FBI to exercise total control over informers and to circumvent supervision by the Justice Department and by the courts.[23]

FBI officials were not committed to maintaining the confidentiality of their informers at all times. Rather, Bureau officials were more concerned with choosing which informers would testify publicly and under what circumstances.[24] This concern arose from the desire to maximize public dissemination of information from informants and other confidential sources—but to do so without embarrassing the Bureau. This could only be done by restricting access to the FBI's so-called "raw" (unevaluated) intelligence files and thereby denying the constitutional right to due process of accused persons—whether before HUAC, federal loyalty boards, or other tribunals.

To further safeguard their informants and, as well, to prevent potential embarrassment to the Bureau when complying with provisions of the Internal Security Act of 1950, the Communist Control Act of 1954, and other Cold War legislation, FBI officials ordered all field offices to prepare "Appendix-Witnesses Sections" detailing the background of individual informants and their willingness to testify publicly against specific investigative targets.[25] Though these Appendix-Witnesses Sections applied primarily to potential prosecutions or the requirement that Communist, Communist-action, and

Communist-front groups register with the SACB, such cataloguing of witnesses was an effective method of control. Furthermore, it could easily have been applied to prospective HUAC witnesses. Whether or not the FBI developed such a formal method of determining which of its informers would appear before HUAC, Bureau officials, in close cooperation with Committee staff, arranged to have dozens of informers testify publicly before the Un-American Activities Committee.

The advantages of such arrangements were obvious. Despite the excesses of the Truman and Eisenhower loyalty-security programs, accused federal employees were accorded at least some semblance of due process and, if not granted access to FBI informer files, were sometimes allowed to cross-examine their accusers. More importantly, loyalty boards, the SACB, and the courts (when interpreting Cold War legislation or reviewing dismissals of federal employees under the Eisenhower loyalty-security program) were required to comply with rules of evidence. The Supreme Court decisions of 1956–1957, in addition, specifically challenged not only federal loyalty-security program standards but most of the legislation designed to contain the CPUSA. Nor surprisingly, these decisions further limited the scope of permissible testimony by FBI informers.

If FBI and Justice Department efforts to prosecute Communists under the Smith Act or to force their registration with the SACB were constrained and if the Eisenhower administration's effort to purge federal employees was similarly checked by the courts, HUAC could at least partially fill the void. For even though one Supreme Court decision (*Watkins*) of 1956–1957 appeared to have dealt a blow to the Committee's freewheeling style and ability to send recalcitrant witnesses to jail, in reality HUAC was henceforth required only to inform hostile witnesses why their testimony was relevant to the Committee's announced investigative task. The other Supreme Court decisions actually enhanced HUAC's status as a supplemental public forum for FBI informers. HUAC, of course, had served such a purpose prior to 1956–1957 during testimony from FBI informers that could not be given under the loyalty-security program, SACB and deportation hearings, and in

Smith Act trials. The Committee was not required to respect rules of evidence, did not demand corroborative evidence, and did not permit cross-examination of FBI informers under any circumstances. No defined set of charges limited the testimony of FBI informers who appeared as friendly HUAC witnesses, and no cooperative witness was ever prosecuted for perjury.

During Smith Act trials, in contrast, defense counsel cross-examination made federal prosecutors reluctant, at times, to introduce hearsay evidence. In some cases, arrangements were then made to present such testimony before HUAC. In April 1954, for instance, four FBI informers, Bernice Baldwin, Milton J. Santwire, Stephen J. Schemanske, and Harold M. Mikkelson, appeared before the Committee in Detroit. All four had recently testified in the Detroit Smith Act trial. (Originally scheduled to begin in November 1953, the HUAC hearings were delayed until after the trial concluded—a decision agreed to after Committee member Kit Clardy conferred with Judge Frank A. Picard and U.S. Attorney Fred W. Kaess.)[26] Mikkelson, who appeared in public session before the Committee, had been a paid FBI informer from November 1948 (he was sent to the FBI by a *Detroit News* reporter who was then completing a series of articles on the CPUSA) until December 1953 when he testified against the Detroit Smith Act defendants. Mikkelson had also received over $3,000 from the Detroit Loyalty Committee. HUAC heard Santwire and Schemanske (FBI informers for fourteen and fifteen years respectively) in executive session but quickly decided to release their testimony to the press.[27] Mikkelson, Schemanske, and Santwire were presented during these hearings, as they had been two months earlier by Smith Act prosecutors, simply as concerned citizens motivated by a sense of patriotic duty. But it was only during the subsequent appeal by Detroit Smith Act defendants that the patriotic motives of Mikkelson, Schemanske, and Santwire were seriously challenged.

Cross-examination by defense counsel revealed that all three were well-paid FBI informers and, further, that Santwire had perjured himself when initially denying the charge that the Ford Motor Company supplemented his $90-per-month FBI salary. Through Schemanske, Santwire received $4,800 from Ford's Investigation Section to act as a labor spy. (The Ford

Investigation Section, which replaced Harry Bennett's head-busting Service Department in 1945, was managed by John Bugas, ex–Special Agent in Charge of the Detroit FBI office.) Under cross-examination and after a compulsory discovery order produced an incriminating Ford memorandum describing Schemanske as a "confidential informant," Santwire admitted his relationship with the Ford Motor Company. (Schemanske received some $70,000 as a Ford spy in addition to the $10,800 he was paid by the FBI.) Santwire also claimed the prosecution had been aware of this relationship at the time he perjured himself. Given an alias and a "cover" job to conceal his connection with Ford, Schemanske remained undercover during the first seven weeks of the Smith Act trial, continuing to report not only to the FBI and Ford but also to his brother-in-law, a policeman assigned to the Detroit subversive squad. Santwire, who committed perjury to protect Schemanske because "he was a holder of Confidential Information," was completely candid with defense attorneys only after learning that Schemanske would also testify. He was not indicted for perjury.[28]

On appeal, the credibility of these FBI informers was undermined. The Circuit Court of Appeals remanded the case to a lower court for a new trial and in September 1958 the government moved to dismiss the Smith Act indictments. But for the hundreds of people whom Santwire, Schmanske, Mikkelson, and Baldwin named before HUAC as Communist conspirators, there was no legal recourse. Persons named before HUAC could not sue for libel as the Committee's public record was considered privileged under the Constitution's speech and debate clause. Nor did they have recourse to the judicial appeals process available to Smith Act defendants—unless they also happened to be indicted and prosecuted for contempt of Congress. HUAC hearings, in short, served the dual purpose of publicizing information in FBI files and creating a permanent, libel-proof record.

COUNTERINTELLIGENCE AND THE INFORMER

HUAC could easily exploit the testimony of Smith Act witnesses Baldwin, Mikkelson, Santwire, and Schemanske, and other FBI informers who testified at Smith Act trials or SACB hearings. Committee staff simply monitored these proceedings, identifying those FBI informers who would serve their purposes. Committee staff, however, also worked closely with the FBI to insure that HUAC's planned hearings would not interfere with other ongoing FBI activities. After interviewing FBI informers, HUAC investigators invariably submitted names of those who could be exposed as CPUSA members to the Bureau for clearance. If for any reason the FBI did not want a particular person identified, the Bureau advised the Committee. To protect active informers, the FBI always submitted the name of their operative along with four or five other names so that the Un-American Activities Committee would not learn which one the Bureau considered sensitive. HUAC invariably deferred to the FBI.[29]

When FBI informer Bernice Baldwin first appeared before the Subversive Activities Control Board on February 12, 1952, for instance, a HUAC staff member advised the *Detroit Times* that she had been under Committee subpoena for weeks. HUAC had delayed public announcement of her scheduled appearance as a Committee witness and did not even talk to her, according to a reporter for the newspaper, "because they [HUAC staff] knew of the key role she was playing for the FBI." Similarly, in Flint, Michigan, an FBI informer known only as "Witness X" in 1954 named numerous auto workers—leading to a rash of firings, harassment, and beatings. And in May 1955, when probing Communist activities in Newark, HUAC relied on yet another anonymous FBI informer, who had named at least seventy-five people as active in local CPUSA clubs. The Committee protected the FBI man's identity, but used the names he provided to discredit union organizers and business agents during public hearings.[30]

These examples were not atypical, but the evolution of FBI-HUAC cooperation on the informant issue was slow and often tortuous. Indeed, the clash of the Bureau and the Committee over the use of informants rivaled the Hoover-Dies feud of 1940. With regard to informants, the FBI wanted it both ways. If pleased with the newspaper headlines generated by FBI informants testifying in whatever city HUAC happened to be in and the "good work" HUAC "is doing . . . generally," FBI officials were concerned with the havoc an unrestrained Committee could wreak on the informant system. Interference with other Bureau priorities would also be likely. For instance, when HUAC investigator William Wheeler contacted one of the Foley Square Smith Act witnesses (apparently Herbert Philbrick) while the trial appeal was still in progress, Hoover dubbed Wheeler's conduct "outrageous." (The FBI Director was more ambivalent toward possible constitutional improprieties after the conviction of the Foley Square defendants was upheld and the government had a solid precedent for sending Communists to jail under the Smith Act.) Similarly, the Committee's habit of sending out one hundred or more subpoenas in any given community inevitably led to five, six, or more FBI informants being caught in the dragnet. Other informants would sometimes be named as Communists during the subsequent hearings because, as FBI officials rightly concluded, "it is not known what the unfriendly witnesses will do if subpoenaed and if they testify."[31]

"The uncovering of these informants," Hoover complained to Attorney General J. Howard McGrath in March 1950, "has resulted in panic and unrest among the remaining informants and it is becoming increasingly difficult to keep them under control." In such cases, local FBI agents were directed to contact the named informants for the purpose of preventing "them from going to the newspapers and discontinuing their services." When uncontrolled HUAC testimony led to situations "wherein the informants jobs [sic] is jeopardized," their employers were "notified of their true status" and, to "assist in the retention of the informant[s]," "additional compensation" was provided.[32] Working with Deputy Attorney General Peyton Ford, FBI officials went to the source of the problem and hammered out an "arrangement . . . wherein the Bureau can look over the names of people to be mentioned before the Committee in order to determine if there is a name of a confidential informant listed."[33]

Hoover did not expect immediate results. "I have little hope," he noted after D. Milton Ladd advised him that this arrangement had been agreed to, "that anything will be done as

headlines mean more to them [HUAC] then ultimate security."
And in a way, Hoover was right. The "definite agreement and
arrangement" which Ford helped negotiate broke down on a
fairly regular basis in the early 1950s, with HUAC counsel
Frank S. Tavenner, Jr., emerging in Hoover's mind as the chief
culprit. The FBI responded by working with carefully selected
staff members and avoiding, whenever possible, all contact
with Tavenner.

This arrangment worked especially well in early 1952 during
the Committee's visit to Detroit. During an in-service training
session on February 8, FBI Assistant Director Nichols directed
the head of the Bureau's Detroit office to work closely with
HUAC investigators in order to protect ongoing FBI investigations and active informants. The Detroit SAC was also
ordered to "cooperate with Mr. [Donald] Appell [the HUAC
investigator in charge of the hearings] in furnishing information
of a general nature, such as addresses of persons in which they
were interested, etc., but that any request of an unusual nature
should be cleared with" FBI headquarters. During the subsequent hearings Appell maintained "almost daily liaison" with
local Bureau agents, prompting the SAC to recommend that
the FBI-HUAC cooperation in this instance serve as a model
for future Bureau policy.[34]

FBI Assistant Director Ladd agreed, in a memorandum
approved by Hoover, and FBI agents immediately began
working with HUAC staff in preparation for the Committee's
visit to Chicago. In addition to coordinating the testimony of
informants in this case, HUAC received blind memorandums
on several unfriendly witnesses and was directed to four FBI
informants. (Louis Russell originally contacted Nichols with a
request for "*old informants whom they* [HUAC] *might utilize*
or . . . anybody whom they might break and use." Nichols,
for his part, considered the submission of the names of "former
Communists who might be in a position to help [the Com-
mittee]" a favor which would be in the FBI's "interest.") When
Hoover approved this specific assistance and more generally a
"close liaison with the House Committee on Un-American
Activities both in Washington and in the field," however, he
cautioned his subordinates: "don't get too optimistic and let our

guard down. I want to see this over a long pull before I will be convinced."[35] The arrangement, as Hoover predicted, never did smooth out completely, but the ex-FBI agents on HUAC's staff and other reliable personnel, including Appell and Wheeler, continued to solicit the names of friendly witnesses and background information on those unfriendly witnesses whom the Committee wanted to subpoena.

As the 1950s wore on the FBI's assistance to HUAC in this area expanded. Particularly after the Supreme Court decisions of 1956–1957 curtailed SACB activity and frustrated Justice Department efforts to prosecute Communists under the Smith Act, the FBI routinely directed HUAC investigators to active FBI informants or "retired" operatives who had not yet revealed their careers as underground agents. Though fairly widespread prior to the restrictions imposed by the Supreme Court, this practice accelerated during the late 1950s. The FBI, indeed, favored unveiling informers for the first time at HUAC hearings as a specific disruptive technique under the counter-intelligence programs.

In one instance, several FBI informers who operated out of the Pittsburgh Field Office decided to terminate their service in May 1958. They complained to the Bureau that as Communists they were "subjected to constant ridicule and embarrass-ment." As a result, "they requested that a public disclosure be made of their cooperation with the Bureau in any manner agreeable to the Bureau." FBI officials arranged to have HUAC contact these informers and, on May 23, they testified in executive session before the Committee. The Pittsburgh SAC was then directed to find out when HUAC would release the testimony provided by these informants or call them to testify in public session. (HUAC returned to Pittsburgh in March 1959 for three days of public hearings.) When the Committee released the testimony, the Pittsburgh Field Office was di-rected to prepare a letter addressed to all Communist party members in the area, signed by the recently surfaced FBI operatives. This letter was then apparently published in a Pittsburgh newspaper, clipped out and reproduced after it appeared in the press, and mailed to carefully selected Communists.[36]

On occasion, the FBI had to persuade its informers to appear before the Committee. In October 1958, the Los Angeles Field Office reported that the CPUSA Southern California District was attempting to identify the source of HUAC's information. The Committee had recently held hearings in Los Angeles, revealing a detailed knowledge of the most mundane proceedings of this unit. To draw suspicion away from a highly productive FBI informer, the Los Angeles SAC requested authority to persuade a less valuable informer to testify before HUAC "inasmuch as the CP could logically conclude that this was the source upon which the HCUA based its first hearing." The appearance of a current Communist as a friendly witness, the SAC noted, "would have a devastating effect on the morale of the CP" by creating "the impression within the CP that, despite all their security precautions, their activities are known to the FBI down to the finest detail." After the earlier HUAC visit to Los Angeles, FBI informers further reported that many local Communists were on the verge of leaving the party "as they felt that their jobs and their ability to earn a living was [sic] being adversely affected." This situation could be fully exploited, the SAC reasoned, only "if the committee could be presented with a current CP member as a cooperative witness."[37]

To convince HUAC to return to Los Angeles, the SAC suggested that "the approach to the committee . . . be made in Los Angeles to" HUAC West Coast investigator William Wheeler. Because the Committee's earlier visit to the city resulted in a civil suit filed against Wheeler by two hostile witnesses, the SAC predicted that Wheeler "would eagerly accept the opportunity to call a further hearing in order to hear a cooperative witness and to actually obtain information." (HUAC did resume its investigation of the CPUSA Southern California District in February 1959 and eight months later launched a new probe.)[38] The only problem, the Los Angeles SAC said, was his informer's reluctance to appear before HUAC.

Neither the SAC nor senior FBI officials were overly concerned: the Bureau granted the Los Angeles office authority to persuade the informer to testify. Senior FBI officials agreed that "this informant's appearance before the HUAC should cause considerable concern and disruption inside Party circles and should add materially to the previous disruption caused by the earlier HCUA Los Angeles hearing." The SAC was only required to request prior Bureau approval before contacting Wheeler and to insure that the informer did not possess any notes, reports, or records of any kind that she may have prepared while in FBI employ. The Los Angeles office was also directed to review her planned HUAC testimony so as not to jeopardize active FBI informers or current "investigative techniques." Finally, the SAC was ordered to submit plans for exploiting her testimony following her HUAC appearance.[39]

The additional plans for exploiting this informer's testimony remain unknown. They may have been similar to a later counterintelligence operation proposed by the same FBI office. In 1960, the Los Angeles SAC planned to discontinue the services of yet another informant by involving her in a "final disruptive action." The SAC specifically recommended that this informant testify before HUAC and apparently FBI officials agreed—though heavy deletions in the FBI documents recording this suggestion make it difficult to determine exactly what took place. In any event, after being advised that the informer had no plans to write a book or to seek other publicity (though she was willing to testify before HUAC or any other appropriate government body), senior FBI officials suggested that additional publicity might be arranged by having "a cooperative newspaper reporter" prepare "an article or series of articles for publication . . . in the Los Angeles area."[40]

Despite wholesale deletions in the documents, it is clear that FBI officials provided informant testimony before HUAC and further ensured newspaper coverage of HUAC hearings and the attendant revelations of discontinued undercover operatives. These strategies were not confined to the Los Angeles and Pittsburgh field offices. In 1959, senior FBI officials directed the Cleveland Field Office to arrange for an informer to testify before HUAC and to gather information that could be used in a parallel effort to gather information that could be regarding CPUSA leader Gus Hall and the "Negro question." This newspaper publicity, to appear simultaneously with the informer's public appearance before the Committee, was contrived by the Crime Records Division, working through its contacts in the "Negro publishing field."[41]

Not all agreements between HUAC and the FBI to unveil undercover operatives were carried out as formal COINTEL-PROs. Julia Brown, for instance, had originally been a CPUSA member for less than a year before leaving the party in 1948. At the FBI's request, she rejoined the Communist party in 1951 and served until May 1960 as confidential informant CV 264-S. Though anxious to testify publicly, Brown waited nearly two years before HUAC summoned her in June 1962 to assist the Committee's investigation of Communist activities in the Cleveland area. (She had testified before HUAC in executive session for four straight days beginning on August 23, 1961; the FBI secured a transcript of her secret testimony and described her as "an effective and cooperative witness, who identified numerous individuals as CP members in Cleveland.") Between May 1960 and June 1962, Brown never revealed her status as a one-time FBI employee, but was confident "I would one day be called to testify [publicly] before the House Committee on Un-American Activities." She found it "frustrating to know that all I had reported remained locked in FBI files, never to become public, never to be used against the enemy, unless I was called before the Committee." If Brown's appearance before HUAC was not listed as part of the counterintelligence program, the FBI's Cleveland Field Office nonetheless used her revelations as the basis for several disruptive actions carried out as formal COINTELPRO operations.[42]

The Bureau not only chronicled the employment problems encountered by uncooperative witnesses named by Brown and other FBI informers in Cleveland, but may have arranged some of these problems. According to recently declassified FBI files, a HUAC witness whom Brown named suffered business losses immediately after his appearance before the Committee. Later, his business "failed completely as a result of newspaper publicity." Furthermore, the local FBI office advised Bureau headquarters of its follow-up strategy: "In accordance with Bureau letter of 6-13-62, the list of individuals named by BROWN before HUAC will be further reviewed for possible counterintelligence plans." Other COINTELPRO documents reported that two people, one an employee of an electrical contractor doing work at NASA, were fired after Brown named them. As a result of newspaper publicity (partly inspired by the FBI) arising from the HUAC hearings, another Bureau source noted that the mother of a local dissident would not permit any more meetings of the Provisional Organizing Committee for a Marxist-Leninist Communist party to be held in her home. And after Violet J. Tarcai, vice-president of the Cleveland chapter of the Women's International League for Peace and Freedom (WILPF), was identified as a "one-time Communist," yet another FBI counterintelligence report advised senior FBI officials of the positive effect the HUAC hearing had in delaying scheduled WILPF elections.[43]

Similarly, a Minneapolis Field Office COINTELPRO report claimed as a "tangible result" that at least one city resident summoned by HUAC and named by an FBI informant in 1964 had been dismissed by his employer. The local FBI office also mailed the transcript of the HUAC hearing to the Superintendent of the Catholic Bureau of Education in Saint Paul—an operation designed to force the dismissal of yet another uncooperative Committee witness.[44] The next year, in Boston, the local FBI office reported (again, in a COINTELPRO report) that someone was fired after "exposure before HUAC hearings." But it abandoned plans for additional economic harassment upon learning that the files of the State Unemployment Security Office were not considered "public source" data and thus might compromise the Bureau. The Boston office had intended to use these files when preparing a blind memorandum regarding the exposed HUAC witness for release to the news media.[45]

A COINTELPRO report of the FBI's Los Angeles Field Office also recorded the difficulties of a HUAC witness and her husband during the early and mid-1960s. The FBI described this couple as Security Index subjects who "have been uncooperative on interview and have refused to testify before the House Committee on Un-American Activities." After the wife appeared before HUAC, a representative of the right-wing Citizens Information Center brought her testimony to the attention of the La Miranda, California, PTA. PTA officials promptly asked her to resign. When she refused, they deactivated the local PTA chapter to which she belonged. Later, this local chapter was reactivated without the recalcitrant witness. Cub Scout Pack 440 used a similar tactic against this woman and her husband, a tactic described by the Los Angeles Special Agent in Charge as an attempt "to discreetly remove the [deleted] from their positions."[46]

FBI officials' efforts to evoke economic sanctions—to punish radicals and, more importantly, to sensitize the community to the "threat" that having even one Communist in a local factory or office posed to the national security—occasionally had unintended results. FBI informers who were unwilling to compromise their relationship with the Bureau suffered economic and other sanctions themselves. When Matthew Cvetic named FBI informers George Dietze and Joseph Mazzei as Communists during HUAC's 1950 hearings in Pittsburgh, both lost their jobs. Though Dietze immediately declared that he, too, was an FBI employee and was rehired, Mazzei remained undercover. Hamp Golden, another FBI informer whom Cvetic identified, was removed as president of Canning Workers Local 325, was blackballed by the American Legion and the Veterans of Foreign Wars, and twice was forced to move. When Golden unveiled himself before HUAC nine years later, he claimed his children "couldn't play out in the yard when we [Mrs. Golden also worked for the FBI] were first disclosed as Communists and the neighbors would call them Commies." Reubin J. Harden—yet another FBI operative inadvertently exposed by Cvetic as a CPUSA organizer from Cambria County—kept his cover despite being fired from his job as a miner, "roughed up," and being evicted from his apartment, which was vandalized (rocks were thrown through the windows). Hardin later appeared as a government witness during the Subversive Activities Control Board investigation of the Civil Rights Congress and, in 1959, testified before HUAC. Harden told the Committee of his extraordinary odyssey as an undercover informant who served the FBI and various other police agencies from 1931 to 1954.[47]

Despite attempts by the FBI and HUAC to coordinate

informant testimony, the experiences of FBI operatives in Pittsburgh were not unusual. Warren Olney III, chief of the Justice Department's Internal Security Section, told of one FBI informer with thirteen years undercover service who stopped attending church because he was hounded by anticommunist neighbors. Another informer's children were ostracized, and his marriage nearly broke up. Joseph A. Poskonka, an FBI informer from 1943 until September 1958, had been inadvertently identified as a Communist in 1952 by FBI informer and HUAC witness Roy Thompson. Poskonka told his story to the Committee seven years later: "But at the same time my family and myself have been discriminated very badly and hurt, cut up to pieces because people pointed and thrown bricks and slapped me in the face and done everything imaginable because the neighborhood I lived in, there are no Communists and they can't stand a Communist."[48]

FBI officials were sensitive to the problems encountered by dedicated informers like Poskonka even after the anticommunist obsessions of the McCarthy era had waned. As part of the FBI's counterintelligence program in 1960, for instance, the Boston Field Office considered a plan to have television cameramen and newspaper reporters force their way into a CPUSA district convention. FBI officials half-heartedly endorsed this proposal, fearing the resultant publicity might attract HUAC's attention. They observed that public hearings at this point "could jeopardize the [deleted] informants participating in the Counterintelligence Program who because of individual employments cannot afford public disclosure since it would result in the loss of their livelihood."[49]

Though the FBI continued to furnish information to HUAC and its successor, widespread use by the Committee of FBI informers ended in the mid-1960s.[50] After Lola Belle Holmes and Lucius Armstrong named over one hundred Chicagoans as Communists in 1965, FBI informers only rarely testified in public. There were notable exceptions—in 1971, for instance, the Bureau culminated a two-year campaign of leaks to HUAC's successor by arranging for informants Lawrence L. and Betty Sue Goff to testify against the Revolutionary Union

(RU), predecessor to the Revolutionary Communist party and the subject of a Bureau "nationalities intelligence" probe. The Goffs' testimony, combined with a ten-page blind memorandum and other FBI information "confidentially furnished" to the Committee, also provided the basis for a detailed staff report on the RU. The Goffs' public testimony regarding this FBI-described "militant, violence-prone, pro-Chicom [Chinese Communist], Marxist-Leninist organization," was in any event the exception rather than the rule. (Senior FBI officials apparently rejected an additional suggestion of the agent in charge of the Revolutionary Union investigation to have the Committee subpoena several RU leaders.)[51]

FBI informant coverage of Communist and other radical groups continued as a top Bureau priority, but unfriendly HUAC witnesses no longer conveniently relied on the Fifth Amendment when confronted with the testimony of FBI informers. Quite simply, the Committee and the Bureau were forced to abandon the practice of public confrontation. This noticeable shift in tactics, however, did not reflect a change in the Cold War assumptions and priorities of FBI officials or HUAC members. Nor was McCarthyism dead. And in some ways, reflected in the escalation of COINTELPRO strategems during the late 1960s, the antiradical political style favored by FBI officials and conservative congressmen was more pervasive than ever.

CHAPTER X

Operation Abolition

From the birth of the Dies Committee to the early Cold War years, opposition to HUAC was one of the few issues capable of uniting the diverse American Left. Thereafter, the coalition of groups and individuals opposed to HUAC was essentially radical. Liberal opposition to the Committee was inconsistent, periodically sacrificed to amorphous notions of national security. Prior to the hardening of the Cold War, congressional debates on the Committee's funding resolutions and contempt of Congress citations were often fierce. And Presidents Roosevelt and Truman, though they sometimes supported the Committee, constantly sought to contain the conservative investigators, some of whom seemed more concerned about the disciples of Franklin D. Roosevelt than Joseph Stalin.

As late as January 1949, the Truman Administration worked closely with Speaker of the House Sam Rayburn to deny two of HUAC's most incorrigible members, John Rankin and F. Edward Hébert (D., La.), reappointment to the Committee.[1] One of the replacements for Rankin and Hébert was Rayburn's protégé, Francis Walter. The new HUAC chairman, John S. Wood, was relatively subdued—at least when compared to his predecessor, J. Parnell Thomas, and his successor, Harold Velde. Moreover, most dissidents, left-wing organizations, civil libertarians, and liberals unequivocally opposed HUAC.

When the Cold War set in things changed. Liberal opposition faltered. Only ten votes were cast in the House from 1950 to 1961 against HUAC's appropriations. Of these ten votes, Minnesota Democrat William Wier cast three. Emanuel Celler (D., N.Y.), Thomas Ashley (D., Ohio), Edith Green (D., Ore.),

255

Robert Kastenmeier (D., Wis.), Barratt O'Hara (D., Ill.), James Roosevelt (D., Cal.), and William F. Ryan (D., N.Y.) also opposed the Committee, but only Celler's vote in 1953 was cast during the depths of the Cold War.[2] And the nation's most prestigious civil liberties group, the American Civil Liberties Union, not only tempered its criticisms of HUAC but unknowingly employed a high-ranking official, Irving Ferman, who regularly reported to the FBI on efforts to enlist ACLU support for a national campaign to abolish the Committee.[3]

HUAC appeared invincible. Congressional opposition to the Committee began to mount only after 1965, when Don Edwards offered a motion to refer the HUAC funding resolution (H.Res. 188) to the Appropriations Committee for public hearings. The House voted 333 to 58 against Edward's motion, and H.Res. 188 passed 360 to 29. The 29 opposition votes, nonetheless, were significant. Not until the climate changed in the mid-1970s were HUAC's critics again able to mobilize even that much congressional support.

The Committee remained entrenched as a standing committee of the House of Representatives. Quite simply, many congressmen ignored the substantive issues raised by the Committee's critics, choosing instead to view any challenge to HUAC as a threat to the congressional committee system itself. A roll-call analysis of the votes on Edwards's motion and HUAC's funding resolution in 1965 revealed that the median seniority of HUAC supporters was three times that of its opponents. Furthermore, the formal congressional leadership was nearly unanimous in supporting the Committee. Of the three most powerful committees in the House (Ways and Means, Rules, and Appropriations), only the Appropriations Committee had a single member opposed to HUAC's funding resolution. Though appalled by the Committee, many otherwise liberal congressmen supported its ever increasing demands for more money because of political expediency. According to former Attorney General Francis Biddle, few congressmen were willing to risk challenging the Committee. A vote for HUAC's appropriation, as civil libertarian Irving Brant observed, was a kind of "insurance premium." If a congressman refused to "pay," he might be red-baited by an opponent when standing for reelection.[4]

Democratic congressional leadership, of course, occasionally challenged the Committee, attempting through indirect means to moderate its behavior. In the late 1940s and 1950s, House Speaker Rayburn banned television cameras from HUAC hearings (a ban that was largely ignored), announced that only attorneys would be appointed to the Democratic side of the Committee, and, to reform HUAC, urged Francis Walter to accept the chair. To save taxpayers' money, Walter eliminated some extravagances—among others, the leather-bound HUAC identification cards favored by his predecessor, Velde. Nevertheless, Walter was not much interested in reform. In the long run he represented little improvement from the full-throttle red-baiting of Velde or Thomas.[5] Walter, too, had grand plans for HUAC. He intended to rename it the Committee on Internal Security, Nationality and Migration and hoped it would assume jurisdiction over immigration, naturalization, and passport legislation.

Given the institutional workings of the House and the incorrigible nature of HUAC personnel, the Committee did not mend its ways under Walter's tutelage. Neither the institutional explanation nor a narrow focus on HUAC members, however, can fully explain the Committee's remarkable longevity. Attempts by Rayburn and others to contain the Committee also failed because HUAC was assisted by one of the most powerful lobbying groups in the capital. "The FBI," as one Washington editor succinctly put it, "will never permit Congress to curb the Committee."[6] FBI officials continuously monitored congressional efforts to moderate HUAC—as well as more radical plans to abolish it. More importantly, the Bureau consciously attempted to influence both the congressional debate over HUAC's future and public perception of the Committee's service to the nation.[7]

Thus, the 1957 HUAC report, *Operation Abolition*, detailed the alleged Communist influence in the New York–based Emergency Civil Liberties Committee (ECLC), the Los Angeles–based Citizens Committee to Preserve American

257

Freedoms (CCPAF), and other activist organizations whose primary goal was to abolish HUAC. The FBI, in turn, kept the ECLC and the CCPAF under constant surveillance and regularly leaked information to HUAC regarding CCPAF strategy. Furthermore, *Operation Abolition* not only contained political dossiers on prominent ECLC activists—among others, Clark Foreman, Corliss Lamont, Harvey O'Connor, Morton Stavis, Carey McWilliams, I. F. Stone, Curtis MacDougall, and Broadus Mitchell—but received Hoover's endorsement. The FBI Director wrote Walter that "real Americans are not going to be fooled . . . by efforts to discredit your vital task."[8] Copies of Hoover's letter were then inserted into every copy of *Operation Abolition* for mass distribution.

The FBI also monitored Communist party efforts in 1958 to have Eleanor Roosevelt pressure Senator John F. Kennedy (D., Mass.) into taking a stand against HUAC's forthcoming visit to Boston. Local Communists, or so the FBI suspected, intended to contact Mrs. Roosevelt through "liberal forces in Boston that . . . 'some of us know.'" The next year, when James Roosevelt introduced a bill to abolish the Committee, Hoover again praised the investigators in a letter to Clyde Doyle. HUAC member Doyle then quoted from the FBI Director's letter when opposing Roosevelt's resolution.[9] FBI officials, however, were not content merely to endorse the Committee or to service HUAC requests for specific Bureau files. They also purposefully sought to discredit the Committee's critics. FBI files on the National Committee Against Repressive Legislation (NCARL), formerly the National Committee to Abolish HUAC (NCAHUAC), for example, confirm that the FBI forwarded derogatory political information regarding the NCAHUAC to HUAC at least twenty different times.[10] In turn, the cooperative Committee gave wide publicity to this information, which it had received either on an ad hoc basis or as part of the FBI's formal counterintelligence program against the Communist party. An FBI memorandum, approved by Hoover, disclosed the purpose of this covert relationship: to "expose, discredit, or disrupt" the NCAHUAC. FBI Assistant Director Fred J. Baumgardner described the Bureau's intent in greater detail:

258

There is considerable agitation for the abolition of the HCUA, much of which is being instigated by communists. Everytime it is possible to expose the communists working behind the scenes, this should be done. . . . Should the communists be successful in having the HCUA abolished, it is believed the next direct target would be the FBI. Therefore, the HCUA, in addition to carrying out its objective of exposing communists, is actually a buffer target between the communists and the FBI.[11]

THE NATIONAL COMMITTEE TO ABOLISH HUAC

Founded in 1960 by retired Wall Street banker James Imbrie, ex–New Dealer Aubrey Williams, civil libertarian Alexander Meiklejohn, and American Friends Service Committee chairman emeritus Clarence Pickett, the Los Angeles–based NCAHUAC's sole purpose had been to abolish the Committee on Un-American Activities.[12] Reflecting the intensity of FBI officials' concern over the possible success of this effort, even before the public anouncement of the National Committee's existence, FBI Director Hoover ordered the Los Angeles SAC to "expedite" an investigation of the NCAHUAC. In addition, memorandums "suitable for dissemination" were to be included with all reports submitted to Bureau headquarters.[13]

One recipient of this dissemination strategy was HUAC. In late August 1960, Cartha DeLoach forwarded information gathered by Bureau informants "to his sources at HCUA." Then, when the National Committee's existence was publicly announced in September, detailed characterizations of the new organization as a Communist front appeared in the *Los Angeles Examiner* and the American Legion's *Firing Line*—apparently based on information contained in FBI files. (The Legion disseminated even more detailed information on NCAHUAC supporters to such prominent citizens as Charles J. Kersten, a former Republican congressman and self-proclaimed "psychological warfare" consultant to Eisenhower.) A HUAC press release to United Press International three weeks later, also based on FBI files and timed to coincide with the NCAHUAC's first formal meeting in New York City, led conservative columnists Fulton Lewis, Jr., and Jack Lotto to reiterate these Communist-front charges. Within the next nine months, at least twenty-three FBI investigative reports and letterhead memorandums on the NCAHUAC were disseminated; in addition, there were a sizeable number of FBI Crime Records Division leaks to its media contacts.[14]

HUAC members, of course, were not content to rely exclusively on the FBI's efforts to discredit their critics. Even before the NCAHUAC was organized, Walter responded to an advertisement in the *Washington Post* that called for the Committee's abolition by releasing dossiers on some of the signers to the *Brooklyn Tablet*. Walter also inserted this derogatory information into the *Congressional Record*, a tactic that HUAC member Gordon Scherer (R., Ohio) repeated in 1962 to discredit the signers of another abolition petition appearing in the *New York Times*. Similarly, HUAC forwarded to its supporters complete dossiers on persons connected to the NCAHUAC for use when debating National Committee representatives.[15]

Both the Committee and the FBI monitored everything said or written about HUAC's activities, including book reviews of William F. Buckley, Jr.'s collection of sympathetic essays, *The Committee and Its Critics*. And when the NCAHUAC was preparing to publish a NCAHUAC- and Southern Conference Educational Fund–sponsored pamphlet by Anne Braden, *HUAC: Bulwark of Segregation*, FBI agents across the country were ordered to secure a copy prior to publication. Braden's husband, Carl, learned of the Bureau's interest in late May 1964 when his printer advised him that FBI agents had discreetly contacted him. Braden responded by forwarding a copy of his wife's pamphlet to the Bureau's Nashville resident agency. "Please let us know," Braden wrote in an accompanying letter, "if you can use more [copies] and we'll be glad to supply them. . . . We appreciate your interest in our work." Unknown to the Bradens, the FBI had obtained a copy of Anne's pamphlet more than three weeks earlier. By May 1, the Bureau had prepared a letterhead memorandum summarizing the pamphlet chapter by chapter—complete with an addendum characterizing Carl and Anne Braden as Communists. After noting that the pamphlet contained "no reference to the FBI or the Director," senior FBI officials forwarded copies of their letterhead memorandum to Assistant Attorneys General J. Walter Yeagley and Burke Marshall, the military intelligence agencies, and possibly other government agencies.[16]

Ostensibly, the Bureau initiated its investigation of the NCAHUAC to ascertain whether it should be required to register as a Communist-front organization under provisions of the Internal Security Act of 1950. FBI reports to the Department of Justice recommending such a listing, however, were consistently rejected in 1962, 1963, 1964, 1966, and 1972. "The evidence is insufficient," Department of Justice officials concluded, to begin proceedings against the NCAHUAC either as a Communist-front or a Communist-infiltrated organization. FBI reports, the Department reiterated, contained "no indication . . . that . . . the CP,USA and its leaders have influenced its activities primarily to advance the objectives of the CP,USA, or the world Communist movement." In July 1963, Yeagley specifically instructed the FBI to discontinue submitting "prospective summary reports" on the NCAHUAC. From February 1962 to July 1963, the Bureau had forwarded twelve summary reports and memorandums to the Department.[17]

Yeagley's order simply reduced the flow of FBI reports to the Justice Department. Unresigned to the decision not to initiate Subversive Activities Control Board hearings, the FBI intensified its surveillance of the NCAHUAC. Field offices were chastised for their reports' "paucity of information," and FBI officials demanded the continued submission of thoroughly analyzed memorandums suitable for dissemination outside the Bureau.[18] Significantly, these efforts were not limited to strengthening the Bureau's case for SACB hearings. Hoover never intended to confine FBI surveillance of HUAC's opponents to ascertaining whether their activities came under provisions of the Internal Security Act of 1950. Almost from the organization's inception, the FBI selected the NCAHUAC for formal counterintelligence attention and subjected it and its sponsors to numerous disruptive actions on an informal basis as well.

THE TARGETING OF FRANK WILKINSON

From the beginning, the primary COINTELPRO target within the NCAHUAC was Frank Wilkinson, an activist identified in secret Bureau documents as a "member of the Los Angeles Communist Party from 1943 to 1952." Beginning in 1952, when he was fired by the Los Angeles City Housing Authority for refusing to cooperate with the California Committee on Un-American Activities, Wilkinson unsuccessfully attempted to organize a broad-based national and liberal coalition against HUAC. For his troubles, HUAC subpoenaed Wilkinson (and a record of telephone calls made from his room at the Biltmore Hotel) in 1958 *after* he arrived in Atlanta to protest against the hearings being conducted by a HUAC subcommittee.[19]

Cited, indicted, and ultimately convicted for contempt of Congress for declining to answer HUAC's questions, Wilkinson served nine months of a one-year prison sentence at the Federal Prison Camp on the Donaldson Air Force Base in Greenville, South Carolina, along with Carl Braden, also imprisoned after an encounter with the Committee. At the FBI's request, prison officials opened Wilkinson's and Braden's mail and turned over photostat copies of all incoming and outgoing correspondence to the Bureau. Following Wilkinson's release from a second federal prison in Allenwood, Pennsylvania, FBI officials widely circulated a blind memorandum reporting that "Wilkinson was publicly identified as having been a Communist Party (CP) member in California at some time during the period from 1951 to 1955 by [FBI informer] Anita Belle Schneider who testified at HCUA hearings . . . in San Diego in 1958." Four years later, yet another FBI informer, Robert C. Ronstadt, identified Wilkinson as a Communist agent. A former private detective and "Communist for the FBI" in Los

Angeles from 1947 to 1954, Ronstadt testified against Wilkinson in executive session before HUAC in April 1962, just three months after revealing, for the first time, his past service to the FBI.[20]

As the NCAHUAC field representative, Wilkinson criss-crossed the country during the 1960s, sometimes speaking ten or more times a week at churches or on college campuses. FBI agents were especially sensitive to Wilkinson's itinerary when it coincided with HUAC's own appearances across the country. Complying with well-defined procedures outlined in the FBI *Manual of Instructions* concerning "public appearances of Party leaders," they sent off "urgent" teletypes detailing Wilkinson's movements and promised to be alert for counter-intelligence opportunities. When the FBI's confidential informants in Los Angeles were unable to determine whether Wilkinson would be in Minneapolis at a time when HUAC was also scheduled to be in town, another source (either a wiretap or a pretext contact) reported: "On 6/24/64 Los Angeles Division informed Minneapolis Division that WILKINSON'S wife informed he would not be in Minneapolis during the HCUA hearings."[21]

FBI informers routinely photographed and secretly taped Wilkinson's lectures, while FBI agents brought his itinerary to the attention of local police red squads and wrote letterhead memorandums detailing the contents of his speeches. When he spoke at Global Books in Detroit, for example, the local FBI office prepared six copies of a letterhead memorandum for distribution outside the Bureau. More importantly, standing instructions from FBI headquarters ordered agents in the field to "be alert for counterintelligence operations that might be effectively employed concerning the various speaking engagements of Wilkinson." The sole constraint seemed to be whether "possible counterintelligence operations" would embarrass the Bureau. In Wilkinson's case, senior FBI officials specifically cautioned the field offices to exercise "the utmost discretion" and "to avoid any basis for allegations that the Bureau is conducting investigations on college campuses, or interfering with academic freedom."[22]

Invariably, during his speaking engagements on college campuses and elsewhere, Wilkinson was asked if he was a Communist or some other "embarrassing" question. That the FBI inspired these queries is suggested by an April 1962 Omaha Field Office report on a debate between Wilkinson and a Birch Society spokesman at Drake University. This report highlighted a question and answer period where a member of the audience (apparently an FBI plant) *"had been able* to ask WILKINSON if he . . . was a Communist" (emphasis added).[23] Again, in May 1962, the Detroit SAC reported the decision of administrators at the University of Michigan to allow Wilkinson to speak on campus: "U of Michigan authorities decided that rather than give cause for 'violation of academic freedom' propaganda and 'martyrdom' propaganda, it was decided in the University's best interest to permit the speech, without publicity, in limited University space." These officials were briefed on Wilkinson's allegedly subversive background by Michigan State University and Wayne State University officials after the FBI had furnished derogatory information on the NCAHUAC field representative to an undisclosed source at Wayne State.[24]

That same month, the Washington, D.C., Field Office drew up a plan calling for the Bureau to station a "friendly newspaperman" at the entrance to a church where Wilkinson and Braden were scheduled to speak. This "inquiring reporter" could then ask persons entering the church their names and addresses in a not-too-subtle effort to dissuade them from attending the meeting rather than risk "exposure in the press." Such a technique would be effective, the SAC concluded, because "the Washington, D.C. area is a particularly sensitive area with regard to publicity for organizations in opposition to HUAC." This disruptive action was apparently carried out. A notation bearing FBI Assistant Director DeLoach's initial on the SAC's airtel recommending this operation indicates something was "handled" on May 4. DeLoach's specific reference, however, is unclear.[25]

In yet another effort to disrupt Wilkinson's speaking engagement in October 1962 at Knox College in Galesburg, Illinois, DeLoach sent derogatory information to *Chicago Tribune*

Washington bureau chief Walter Trohan. The Springfield Field Office also monitored the plans of a local chapter of the Young Republican League to harass Wilkinson. Other possible recipients of FBI leaks on this occasion included HUAC, Fulton Lewis, Jr., the *Galesburg Register-Mail*, and United States Senator John Tower (R., Tex.). Characterizing Tower as a man who considered "the Director to be his hero" and noting that DeLoach had presented him with an autographed copy of Hoover's *Masters of Deceit*, senior FBI officials readily approved this proposal. Whether Tower actually received derogatory information on Wilkinson is not known.[26]

Similarly, a May 1964 memorandum from the Cincinnati SAC advised FBI headquarters that University of Cincinnati officials had decided to cancel Wilkinson's scheduled talk.[27] And in November 1965 the Omaha SAC reported that the executive committee of Local 46, United Packinghouse Workers Union, had withdrawn its sponsorship of Wilkinson's appearance. Union officials were not aware of his "subversive" background, the SAC reported, until two exposé articles appeared in the *Waterloo* (Iowa) *Courier*.[28] Extensive deletions in released FBI documents and the nonrelease to date of other FBI-referenced documents again make it difficult to determine the Bureau's precise role in Wilkinson's scheduling problems.

That the FBI was responsible for many of these difficulties is further suggested by the Bureau's counterintelligence files and the routine investigation under the COMINFIL program of anyone who opposed HUAC. A modest financial contribution to the NCAHUAC was enough to attract FBI attention and, on one occasion, the Bureau offered Martin Luther King, Jr.'s signature on an abolition petition as evidence of his subversiveness. Even Democratic party fund raisers and non-Communist candidates for national office were considered valid COINTELPRO and COMINFIL targets if they were active in the drive to abolish HUAC.[29] Most FBI operations intended to immobilize Wilkinson and other Committee opponents, however, involved private citizens and not public personalities who were, in some ways, less vulnerable to covert COINTELPRO and COINTELPRO-like tactics.

In 1964, for example, a local FBI field office arranged a "propaganda campaign" to counter the extensive media publicity Wilkinson and others had arranged to greet HUAC members upon their arrival in Buffalo. Though the opposition to HUAC on this occasion was organized primarily by Buffalo residents, Wilkinson's movements and activities in Buffalo on the NCAHUAC's behalf were carefully monitored. (At this HUAC hearing a long-time FBI informer was scheduled to identify dozens of Buffalo residents as subversives; fifteen of them were to be subpoenaed.) Local FBI agents were primarily concerned about the success of a recently formed committee to oppose HUAC. Operating from the campus of the State University of New York at Buffalo, where the student senate and the weekly campus newspaper had already condemned HUAC's visit, this committee provided mainstream newspaper reporters with a steady supply of anti-HUAC literature, which in turn inspired several newspaper stories and editorials critical of the Committee.

To counter this publicity, the Buffalo Field Office forwarded information to its "sources" at the *Buffalo Courier Express* and the *Buffalo Evening News*. They also arranged a counter-flood of FBI-prepared anonymous letters and newspaper clippings to local newspapers and SUNY-Buffalo officials and student leaders. In one case, authority to mail anonymous letters was sent in the form of a "radiogram . . . in view of imminence of HCUA hearing . . . and necessity for immediate counterintelligence action." In another case, several pro-HUAC letters to the *Buffalo Courier Express* and the *Buffalo Evening News* were "signed with the married names of two sisters of Special Agents assigned to the Buffalo Office." Buffalo agents also proposed that two highly respected community leaders be contacted to issue news release favorable to HUAC. One candidate for this FBI-directed task, described as an active Legionnaire and a "colorful individual who commands a good press," was especially attractive. Both individuals had been investigated by the Buffalo FBI office and were "known to be reliable and discreet." Senior FBI officials at Bureau headquarters, nonetheless, rejected this proposal "because of inherent risks in contacting individuals on whom we do not have extensive knowledge and experience regarding their discretion." For similar reasons, FBI officials rejected yet another plan to form a "paper committee" to counter the Buffalo Committee to Oppose HUAC. All candidates for membership on this paper committee were again described as discreet, well disposed toward the Bureau, and close personal friends of local FBI agents. FBI Assistant Director Baumgardner specifically directed the Buffalo SAC not to organize this paper committee, but to consider furnishing it with information from FBI files if it could be formed independently.[30]

Other counterintelligence operations included the mailing of FBI-authored anonymous letters and a pamphlet, *Freedom or Imperialism*, to various fraternities and sororities at the Carnegie Institute of Technology in Pittsburgh, where Wilkinson was scheduled to speak. The FBI prepared *Freedom or Imperialism* specifically for the Communist party counterintelligence program, designing the pamphlet to appeal to college students who were occasionally subjected to "Communist propaganda." On October 9, 1963, the day before Wilkinson and NCAHUAC founder Aubrey Williams were to speak at American University in Washington, D.C., DeLoach leaked derogatory information on their subversive backgrounds to a media contact for his use when interviewing University officials. In Minneapolis, officials of the Floyd B. Olson Memorial Labor Temple canceled Wilkinson's reservation for the hall after a former FBI security informant brought Wilkinson's alleged CPUSA membership to their attention. In Cleveland, after noise from pro-HUAC demonstrators interrupted Wilkinson's address at the Jewish Cultural Center on a hot summer night, the building custodian closed the windows and—according to an FBI informant—turned on "what he believed to be the air-conditioning unit." Whether inadvertently or not, the janitor had turned on the furnace instead. The doors and windows of the Jewish Cultural Center then had to be opened for relief, allowing the pro-HUAC picketers to enter and heckle Wilkinson at closer range. FBI officials later relayed

Wilkinson's problems with the air-conditioning to all field offices as an example of an outstanding counterintelligence action.[31]

FBI COINTELPRO operations aimed at other persons also affected Wilkinson and his abolition movement. In May 1962, when Jack Kling, editor of the left-wing *Morning Freiheit*, reserved the Ohio Savings Association auditorium in South Euclid, the FBI immediately countered. Officers of the Savings Association canceled Kling's reservation after they were "discreetly influenced" by an FBI operative. (Apparently, this unnamed informant was an employee of Cleveland television station KYW.) To protest against this action, Wilkinson's sponsors, the Citizens for Constitutional Rights, canceled their reservation to use the same hall. As a result, they lost their deposit and were unable to find another suitable meeting place. The FBI's Cleveland Field Office then advised Bureau headquarters that it would continue to monitor Wilkinson's activities and promptly report "any further tangible results."

When Wilkinson returned to Cleveland in February and again in October 1963, additional counterintelligence actions were carried out. One involved Wilkinson's anticipated appearance before a gathering of thirty persons at the home of a woman active in the Cleveland branch of the Women's International League for Peace and Freedom. To persuade this woman to cancel this visit, the FBI mailed her a copy of a highly unfavorable article concerning Wilkinson that had appeared in the *Cleveland Plain Dealer*. Then, after learning of Wilkinson's plans to speak at the Unitarian Church in Youngstown on October 12 and before the Unitarian Society in Cleveland on October 13, the FBI furnished derogatory "public source data" to its contacts on the *Plain Dealer* and the *Youngstown Vindicator*. "This action," FBI officials concluded, "will serve to publicly warn people, who may be thinking of attending the . . . events, of the subversive character of Wilkinson and the NCAHUAC."[32]

The Bureau also attempted to discredit Wilkinson's sponsors, particularly the Reverend Dennis Kuby of the Cleveland Unitarian Society Social Action Committee. First, FBI agents compiled information alleging that Kuby, his Social Action Committee, the NCAHUAC, Wilkinson, and the Cleveland-based Citizens for Constitutional Rights were involved in a Communist plot to abolish HUAC. Then, the FBI leaked part of this information to Leta Woods, head of the far-right Organization to Fight Communism (OFC) and publisher of the *Cleveland Times*, a "self-described conservative weekly newspaper." The FBI's purpose, to "alert responsible people to the nature of the local effort to abolish the House Committee on Un-American Activities," was partially fulfilled when the *Cleveland Times* published an article, "Locals to Aid Red Line Here," based upon these FBI leaks. A copy of this article was also sent to every member of the Cleveland Unitarian Society, and KYW TV Eyewitness News publicized the charges against Kuby. (The Bureau source at KYW TV was a veteran, if unwitting, COINTELPRO participant who may have been responsible for this additional publicity.)[33]

By bringing Wilkinson's itinerary to the attention of Leta Woods and her Organization to Fight Communism, the FBI may have consciously sought to promote vigilantism. Indeed, the OFC had disrupted Wilkinson's speaking engagement at the Unitarian Church on October 13, 1963, and had also harassed him when he spoke at Oberlin College in February. Reverend Kuby filed an affidavit charging the OFC with resorting to "fist fights" in their crude efforts to disrupt his activities.[34] An FBI favorite, Woods was on the Bureau's "Special Correspondents' List" and regularly received anonymous COINTELPRO mailings regarding the itineraries of such top CPUSA functionaries as Henry Winston. Woods also received additional derogatory information from the FBI regarding the anti-HUAC activities of the Women's International League for Peace and Freedom and the Citizens for Constitutional Rights. She did not, of course, always need prodding from the FBI. Even when taking independent action, her organization's activities were closely monitored because the Bureau desired to maximize her efforts to discredit the abolition movement. For example, when KYW TV scheduled an interview with HUAC critic Frank J. Donner in January 1963, the FBI source at the television station requested background information on him. The FBI failed to comply with this request only because the OFC and other anticommunist groups were already circulating public source information detailing

Donner's alleged red record. A series of earlier Bureau leaks to reporter Edward Mowery had inspired several newspaper stories regarding Donner, which Karl Mundt had read into the *Congressional Record*.[35]

GRASS ROOTS COUNTERINTELLIGENCE

Because senior Bureau officials considered opposition to HUAC prima facie evidence of communism, FBI agents were instructed to foster dissension within the NCAHUAC's local affiliates and to open a file on all anti-HUAC organizations.[36] Thus, when an abolition committee was organized in Salt Lake City, Utah, FBI officials ordered the local SAC to consider counterintelligence operations designed to prevent "influential people" from participating "in the activities of this committee."[37] But if the Bureau lacked the resources to expose, discredit, or disrupt all of HUAC's opponents, the FBI did investigate as many of the Committee's opponents as possible. A student demonstration at a Chicago shopping center sponsored by an abolition committee at the University of Chicago, for instance, inspired two FBI agents to masquerade "as representatives of the City News Bureau" (apparently, with the cooperation of a confidential source at City News) and to take photographs of individuals handing out literature. As a result, the FBI opened files on five students, including a "Negro Male, 5'8" tall, slender build, light skin."[38]

In Milwaukee, the local FBI Field Office and senior FBI officials concluded that the Wisconsin Committee for Constitutional Freedom's "only activity to date has been to urge the abolition of the House Committee on Un-American Activities." Such credentials made the group a likely candidate for the counterintelligence program. Predictably, then, in December 1960 the Milwaukee SAC recommended furnishing derogatory public source data exposing the Communist background of John Gilman and other officers of the Wisconsin Committee to a *Milwaukee Journal* reporter. Rejecting this proposal, FBI officials instead directed the SAC to forward the information to Bureau headquarters "so that prompt counterintelligence action can be taken" by FBI Assistant Director DeLoach. DeLoach's Crime Records Division, not the Milwaukee Field Office, handled this leak, which was routed through CRD contacts on the *Milwaukee Sentinel*, then "a Hearst publication" (as approvingly noted by FBI officials); the more liberal *Milwaukee Journal* had not always demonstrated a friendly attitude toward the FBI.[39] The Milwaukee Field Office, however, did not limit its activities on behalf of HUAC to formal COINTELPRO operations. It disseminated on an ad hoc basis several Supreme Court decisions favorable to Bureau interests, particularly decisions upholding HUAC and the registration requirements of the Communist Control Act.[40]

In Cleveland, the Women's International League for Peace and Freedom and the Citizens for Constitutional Rights were also investigated under the counterintelligence program. The FBI attempted to disrupt the WILPF not only because it was "a pacifist-type organization," but because one of its officers, Edna Kaufman, was "spearing the propaganda activity in the Cleveland area to abolish the House Committee on Un-American Activities." More importantly, as secretary of the WILPF's Cleveland chapter, Kaufman could utilize the group's membership and mailing lists "in this propaganda effort and for the dissemination of other Communist propaganda." To discredit Kaufman, the FBI reviewed its files for suitable public source information. According to the Cleveland SAC, the most derogatory item the Bureau could safely use was contained in HUAC's public record. The SAC recommended that transcripts of Kaufman's 1956 testimony before the Committee be mailed anonymously to several non-Communist WILPF members and to Leta Wood's OFC. (Kaufman had invoked the First and Fifth Amendments when testifying before HUAC after FBI informers described her farm as the "nerve center" of the Ohio Communist party underground.)

When considering this proposal, FBI Assistant Director Sullivan noted that the WILPF had been founded at The Hague by Jane Addams and others and further that "there is no significant communist control on a national basis." But this did not exempt the group from COINTELPRO consideration, because Sullivan nonetheless concluded that the WILPF was a prime target for Communist infiltration. The suggested counterintelligence operation was approved and carried out with minor modifications. Only one WILPF member, selected because she "might instigate some action against Kaufman within the chapter," received a copy of the HUAC transcript, along with the Organization to Fight Communism.[41]

Similarly, the FBI attempted to disrupt a dinner party held by the Citizens for Constitutional Rights in rural Ohio. KYW Radio and TV, the *Cleveland Plain Dealer*, the *Cleveland Press*, and the OFC were notified of the dinner party and advised that it was a CPUSA-sponsored function intended to promote HUAC's abolition. The press, however, did not cover the dinner party, either because—as the Cleveland SAC explained to his superiors—it was held at a private residence in an isolated area outside of Cuyahoga County or because no prominent Communist was scheduled to speak; moreover, he surmised, the media may have concluded that their invitations had been sent by the CPUSA. Nonetheless, the FBI assigned an informant to monitor the dinner party and apparently alerted the Twinsburg Police Department. Officers in two patrol cars maintained a highly visible surveillance of the dinner party, jotting down license plate numbers and ordering all those parked on the street to move their cars.[42]

Richard Criley, director of the NCAHUAC-affiliated Chicago Committee to Defend the Bill of Rights (CCDBR), was the subject of even more ambitious COINTELPRO efforts. "The success of a good counterintelligence operation on an organization," the Chicago SAC mused in April 1962, "depends to a large degree in being able to decipher for public consumption the direction and control of the CP." The FBI's decision to concentrate on Criley thus stemmed from his identification as a Communist before the Dies Committee in 1938 and his testimony before HUAC in 1959. Significantly, HUAC only summoned Criley after he and an associate mailed (under their own signatures) 8,000 leaflets opposing the Chicago hearings. Criley and his fellow activist received their subpoenas four weeks after all other Committee subpoenas had been served. (Another reason Criley and the CCDBR were

272

selected by the FBI was the size—some 10,000 names—of their mailing list.) The Chicago SAC pointedly described Criley as "probably the only communist of importance in Chicago who will do battle with anyone, government or press, as a means to publicize his fight for civil rights." At the same time they attributed his frequent deviation from the CPUSA line to his being a member of the party's "left wing faction." In fact, Criley had already left the CPUSA, and the FBI knew it.[43]

The FBI's disruptive actions also included preparing questions for Mike Douglas's anticipated May 1962 television interview with Criley and Wilkinson. This COINTELPRO project was to be handled by the FBI's established source at KYW TV in Cleveland. Before approving this action, FBI officials ordered the Cleveland SAC to determine whether Douglas would be involved with the programming and, if so, to "furnish background information on him." Whether because of lingering doubts about Douglas's reliability (despite the assurance of the Assistant Special Agent in Charge [ASAC] that his source "would handle all arrangements . . . and no other employees at the television station would be aware of the Bureau's interest") or because of Criley's inability to make it to Cleveland, this particular recommendation was not carried out for the *Mike Douglas Show*. Instead, it was handled during a videotaped interview with Wilkinson for the noon news. FBI headquarters nonetheless sent public source data describing Wilkinson and Criley as CPUSA members to Cleveland. The ASAC forwarded this information to his operative at KYW TV, who had also received several FBI-authored questions for his use when arranging the interview. Because Wilkinson was asked if he was a Communist and other "embarrassing" questions by the interviewer, FBI officials touted this operation as well-executed and effective.[44]

In an effort to isolate Criley from the "liberal element," the next month two FBI agents interviewed a CCDBR board member who promptly resigned when informed of Criley's allegedly subversive intentions. The Bureau then mailed (in a "commercially purchased envelope," under the name of "true believers in democratic and constitutional process") a five-page FBI-authored document entitled "What is the Chicago

273

Committee to Defend the Bill of Rights?" to over twenty members of the CCDBR board of directors. To monitor responses to this mailing, the Chicago Field Office had originally proposed renting a Post Office box under false pretenses. COINTELPRO supervisors rejected this portion of the proposal because "too many unforeseen and uncontrollable factors arise in such a procedure." If, as a result, it was more difficult to assess the results of this mailing, the Chicago Field Office nonetheless credited its poison-pen letter with undermining CCDBR fund-raising efforts and "keeping members away from meetings, thereby depriving Criley of the services of those liberals and possibly the use of their names in the future."[45]

The FBI also mailed this anonymous statement, characterizing Criley as the "propaganda commissar of the Illinois CP," to Arnold Rosenzweig, publisher of the Chicago-based *National Jewish Post and Opinion*, and to Illinois State Senator Paul Broyles. The FBI selected Rosenzweig, a frequent though perhaps unwitting participant in the counterintelligence program, because he was "an orthodox Jew who equates Communism with Nazism in its dangers to the Jewish community." Broyles was chosen because he had headed the Illinois Seditious Activities Investigation Commission during the late 1940s, a "little HUAC" popularly known as the Broyles Commission. The Chicago Field Office hoped Broyles would place the FBI characterization of the CCDBR "in the hands of the press, raise the issue on the Senate floor, or perhaps cause an investigation" by the Illinois State Senate. Broyles's fellow Senator James Monroe was a peripheral target of this COINTELPRO operation. Because Monroe was listed on CCDBR letterhead as a member of the group's board of directors, the FBI included a copy of this letterhead in its anonymous mailing to Broyles.[46]

To neutralize anti-HUAC organizations, particularly the NCAHUAC and its affiliates in Chicago and elsewhere, FBI officials regularly forwarded field office reports to the Immigration and Naturalization Service and to the IRS red squad—the Special Service Staff. Bureau officials even enlisted the support of other intelligence agencies. U. S. Army Counter-

Intelligence Analysis Branch operators kept a file on the NCAHUAC, and the Army and Navy both censored anti-HUAC literature. CIA agents opened Richard Criley's mail; apparently supplied the FBI with information regarding the CPUSA membership of the parents of a young activist working to establish an abolition committee at Oberlin College; kept a dossier on former Congresswoman Bella Abzug that noted her counsel to subpoenaed HUAC witnesses during the early 1950s;[47] and attempted to discredit Warren Commission critic Mark Lane by publicizing his position as vice-chairman of the NCAHUAC's New York affiliate.[48] Not content to rely on its own informers or other intelligence agency operatives, in January 1966 FBI agents burglarized at least one NCAHUAC affiliate, the Chicago Committee to Defend the Bill of Rights, to photograph a list of that organization's regular financial contributors. FBI Assistant Director Sullivan authorized this "black bag job" in a telephone conversation with Chicago SAC Marlin Johnson. In time, Johnson went on to head the Chicago Police Board, whose responsibilities included disciplining overzealous police officers.[49]

NEUTRALIZING THE HILL

The FBI's monitoring of anti-HUAC activists in the NCAHUAC and other abolition committees inevitably led to the surveillance of United States congressmen. The NCAHUAC, after all, functioned primarily as a civil liberties lobby, and the FBI carefully scrutinized its efforts to rally congressional opposition to HUAC. The full extent of this surveillance, however, is difficult to document. Because of their sensitive nature, Bureau files recording surveillance of congressmen were generally filed separately from regular FBI files or were destroyed to preclude the possibility of public disclosure. Furthermore, of the FBI's files released under the Freedom of Information Act, those recording contacts with congressmen show heavy deletions. A Washington Field Office airtel of December 1960, for instance, reported that FBI agents planned to monitor a NCAHUAC-sponsored demonstration

275

scheduled to take place in front of the White House. The report also states that these FBI agents would not monitor "by physical surveillance" a meeting between picketers and congressmen later that day "because of the possibility of embarrassment." The next paragraph has been deleted in its entirety, suggesting that an FBI informant had "covered" this meeting.[50]

Despite the extensive deletions, these documents reveal that FBI surveillance activities and related attempts to neutralize HUAC's critics extended into the House of Representatives. Because FBI officials were concerned about NCAHUAC efforts to "influence various Congressmen to vote against the HCUA's appropriation" and thereby insisted upon full coverage of all debates involving the Committee, FBI agents regularly monitored the *Congressional Record*. Hoover specifically ordered the Los Angeles Field Office (the office of origin in the NCAHUAC investigation) to report any "action taken by Congress regarding the House Committee on Un-American Activities." Furthermore, to discredit liberal Congressman James Roosevelt, the leader of the abolition campaign in the House, the FBI disseminated his opinions on HUAC. The FBI also disseminated a summary of a speech by John Conyers, Jr. (D., Mich.) at a CCDBR conference and closely followed the anti-Committee activities of former congressmen Maury Maverick and Charles O. Porter.[51]

Occasionally, passive surveillance gave way to aggressive counterintelligence. FBI agents were ordered to determine not only the "pertinent activities" of NCAHUAC legislative representative Donna Allen, "but also . . . what *further* counterintelligence activities we will be able to utilize as a disruptive measure" (emphasis added). In anticipation of Frank Wilkinson's visit to the capital, the Washington SAC reported that his office was "considering [the] possibility of counterintelligence activity in connection with [Wilkinson's] presentation of petitions to Congressman CARLTON SICKLES [D., Md.]." Not satisfied with this single proposal, FBI officials ordered the Washington SAC to "immediately consider possible counterintelligence action in an effort to expose, discredit, or disrupt Wilkinson's activities . . . you should consider furnishing pertinent data relating to his activities to cooperative news media sources of your office or at the Seat of Government [FBI headquarters] . . . [and] to the HCUA through the Bureau." DeLoach did brief HUAC. The SAC, however, could not fully comply with this order, but that was because Wilkinson "held no public meetings [while contacting congressmen on Capitol Hill] and no situation arose which would offer an opportunity to employ counterintelligence measures."[52]

To deter congressmen from challenging HUAC, the FBI furnished derogatory information about the NCAHUAC to HUAC and to certain favored newspaper reporters. In December 1960, for example, the New York Field Office learned that plates used to address copies of the CPUSA weekly newspaper, the *Worker*, had also been used by the NCAHUAC's local affiliate, suggesting a close tie between the Communist party and the New York Council to Abolish the Un-American Activities Committee (NYCAUAC). The New York SAC then alerted senior Bureau officials and suggested that this discovery be routed "through appropriate liaison channels to the House Committee on Un-American Activities." If this leak and the attendant "publicity" could be "arranged [by Crime Records Division] prior to the reconvening of Congress on 1–3–61," FBI Internal Security section chief Baumgardner advised, it would "discredit the [NCAHUAC] and weaken its attack on the HCUA." Ordered by Hoover to "get this out," DeLoach promptly dispensed the information to HUAC and also to Fulton Lewis, Jr.—and both beat Baumgardner's deadline. On December 27, during his nationally syndicated radio program, Lewis reported on NYCAUAC's use of the *Worker's* addressograph plates. The next day, HUAC Chairman Walter issued a special press release on the addressograph exposé, a copy of which DeLoach sent directly to Hoover.[53]

When later summarizing the "tangible results" of this operation, FBI officials stressed the "increasing public support of the HCUA" resulting from the "current publicity showing communist activity in the [abolition] movement." More importantly, FBI officials were pleased that James Roosevelt, still the leader of the anti-HUAC movement in the House, "has retreated from his former position of calling for the abolition of

277

the HCUA to a less drastic position of calling for a reduction in the appropriation granted to the HCUA."[54] In early December 1960, Roosevelt had been undecided about how to proceed in his campaign against the Committee. At the end of the month, he wrote his colleagues in the House about what he believed to be the Committee's recent "massive propaganda effort designed to prove that all its opponents are Communists." Roosevelt had also decided not to pressure his colleagues to vote against the Un-American Activities Committee in that climate of opinion.[55]

These specific efforts to discredit the NCAHUAC and to influence congressional debate over HUAC's future were supplemented two weeks later in a similar leak regarding the Chicago Committee to Defend the Bill of Rights. (This leak was not carried out as a formal COINTELPRO project. Instead, documents recording it were filed in the FBI case file on the CCDBR.) On January 9, 1961, Hoover and his top aides approved a plan to disseminate an FBI "statement on unwatermarked bond paper . . . to our friendly press contacts in the Chicago area." In it, Richard Criley was characterized as having been identified as a Communist in sworn testimony by an FBI informer appearing before HUAC. This statement ("a new communist front has reared its head . . . to join the cacophony which has swelled in recent weeks to abolish [HUAC] . . . ") was then forwarded to DeLoach, who presumably made it available to carefully selected Chicago-area journalists. DeLoach, moreover, decided to seek national publicity. In an addendum to the document recording this non-COINTELPRO action, he advised that within two days "Fulton Lewis carried an exposé . . . on his radio program covering 422 stations . . . [and] the House Committee on Un-American Activities issued a wire release in connection with the same matter."[56]

In December 1961, DeLoach also gave Lewis information from other FBI reports regarding a meeting of the national officers of the NCAHUAC, including data on six congressmen who recently voted against HUAC's appropriation and a list of congressmen whom the NCAHUAC proposed to lobby. (An FBI informer apparently turned over the minutes of this

278

meeting to the Bureau.) Because of the extensive deletions in the released FBI files, it is impossible to determine exactly what information Lewis received. In any event, Hoover had specifically approved this leak, admonishing DeLoach to "get this widely exposed."[57]

This action, furthermore, was part of a strategy to disrupt the NCAHUAC's attempt to establish a legislative office in Washington, D.C. Conservative radio commentator Paul Harvey and others apparently received similar information on NCAHUAC lobbying efforts and on congressional resolutions intended to cripple HUAC. To gather data for these operations, the FBI carefully monitored the activities of HUAC's liberal congressional critics William F. Ryan (D., N.Y.), Phillip Burton (D., Cal.), and Don Edwards (D., Cal.). Ryan in particular attracted Bureau attention because of his allegedly close association with NCAHUAC legislative representative Donna Allen. In November 1962, FBI Assistant Director Baumgardner first advised William Sullivan of Ryan's anticipated anti-HUAC meeting in Los Angeles with recently elected California Democratic congressmen Roosevelt, Edward R. Roybal, George E. Brown, Jr., and Augustus F. Hawkins. He then directed DeLoach "to alert his sources at HCUA . . . on a confidential basis."[58]

In January 1965, the Washington Field Office identified thirteen congressmen who supported abolition and then forwarded their names in "URGENT" teletypes to FBI headquarters and to the Los Angeles, New York, Chicago, San Francisco, and Philadelphia field offices.[59] Reporting that Edwards and Burton planned to introduce anti-HUAC resolutions in the House, FBI informants secured a draft copy of Edwards's resolution even before it was introduced. With Hoover's approval, DeLoach briefed HUAC staff director Francis J. McNamara. The Washington Field Office also covered a meeting the next year between anti-HUAC activists and newly elected Congressman Gilbert Gude (R., Md.). In 1967, another informer reported that Edwards had written twenty-five colleagues urging them to speak against HUAC. Two years later, the Bureau monitored House Judiciary Committee Chairman Emanuel Celler's plans to speak at a

NCAHUAC function. Another FBI report identified the ten or twelve anti-Committee congressmen, including Thomas S. Foley (D., Wash.), Bob Eckhardt (D., Tex.), William L. St. Onge (D., Conn.), and Allard K. Lowenstein (D., N.Y.), who had attended a NCAHUAC-sponsored reception.[60]

FBI officials also occasionally forwarded political intelligence regarding NCAHUAC attempts to lobby congressmen to the White House. In November 1960, and again in early January 1961, Hoover advised Eisenhower aide Wilton Persons of NCAHUAC plans to picket the White House and to meet with various congressmen. Four years later, the FBI alerted presidential assistant Walter Jenkins about NCAHUAC plans to invite twenty-five congressmen and senators to a luncheon honoring civil rights activist and NCAHUAC founder Aubrey Williams. Four FBI field offices investigated the anticipated luncheon, and DeLoach again briefed HUAC staff director McNamara. At least one FBI informer infiltrated the March 16 affair, reporting that only one congressman and several legislative assistants had attended.[61]

Despite the Bureau's continuous surveillance of NCAHUAC meetings with congressmen, a shift in the priorities of FBI officials by late 1967 (occasioned by the initiation of "Black Hate Group" and "New Left" COINTELPROs) led to a decline in FBI surveillance of the NCAHUAC.[62] FBI officials also formally terminated their covert briefings of HUAC on NCAHUAC activities after 1967. In a memorandum to Sullivan, Domestic Intelligence Division official Charles D. Brennan explained this policy shift: "Our relations with the House Committee on Un-American Activities have been strained and the Director has instructed that no contact be made with it."[63] Whether or not Hoover's order was intended only to create a paper record of disapproval (much like his July 19, 1966, directive prohibiting "black bag jobs"), the FBI-HUAC feud was short-lived. Bureau officials continued to share with HUAC (and later the House Internal Security Committee) political intelligence gathered during FBI investigations of other organizations and individuals.

The FBI assault on the Committee's critics underscores the

Bureau's political activism and belies its posturing as a disinterested investigative agency. More importantly, the Bureau's support of the House Committee on Un-American Activities and its dated methods illustrates an enduring commitment to Cold War values—a commitment to the anticommunist consensus that the Bureau and the Committee had nurtured for nearly thirty years. The increased appeal of the abolition campaign in the 1960s marked the beginning of a substantive challenge to anticommunist orthodoxy. And the FBI knew it. That the Bureau responded as it did, by radically expanding its counterintelligence and other political activities in the face of a disintegrating anticommunist consensus, reflected the degree to which the FBI had become a law unto itself, seemingly invulnerable, not because it remained aloof from partisan considerations, but precisely because Bureau officials were so deeply and effectively involved in national politics.

Conclusion

For much of the 1960s and early 1970s, the House Committee on Un-American Activities (and its successor) appeared to be an anachronism, a relic of an ugly past. Student rioting at subcommittee hearings in San Francisco in 1960 marked the beginnings of a new American activism, with the so-called New Left developing in part from the abolition movement.[1] HUAC's visit to Chicago in 1965 represented the last of the old-style hearings where middle-aged, former radicals with distant Communist party ties took refuge in the Fifth Amendment. When HUAC counsel Alfred Nittle, aided by FBI informers Lola Belle Holmes and Lucius Armstrong, attempted to establish the presence of foreign influence in the peace and civil rights movements, demonstrations within and without the hearing room indicated widespread disfavor toward such political trials.

Some thirty separate groups, led by the Chicago Committee to Defend the Bill of Rights and including local chapters of the NAACP and the Congress of Racial Equality, organized to protest HUAC's visit. The FBI's Chicago Field Office, furthermore, had infiltrated the CCDBR and disseminated reports on the planned protest for at least two weeks before the hearing. And after an "urgent" teletype of May 24 advised senior FBI officials of the imminent demonstrations (including the intent of the pacifist Women Strike for Peace to form a "separate picket line with women dressed as witches"), the Crime Records Division alerted HUAC staff director McNamara's office. When the hearings opened, over 200 policemen and United States marshals (and local Nazis as well) were on hand to greet the more than 500 demonstrators who marched down Lake Shore Drive. When some of the demonstrators attempted to enter the old Federal Court of Appeals Building where HUAC was in session, nineteen were arrested. When a police paddy wagon attempted to cart them away, other demonstrators lay down in front of it. Similar protest activities took place during the remaining two days of Committee hearings, inspiring the FBI to film the confrontation from a strategic location on the second floor of the Court of Appeals Building, while Chicago Police arrested fifty-one more demonstrators.[2]

Thereafter, HUAC was less likely to venture beyond Washington, D.C., less likely to summon hostile witnesses, and less likely to issue contempt citations. Unfriendly witnesses were also less likely to lose their jobs. The dissent of the 1960s and early 1970s and the concomitant breakdown in the Cold War's overt internal security machinery necessitated a change in style for the FBI and HUAC. Bureau officials responded reflexively. They expanded their activities, relying almost exclusively on covert action, and launched new counterintelligence programs in 1967 against "Black Nationalist Hate Groups" and in 1968 against the New Left.[3] Committed to stopping the erosion of the Cold War consensus, FBI officials were constrained only by their fear of public disclosure. The Committee was no longer able to cite membership in the Soviet-dominated CPUSA or witnesses' rote recitation of the Fifth Amendment, because the new social protest was not tainted by the Communist specter and the new activists were only too willing to exploit the Committee's public forum to get their own information into the record. So HUAC began to specialize in the compilation of elaborate dossiers complete with mug shots of dissidents and to favor the testimony of local police officers and their informants rather than ex-FBI operatives. Although they realized that the ritualized hearings of Harold Velde's or Francis Walter's heyday were no longer tenable, the Bureau and the Committee nonetheless continued their symbiotic relationship. Former HUAC staff director NcNamara claimed the Committee's noticeably different style under Chairman Richard Ichord and chief counsel Donald Sanders, a former FBI agent, was inspired by increased FBI influence.[4]

Never able to adapt to the new social protest, despite a new name and mandate, the Committee was further frustrated by Supreme Court decisions in 1969 and 1972 that outlawed electronic surveillance without warrants in domestic intelligence investigations; permitted defense counsel to examine wiretap records; and prohibited, at any stage of prosecution, the submission of any evidence gathered by electronic surveillance without a warrant or prior court approval.[5] For all practical purposes, these decisions emasculated HISC's ability to compel testimony by threatening recalcitrant witnesses with contempt of Congress proceedings.

After these court decisions, the only outstanding HUAC/HISC contempt of Congress indictments, against Communist party functionary Arnold Johnson and Chicago residents Jeremiah Stamler, Yolanda Hall, and Milton Cohen, were dismissed. Had the indictments been pursued, the Justice Department anticipated "evidentiary problems" involving "intercepted communications" or "conversations" that, if disclosed, would "prejudice the national interest."[6] Apparently, information gathered by FBI electronic eavesdropping had been sanitized and forwarded to HUAC and its successor.

In an off-the-record boast to the FBI, Martin Dies admitted "that he had tapped wires all over the country" and his successors occasionally did their own tapping and bugging.[7] In any event, the Committee's limited resources would not permit the widespread electronic work suggested by the Johnson and Stamler, Hall, and Cohen cases. FBI electronic surveillance, in contrast, was incredibly pervasive—for instance, in 1968, when President Johnson wanted Communist critics of his Vietnam policy hauled before the moribund Subversive Activities Control Board, the FBI could only identify six relatively insignificant Communist functionaries and officials who had *not* been subjected to some type of electronic surveillance.[8] More importantly, the Committee claimed all along that it had evidence from "reliable sources" conclusively documenting the Communist associations of Stamler, Hall, and Cohen, but the Justice Department concluded that it could not establish these associations without recourse to tainted evidence. When preparing to prosecute Stamler, Hall, and Cohen for contempt

284

of Congress, Justice Department attorneys requested and received from the FBI dozens of intelligence reports—including
at least forty-one FBI reports (dating from September 1941 to
May 1967) on Cohen.[9]

The contempt of Congress indictment against Arnold Johnson was also indicative of the scope of FBI surveillance and the
implicit cooperation between the Bureau and the Committee.
Johnson, a well-known veteran Communist who, according to
HISC member John Ashbrook, "conveniently looks like any-
one's grandfather," was a steering committee member of
the New Mobilization Committee to End the War in Vietnam
(New Mobe). On November 5, 1969, in anticipation of a "large"
antiwar demonstration, FBI Director Hoover asked Attorney
General Mitchell to authorize a tap on New Mobe's telephone.
Mitchell approved a wiretap the next day. New Mobe was then
investigated under such Bureau programs as COMINFIL and
VIDEM (Vietnam Demonstrations); subjected to formal
COINTELPRO-New Left and COINTELPRO-Socialist
Workers Party actions (including an FBI-authored anonymous
memorandum to Johnson and other steering committee members and a leak to "a nationally syndicated columnist"); and
selected for extra-COINTELPRO harassment as well. (FBI
agents openly solicited New Mobe volunteers to become
informers in the very building that housed New Mobe's
offices.) Ultimately, in 1970, HISC held hearings on New Mobe
and it was during these hearings that Johnson was alleged to
have been in contempt of Congress.[10]

The Committee's FBI benefactors also encountered problems. While the events of the pre-Watergate 1970s (notably the
break-in at the FBI resident agency in Media, Pennsylvania)
had done much to dissolve the Bureau's long-standing immunity from public and congressional scrutiny, by its own
aggressive efforts and a reservoir of support in the Congress the
FBI had been able at the time to avert any serious congressional
inquiry—particularly involving congressional access to its
domestic intelligence files. In some ways, the Bureau remained
relatively invulnerable until the Watergate affair broke with its
attendant investigations of the intelligence community by the
Church Committee. Only in 1975–1976 did the Church Com-

mittee partially reveal, by concentrating principally on the counterintelligence programs, the FBI's political activities. Combined with the already well-publicized Watergate scandals, the Church Committee investigations challenged the once-dominant Cold War consensus. But although Cold War values were eviscerated, the consequences were not inevitable. For without the searing impact of Watergate and the chain of events which that burglary set in motion, the Bureau and the Un-American Activities Committee might still be doing business as usual.

The fortuitous occurrence of the Watergate scandal revealed the often fraudulent nature of expansive executive privilege claims that were based more on political criteria than a legitimate concern for the national security. In this altered political climate, Gerald Ford, Richard Nixon's successor, was compelled to comply with congressional requests for access to FBI documents, thereby permitting a serious congressional investigation of FBI practices and programs. Seymour Hersh's story in the *New York Times* on December 22, 1974, revealing CIA involvement in domestic surveillance, also encouraged a favorable climate for an inquiry. And in January 1975 the press revealed that President Johnson had received FBI reports on the strategies of members of Congress, Robert F. Kennedy, and civil rights leaders at the 1964 Democratic National Convention. Finally, Attorney General Edward Levy announced that Hoover had kept secret files containing derogatory information on prominent personalities—including members of Congress.[11]

These numbing disclosures had a cumulative effect, propelling both the executive and Congress into action. On December 23, 1974, President Ford ordered Secretary of State Henry Kissinger to file a report on Hersh's allegations. Kissinger's report, in turn, prompted Ford to issue Executive Order 11828 on January 4, which created the Rockefeller Commission on CIA Activities Within the United States. On January 27 the Senate established its Select Committee to Study Intelligence Activities, chaired by Idaho Democrat Frank Church, and on February 19 the House created its own Select Committee, chaired initially by Lucien N. Nedzi (D., Mich.) and then by Otis Pike (D., N.Y.).[12]

The fate of HUAC's successor further illustrated an abrupt shift in the climate of opinion. Like the FBI, the House Internal Security Committee faced the challenge of a disintegrating Cold War consensus. Its problems were also exacerbated as the Watergate scandals unraveled. Involved (both directly and indirectly) in illegal electronic surveillance and other abuses, notably the FBI's counterintelligence programs and the tax harassment adventures of the IRS Special Service Staff, HISC's position was tenuous. Though the Committee tried to adapt to the new climate by launching an ambitious investigation of terrorism,[13] its base of support in the House collapsed. Sensitized to the fragility of civil liberties and buttressed by the recent election of seventy-five freshman Democrats, the House Democratic Caucus decided by voice vote on January 13, 1975, to abolish HISC. (Led by Phillip Burton, Don Edwards, and Robert F. Drinan, S.J.—a HISC member who had joined the Committee to seek its abolition—the Caucus had agreed to this strategy a month earlier, refusing to assign any Democrats to the Committee except Chairman Ichord.) Unwilling to risk a roll call vote, the full House formally disbanded the Internal Security Committee on January 14 when approving a new House reorganization plan by a vote of 259 to 160. Assuming possession of HISC's property, the Committee on the Judiciary transferred its files to the National Archives under seal for at least fifty years. HISC's counterpart, the Senate Internal Security Subcommittee, met a similar fate two years later when it was merged with the Criminal Activities Subcommittee and became dormant.[14]

The Church Committee's highly publicized investigations of the counterintelligence programs and other questionable FBI activities had for the first time directly challenged a McCarthyite politics and, in the process, revealed the Cold War's impact on American values. Intelligence agency bureaucrats had not been principally concerned whether their domestic or international activities violated the law or the Constitution. Former FBI Assistant Director Sullivan encapsulated this disdain for traditional legal and constitutional constraints during his executive session testimony before the Church Committee:

> During the ten years [1961-1971] that I was on the U.S. Intelligence Board . . . never once did I hear anybody, including myself, raise the question: "Is this course of action which we have agreed upon lawful, is it legal, is it ethical or moral?" We never gave any thought to this realm of reasoning, because we were just naturally pragmatists. The one thing we were concerned about was this: will this course of action work, will it get us what we want, will we reach the objective that we desire to reach? . . . We did what we were expected to do.[15]

From the early Cold War years until Watergate, responsible elected officials had tolerated this lawlessness or, at the least, had willingly looked the other way. The House Internal Security Committee investigation of the FBI in 1974, and not the Church Committee probe in 1975-1976, more aptly represented congressional politics and priorities during the Cold War years. When the National Lawyers Guild publicized illegal FBI wiretapping and other improper surveillance in 1950, Congress responded through HUAC by investigating the NLG. Nor did the Congress and the Justice Department investigate the FBI in 1954 following Karl Mundt's inadvertent confirmation of what many on the Left had long suspected—that the FBI was aiding and abetting HUAC and the junior Senator from Wisconsin. Instead, Attorney General Brownell and President Eisenhower reflexively defended the Bureau while key congressmen uncritically accepted the fraudulent denials of FBI Director Hoover, Senator Mundt, and Senator McCarthy. Again in 1965-1966, when the Senate Subcommittee on Administrative Practice and Procedure threatened to extend its investigation of IRS activities in a manner that might expose several sensitive FBI surveillance techniques (including mail openings and separate filing procedures for burglaries), Bureau officials, the Attorney General, Vice-President Hubert H. Humphrey, and possibly President Johnson convinced Subcommittee Chairman Edward V. Long (D., Mo.) to redirect his inquiry.[16] Finally, when in 1971 the Media burglary exposed COINTELPRO–New Left, Congress did not initiate an investigation but instead increased FBI appropriations to enable the FBI to hire additional agents to handle what Hoover described as the "ever increasing investigative work . . . in the internal security area."[17]

Events since 1976 have further highlighted the aberrant nature of the Church Committee probe. By employing the Freedom of Information Act to gain access to FBI files, independent scholars, journalists, and political activists have documented a record of abuse going far beyond the Church Committee revelations. And yet Congress has failed to enact legislation to prevent these abuses from recurring. Indeed, Senator Paul Laxalt (R., Nev.) introduced a bill, S. 2928, in July 1980 that would legitimize for the first time some of the most questionable intelligence community activities—including provisions that, in effect, authorize the FBI to forward information on dissidents to private employers and congressional committees.

Conservative success in the 1980 elections and the Reagan administration's internal security agenda do little to reassure those troubled by the efforts of conservative Republican Senator Laxalt, a close friend of Ronald Reagan, to legitimize blacklisting by statute. The Heritage Foundation, a right-wing think tank with ties to Edwin Meese III and other top Reagan advisers, has called upon the administration to lead yet another campaign alerting the nation to the "reality of subversion and . . . the un-American nature of much so-called 'dissidence.'" The Foundation advocates surveillance of all "terrorist" and "potentially subversive" political groups, including "anti-defense and anti-nuclear lobbies."[18]

When the Heritage Foundation also called for revival of the congressional internal security committees immediately after the 1980 elections, the Senate Judiciary Committee and its new Republican Chairman, Strom Thurmond, quickly obliged—reestablishing SISS in December 1980 under a new name, the Subcommittee on Security and Terrorism (SST). Subcommittee Chairman Jeremiah A. Denton, an Alabama Republican who spent over seven years in a North Vietnamese prisoner of

war camp, hired former FBI agent Joel Lisker as chief counsel
and has held hearings on such subjects as international terrorism, Communist manipulation of the press, and the so-called
Levy guidelines—promulgated by Gerald Ford's Attorney
General, Edward Levy, and intended to prohibit FBI surveillance of any political group unless there is reasonable
grounds to suspect that the group intends to engage in criminal
activity. Like the Fish Committee of 1930, SST serves as a
standard bearer in the current campaign to revive the FBI's
domestic intelligence probes. In the tradition of J. B. ("Doc")
Matthews, the Subcommittee also has an intellectual in residence. The chief theoretician of the new antiterrorist campaign, Samuel T. Francis, is an aide to SST member John P.
East (R., N.C.) and the author of a Heritage Foundation study
on internal security. Francis holds a Ph.D. from the University of North Carolina with a thesis on the foreign policy of
Edward Hyde, the first Earl of Clarendon.[19]

If the anemic CPUSA could be sold as a serious threat to
national security in the 1940s and 1950s, then the concern over
terrorists in the 1980s might yet prove equally successful in
establishing a neo-McCarthyite politics. Senator Thurmond,
for his part, is a former available channel of the FBI and a
COINTELPRO participant who is also supporting Senate
efforts to roll back the Freedom of Information Act. In the
House, the effort to revive HUAC is being led by ultra-
conservative Georgia Democrat Larry McDonald, the youn-
gest member of the national council of the John Birch Society.
As early as the summer of 1978, McDonald had secured 178
(out of a needed 218) cosponsors to force a HUAC revival
resolution out of the Rules Committee for a roll call vote.

Signs of a born-again McCarthyism in the 1980s are common.
Assistant Secretary of Agriculture John B. Crowell claimed, in
March 1982, that at least two environmental protection groups,
the Audubon Society and the Sierra Club, had been infiltrated
by Socialists and Communists. Two months later James
Handley, special assistant to Secretary of Agriculture John R.
Block, requested loyalty checks of scientists who provide advice on the scientific merit of applications to the Department's
competitive grants program. Handley wanted the "scientists
checked for philosophical compatibility" with the Reagan

administration's political views. (The loyalty probes were cancelled by Block the day after the practice was disclosed by the *Washington Post*.) And the rumblings in the entertainment industry, particularly the Ed Asner–Charlton Heston confrontation over Asner's support of Salvadoran guerrillas and the Boston Symphony Orchestra's cancellation of a 1982 performance of Stravinsky's *Oedipus Rex* narrated by Vanessa Redgrave, recalls those bygone days when blacklisting was the rule and not the exception. In Congress, the so-called Blitz Amendment (named after Dorothy Blitz, who refused to take a loyalty oath in Virginia when applying for a Comprehensive Employment and Training Act job), was signed into law on December 14, 1981, without public or congressional debate, having been tacked on to the Labor, Health and Human Services, and Education Appropriations Act of 1981. The amendment, which was intended to deny CETA funds to individuals who publicly advocated the violent overthrow of the federal government, was aborted by the courts in May 1982. Later in the year the Intelligence Agents Identities Protection Act was signed into law—legislation criminalizing, for the first time, the publication of information disclosing the identities of undercover intelligence agents, even if that information was already public or could be gleaned from public sources.

The Reagan administration, moreover, has returned the pre–Church Committee zest to the intelligence community, with the mainstream press reporting evidence of CIA covert operations in Libya, Iran, Cambodia, Afghanistan, and Nicaragua. On the home front, a proposed executive order authorizing surveillance of American citizens within the United States by the CIA and the use of illegal intelligence gathering techniques was temporarily aborted in March 1981, after a leak to the *New York Times*. (That same month the President, a former member of the Rockefeller Commission, pardoned FBI officials W. Mark Felt and Edward Miller, who had been indicted in April 1978 for illegally authorizing break-ins in 1971–1974 of the "Weather Underground." Reagan justified the pardon of Felt and Miller on the grounds of their intent to safeguard the national security.) A revised version of the executive order, dropping the section that permitted CIA agents to infiltrate and influence domestic organizations, was finally signed on December 4, 1981. Executive Order 12333 authorized the CIA to "conduct administrative and support activities within the United States" (including "counterintelligence activities" if coordinated with the FBI), to acquire and disseminate information regarding "the domestic activities of United States persons" if "necessary for administrative purposes" or "incidentally obtained," and to perform "such other intelligence activities as the President may from time to time direct."

Even more troubling is the administration's declaration of war on the right to know. When the *Washington Post* reported that Richard D. DeLauer, head of weapons research and procurement at the Defense Department, told the Joint Chiefs of Staff in late 1981 that Reagan's proposed defense build-up would cost some fifty percent (or $750 billion) more than anticipated, the administration ordered an all-out investigation of this leak. Senior Pentagon officials submitted to a series of lie detector tests and all government officials below the rank of deputy secretary were required thereafter to obtain prior approval before talking to any member of the press and to write a memorandum afterwards describing what information had been discussed. This overreaction to a case of Defense Department whistle-blowing was quickly scaled down, but not before a Pentagon press spokesman revealed the all-too-clear impetus. The "official information" had been leaked not to an enemy but to an "adversary"—Congress. On the nation's campuses, administration officials are urging voluntary censorship and prior restraint—in the words of then CIA Deputy Director Bobby R. Inman, "prior to the start of research and prior to publication"—in order to halt the "hemorrhage" of scientific and technological data to the Soviet Union. The alternative, they warn, is mandatory government controls in the future. Similarly, Lawrence J. Brady, Assistant Secretary of Commerce for trade administration, denounced the "strong belief in the academic community that they have an inherent right to teach, conduct research and develop exchange programs free of government review or oversight."[20]

If the Reagan administration distrusts government bureaucracy, it distrusts an open society even more. Nowhere is this more apparent than in the administration's effort to shelve the Freedom of Information Act. Conservative Senator Orrin Hatch (R., Utah) and the administration each have introduced bills (S. 1730 and S. 1751 respectively) to amend the FOIA. Hatch's bill has since been substantially amended; the full Judiciary Committee either rewrote or revised most of the restrictive provisions—a compromise reluctantly agreed to by Hatch after receiving adverse newspaper publicity in his home state. The Reagan administration's bill would exempt all records pertaining to terrorism, organized crime, and foreign counterintelligence and all information related to "ongoing" investigations. (How the FBI and other intelligence agencies would interpret "ongoing" is impossible to say; it should be remembered, in any event, that the FBI kept its file on Frank Wilkinson and the National Committee to Abolish HUAC open until the mid-1970s in an effort to determine whether Wilkinson planned to file an FOIA request.) Not content to wait for congressional action on S. 1751, on May 4, 1981, Attorney General William French Smith rescinded a requirement of his predecessor that all government agencies, when withholding information, must demonstrate that disclosure under FOIA would be "demonstrably harmful" to the national security. In addition, according to Smith's new policy, the Justice Department will hereafter defend all decisions, no matter how capricious, to withhold information. Perhaps coincidentally, the day before Smith reversed Griffin Bell's requirement, 50,000 demonstrators marched on the Pentagon to protest United States military aid to El Salvador—the largest anti-military demonstration since the Vietnam War era.

Nearly a year later, on April 3, 1982, President Reagan issued Executive Order 12356 on classifying government documents. By executive fiat, this order eliminated previous requirements that government officials must consider the public's right to know before classifying documents and that classification must be based on "identifiable" potential damage to the national security. The executive order also eliminated the ban on the reclassification of documents and information already released; radically expanded the definition of "foreign government information"; created a presumption that intelligence sources and methods are classified; removed the requirement that doubts be resolved in favor of declassification; and curtailed declassification review practices in the National Archives and all executive agencies and departments. The administration has pursued a strategy of "soft" criticism more than of frontal assault on the Freedom of Information Act, using grounds of cost and FOIA's adverse impact on collection of intelligence. Even if the inflated figure of $50 million or more per year to administer the FOIA is accepted (the annual budget for military marching bands is often nearly twice that amount), the Act has resulted in savings by identifying "fraud, waste, and abuse" in government, as well as dangers to public health and safety. More importantly, a recent FBI study, obtained through FOIA, flatly contradicts the well-publicized FBI claim that the Act has reduced informants' willingness to cooperate with the Bureau.[21]

Ronald Reagan's conception of the "truth" helps explain his administration's across-the-board attack on access to information. In a speech at the fortieth anniversary celebration of the Voice of America, the President recalled his days as a baseball broadcaster in Illinois. When word came over the wire noting a routine out, Reagan said, he would describe the play as "a hard-hit ball down toward second base. The shortstop is going over after the ball and makes a wild stab, picks it up, turns and gets him out just in time. . . . Now, I submit to you," Reagan continued, "that I told the truth. . . . The truth got there and, in other words, it can be attractively packaged." For the President, as Alan Wolfe put it,

> truth . . . lies in the intention. Since Reagan's goals are, to him, honorable, then any statements that help realize them are true and any that hinder them are false. It is, to be blunt, an instrumental conception of truth, one developed in the propaganda wars that brought the right to power and sharing the right-wing vision of a world under siege.[22]

Even if Wolfe exaggerates the President's cavalier attitude toward the truth, those who fear the rise of a neo-McCarthyism in the current decade might not be unduly paranoid. When

294

coming to political maturity in the days when Cold War I was hardening, Reagan headed the Screen Actors Guild, testified as a friendly witness before HUAC, and even ran a security check of sorts on the future first lady before they met. In the 1970s, candidate Reagan denied the existence of a blacklist in Hollywood during those dark days. And in October 1982 he charged that the antinuclear movement was influenced by Soviet agents and others "who want the weakening of America and who are manipulating many honest and sincere people." (An FBI spokesman said the President's contention was based in part on reports submitted to the White House by the Bureau.) Nor is it comforting to know that the President's national security adviser, William Clark, hired Jeremiah O'Leary as his special assistant for press relations. O'Leary, a retired Marine colonel and White House correspondent for the *Washington Star*, brought appropriate credentials to the job—having served J. Edgar Hoover and Cartha DeLoach as one of the FBI's available channels.

The Laxalt bill, the rebirth under a new name of the McCarthy-era SISS, the effort to reconstitute HUAC, the antinuclear smear campaign, and the Reagan administration's backdoor gutting of the FOIA and general hostility toward an open society all suggest that the erosion during the Cold War years of such traditional American values as the right to privacy, the right to dissent, and freedom of speech has taken a heavy toll on the Constitution. While the lingering Watergate and Church Committee revelations of past abuses will no doubt temper any future efforts to reopen FBI domestic intelligence operations on a truly grand scale, FBI efforts in the past to socialize Americans into the anticommunist world view succeeded perhaps to an extent beyond the late FBI Director's wildest dreams. Hoover, after all, received his political baptism during the Teapot Dome scandals of the 1920s, when the Bureau was nearly destroyed by its well-publicized abuses. The FBI today has managed to withstand what Hoover never thought it could—a second public airing of even seamier political adventures.[23] Elite opinion has treated these revelations as a policy problem rather than a constitutional problem. The fundamental question—Can a democratic society tolerate a political police and remain democratic?—has been pushed aside in favor of another question: how can we be assured of an efficient and effective intelligence capability to meet the complex law enforcement problems of a modern industrial society? American political leaders today tend to prefer security and order rather than liberty. For that the FBI, along with the old House Committee on Un-American Activities and its constituency, must be granted some of the credit.

Notes

ALH	Archives of Labor History. Wayne State University. Detroit.
CF	Confidential File.
DDE	Dwight D. Eisenhower Library. Abilene, Kansas.
DIOISP	House Committee on Internal Security. *Domestic Intelligence Operations for Internal Security Purposes.* 93d Cong., 2d sess., 1974.
FBI CCDBR Files	FBI Chicago Committee to Defend the Bill of Rights Files. Chicago.
FBI CPJ Files	FBI Committee for Public Justice Files. New York City.
FBI HUAC Files	FBI House Committee on Un-American Activities Files. To be deposited at the Marquette University Library. Milwaukee.
FBI NCARL Files	FBI National Committee Against Repressive Legislation/National Committee to Abolish HUAC Files. Los Angeles.
FBI NLG Files	FBI National Lawyers Guild Files. New York City.
FDR	Franklin D. Roosevelt Library. Hyde Park, New York.
HCH	Herbert C. Hoover Library. West Branch, Iowa.
HIA, vol. 6, *FBI*	Senate Select Committee to Study Governmental Operations with Respect to Intelligence Activities. *Hearings on Intelligence Activities.* Vol. 6. *Federal Bureau of Investigation.* 94th Cong., 1st sess., 1975.
Hoover O&C FBI Files	Unserialized Official and Confidential Files of former FBI Director J. Edgar Hoover. To be deposited at the Marquette University Library. Milwaukee.
HST	Harry S. Truman Library. Independence, Missouri.
IARA	Senate Select Committee to Study Governmental Operations with Respect to Intelligence Activities. *Final Report.* S.Rept. 755. Book II. *Intelligence Activities*

	and the Rights of Americans. 94th Cong., 2d sess., 1976 (Serial 13133–4).
JEH	J. Edgar Hoover FBI Building. Washington, D.C.
KEM	Karl E. Mundt Papers. Karl E. Mundt Archival Library. Dakota State College. Madison, South Dakota.
LBJ	Lyndon B. Johnson Library. Austin, Texas.
Nichols O&C FBI Files	Unserialized Official and Confidential Files of former FBI Assistant Director Louis B. Nichols. To be deposited at the Marquette University Library.
OF	Official File
Post-Pres. File	Post-Presidential File
PPF	President's Personal File
PPI	Post-Presidential Individual Name File
PSF	President's Secretary's File
RG	Record Group
SDSRIARA	Senate Select Committee to Study Governmental Operations with Respect to Intelligence Activities. *Final Report*. S.Rept. 755. Book III. *Supplementary Detailed Staff Reports on Intelligence Activities and the Rights of Americans*. 94th Cong., 2d sess., 1976 (Serial 13133–5).
SHSW	State Historical Society of Wisconsin. Madison.
SRIA	Senate Select Committee to Study Governmental Operations with Respect to Intelligence Activities. *Final Report*. S.Rept. 755. Book VI. *Supplementary Reports on Intelligence Activities*. 94th Cong., 2d sess., 1976 (Serial 13133–8).
WHCF	White House Central File

INTRODUCTION

1. Daniel Bell, "The Dispossessed," in Daniel Bell, ed., *The Radical Right* (Garden City, N.Y.: Doubleday, 1963), pp. 5–7. See also Frank J. Donner, *The Age of Surveillance* (New York: Knopf, 1980), p. 293; U.S., Senate, Special Preparedness Subcommittee of the Committee on Armed Services, *Military Cold War Education and Speech Review Policies*, 87th Cong., 2d sess., 1962, pts. 1–8.

2. U.S., Senate, Select Committee to Study Governmental Operations with Respect to Intelligence Activities, *Final Report*, Book I, *Foreign and Military Intelligence*, S.Rept. 755, 94th Cong., 2d sess., 1976 (Serial 13133–3), pp. 193–94; idem, *Final Report*, Book IV, *Supplementary Detailed Staff Reports on Foreign and Military Intelligence*, S.Rept. 755, 94th Cong., 2d sess., 1976 (Serial 13133–6), p. 50.

3. Ibid., p. 52 n9.

4. Historians and others have explained the rise of McCarthyism in several

ways. One interpretation contends that McCarthyism was a justifiable response to a serious internal security threat. See William F. Buckley, Jr., and L. Brent Bozell, *McCarthy and His Enemies* (Chicago: Henry Regnery, 1954); James Burnham, *The Web of Subversion* (New York: John Day, 1954); David Y. Dallin, *Soviet Espionage* (New Haven, Conn.: Yale University Press, 1955). Earl Latham's *The Communist Controversy in Washington: From the New Deal to McCarthy* (Cambridge, Mass.: Harvard University Press, 1966) also emphasizes the threat posed by the CPUSA but is more critical of the McCarthyites' methods. Others have explained McCarthyism as a mass movement of a so-called radical Right unduly susceptible to the wildest conspiracy theories. See essays by Richard Hofstadter, Nathan Glazer, Peter Viereck, Talcott Parsons, Daniel Bell, and Seymour Martin Lipset in Bell, *The Radical Right*. More recently, scholars have looked to Harry S Truman and his domestic anticommunist program—the Attorney General's list, the loyalty program, and the Smith Act prosecutions. One school of thought views Truman's anticommunism as benign, an attempt to contain the excessive internal security measures advocated by congressional red-hunters. See Alan D. Harper, *The Politics of Loyalty: The White House and the Communist Issue, 1946–1952* (Westport, Conn.: Greenwood, 1969); Alonzo L. Hamby, *Beyond the New Deal: Harry S. Truman and American Liberalism* (New York: Columbia University Press, 1976); Richard Fried, *Men Against McCarthy* (New York: Columbia University Press, 1976); Francis H. Thompson, *The Frustration of Politics: Truman, Congress, and the Loyalty Issue, 1945–1953* (Rutherford, N.J.: Fairleigh Dickinson University Press, 1979). To the revisionists, in contrast, Truman's anticommunism was part of a purposeful strategy to silence critics of the pax Americana and to mobilize public opinion behind the administration's pursuit of an open-door world. Truman emerged after 1950 as the favorite target of the McCarthyites for his softness on communism only because he promised more than he could deliver. For the leading revisionist studies, see Athan Theoharis, *Seeds of Repression: Harry S. Truman and the Origins of McCarthyism* (Chicago: Quadrangle, 1971); Richard M. Freeland, *The Truman Doctrine and the Origins of McCarthyism: Foreign Policy, Domestic Politics, and Internal Security, 1946–1948* (New York: Schocken, 1974); Robert Griffith and Athan Theoharis, eds., *The Specter: Original Essays on the Cold War and the Origins of McCarthyism* (New York: New Viewpoints, 1974).

5. I.F. Stone, "Is the Constitution Un-American?," *Nation*, Sept. 6, 1947, p. 224. For the Committee, see August R. Ogden, *The Dies Committee* (Washington, D.C.: Catholic University of American Press, 1945); Robert K. Carr, *The House Committee on Un-American Activities, 1945–1950* (Ithaca, N.Y.: Cornell University Press, 1952); Frank J. Donner, *The Un-Americans* (New York: Ballantine, 1961); Walter Goodman, *The Committee: The Extraordinary Career of the House Committee on Un-American Activities* (New York: Farrar, Straus and Giroux, 1968).

6. Mundt is quoted in *Cong. Rec.*, 79th Cong., 2d sess., May 17, 1946, pp. 5217–18. Hoover is quoted ibid., 93d Cong., 2d sess., April 1, 1974, p. 8936.

7. Ronald R. May, "Genetics and Subversion," *Nation*, May 16, 1960, pp. 420-22.

8. For Roudebush, see George O'Toole, *The Private Sector: Private Spies, Rent-a-Cops, and the Police Industrial Complex* (New York: Norton, 1978), pp. 203-04, 206-09, 214-15. For Russell, see Jim Hougan, *Spooks: The Haunting of America—The Private Use of Secret Agents* (New York: William Morrow, 1978), pp. 280, 287-89; Carl Oglesby, *The Yankee and Cowboy War: Conspiracies from Dallas to Watergate* (Kansas City: Sheed Andrews and McMeel, 1976), pp. 300-01.

9. See Ehrlichman's handwritten notes on his June and July 1971 meetings with Nixon, in U.S., House, Committee on the Judiciary, *Statement of Information*, Appendix III, *Supplementary Documents*, 93d Cong., 2d sess., 1974, pp. 91, 109, 115-16, 121, 124-29, 146, 188, 190-91. For the FBI leak, see *HIA*, vol. 6, *FBI*, pp. 486-88.

10. U.S., House, Committee on the Judiciary, *Statement of Information*, Book VII, pt. 2, *White House Surveillance and Campaign Activities*, 93d Cong., 2d sess., 1974, pp. 633, 835-36; idem, Appendix III, *Supplementary Documents*, p. 146.

11. While it is now possible to research FBI files, Congress exempted itself from the FOIA, and HUAC's internal records (memorandums, staff reports and assignments, executive session minutes) remain inaccessible.

12. During the past few years scholars have begun to give FBI activities the attention they deserve. See especially Athan Theoharis, *Spying on Americans: Political Surveillance from Hoover to the Huston Plan* (Philadelphia: Temple University Press, 1978); Donner, *Age of Surveillance*. Both Theoharis and Donner go well beyond the narrow purview of federal surveillance policy to consider questions of more salient interest. At the same time, Theoharis and Donner are more concerned with the development of the FBI's domestic intelligence activities than the development of an anticommunist or McCarthyite politics. There has been little written thus far focusing specifically on the development of the domestic Communist issue during the McCarthy era (1946-1954). Most of what has been written recently on the FBI focuses disproportionately on the 1960s and particularly on the counterintelligence programs (COINTELPROs). For several notable exceptions to this trend, see the essays in Athan Theoharis, ed., *Beyond the Hiss Case: The FBI, Congress, and the Cold War* (Philadelphia: Temple University Press, 1982).

13. Michael Ledeen, "Hiss, Oswald, the KGB, and Us," *Commentary*, May 1978, p. 30.

I. FEDERAL SURVEILLANCE AND THE MENACE, 1919-1940

1. *SDSRIARA*, p. 391.

2. U.S., Senate, Subcommittee of the Judiciary Committee, *Hearings Regarding Brewing and Liquor Interests and German and Bolshevik Propaganda*, 66th Cong., 1st sess., 1919 (Serial 7597-99), passim. See also

Robert J. Goldstein, *Political Repression in Modern America* (Cambridge, Mass.: Schenkman, 1978), p. 148; Max Lowenthal, *The Federal Bureau of Investigation* (New York: William Sloane, 1950), pp. 36–66.

3. U.S., Senate, *Investigation Activities of the Department of Justice*, S.Doc. 153, 66th Cong., 1st sess., 1919 (Serial 7607).

4. U.S., Senate, Subcommittee of the Foreign Relations Committee, *Hearings Regarding Recognition of Russia*, 68th Cong., 1st sess., 1923; Don Whitehead, *The FBI Story* (New York: Pocket Books, 1963), p. 433.

5. U.S., Senate, *Attempts of the Communists to Seize the American Labor Movement*, S.Doc. 14, 68th Cong., 1st sess., 1923 (Serial 8253); Ogden, *The Dies Committee*, p. 19.

6. *Cong. Rec.*, 71st Cong., 2d sess., May 22, 1930, p. 9390; Ogden, *The Dies Committee*, pp. 20–23. For Whalen and Fish, see also Goodman, *The Committee*, pp. 6–7. For the Bureau, see Donner, *Age of Surveillance*, p. 48.

7. U.S., House, Special Committee to Investigate Communist Activities in the United States, *Investigation of Communist Propaganda*, 71st Cong., 2d sess., 1930, passim. For Hoover's testimony, see Donner, *Age of Surveillance*, p. 48.

8. *SDSRIARA*, p. 391; *HIA*, vol. 6, *FBI*, p. 556.

9. Ogden, *The Dies Committee*, pp. 32–36.

10. *HIA*, vol. 6, *FBI*, p. 557. For the report, see *Investigation of Nazi and Other Propaganda*, H.Rept. 153, 74th Cong., 1st sess., 1935 (Serial 9890).

11. *SRIA*, pp. 94–95. For the APL, see Joan M. Jensen, *The Price of Vigilance* (Chicago: Rand McNally, 1968). Microfilm of Bureau of Investigation records for the 1908–1922 period, including an index comprising 111 rolls, are available in the National Archives (RG65).

12. Lowenthal, *Federal Bureau of Investigation*, pp. 83–92, 149; *SRIA*, pp. 98–101, 114.

13. Burns is quoted in Goldstein, *Political Repression*, p. 175. For Frankfurter et al., see David Williams, "The Bureau of Investigation and Its Critics: The Origins of Federal Political Surveillance," *Journal of American History* 68 (Dec. 1981): 569–74. For Whitney and Easley, see Norman Hapgood, ed., *Professional Patriots* (New York: Albert and Charles Boni, 1927), pp. 97–102.

14. Lowenthal, *Federal Bureau of Investigation*, pp. 289–93; Sanford J. Ungar, *FBI* (Boston: Little, Brown, 1975), p. 47.

15. Theoharis, *Spying on Americans*, p. 255 n8; *HIA*, vol. 6, *FBI*, p. 553; Donner, *Age of Surveillance*, p. 46.

16. For the ACLU, see FBI ACLU Files, JEH, passim. The other Bureau surveillance is referred to in memos, re Leo Gallagher and Herbert Resner, May 6, 1942, Nichols O&C FBI Files-Carol King.

17. As an early White House "plumber" of sorts who investigated press leaks and maintained an informal blacklist of the President's critics, Richey was rumored to have directed an organization active in the assembling of derogatory information on Democratic party officials. Memo, [Hoover?] to [File], May 2, 1933, Nichols O&C FBI Files-Val O'Farrell. See also Craig Lloyd, *Aggressive Introvert: A Study of Herbert Hoover and Public Relations*

Management, 1912-1932 (Columbus: Ohio State University Press), p. 180n.
18. Letter, Lincoln to the President, Nov. 16, 1929, Subject File-Sentinels of the Republic, HCH; letter, R. E. Vetterli to Director, Nov. 21, 1929, ibid.; letter, Hoover to Richey, Nov. 21, 1929, ibid.
19. See the correspondence in Subject File-American Civil Liberties Union, HCH; Subject File-Colored Question, HCH; Foreign Affairs-Italy Correspondence 1930, HCH; PSF-Moorhead, H. to Moos, A., HCH; Subject File-FBI, HCH; Subject File-American Citizens Political Awakening Association, HCH; Cabinet Office-Justice Dept., Farmers' Strike, HCH.
20. Letter, Nutt to Joslin, Oct. 6, 1931, PSF-Menh to Menl, HCH; letter, Joslin to Nutt, Oct. 13, 1931, ibid.; memo, Hoover to Attorney General, Oct. 10, 1931, ibid.
21. For the Bureau's reports on the League, see letters, Hoover to Richey, Oct. 30 and 31, 1931, and Nov. 2, 1931, Subject File-Navy League of the U.S. Investigation, HCH. For a history of the League, see Armin Rappaport, *The Navy League of the United States* (Detroit: Wayne State University Press, 1962).
22. Letters, Hoover to Early, Aug. 19, 1933 and Dec. 5, 1934, OF10-B (FBI 1933-34), FDR; memo, Early to Hoover, Feb. 24, 1934, ibid. See also memo, Hoover to Attorney General, Oct. 18, 1934, Memoranda-FBI, Homer S. Cummings Papers, University of Virginia, Charlottesville.
23. For "Mother" Bloor, see Monty N. Penkower, *The Federal Writers' Project: A Study in Government Patronage of the Arts* (Urbana: University of Illinois Press, 1977), p. 182. For the Scottsboro boys et al., see memos, re Leo Gallagher, Herbert Resner, and Arthur Goldberg, May 6, 1942, Nichols O&C FBI Files-Carol King.
24. *SDSRIARA*, p. 393; *HIA*, vol. 6, *FBI*, pp. 558-59.
25. Ibid., p. 562; *IARA*, p. 25; *SDSRIARA*, pp. 393-97; *SRIA*, p. 99.
26. Diary entries, Sept. 17 and 18, 1936, Cummings Papers. See also the correspondence in PPF2282, FDR; OF10-B (FBI 1937-38), FDR; PSF-Justice Dept. (J. Edgar Hoover), FDR; PSF-Justice Dept. (Homer Cummings 1938-39), FDR.
27. In December 1939, moreover, Roosevelt granted Bureau agents, along with Army G-2 and Office of Naval Intelligence investigators, limited access to Census Bureau records. Memo, Edwin Watson to FDR, Dec. 7, 1939, OF10-B (FBI 1939), FDR; memo, FDR to Watson, Dec. 8, 1939, ibid. And in June 1941 Roosevelt authorized an expansion of FBI responsibilities "in the fields of subversive control of labor." (The Bureau had been investigating CPUSA influence in strikes with the administration's knowledge since at least October 1939.) Memo, FDR to Secretary of War and Secretary of the Navy, June 4, 1941, OF10-B (FBI 1940-41), FDR; memo, dj [Dorothy Jones] to Early, Oct. 5, 1939, OF407-B (Strikes 1939-40), FDR.
28. Memo, re Present Status of Espionage Operations, Oct. 24, 1940, no. 408, OF10-B, FDR.
29. Walter Trohan, *Political Animals: Memoirs of a Sentimental Cynic* (Garden City, N.Y.: Doubleday, 1975), p. 169.

30. See, for example, letter, Hoover to Early, June 4, 1940, no. 112, OF10-B, FDR; letter, Hoover to Early, Aug. 2, 1940, OF10-B (FBI 1940–41), FDR; memos, FDR to STE [Early], May 21 and 22, 1940, ibid.; memos, Early to Hoover, May 18, 21 and 29, 1940, and June 17, 1940, all ibid. For the thank-you note, see memo, FDR to Watson, June 12, 1940, ibid.; letter, FDR to Hoover, June 14, 1940, ibid.

31. Letters, Hoover to Watson, March 19, 1941, no. 690, July 10, 1941, no. 860, Oct. 13, 1941, no. 937, Aug. 14, 1941, no. 891, and Aug. 26, 1941, no. 899, all in OF10-B, FDR.

32. For Fish, see FBI Repts. no. 400, Oct. 22, 1940 and no. 533, Dec. 13, 1940 (summaries only), ibid. For Nye et al., see letter, Hoover to Watson, Aug. 28, 1941, no. 902, ibid. For the radio station, see memo, FDR to Hoover, May 20, 1940, PSF-Justice Dept. (J. Edgar Hoover), FDR; letter, Hoover to Watson, May 22, 1940, ibid. For Seldes, see memo, Early to the President, Feb. 18, 1941, OF4185, FDR; letters, Hoover to Early, Dec. 11, 1940 and Feb. 15, 1941, ibid.

33. See especially memos, FDR to Hoover, Sept. 7, 1943 and July 11, 1944, PSF-Justice Dept. (J. Edgar Hoover), FDR; letter, Hoover to Grace Tully, July 19, 1944, ibid.; memo, re Reuben Hollis Fleet, July 18, 1944, ibid.; memo, Walter Winchell to [Early?], July 7, 1944, ibid.; letter, Hoover to Watson, Nov. 30, 1939, no. 11, OF10-B, FDR.

34. Memos, Tamm to Director, July 2 and 10, 1940, Nichols O&C FBI Files-Herbert Hoover.

35. Letter, Hoover to Watson, Feb. 8, 1941, no. 634, OF10-B, FDR; memo, March 29, 1943, FBI Repts. (Misc. 1943), Harry Hopkins Papers, FDR.

36. Robert Conway, a reporter for the *New York Daily News*, had made arrangements in late 1939 with a switchboard operator at Washington's Carlton Hotel, where Secretary of State Cordell Hull lived, allowing him to listen in on telephone conversations between FDR and Hull. See Nichols O&C FBI Files-*New York Daily News*. *Daily News* columnist John O'Donnell, a relentless critic of the President's defense policies (and of the FBI's effort to keep tabs on "fifth columnists" in Hawaii prior to Pearl Harbor), was investigated by the Bureau, denied press credentials by the War Department, and awarded (in absentia) the "Nazi Iron Cross" by FDR at a White House press conference. Letter, Hoover to Early, Dec. 29, 1941, FBI, Stephen T. Early Papers, FDR; Richard W. Steele, "Franklin D. Roosevelt and His Foreign Policy Critics," *Political Science Quarterly* 94 (Spring 1979): 29.

37. See Propaganda-Domestic, Francis Biddle Papers, FDR, passim.

38. Memo, FDR to Attorney General, May 11, 1942, OF419 (Congress 1942), FDR. According to Kahn, Viereck had also worked closely with Hamilton Fish and the late Senator Ernest Lundeen (Farmer-Labor, Minn.) prior to Pearl Harbor. Other congressmen—including Senators D. Worth Clark (D., Iowa), Rush D. Holt (D., W.Va.), E. C. Johnson (D., Col.), Gerald P. Nye (R., N.D.), and Burton K. Wheeler (D., Mont.) and Congressmen Philip Bennett (R., Mo.), Stephen Day (R., Ill.), Henry Dworshak (R., Idaho),

and Clare E. Hoffman (R., Mich.)—had allowed (whether inadvertently or deliberately) their franking privileges to be "used to further the schemes of the Axis." Michael Sayers and Albert E. Kahn, *Sabotage! The Secret War Against America* (New York: Harper and Brothers, 1942), pp. 177–95. One man's patriot, however, can often be another man's subversive. When Sayers and Kahn later published *The Great Conspiracy: The Secret War Against Soviet Russia* (New York: Boni and Gaer, 1946), Herbert Hoover wrote to the FBI Director requesting information regarding the authors' ties to the CPUSA. Letters, Hoover to Hoover, Feb. 7 and 15, 1946, PPI-J. Edgar Hoover, HCH.

39. FBI Rept. no. 1091, Jan. 1, 1942 (summary only), OF10-B, FDR; letters, Hoover to Hopkins, Nov. 9, 1942, no. 2271-B and May 1, 1943, no. 2331-A, ibid.; letter, Hoover to Marvin H. McIntyre, Sept. 17, 1943, PSF-Justice Dept. (J. Edgar Hoover), FDR; letters, Hoover to Hopkins, July 22, 1942, FBI Repts. (Communist Party), Hopkins Papers; letter, Hopkins to Hoover, July 28, 1942, ibid.

40. For specific examples, see memo, Hoover to Attorney General, Oct. 20, 1938, OF10-B (FBI 1937–38), FDR; memo, FDR to Attorney General, Nov. 16, 1938, ibid.; letter, Hoover to Watson, Oct. 3, 1940, no. 341, OF10-B, FDR; memo, FDR to Cummings, Oct. 10, 1940, no. 341, ibid.; letter, FDR to Rexford Tugwell, Feb. 3, 1942, CF-Puerto Rico, FDR; letters, Tugwell to FDR, Feb. 11, 1942 and Jan. 29, 1942, ibid.; memo, FDR to Secretary of the Interior, Feb. 23, 1942, ibid.; letter, Harold Ickes to FDR, Feb. 25, 1942, ibid.

41. Lewis was the subject of at least three FBI wiretaps in 1938. See Nichols O&C FBI Files-John L. Lewis.

42. For Cummings, see letter, Hoover to Watson, Oct. 3, 1940, no. 341, OF10-B, FDR; memo, FDR to Cummings, Oct. 10, 1940, ibid. For Randolph, see letters, Hoover to Watson, June 19, 1941, no. 835 and June 26, 1942, no. 2194, ibid.; letters, Hoover to Hopkins, Sept. 4, 1942, no. 2248-B, Feb. 1, 1943, no. 2304-A, July 3, 1943, no. 2355-C, July 6, 1943, no. 2356-A and -B, July 8, 1943, no. 2357-A, and Sept. 15, 1943, no. 2416-A, all ibid. For Lewis and Hillman, see FBI Rept. no. 441, Nov. 4, 1940 (summary only), ibid. For the Republican party, see letter, Hoover to Hopkins, Feb. 24, 1943, no. 2312-B, ibid.; letter, Hoover to Watson, April 13, 1944, no. 2530-A, ibid. See also letter, Hoover to Hopkins, Aug. 22, 1942, FBI Repts. (Communist Party), Hopkins Papers. For the political climate, see General Intelligence Survey in the U.S., ibid., passim. For Dewey, see letter, Hoover to McIntyre, June 5, 1940, PSF-Justice Dept. (J. Edgar Hoover), FDR.

43. For the crime control program, see Arthur C. Millspaugh, *Crime Control by the National Government* (Washington, D.C.: Brookings Institution, 1937).

44. Ungar, *FBI*, p. 60. The "soft-shoe" quote is from Milton S. Mayer, "Myth of the 'G-Men,'" *Forum*, Sept. 1935, p. 145.

45. Ungar, *FBI*, pp. 60–61. See also Mayer, "Myth," p. 145; Jack Alexander, "The Director," *New Yorker*, Oct. 2, 1937 (pt. 2), p. 25. For O'Farrell, see Fred J. Cook, *The FBI Nobody Knows* (New York: Pyramid, 1965), pp.

147–48; memo, [Hoover?] to [File], May 2, 1933, Nichols O&C FBI Files-Val O'Farrell. For whatever reasons, this FBI folder on O'Farrell also records the allegation that Homer Cummings's "relations with [a] Mrs. Mara had been very intimate."

46. Max Freedman, ed., *Roosevelt and Frankfurter: Their Correspondence, 1928-1945* (Boston: Little, Brown, 1967), p. 129. For Herbert Hoover, see Whitehead, *The FBI Story*, p. 107.

47. Samuel Rosenman, ed., *The Public Papers and Addresses of Franklin D. Roosevelt*, 13 vols. (New York: Random House, 1938-1950), 3: 12-13.

48. Howard McLellan, "Shoot to Kill? A Note on the G-Men's Methods," *Harper's*, Jan. 1936, pp. 236-44. See also Cook, *The FBI Nobody Knows*, p. 151.

49. Millspaugh, *Crime Control*, pp. 51-53.

50. Rosenman, *Public Papers*, 3: 242-45, 492-95.

51. Though ideologically opposed to New Deal liberalism, Oursler would occasionally submit articles scheduled to be published in *Liberty* for the President's inspection—including an essay on FDR's personal income taxes and galleys of the first two installments of Martin Dies's autobiography. While the White House declined to respond to the charges raised by the Dies series, Roosevelt did comment extensively on the proposed income tax exposé, and Oursler killed it. Letter, Oursler to Early, Dec. 18, 1939, OF880, FDR; letter, Early to Oursler, Dec. 28, 1939, ibid.; letter, M. A. LeHand to Oursler, Jan. 15, 1937, PPF2993, FDR; letter, Oursler to LeHand, Jan. 8, 1937, ibid.; telegram, Oursler to LeHand, Jan. 18, 1937, ibid.

52. Memo, Early to the President, July 12, 1940, ibid.; memo, Early to Lowell Mellett, July 30, 1940, OF880, FDR; letter, FDR to Suydam, March 5, 1937, PPF4455, FDR. When recalling Oursler's contribution to "Homer Cummings' publicity drive against Dillinger's gang and their ilk," Early urged FDR to approve Oursler's more recent "practical ideas as to a far-flung all-covering campaign he wants to inaugurate, for the purpose of firmly instilling in the minds of American youth, the ideas of loyalty, patriotism, discipline and duty." A meeting between Oursler, a close friend of the FBI's public relations specialist, Louis Nichols, and the President was then arranged. FDR approved Oursler's plan but the administration's media expert, Lowell Mellett, balked. Mellett, then director of the Office of Government Reports and later chief of the Bureau of Motion Pictures in the Office of War Information, refused to manage the proposed "Americanism educational program" because "any campaign satisfactory to Mr. Oursler would be in line with his conception of American principles and therefore opposed to practically everything this Administration represents." Mellett objected, according to Oursler, because "there were some things" in the plan that he felt "could not be done under a democracy." See the two memos cited above and memo, Mellett to Early, Aug. 27, 1940, OF880, FDR; telegram, Watson to Oursler, July 16, 1940, PPF2993, FDR; telegram, Oursler to Watson, July 16, 1940, ibid.

53. Mayer, "Myth," p. 147.

54. In *Who's Who* (1940), Cooper described himself as a "collaborator with J. Edgar Hoover . . . on magazine articles, books and motion pictures on crime subjects."

55. This last quote is from Richard G. Powers, "One G-Man's Family: Popular Entertainment Formulas and J. Edgar Hoover's F.B.I.," *American Quarterly* 30 (Fall 1978): 473. Pegler is quoted in Cook, *The FBI Nobody Knows*, p. 196. See also Jack Alexander, "The Director," *New Yorker*, Sept. 25, 1937 (pt. 1), pp. 20, 25 and Oct. 9, 1937 (pt. 3), p. 24; Donner, *Age of Surveillance*, p. 90; Lowenthal, *Federal Bureau of Investigation*, pp. 391-93. For the FBI's mid-1930s surveillance of its critics, see Curtis D. MacDougall FBI Files, Evanston, Illinois; Roy Turnbaugh, "The FBI and Harry Elmer Barnes: 1936-1944," *Historian* 42 (May 1980): 388.

56. Lowenthal, *Federal Bureau of Investigation*, p. 393; Alexander, "The Director," pt. 1, pp. 20-22; Millspaugh, *Crime Control*, p. 296.

57. Ibid., pp. 96, 112, 295; Alexander, "The Director," pt. 2, p. 26.

58. Millspaugh, *Crime Control*, p. 79.

59. Diary entry, April 11, 1938, Cummings Papers. Cummings's concern did not extend to questions of impropriety. He was concerned exclusively with the image of the Bureau (and the Justice Department). Indeed, he requested FBI file checks on at least two publishers interested in FBI activities and received Hoover's report in January 1939—after he had resigned as Attorney General. Letter, Hoover to Cummings, Jan. 30, 1939, Personal File, ibid.

60. For the Hearst press, see Arthur M. Schlesinger, Jr., *The Age of Roosevelt*, vol. 3: *The Politics of Upheaval* (Boston: Houghton-Mifflin, 1960), pp. 84-86. For Pegler's access to McCormack-Dickstein Committee documents, see the correspondence in Communism . . . Dickstein, McCormack, Dies Committee 1934-42, Westbrook Pegler Papers, HCH.

61. William Gellermann, *The American Legion as Educator* (New York: Columbia University Teachers College, 1938), pp. 99, 130-32; Elizabeth Dilling, *The Red Network: A "Who's Who" and Handbook of Radicalism for Patriots* (Chicago: privately published, 1934). By the time the Dies Committee was established, the Progressive Era's antiradicalism, the postwar red scare, and the specter of class warfare during the Great Depression contributed to the enactment of red-flag laws in thirty-one states; criminal syndicalism laws in eighteen states; anarchy and sedition laws in twenty-six states; and teacher loyalty oath requirements in twenty-one states. Eldridge F. Dowell, *A History of Criminal Syndicalism Legislation in the United States* (Baltimore: Johns Hopkins Press 1939), pp. 14-16, passim.

62. U.S., Senate, Committee on Education and Labor, *Violations of Free Speech and Rights of Labor*, pt. 6, *Labor Policies of Employers' Associations (The NAM)*, S.Rept. 6, 76th Cong., 1st sess., 1939 (Serial 10289-90), pp. 166-67, 170, 184-85, 203-06.

63. Idem, *Violations of Free Speech and Rights of Labor*, pt. 3, *Industrial Munitions*, pp. 15, 157-63.

1. *Cong. Rec.*, 75th Cong., 3d sess., May 26, 1938, pp. 7567–86. For Dickstein's role in fathering the Committee, see Goodman, *The Committee*, pp. 3–23.

2. Martin Dies, *Martin Dies' Story* (New York: Bookmailer, 1963), p. 159.

3. Whitehead, *The FBI Story*, pp. 196–97; memos, K. R. McIntire to Edward A. Tamm, May 27, 1938, no. 1 and May 31, 1938, no. 4X, FBI HUAC Files (61–7582). Whenever possible, serial numbers for FBI documents will be provided. The FBI file classification number and file number (in this case 61 and 7582 respectively) will be provided following the first citation of a document from a particular FBI file.

4. For Dies's efforts to solicit the FBI report on the Bund, see letter, Dies to Cummings, July 6, 1938, 235343(13), RG60, Department of Justice Central Files, Numerical Files, National Archives; letter, Dies to Roosevelt, Aug. 24, 1938, 235343(14), ibid.; letter, Jackson to Dies, Aug. 13, 1938, reprinted in Dies Committee, *Annual Report*, H.Rept. 2, 76th Cong., 1st sess., 1939 (Serial 10296), pp. 3–4. For the Metcalfe brothers, see letter, Hoover to SAC Chicago, July 11, 1938, no. 4, FBI HUAC Files; letter, Hoover to Thomas F. Cullen, June 29, 1938, no. 5, ibid. For the FBI report on the Bund, see "Investigation . . . into Nazi Military Training Camps in the United States," Dec. 31, 1937, JEH. For the Committee's access to this report, see memo, Tamm to Director, March 19, 1939, no. 94, FBI HUAC Files. For Starnes, see memo, re Data Furnished Directly or Indirectly by Dies Committee, Nov. 30, 1940, no. 684, ibid.

5. Goldstein, *Political Repression*, pp. 266, 269, 271–72; *Cong. Rec.* 78th Cong., 2d sess., March 26, 1944, pp. A1523–24. For the trial, see Leo P. Ribuffo, "*United States vs. McWilliams*: The Roosevelt Administration and the Far Right," in Michal R. Belknap, ed., *American Political Trials* (Westport, Conn.: Greenwood, 1981), pp. 201–32. The decision to prosecute the so-called native fascists was supported if not initiated by the President. Roosevelt advised Hoover in January 1942 that America's entry into the war provided "a good chance to clean up a number of . . . [the native fascists'] vile publications," some of which came "pretty close to being seditious." Memo, FDR to Hoover, Jan. 21, 1942, PSF-Justice Dept. (J. Edgar Hoover), FDR.

6. Goodman, *The Committee*, p. 28.

7. As late as June 1939 Hoover maintained close contact with top Nazi police officials, including W. Fleischer, counselor to the Reich criminal police bureau. Donner, *Age of Surveillance*, p. 86.

8. When Kamp's Constitutional Educational League published a pamphlet in 1941 entitled *The Fifth Column versus the Dies Committee*, Roosevelt ordered the FBI to investigate the pamphlet's sponsors for the purpose of having "the mails forbidden to" them. Letter, Hoover to Edwin Watson, March 10, 1941, no. 663, 0F10-B, FDR; letter, Gardner Jackson to FDR, Jan.

28, 1941, no. 663, ibid.; letter, Watson to Hoover, Feb. 27, 1941, no. 663, ibid.; memo, FDR to Hoover, Feb. 29, 1941, no. 663, ibid.

9. Transcript, President's Conference with Dies, Nov. 29, 1940, OF320 (Dies Committee 1940–41), FDR.

10. Stripling quickly aligned himself with J. Parnell Thomas and worked with Thomas (sometimes successfully) to solicit information from the FBI. Note, CRW, Nov. 29, 1938, no. 38, FBI HUAC Files; letter, [Hoover] to Thomas, Nov. 29, 1938, no. 38, ibid.

11. For Sullivan, see Dies, *Martin Dies' Story*, p. 62; Goodman, *The Committee*, pp. 25, 34; Allan A. Michie and Frank Rhylick, *Dixie Demagogues* (New York: Vanguard Press, 1939), p. 58; D. A. Saunders, "The Dies Committee: First Phase," *Public Opinion Quarterly* 3 (April 1939): 229–30; Albert E. Kahn, *Treason in Congress* (New York: Progressive Citizens of America, 1948), pp. 5–6; *New York Times*, Sept. 21, 1938, p. 11.

12. Memos, Hoover to Attorney General, June 11, 1938, no. 3 and June 21, 1938, no. 3, FBI HUAC Files; memo, McIntire to Tamm, May 27, 1938, no. 2, ibid.; letter, Hoover to Dies, June 21, 1938, no. 3, ibid.; letter, Dies to Hoover, June 17, 1938, no. 3, ibid. For the G-2 investigator, see memo, [deleted] to D. Milton Ladd, Nov. 3, 1942, no. 1197, ibid.

13. Memo, Glavin to Tolson, July 6, 1938, no. 6, ibid.

14. For the fingerprint check, see memo, Dec. 9, 1940, no. 781, ibid. For Randall et al., see memo, re Direct Requests of Dies Committee Upon FBI for Assistance, April 18, 1941, no. 938X, ibid. For Starnes and Voorhis, see note, sbr, Feb. 9, 1939, no. 54, ibid.; memos, Tamm to Director, Feb. 9, 1939, no. 55 and Feb. 15, 1939, no. 57, ibid.; memos, Tamm to File, Feb. 14, 1939, no. 61 and Feb. 20, 1939, no. 62, ibid.; memo, J. L. Brennan to Tamm, March 28, 1939, no. 105, ibid. For Whitley, see memo (routed to Tolson and Tamm), June 24, 1939, no. 120, ibid.; letter, Hoover to Whitley, Aug. 2, 1939, no. 123, ibid.; memo, Tamm to File, Aug. 2, 1939, no. 126, ibid.; memo, Leo J. Gauthier to Hugh H. Clegg, Aug. 8, 1939, no. 131, ibid. For FBI surveillance of Dies Committee investigators, see, for example, memo, Nichols to Tolson, Aug. 9, 1938, no. 11, ibid.; letter, Ladd to Director, March 2, 1939, no. 85, ibid.; teletype, Dwight Brantley to Guy Hottel, July 11, 1939, no. 122, ibid. For Tamm and Nichols, see memo, Nichols to Director, Oct. 4, 1941, Nichols O&C FBI Files-Dies Committee; memo, Tamm to Director, Oct. 17, 1941, ibid.

15. Richard Rovere, "J. B. Matthews—The Informer," *Nation*, Oct. 3, 1942, p. 315. For Matthews's career, see Murray Kempton, *Part of Our Time: Some Monuments and Ruins of the Thirties* (New York: Simon and Schuster, 1955), pp. 154–79; J. B. Matthews, *Odyssey of a Fellow Traveller* (New York: Mount Vernon Publishers, 1938). For Dies's book, see *The Trojan Horse in America* (New York: Dodd, Mead, 1940). For the FBI's use of Matthews's *Odyssey*, see memo, re Leo Gallagher, May 6, 1942, Nichols O&C FBI Files-Carol King.

16. Harold L. Ickes, *The Secret Diary of Harold L. Ickes*, vol. 2, *The Inside Struggle* (New York: Simon and Schuster, 1954), p. 455.

Notes to pp. 44–47

17. Memo, Glavin to Tolson, July 6, 1938, no. 6, FBI HUAC Files.

18. For these and other Dies Committee raids, see memo, Starling to Early, March 30, 1940, PPF1-A, FDR; letter, Hutchinson to Wilson, March 25, 1940, ibid.; letters, Hoover to Watson, March 5, 1941, no. 666-A and March 7, 1941, no. 672, OF10-B, FDR; FBI Rept. no. 66, May 10, 1940 (summary only), ibid.; "The Dies Offensive," *Nation*, April 13, 1940, p. 465; Ickes, *Secret Diary*, vol. 3, *The Lowering Clouds, 1939–1941*, p. 33; letter, Harris to all Branches, n.d. (ca. Oct. 1939), Box 2, American League for Peace and Democracy Papers (Madison Branch), SHSW; *New York Times*, Oct. 4, 1939, p. 19; James B. Jacobs, "The Conduct of Local Political Intelligence" (Ph.D. diss., Princeton University, 1977), pp. 111–12; press release, Oct. 5, 1938, Series 4, Box 31, Civil Rights Congress of Michigan Papers, ALH. In February 1942 the FBI encouraged at least one "little Dies Committee," the California Fact-Finding Committee on Un-American Activities, to obtain a membership list of the Friends of Progress. The California Committee arranged a meeting with the Friends of Progress, served subpoenas *duces tecum*, and seized boxes containing donation envelopes with the names and addresses of financial contributors. Presumably, these files were turned over to the FBI. Edward L. Barrett, Jr., *The Tenney Committee: Legislative Investigation of Subversive Activities in California* (Ithaca, N.Y.: Cornell University Press, 1951), pp. 28–29.

19. For the Philadelphia raid, See *Cong. Rec.*, 78th Cong., 3d sess., April 17, 1940, p. 2184; Martin Dies, "They Tried to Get Me, Too," *U.S. News and World Report*, Aug. 20, 1954, p. 66. For Welsh's decision, see *Reeve v. Howe*, 33 F. Supp. 619 (1940). For the New York and Chicago raids, see *Detroit Times*, Nov. 20, 1940, p. 1 and Nov. 22, 1940, p. 1; memo, Hoover to Attorney General, Sept. 14, 1940, no. 470X1, FBI HUAC Files.

20. For the Chicago Police–HUAC relationship, see speech, Chicago Police Lieutenant Frank J. Heimoski to the Law Enforcement Intelligence Unit Eastern Regional Conference, Chicago, Nov. 1, 1963. For Mikuliak and Maciosek, see Jacobs, "The Conduct of Local Political Intelligence," pp. 111–12.

21. Dies Committee, Public Hearings (17 vols., 1938–1944), 75th Cong., 2d sess., 1938, vol. 2, pp. 1605–32.

22. For Birmingham, see Dies Committee, Public Hearings, 77th Cong., 1st sess., 1941, vol. 14, p. 8467; NYPD Alien Squad Rept., Sept. 4, 1941, Communism . . . Dies Committee 1934–42, Westbrook Pegler Papers, HCH; NYPD Rept. no. 695, Oct. 14, 1941, ibid. For Barker, see letter, Barker to Birmingham, Feb. 22, 1941, Dies Committee 1934–42, Pegler Papers. In 1946 Barker became chief investigator for the red-hunting House Special Committee to Investigate Campaign Expenditures.

23. For the license plate checks, see memo, SAC New York to Director, Oct. 4, 1940, no. 478, FBI HUAC Files. For the Social Security Board, see letter, Hoover to Matthew F. McGuire, Oct. 11, 1940, no. 484, ibid. For the FBI's role, see memo, Hoover to Attorney General, Oct. 21, 1940, Hoover O&C FBI Files-Martin Dies. For the Dies Committee staff surveillance, see J.

Parnell Thomas, "Sabotage? You Haven't Seen Anything Yet," *Factory Management and Maintenance*, Dec. 1940, p. 46.

24. Dies, "They Tried to Get Me," pp. 66–67; Dies Committee, *Annual Report*, H.Rept. 2748, 77th Cong., 2d sess., 1943 (Serial 10665), p. 3. For FBI applicants, see memo, for the File, Jan. 14, 1947, Pres. Temp. Comm. on Employee Loyalty—Vol. II(1), Stephen J. Spingarn Papers, HST.

25. *SDSRIARA*, pp. 359–60; *IARA*, pp. 12, 66, 211 nl; William C. Sullivan and Bill Brown, *The Bureau: My Thirty Years in Hoover's FBI* (New York: Norton, 1979), p. 21.

26. Memo, Hoover to Tolson and Tamm, Feb. 11, 1941, Nichols O&C FBI Files-Walter Krivitsky; memo, [Hottel] to File, Feb. 11, 1941, ibid.; memo, E. J. Connelley to Director, Feb. 21, 1941, ibid. FBI agents also maintained surveillance of the city editor's home.

27. Dies Committee, Public Hearings, 75th Cong., 3d sess., 1938, vol. 1, passim.

28. For Green, see letter, Frey to Thomas J. Donnelly, Dec. 2, 1938, Box 8, Dies Committee(3–4), John P. Frey Papers, Library of Congress; letter, W. C. Hushing to Green, Sept. 30, 1938, ibid. For Dies, see statement to FBI, re Willis Morgan, Dec. 27, 1948, ibid. For Frey's testimony, see Dies Committee, Public Hearings, vol. 1, pp. 92–277. For the FBI's use of Frey's testimony, see memo, re Abraham J. Isserman, May 6, 1942, Nichols O&C FBI Files-Carol King.

29. See, for example, memo, re Communist party Central Committee Directive, Nov. 16, 1935, Box 5, Communism(5), Frey Papers; letter, Frey to Dies, Aug. 30, 1938, Box 7, Dies Committee(1), Frey Papers; telegram, Joe Curran to Dies, Aug. 15, 1938, ibid.; letter, Frey to Dies, Jan. 3, 1939, Box 8, Dies Committee(3), Frey Papers; letter, Whitley to Frey, April 21, 1939, ibid.; letter, Frey to H. G. Flaugh, April 19, 1939, ibid.

30. Letter, Frey to Vandenberg, Aug. 16, 1938, Box 7, Dies Committee(1), Frey Papers; letter, Vandenberg to Frey, Aug. 18, 1938, ibid.

31. Memo, McIntire to Mumford, Oct. 5, 1942, Vito Marcantonio FBI Files (100-28126), JEH; letter, Hoover to Steele, Dec. 19, 1940, no. 838X, FBI HUAC Files; letter, Steele to Hoover, Dec. 6, 1940, no. 838X, ibid. Most of the organizations Steele claimed to represent—in particular those that supported the Dies Committee—were subjected to FBI surveillance as part of the Bureau's "study of patriotic and vigilante organizations." Memo, re Dies Committee, Oct. 6, 1938, no. 27, ibid.

32. Dies Committee, Public Hearings, vol. 1, pp. 277–428, 455–706.

33. Ibid., pp. 284–85, 304, 311.

34. For Hoover, see the notation on memo, P. E. Foxworth to Director, Aug. 22, 1938, no. 13, FBI HUAC Files. See also memo, Glavin to Director, Aug. 15, 1938, no. 12X, ibid.; memo, Foxworth to Tamm, Jan. 5, 1939, no. 43, ibid.; memo, McIntire to Tamm, Dec. 29, 1938, no. 43, ibid; memo, Foxworth to Director, Aug. 16, 1938, no. 12, ibid.

35. Memos, FDR to Secretary of Labor, Aug. 29 and Sept. 18, 1935, OF1750, FDR.

36. Letter, Dies to Jackson, Oct. 29, 1938, OF320 (Dies Committee 1938), FDR; Dies Committee, Public Hearings, vol. 14, pp. 8563–64. Although Roosevelt was no longer anxious to deport Bridges after America entered the war, his reluctance was not shared by Attorney General Biddle. According to Biddle, FDR "was inclined at first to suggest that we could not deport Communists. I suggested that we could and would." Notes, re luncheon with the President, May 4, 1942, Roosevelt, Francis Biddle Papers, FDR.

37. For Mrs. Roosevelt's close relationship with the AYC and subsequent break with the Youth Congress in mid-1941, see Joseph P. Lash, *Eleanor and Franklin* (New York: Norton, 1971), pp. 543–54, 597–611.

38. For the AYC, see letters, Eleanor Roosevelt to Hoover, May 31 and June 15, 1939, Hom-Hoz 1939, Eleanor Roosevelt Papers, FDR; letters, Eleanor Roosevelt to Hoover, May 12 and July 25, 1940, Hej-Hoz 1940, ibid. For the other FBI reports, see letters, [Malvina Thompson] to Hoover, Aug. 27 and Dec. 31, 1942, He-Ho 1942, ibid.; letter, Hoover to Eleanor Roosevelt, Jan. 6, 1943, He-Ho 1942, ibid.; letter, Adams to Eleanor Roosevelt, Dec. 22, 1942, He-Ho 1942, ibid.; letter, Thompson to Mrs. David Honeyman, Aug. 21, 1943, Ho-I 1943, ibid.; letter, Hoover to Early, Aug. 4, 1943, Ho-I 1943, ibid.; memo, Early to Thompson, Aug. 9, 1943, Ho-I 1943, ibid.; memo, Thompson to Early, July 30, 1943, Ho-I 1943, ibid.; letter, Hoover to Watson, Dec. 28, 1942, no. 2294, OF10-B, FDR; memo, GGT [Grace Tully] to Thompson, Jan. 8, 1943, ibid.; memo, Tully to Hoover, Dec. 11, 1942, PSF-Justice Dept. (J. Edgar Hoover), FDR. For HUAC, see *Milwaukee Journal*, June 14, 1982, p. 12.

39. Sullivan, *The Bureau*, p. 276.

40. Documents recording this break-in and copies of the correspondence are in Nichols O&C FBI Files-American Youth Congress. Mrs. Roosevelt and Lash were also the subjects of G-2 surveillance, with Army counterespionage agents opening the First Lady's mail and bugging her hotel rooms. Both the Army and the FBI erroneously concluded that Lash and Eleanor Roosevelt were having an affair—a conclusion which Hoover brought to the President's attention in 1943. FDR responded by ordering a shake-up of G-2. Joseph P. Lash, *Love, Eleanor: Eleanor Roosevelt and Her Friends* (Garden City, N.Y.: Doubleday, 1982), pp. 450, 459–93.

41. For Knowles, see Dies Committee, Public Hearings, 75th Cong., 3d sess., 1938, vol. 3, pp. 1717–2060; *New York Times*, Oct. 25, 1938, p. 1. For the FBI's use of Knowles's testimony, see memo, re Leo Gallagher, May 6, 1942, Nichols O&C FBI Files-Carol King. For the Western Research Foundation, see Bill Wallace, "The Intelligence Laundry: Blacklisting Lives On," *Nation*, May 6, 1978, pp. 539–41.

42. For Gehan, see Paul Y. Anderson, "Behind the Dies Intrigue," *Nation*, Nov. 12, 1938, p. 499; Michie and Ryhlick, *Dixie Demagogues*, pp. 57–58. For Fowler, see letters, R. J. Abbaticchio to Director, Sept. 24, 1940, no. 473 and Oct. 3, 1940, no. 480, FBI HUAC Files. The leak of Congressman Frank Havenner's (D., Cal.) name offers another example of the Dies Committee's partisan purposes and incorrigible personnel. On July 16, 1940, ex-Com-

munist John J. Leech named Havenner as a CPUSA member before Dies, then sitting as a one-man executive committee in Beaumont, Texas. In the midst of a reelection campaign four years later, an ad appeared in the *San Francisco Chronicle* accusing Havenner of being a Communist and printing portions of Leech's executive session testimony. Though responsibility for this development has never been determined conclusively, James H. Steadman, a former Dies aide in charge of the Committee's Los Angeles office, who had participated in Leech's interview, may have been responsible. In 1944 Steadman was working for Albert C. Mattei, the chief financial backer of Havenner's Republican opponent in the 1944 elections. Goodman, *The Committee*, p. 102n; *Cong. Rec.*, 79th Cong., 1st sess., Jan. 11, 1945, p. 206. Another congressman named by Leech, Lee E. Geyer (D., Cal.), was apparently investigated by the FBI. Memo, Clegg to Director, Nov. 1, 1940, Nichols O&C FBI Files-Harry McMullin.

43. Jerry Voorhis, *Confessions of a Congressman* (Garden City, N.Y.: Doubleday, 1947), pp. 212–13. A copy of Matthews's report is in Consumers, Gardner Jackson Papers, FDR.

44. Berlin's telegram is referred to in memo, Berlin to Advertisers and Manufacturers, Dec. 9, 1939, Series 1, Box 3, Donald Montgomery Papers, ALH. See also letter, Montgomery to Dies, April 15, 1940, Series 1, Box 2, Montgomery Papers; letter, Anne Simmons to Montgomery, Jan. 4, 1940, ibid.; letter, Corliss Lamont to Montgomery, Dec. 13, 1940, ibid.; Frank Jellinek, "Dies, Hearst and the Consumer," *New Republic*, Jan. 1, 1940, pp. 10, 12; *New York Times*, Aug. 21, 1939, p. 20. Montgomery would later be smeared by the FBI as well—in 1957 the Bureau leaked a blind memorandum regarding his activities to former HUAC member Karl Mundt for Mundt's use as a member of the Senate Select Labor Management Committee (the so-called Rackets Committee). Memo, re Donald Ewan Montgomery, Feb. 27, 1957, Box 701(3), KEM.

45. Memo, Berlin to Advertisers and Manufacturers, Dec. 9, 1939, Series 1, Box 3, Montgomery Papers.

46. *New York Times*, Oct. 15, 1938, p. 3. The Dies Committee was not the only congressional committee probing New Deal programs and personnel. After Thomas finished his FBI-assisted probe of the Federal Theatre and Writers' projects, Clifton A. Woodrum's (D., Va.) House Appropriations Subcommittee launched a new probe. And Howard Smith's (D., Va.) Special House Committee to Investigate Executive Agencies was established in 1943 with the implicit purpose of discrediting the New Deal.

47. Dies Committee, *Annual Report*, H.Rept. 2277, 77th Cong., 2d sess., 1942 (Serial 10664), p. 2.

48. Other liberal investigating efforts included the Senate Banking and Currency Committee probe of 1933–1934, the munitions inquiry of 1934–1936, and the mid-1930s exposé of the utilities lobby.

49. Letter, Wallace to Early, Dec. 12, 1939, OF320 (Dies Committee 1939), FDR; letter, Gardner Jackson to Eleanor Roosevelt, Dec. 18, 1939, OF320 (Americanization 1939), FDR; memo, FDR to Eleanor Roosevelt, Dec. 22, 1939, ibid. By mid-1943 Hoover was forwarding FBI reports to the White

House regarding CPUSA efforts to infiltrate the consumer movement. Letter, Hoover to Hopkins, May 18, 1943, no. 2335-A, OF10-B, FDR.

50. Dies, *Martin Dies' Story*, pp. 82, 254–55; Ickes, *The Lowering Clouds*, p. 526. For Rayburn and Arnold, see memo, FDR to Mac [McIntyre], Nov. 23, 1938, OF320 (Dies Committee 1938), FDR. For Ickes on Jemison, see *The Inside Struggle*, pp. 506–07. Income tax questions continued to plague Dies. In 1943 Treasury Department agents spent six months auditing his returns and Dies claimed it was part of an administration plot to harass him. Other anti–New Deal countersubversives, such as Hamilton Fish, also claimed to have been harassed. Indeed, a tax investigation of Father Charles Coughlin's financial affairs lasted from the mid-1930s into the early 1940s. Victor Lasky, *It Didn't Start with Watergate* (New York: Dial, 1977), pp. 160-61; memo, Guy Helvering to Secretary of the Treasury, Sept. 18, 1940, Confidential Reports About People, Henry M. Morgenthau, Jr., Papers, FDR. On the other side of the political spectrum, Treasury Secretary Morgenthau ordered an investigation of singer Paul Robeson, the CPUSA's most prominent black spokesman. The report to Morgenthau highlighted Robeson's opposition to the Dies Committee. Memo, Elmer Irey to Secretary of the Treasury, Aug. 7, 1941, ibid.; Bureau of Internal Revenue Intelligence Unit Report, July 31, 1941, ibid.

51. For Dies's father, see memo, RWJ [Jackson] to Hoover and James Allen, Nov. 29, 1940, no. 819X, FBI HUAC Files. For the Senate election, see Ronnie Dugger, *The Politician: The Life and Times of Lyndon Johnson— The Drive for Power, From the Frontier to Master of the Senate* (New York: Norton, 1982), pp. 225–26, 233, 235, 333, 442n. For Westrick, see memo, for the President, April 15, 1942, CF-D, FDR; memo, FDR to Attorney General, April 16, 1942, ibid.; memo, Biddle to the President, April 20, 1942, ibid. Although Roosevelt apparently did not know it, Dies had requested the FBI file on Westrick in mid-1940. See Thomas, "Sabotage?," p. 48.

52. Memo, for Watson, Sept. 29, 1943, PSF-Justice Dept. (J. Edgar Hoover), FDR. For White House interest in the Dies Committee and its constituency, see memo, McIntyre to Hoover, Nov. 14, 1938, OF3474, FDR; memo, FDR to McIntyre, Nov. 12, 1938, ibid.; letter, Hoover to McIntyre, Nov. 19, 1938, ibid.; letter, Perry F. Ramey to FDR, Nov. 9, 1938, ibid.; FBI Repts. no. 66, May 10, 1940, no. 190, July 30, 1940, and no. 535, Dec. 13, 1940 (summaries only), OF10-B, FDR; letters, Hoover to Watson, March 5, 1941, no. 666-A and March 6, 1941, no. 672, ibid.; letter, Hoover to Watson, n.d. (ca. Sept. 18, 1943), PSF-Justice Dept. (J. Edgar Hoover), FDR; memo, FDR to Hoover, March 25, 1943, ibid.; letter, Hoover to McIntyre, March 31, 1943, ibid.; memos, Hoover to Attorney General, Oct. 21, 1940, no. 497 and Oct. 23, 1940, no. 496, FBI HUAC Files; letter, Hoover to Watson, July 3, 1940, no. 446, ibid.; letter, Hoover to Attorney General, July 3, 1940, no. 448, ibid.; letter, Whitley to Hoover, July 1, 1940, no. 448, ibid.

53. FBI Rept. no. 54, April 10, 1940 (summary only), OF10-B, FDR; letter, Hoover to Watson, Jan. 28, 1941, no. 616, ibid. For Riley, see letter, Hoover to Watson, March 26, 1941, no. 700, ibid.

54. FDR publicly censured the Committee on two lone occasions. The

first, deemed by Roosevelt "a flagrantly unfair and un-American attempt to influence an election," involved Michigan Governor Frank Murphy's unsuccessful reelection campaign in 1938. The second and last time FDR publicly censured the Committee occurred in October 1939 when Committee investigators seized the mailing list of the American League for Peace and Democracy's Washington chapter. After Dies released the names of 563 federal employees on this list to the press, Roosevelt labeled this action a "sordid procedure." Richard Polenberg, "Franklin Roosevelt and Civil Liberties: The Case of the Dies Committee," *Historian* 30 (Feb. 1968): 169.

55. For Voorhis, Dempsey, and Starnes, see ibid. pp. 170–71; Ickes, *The Inside Struggle*, pp. 546–49, 573–74; memo, LeHand to the President, Jan. 13, 1939, PSF-Harold Ickes 1937–39, FDR; memo, LeHand to STE [Early], Feb. 18, 1939, OF320 (Dies Committee 1939), FDR; memo, Rowe to Early, Jan. 4, 1940, OF320 (Dies Committee 1940–41), FDR; memos, FDR to Steve [Early], Nov. 1, 1939 and Nov. 2, 1939, OF320 (Americanization 1939), FDR. For McIntyre and Byrnes, see memo, FDR to Mac [McIntyre], Jan. 13, 1942, OF133 (Immigration 1942), FDR; memo, MHM [McIntyre] to the President, Jan. 10, 1942, ibid.; memo, JFB [Byrnes] to the President, n.d. (ca. Jan. 1942), ibid.

56. Ickes, *The Lowering Clouds*, pp. 76–77. For the FBI file on Murphy, see Donner, *Age of Surveillance*, p. 99. For Hoover's similar attempt to pressure Murphy's successor, see Hoover O&C FBI Files-Martin Dies, passim. The Bureau kept a file on another New Dealer and Supreme Court Justice, Felix Frankfurter. For this file, captioned with the name of Frankfurter's brother, see Nichols O&C FBI Files-Otto N. Frankfurter.

57. Memo, Tamm to Director, Jan. 25, 1939, no. 46X, FBI HUAC Files; memo, S. J. Tracy to Tamm, Jan. 26, 1939, no. 46, ibid.; memo, Tamm to File, Jan. 26, 1939, no. 47, ibid. See also the newspaper clippings in no. 40X10 and no. 80X1, ibid. For the Justice Department's interest in Committee files, see letters, Murphy to Dies, Nov. 2 and 27, 1939, 236377(1–2), Department of Justice Central Files; letters, Dies to Murphy, Nov. 22 and Oct. 26, 1939, ibid.; memo, re Important Matters Found on Review of Dept. Files, Oct. 26, 1939, ibid.; memo, re American League for Peace and Democracy, May 23, 1939, ibid.

58. For the Workers Alliance, see Ickes, *The Inside Struggle*, p. 642. For the tax question, see letter, Murphy to the President, March 30, 1939, OF320 (Dies Committee 1939), FDR; memo, K to Watson, May 11, 1939, ibid. Dies had also been granted access to income tax records in 1938. See letters, Morgenthau to the President, June 29 and July 1, 1938, OF962 (1938), FDR; letter, Dies to FDR, June 17, 1938, ibid.; letter, D. W. Bell to Attorney General, July 7, 1938, ibid.

59. Quoted in *Cong. Rec.*, 77th Cong., 1st sess., Feb. 11, 1941, pp. 887, 889. See also ibid., 76th Cong., 3d sess., Dec. 12, 1940, pp. 13912–13; Voorhis, *Confessions*, p. 224; Richard B. Henderson, *Maury Maverick: A Political Biography* (Austin: University of Texas Press, 1970), pp. 284–85.

60. Dies, *Martin Dies' Story*, pp. 35, 75; Ickes, *The Inside Struggle*, p. 529.

61. *New York Times*, Sept. 27, 1939, p. 1; Ogden, *The Dies Committee*,

pp. 141–42. For Thomas's request, see note, cek, n.d. (ca. Dec. 12, 1938), no. 41, FBI HUAC Files; letter, Thomas to Hoover, Dec. 12, 1938, no. 41, ibid.; [Hoover] to Thomas, Dec. 13, 1938, no. 41, ibid.

62. Eleanor Roosevelt, *This I Remember* (New York: Harper, 1949), pp. 202–03.

63. Whitehead, *The FBI Story*, p. 434 nl; Benjamin Ginzburg, *Rededication to Freedom* (New York: Simon and Schuster, 1959), pp. 90–91; *Report of F.B.I. Relative to Investigation of Government Employees Charged with Un-American Activities*, H. Doc. 833, 77th Cong., 2d sess., 1942 (Serial 10695), pp. 12–13; Goldstein, *Political Repression*, pp. 278–79. For Hoover's report to the White House, see letter, Hoover to Watson, Feb. 27, 1941, no. 661, OF10-B, FDR.

64. In September 1942 Dies obtained a "strictly confidential" memorandum of the Attorney General containing FBI data on all twelve Communist and Communist-front groups included on the Attorney General's list. *Cong. Rec.*, 77th Cong., 2d sess., Sept. 24, 1942, pp. 7442–48.

65. Note, June 30, 1942, no. 2196, OF10-B, FDR; memo, FDR to Berle, Aug. 12, 1941, OF4514, FDR; memo, Berle to the President, July 29, 1941, ibid.; memo, Smith to the President, Oct. 16, 1941, ibid.; diary entry, Jan. 16, 1942, Smith Papers. See also John Franklin Carter, "Report on 'Blacklisting' Government Employees," June 11, 1942, no. 1160, FBI HUAC Files; memo, FDR to Hoover, June 13, 1942, no. 1160, ibid.; letter, Hoover to Watson, n.d. (ca. June 14, 1942), no. 1160, ibid. For Carter's reports, see PSF-John Franklin Carter, Boxes 120–37, FDR. For another quasi-official intelligence operation, see Jeffery M. Dorwart, "The Roosevelt-Astor Espionage Ring," *New York History* 62 (July 1981): 307–22.

66. Letter, Ugo Carusi to Watson, Oct. 7, 1941, OF252 (Government Employees 1941), FDR; letter, Attorney General to Dies, Oct. 7, 1941, ibid. For Hoover on "overt acts," see memo, Hoover to Attorney General, April 5, 1941, no. 966, FBI HUAC Files.

67. Voorhis, *Confessions*, p. 224. For the break-ins, see memo, Tamm to Director, May 31, 1941, Nichols O&C FBI Files-Justice Dept.; note, re confidential informants, n.d. (ca. May 1941), ibid.; memo, Hoover to Matthew F. McGuire, May 13, 1941, ibid. For Mattei, see memo, Nichols to Tolson, Oct. 14, 1941, Nichols O&C FBI Files-Dies Committee. For the "blind" memorandum, see memo, P. E. Foxworth to Director, Sept. 8, 1941, no. 1019, FBI HUAC Files. The FBI apparently gave a copy of the Washington Committee for Democratic Action list to the Washington Police Department and a policeman forwarded yet another copy to Mary Spargo, a Dies Committee investigator. Memo, Ladd to Director, Oct. 22, 1941, no. 1021, ibid.; memo, S. K. McKee to Director, Nov. 27, 1941, no. 1040, ibid.

68. *Report of F.B.I.* (1942), pp. 11, 13–17.

69. *Cong. Rec.*, 77th Cong., 2d sess., Sept. 24, 1942, pp. 7442–48; *Report of F.B.I. Relative to Investigation of Government Employees Charged with Un-American Activities*, H.Doc. 51, 78th Cong., 1st sess., 1943 (Serial 10792), pp. 4–5.

70. Letter, Ickes to the President, June 3, 1943, OF1661-A (1941–45), FDR.

71. Memo, Hoover to Attorney General, Sept. 1, 1942, Hoover O&C FBI Files-Martin Dies; memo, Ladd to Director, Nov. 27, 1953, ibid.; memo, E. W. Timm to Ladd, Sept. 24, 1942, no. 1186, FBI HUAC Files.

72. Memo, Ladd to Callan, May 4, 1943, FBI ACLU Files, JEH. Wallace is quoted in Goodman, *The Committee*, p. 132. For the Kerr Committee, see generally Goldstein, *Political Repression*, pp. 279-80; Frederick L. Schuman, "'Bill of Attainder' in the Seventy-Eighth Congress," *American Political Science Review* 37 (Oct. 1943): 821; memo, re *U.S. v. Lovett*, n.d. (ca. Jan. 1947), Pres. Temp. Comm. on Employee Loyalty-Vol. II(3), Spingarn Papers; Robert E. Cushman, "The Purge of Federal Employees Accused of Disloyalty," *Public Administration Review* 3 (Autumn 1943): 306; memo, Ickes to the President, May 15, 1943, OF1661-A, FDR; letter, Ickes to the President, June 3, 1943, ibid.

73. Letter, Kerr to Tolson, March 5, 1945, Nichols O&C FBI Files-John H. Kerr; letter, Tolson to Kerr, March 5, 1945, ibid.; memo, Hoover to Tolson, Nichols, and Glavin, Feb. 3, 1945, ibid.

74. Memo, Tracy to Tamm, Jan. 26, 1939, no. 49X, FBI HUAC Files; memo, Tamm to Director, Jan. 30, 1939, no. 52, ibid.

75. Letter, Hoover to Watson, June 3, 1940, no. 109, OF10-B, FDR. For Dies on the FBI's agents, see Lewis H. Carlson, "J. Parnell Thomas and the House Committee on Un-American Activities, 1938-1948" (Ph.D. diss., Michigan State University, 1967), p. 139. For Dies on Detroit, see Goodman, *The Committee*, p. 105.

76. Ibid., pp. 105-07; Ogden, *The Dies Committee*, pp. 220, 223; memo, Hoover to Attorney General, Sept. 14, 1940, no. 470X1, FBI HUAC Files. For the white paper, see Appendix II, *A Preliminary Digest and Report on the Un-American Activities of Various Nazi Organizations and Individuals in the United States, Including Diplomatic and Consular Agents of the German Government*, 76th Cong., 3d sess., 1940.

77. Letter, Hoover to Cobbie (Edmond D. Coblentz), Oct. 19, 1940, Nichols O&C FBI Files-Paul Mallon; memo, Nichols to Tolson, Oct. 19, 1940, ibid. For the "on top" quote, see memo, Tamm to Director, Oct. 3, 1940, no. 483X, FBI HUAC Files.

78. FBI Rept. no. 429, Oct. 29, 1940 (summary only), OF10-B, FDR. By November 18 the FBI had agents from nineteen field offices working on the Zapp case. Memo, Hoover to Attorney General, Nov. 18, 1940, Hoover O&C FBI Files-Martin Dies.

79. For Jackson, see Ogden, *The Dies Committee*, pp. 220, 224; *Cong. Rec.*, 76th Cong., 3d sess., Nov. 28, 1940, pp. A6724-25; *New York Times*, Nov. 28, 1940, p. 1; FBI Repts. no. 480, Nov. 20, 1940 and no. 491, Nov. 25, 1940 (summaries only), OF10-B, FDR. Two weeks later Hoover advised Jackson that Fassbender was wanted on a "serious charge" in France and Germany and, fearing deportation, "resorted to 'an array of ghost stories to satisfy the purposes of Mr. Dies.'" Memo, Hoover to Attorney General, Dec. 3, 1940, no. 632, FBI HUAC Files.

80. Teletype, Hoover to all SACs, Nov. 23, 1940, no. 536, ibid. See also

memo, Nichols to Director, Nov. 25, 1940, Hoover O&C FBI Files-Martin Dies. For Schoenstein, see memos, Nichols to Tolson, Nov. 18, 1940, no. 692 and Nov. 20, 1940, no. 693, FBI HUAC Files.

81. Memo, Fletcher to Director, Dec. 7, 1940, no. 683, ibid.; memos, Tracy to Director, Dec. 11, 1940, no. 785, Nov. 19, 1940, no. 517, and Nov. 28, 1940, no. 673, ibid.; note, st, Nov. 19, 1940, no. 516, ibid.; memo, C. H. Carson to Tamm, Nov. 23, 1940, no. 583, ibid.; memos, Hoover to Attorney General, Nov. 27, 1940, no. 583, Nov. 28, 1940, no. 673, Dec. 2, 1940, no. 700, and Dec. 17, 1940, no. 841, all ibid.

82. Ogden, *The Dies Committee*, p. 224; Dies, *Martin Dies' Story*, p. 73; Cook, *The FBI Nobody Knows*, pp. 238-41.

83. See generally *New York Times*, Nov. 28, 1940, p. 1 and Dec. 1, 1940, p. 47; FBI Rept. no. 404, Oct. 23, 1940 (summary only), OF10-B, FDR; memo, Attorney General to the President, Nov. 28, 1940, OF320 (Dies Committee 1940-41), FDR; transcript, President's Conference with Dies, Nov. 29, 1940, ibid.; letter, Dies to FDR, Dec. 3, 1940, PPF3458, FDR; letter, Early to Dies, Dec. 19, 1940, ibid. Dies's seven-point program included proposals to outlaw the CPUSA; purge all Communists from government service; permit federal action against alleged subversives before overt acts of disloyalty occurred; train and plant spies in every federal agency; require a loyalty oath for all government employees; refuse government sanction of labor negotiations involving Communist-controlled unions; and strengthen the Justice Department's powers regarding subversion and disloyalty.

84. For the Roosevelt-Dies meeting, see transcript, President's Conference with Dies, Nov. 29, 1940, OF320 (Dies Committee 1940-41), FDR; letter, Dies to FDR, Dec. 4, 1940, ibid.; letter, Watson to Dies, Dec. 20, 1940, ibid. For the agreement and Jackson's remarks, see *Cong. Rec.* 76th Cong., 3d sess., Dec. 12, 1940, p. 6847; *New York Times*, Dec. 11, 1940, p. 17.

85. Ogden, *The Dies Committee*, p. 228; *New York Times*, Dec. 14, 1940, p. 1. For Appendix I, see *A Compilation of Original Sources Used as Exhibits to Show the Nature and Aims of the Communist Party, Its Connections with the U.S.S.R. and Its Advocacy of Force and Violence*, 76th Cong., 3d sess., 1940. The "defense index" Hoover alluded to was part of the FBI Custodial Detention list of people whose "presence at liberty in this country in time of war or national emergency would be dangerous to the public peace and safety of the United States Government." Begun on September 2, 1939, the day after the Nazi invasion of Poland, the detention program was terminated at the order of Attorney General Biddle in July 1943. Biddle's conclusion, however, that "no useful purpose" was served by "classifying persons as to dangerousness" was not shared by FBI officials. Hoover circumvented Biddle's order by changing the program's title to Security Index and informing the Attorney General that the Custodial Detention program had been terminated. Three years later Bureau officials convinced Biddle's successor, Tom Clark, to provide formal authority for a preventive detention program. They did not inform Clark of their ongoing program. Moreover, when the Internal Security Act of 1950 provided legislative authorization for

the first time, the FBI and the Justice Department ignored the standards set by Congress. And when Congress repealed the emergency detention provisions of the Internal Security Act in September 1971, Bureau officials again responded—this time with Attorney General John Mitchell's consent—by changing the program's name to Administrative Index. See FBI Security Index Files, JEH, passim.

86. Memo, Nichols to Tolson, Oct. 14, 1941, Nichols O&C FBI Files-Dies Committee.

87. See Hoover's handwritten notation on newspaper clipping, Feb. 17, 1941, no. 928, FBI HUAC Files.

88. See, for example, Richard M. Nixon, *RN: The Memoirs of Richard Nixon* (New York: Grosset and Dunlap, 1978), pp. 44–45; Louis F. Budenz, *The Cry Is Peace* (Chicago: Henry Regnery, 1952), p. 15.

89. Goodman, *The Committee*, p. 163. Dies is quoted in *Martin Dies' Story*, p. 10. For Dies on HUAC, see *New York Times*, Nov. 25, 1952, p. 18 and Nov. 24, 1952, p. 12. For McCarthy on Dies, see ibid., Jan. 15, 1955, p. 7. For the Eisenhower aide, see memo, re suggested Statement for President Eisenhower, n.d., Whitman File-Brownell 1952–54(1), DDE.

90. Harry S. Truman, *Memoirs*, 2 vols. (Garden City, N.Y.: Doubleday, 1956), 2, *Years of Trial and Hope*, p. 275.

91. Robert Griffith, *The Politics of Fear: Joseph R. McCarthy and the Senate* (Lexington: University of Kentucky Press, 1970), pp. 32–33.

III. MAKING THE COLD WAR: SHAPING PUBLIC OPINION

1. *Cong. Rec.*, 79th Cong., 1st sess., Jan. 3, 1945, pp. 6–15. Rankin is quoted in Goodman, *The Committee*, pp. 168–69.

2. Between 1945 and 1950 the Committee had a high turnover and only a handful of the twenty-two congressmen who served on HUAC during those years made substantive contributions. The Committee had three chairmen (Hart, Thomas, and John S. Wood, a Georgia Democrat), two acting chairmen (Rankin in 1945 and Mundt in late 1948), and four staff directors.

3. For Rankin's racism, see *Cong. Rec.*, 79th Cong., 1st sess., July 18, 1945, p. 7739 and Oct. 24, 1945, p. 10032; ibid., 79th Cong., 2d sess., Feb. 11, 1946, p. 1225, Feb. 19, 1946, p. A872, and Feb. 27, 1946, p. 1727.

4. Letter, Hoover to Harry Vaughan, June 21, 1946, PSF-FBI Communist Data, HST. For the hearings, see *Hearings on Office of Price Administration* and *Hearings on Communist Party*, 79th Cong., 1st sess., 1945.

5. *IARA*, p. 66; *SDSRIARA*, p. 430.

6. HUAC, *Hearings on H.R. 1884 and H.R. 2122, Bills to Curb or Outlaw the Communist Party of the U.S.*, pt. 2, *Testimony of J. Edgar Hoover*, 80th Cong., 1st sess., 1947.

7. J. Edgar Hoover, "How to Fight Communism," *Newsweek*, June 9, 1947, pp. 30–32; Donner, *Age of Surveillance*, pp. 91–92, 467–77; Sullivan, *The Bureau*, p. 90. For Hoover's classic statement on the red menace, see "Red Fascism in the United States Today," *American Magazine*, Feb. 1947,

pp. 24–25, 87–90. See also James D. Bales, comp., *J. Edgar Hoover Speaks Concerning Communism* (Washington, D.C.: Capitol Hill Press, 1971).

8. See the documents in Nichols O&C FBI Files-John D. Rockefeller III. For the Dies index, see memo, O. H. Patterson to Tolson, Sept. 10, 1940, no. 474, FBI HUAC Files. For Cooper, see Ovid Demaris, *The Director: An Oral Biography of J. Edgar Hoover* (New York: Harper's Magazine Press, 1975), p. 65. For Rockefeller and a select few, the FBI was not unlike a private detective agency. Acting at the request of Supreme Court Chief Justice Earl Warren in 1955, for instance, the Bureau investigated his daughter's fiance, Dr. Stuart Brien. Nichols O&C FBI Files-Earl Warren.

9. Hoover proved his confidence in Nichols by his October 1941 decision to create an "Official and Confidential" file to be maintained in Nichols's office.

10. Quoted in Demaris, *The Director*, p. 67. Nichols was not above lying when pursuing his mission. Following the *Harvard Crimson*'s attack on FBI investigative techniques and standards in 1949, he worked closely with *Yale Daily News* editor William F. Buckley, Jr., then an undergraduate at Yale, to discredit the *Crimson*'s charges. When appearing at a general meeting at Yale on October 24, Nichols responded to Yale Law Professor Fred Rodell's query regarding the alleged FBI practice of keeping files on congressmen by dismissing it categorically. "I branded this a lie," Nichols later advised Hoover. In fact, Hoover had kept files containing derogatory information on the personal lives of various congressmen and Nichols had been aware of them for nearly ten years. Sigmund Diamond, "Heeling for Hoover: God and the F.B.I. at Yale," *Nation*, April 12, 1980, pp. 423–28. See also Diamond's letter to the editor, ibid., Sept. 13, 1980, pp. 202, 206.

11. For Nichols's career, see Demaris, *The Director*, p. 67; *New York Times*, Nov. 2, 1957, p. 11; Ungar, *FBI*, pp. 277–78; Sullivan, *The Bureau*, p. 39; interview (telephone conversation) with Karl Hess, Washington, D.C., Oct. 1, 1979; Drew Pearson, *Diaries, 1949–1959*, ed. Tyler Abell (New York: Holt, Rinehart and Winston, 1974), pp. 516–17; Hank Messick, "J. Edgar's Image: The Schenley Chapter," *Nation*, April 5, 1971, pp. 428–31.

12. Donner, *Age of Surveillance*, p. 92. The slick *FBI Law Enforcement Bulletin*, moreover, had a key circulation (estimated at 46,000 in 1964) to police officers, judges, mayors, and other state and local officials. See note, Deke [Cartha DeLoach] to Walter [Jenkins], May 28, 1964, WHCF, Gen FG135-6, LBJ.

13. Hess interview. For the "not to contact list," see *IARA*, p. 239. The FBI's practice of disseminating derogatory information on its media critics dated at least from early 1941. And when these critics—such as *New York Daily News* editor Joseph M. Patterson—were also critical of the incumbent administration, the FBI filed reports with the White House. See Nichols O&C FBI Files-*New York Daily News*, passim; letter, Hoover to Watson, Feb. 28, 1941, no. 66, OF10-B, FDR; letter, Hoover to Early, Dec. 29, 1941, FBI, Stephen T. Early Papers, FDR. FBI efforts to gather information on its media critics included unauthorized entries. On one occasion in 1959, FBI agents

gained access to the Washington hotel room of a *New York Post* investigative team that had planned a series on the Bureau. Donner, *Age of Surveillance*, p. 112.

14. Others included Charles McHarry of the *New York Daily News*, Jimmy Ward of the *Jackson* (Miss.) *Daily News*, Miami television news director Gene Strul, Boston radio and television investigator Gordon Hall, Ray Richards, Ralph McGill, Bill Shipp, Sid Epstein, Paul Palmer, Edward Nellor, Leo Rosten, Thomas Lubenow, Julian Morrison, Ray McHugh, Miriam Ottenberg, Bob Allen, Ray Cromley, Gardner Cowles, Jr., Edward J. Mowery, Ed O'Brien, and Warren Rogers. For the FBI's relationship with "friendly media," see Nichols O&C FBI Files, passim; *HIA*, vol. 6, *FBI*, pp. 762–817; *IARA*, pp. 11, 15–16, 89, 221–23, 242–47; *SDSRIARA*, pp. 34–36, 61, 161, 174–77, 182, 219–20; Ungar, *FBI*, pp. 277, 284–85, 385; Sullivan, *The Bureau*, pp. 84–85, 93–94; Hess interview; *Milwaukee Journal*, Nov. 23, 1977, pp. 1, 8; ibid., Nov. 24, 1977, pp. 1, 9; ibid., Dec. 11, 1977, Accent section, pp. 1, 15; Donner, *Age of Surveillance*, pp. 239, 240n, 490 n23; Herman Klurfeld, *Winchell: His Life and Times* (New York: Praeger, 1976), pp. 68–70; Robert Friedman, "FBI: Manipulating the Media," *Rights*, May–June 1977, pp. 13–14; Kenneth O'Reilly, "Friendly Journalists' Access to FBI Files," *USA Today*, Sept. 1980, pp. 29–31; David J. Garrow, *The FBI and Martin Luther King, Jr.: From "Solo" to Memphis* (New York: Norton, 1981), pp. 53, 66, 179.

15. Edwin R. Bayley, *Joe McCarthy and the Press* (Madison: University of Wisconsin Press, 1981), pp. 131–32.

16. Quoted in Whitehead, *The FBI Story*, pp. 353–54.

17. Hoover's statement before the Senate Foreign Relations subcommittee was reproduced and distributed by the Democratic National Committee prior to the 1950 congressional elections.

18. Thus, Rea S. Van Fosson, a much-decorated bombardier and former captain in the Air Force Office of Special Investigations, was ultimately prosecuted for forwarding a photostat of an FBI report on ex-Communist Jay Lovestone to HUAC. This leak ultimately led to Van Fosson's resignation from the Air Force on November 23, 1954. He was hired as an investigator by HUAC Chairman Harold Velde the very next day. His career with the Committee, however, was brief. Fired in January 1955, he was arrested the following August and indicted. After obtaining the services of attorney Edward Bennett Williams, Van Fosson pleaded guilty to the charge of "unlawfully converting to his own use 113 sheets of paper" owned by the government, valued at less than $100. Given a six-month suspended sentence and probation, Van Fosson next found work with Robert Aime Maheu's investigative service and, more recently, as a free-lance private investigator in Washington, D.C. *New York Times*, Dec. 22, 1954, p. 15; ibid., Aug. 13, 1955, p. 30; ibid., Sept. 10, 1955, p. 9; ibid., Jan. 13, 1956, p. 5; ibid., Feb. 4, 1956, p. 40; *Washington Evening Star*, April 28, 1957, p. A-27; Hougan, *Spooks*, p. 274n.

19. Memo, FBI Executives' Conference to Director, Oct. 14, 1953, FBI HUAC Files.

20. Ungar, *FBI*, pp. 373–74. Whitehead also had access to FBI files for *Attack on Terror: The FBI Against the Ku Klux Klan in Mississippi* (New York: Funk and Wagnalls, 1970). When Whitehead retired, the Bureau's Knoxville and then Miami field office looked after his needs. Similarly, when Walter Trohan travelled to California, Nichols's successor placed the services of San Francisco SAC Charles W. Bates at his disposal. Letter, DeLoach to Trohan, Jan. 26, 1968, Correspondence-DeLoach, Walter Trohan Papers, HCH.

21. Ungar, *FBI*, pp. 77, 375.

22. Others included the NBC *Monitor* serial (1962–1965), which contained such segments as "Know Your FBI," and "National Alert," and *FBI Washington*, produced from 1962 to 1975 by ABC. Yet another serial, *The FBI in Peace and War* (1944–1958), was based on a book of the same name written by Frederick L. Collins with research help from the Bureau.

23. The Bureau also assisted with the production of two CBS made-for-TV movies, *The FBI vs. Alvin Karpis* (1974) and *Attack on Terror* (1975). Although the CBS series *I Led Three Lives* (1957–1959) was produced without Bureau assistance, it was based on FBI informer Herbert Philbrick's memoirs, which had been prepared with FBI help.

24. For Wayne, see *Atlanta Constitution*, Dec. 28, 1979, p. A-4. For Wheeler, see Victor S. Navasky, *Naming Names* (New York: Viking, 1980), p. 42n. Other FBI-assisted films included *The House on 92d Street* (1945), *Walk a Crooked Mile* (1948), *I Was a Communist for the FBI* (1951), *Walk East on Beacon* (1952), and *The FBI Story* (1959).

25. Memo, Nichols to Tolson, Dec. 20, 1948, Nichols O&C FBI Files-Morris Ernst.

26. Letter, Hoover to Oxnam, April 3, 1947, Louis B. Nichols, G. Bromley Oxnam Papers, Library of Congress; letters, Oxnam to Nichols, Feb. 16, 1950, Jan. 9, 1951, Oct. 4, 1955, and June 20, 1956, all ibid.; letters, Nichols to Oxnam, March 16, 1949 and Jan. 25, 1951, and Oct. 19, 1955, ibid.; letter, Oxnam to McMichael, March 2, 1949, ibid.; letters, McMichael to Oxnam, March 4 and 25, 1949, ibid.; memo, Oxnam to File, Oct. 20, 1955, ibid.

27. HUAC, *Communism in the Detroit Area*, 82d Cong., 2d sess., 1952, pt. 1, p. 2832. For the Bureau, HUAC, and Communist infiltration of the clergy, see Ungar, *FBI*, p. 306; Sullivan, *The Bureau*, p. 267; deposition of Francis J. McNamara, Sept. 16, 1971, pp. 232–33, Jeremiah Stamler Papers, SHSW; *Cong. Rec.*, 87th Cong., 2d sess., March 8, 1962, pp. 3776–79 and Aug. 30, 1962, pp. 18279–82; Corliss Lamont, *Freedom Is as Freedom Does* (New York: Horizon, 1956), pp. 55–56; Wesley, *Hate Groups*, p. 12; letter, Henry M. Bullock to Mundt, May 20, 1950, Box 689(4), KEM; letter, Mundt to Ann Turner, May 24, 1950, ibid. For the Communist front charge, see U.S. House, Committee on Foreign Affairs, *American Neutrality Policy*, 74th Cong., 1st sess., 1935, p. 46.

28. For the FBI's investigation of Oxnam, see memo, Ladd to Director, June 12, 1948, FBI ACLU Files, JEH. For Byrd, see *New York Times*, July 30, 1953, pp. 1, 6. For Carr, see I. F. Stone, "J. Edgar Hoover and the Witch

Hunters," *I. F. Stone's Weekly*, Nov. 9, 1959, p. 3. For McMichael's and Oxnam's HUAC testimony, see *Testimony of G. Bromley Oxnam* and *Hearings Regarding Jack R. McMichael*, 83rd Cong., 1st sess., 1953. One apparent result of the Matthews-Protestant clergy flap was the FBI's decision to stop the covert dissemination of information to McCarthy's Permanent Subcommittee on Investigations. From Carr's appointment to mid-October, the Bureau furnished "no information . . . to this Committee." It is not known if the Bureau resumed its assistance to McCarthy after this date or if the Bureau simply worked through Carr. Memo, Executives' Conference to Director, Oct. 14, 1953, FBI HUAC Files.

29. Letter, Oxnam to Rogers, Jan. 8, 1960, SCEF, Oxnam Papers.

30. Airtel, Director to SAC Los Angeles, June 5, 1962, no. 210, FBI NCARL Files (100-433447). For the Klan, see Brooks R. Walker, *The Christian Fright Peddlers* (Garden City, N.Y.: Doubleday, 1964), p. 21. For Hoover, see Sullivan, *The Bureau*, p. 267; Ungar, *FBI*, p. 306.

31. For Wackenhut and the Church League, see Donner, *Age of Surveillance*, pp. 422-23, 425; Hougan, *Spooks*, pp. 13-15, 52, 72; O'Toole, *The Private Sector*, pp. 30-33, 161-65. See also Arnold Forster and Benjamin R. Epstein, *Danger on the Right* (New York: Random House, 1964), pp. 144-50; Cedric Belfrage, *The American Inquisition, 1945-1960* (Indianapolis: Bobbs-Merrill, 1973), p. 266n; William W. Turner, *Hoover's F.B.I.: The Men and the Myth* (New York: Dell, 1971), p. 294; Privacy Protection Study Commission, *Personal Privacy in an Information Society* (Washington, D.C.: Government Printing Office, 1977), pp. 333-34. For Mundt, see letters, Mundt to Robnett, April 20, 1946, Box 679(3) and April 24, 1947, Box 681(3), KEM.

32. Donner, *Age of Surveillance*, pp. 239, 389-90, 423. See also Turner, *Hoover's F.B.I.*, p. 296; O'Toole, *The Private Sector*, p. 160; deposition of Donald I. Sweany, Aug. 30, 1971, pp. 34-36, 137, Stamler Papers; *New York Times*, Aug. 17, 1970, p. 21.

33. *SDSRIARA*, p. 255; memo, Hoover to Edward A. Tamm and Hugh H. Clegg, Nov. 18, 1940, no. 2, FBI American Legion Contact Program File (66-9330); memos, FBI Executives' Conference to Director, Nov. 1, 1945, no. 171 and July 17, 1950, no. 205, ibid; memo, Fred J. Baumgardner to William C. Sullivan, March 7, 1966, no. 417, ibid. For the ABA et al., see the undated Bureau Bulletin, ca. Nov. 1945 (serial no. 707 recorded in 66-03 file), ibid. The "Bolshevik bouncers" quote is from Jacobs, "The Conduct of Local Political Intelligence," p. 101.

34. For the Legion's anticommunist politics, see generally John Cogley, *Report on Blacklisting*, 2 vols. (New York: Fund for the Republic, 1956), vol. 2: *Radio-Television*, pp. 110-12; Robert Vaughn, *Only Victims: A Study of Show Business Blacklisting* (New York: G. P. Putnam's Sons, 1972), p. 209; Robert W. Iverson, *The Communists and the Schools* (New York: Harcourt, Brace, 1959), p. 242; Roscoe Baker, *The American Legion and Foreign Policy* (New York: Bookman, 1954), pp. 16, 20-21, 89-90.

35. J. Edgar Hoover, "Our Achilles' Heel," *Vital Speeches of the Day*, Oct. 15, 1946, pp. 10-11.

36. Letter, Trohan to Comrade [Hoover], Sept. 24, 1964, Correspondence-Hoover, Trohan Papers; letter, DeLoach to Trohan, Sept. 14, 1964, Correspondence-DeLoach, ibid. See also Ungar, *FBI*, pp. 282-83, and Nichols's report to Clyde Tolson (Oct. 17, 1955, FBI ACLU Files) on the 1955 Legion National Convention in Miami. After the Legion approved a resolution commending Constantine Brown, George Sokolsky, Paul Harvey, Victor Riesel, and Earl Godwin for their "unceasing fight against Communism," Nichols advised Tolson that "these individuals [were] notified unofficially of this action by my office." Nichols then lamented the intrusive efforts of another government body to lobby the Legion: "A disconcerting note was represented by State Department campaign to 'force' favorable reaction to UNESCO upon Legionnaires." By the mid-1960s, DeLoach was working closely with the Legion and Lyndon B. Johnson in support of the President's Vietnam and Dominican Republic policies. See memo, DeLoach to Marvin Watson, Sept. 7, 1965, Appointments File, Diary Back-up, LBJ; President's Schedule, March 3, 1966, ibid.; letter, Watson to L. Eldon James, Feb. 28, 1966, ibid.; letter, James to the President, Feb. 25, 1966, ibid.

37. *SDSRIARA*, p. 49.

38. Hess interview; McNamara deposition, pp. 6, 8-9, 11. For ABC, see Cogley, *Radio-Television*, pp. 1-21; Merle Miller, *The Judges and the Judged* (Garden City, N.Y.: Doubleday, 1952), pp. 63-148. See also memo, re *Plain Talk*, Aug. 31, 1951, PSF-China Lobby (Justice Dept.), HST; Joseph Keeley, *The China Lobby Man: The Story of Alfred Kohlberg* (New Rochelle, N.Y.: Arlington House, 1969), pp. 1, 87, 196-97; Turner, *Hoover's F.B.I.*, pp. 177-78. For ABC's most important publication, see *Red Channels: The Report of Communist Influence in Radio and Television* (New York: American Business Consultants, 1950).

39. McNamara deposition, pp. 6-7; Hannah Bloom, "The Hollywood Hearings," *Nation*, Oct. 13, 1951, p. 304. For the Legion's role in policing the blacklists, see Cogley, *Report on Blacklisting*, vol. 1, *Movies*, pp. 118-43.

40. Newspaper clipping, Aug. 21, 1938, no. 11X3, FBI HUAC Files; memo, Nichols to Tolson, March 10, 1941, no. 968, ibid.; *New York Times*, Feb. 16, 1940, p. 11. See also Goodman, *The Committee*, pp. 101-02.

41. Letter, Richard B. Hood to Director, Sept. 5, 1941, no. 1016, FBI HUAC Files; memos, Hood to Director, Aug. 10, 1945, no. 1327, Aug. 11, 1945, no. 1328, and Aug. 17, 1945, no. 1329, ibid.

42. Memo, R. H. Cunningham to P. E. Foxworth, Aug. 7, 1941, no. 1014, ibid.

43. Memo, Nichols to Tolson, May 13, 1947, no. 1464, ibid. See also memo, Tolson to Director, May 12, 1947, no. 1462, ibid.; letter, Hood to Director, May 12, 1947, no. 1465, ibid.; teletype, Hoover to SAC Los Angeles, May 13, 1947, no. 1464, ibid. For the "dank air" quote, see Hoover's handwritten notation on newspaper clipping, April 9, 1947, no. 1447, ibid.

44. Memo, re Communist Activities in Hollywood, May 13, 1947, no. 1468, ibid. For Hood, see teletypes, SAC Los Angeles to Director, May 13, 1947, no. 1463 and no. 1464, ibid.; letter, Hood to Director, May 14, 1947, no. 1468, ibid.

45. For Russell, Leckie, and Smith, see Freeland, *The Truman Doctrine*, p. 240; memo, SAC Los Angeles to Director, Aug. 12, 1947, no. 1471, FBI HUAC Files; memo, Hood to Director, Sept. 13, 1947, no. 1476, ibid.; memo, re Possible Schedule of Witnesses, Sept. 10, 1947, no. 1476, ibid.; letter, Hood to Director, Oct. 13, 1947, no. 1478, ibid. For Parks, see Navasky, *Naming Names*, p. 317n. For Brecht, see James K. Lyon, *Bertolt Brecht in America* (Princeton, N.J.: Princeton University Press, 1980), pp. 298, 315, 331. For the Hollywood Ten hearings, see *Hearings Regarding Communist Infiltration of the Motion-Picture Industry*, 80th Cong., 1st sess., 1947.

46. Letter, Hoover to Vaughan, April 7, 1948, PSF-FBI Communist Data, HST. For the FBI report, see letter, Tom [Clark] to Matthew Connelly, April 14, 1947, OF263 (1945–47), HST; memo, Director to Attorney General, May 3, 1947, ibid. The administration's request for an FBI report on communism in Hollywood was not an isolated request. In February 1950, as the Committee was preparing for hearings on communism in Hawaii, the White House requested a file check "for information of a derogatory nature" on the Democratic Committee of Hawaii. Letter, Hoover to Donald S. Dawson, Feb. 21, 1950, CF-Justice Dept.(1), HST.

47. Memo, Baumgardner to Alan H. Belmont, April 25, 1960, FBI COINTELPRO-CPUSA Files (100-3-104), JEH. For the FBI's early interest in the motion picture industry, see *SDSRIARA*, pp. 437–38. For Bright, Decker, and Wheeler, see memos, SAC Los Angeles to Director, Sept. 8, 1952 and Aug. 9, 1951, no. 1776, FBI HUAC Files; airtel, SAC Los Angeles to Director, March 6, 1953, no. 1877, ibid.; teletype, Director to SAC Los Angeles, March 11, 1953, no. 1877, ibid. Russell also kept Nichols posted on how the "Hollywood hearings are shaping up." Memo, Nichols to Tolson, March 30, 1951, no. 1752, ibid. For Hoover on the "Committee 'whitewash,'" see memo, Nichols to Tolson, March 30, 1951, no. 1752, ibid. For Lucille Ball, see memo, SAC Los Angeles to Director, Aug. 26, 1953, ibid.; airtel, SAC Los Angeles to Director, Sept. 11, 1953, no. 1965, ibid. HUAC member Clyde Doyle intended to leak the fact that Ball had once registered as a CPUSA voter but was scooped by Walter Winchell. Winchell did not mention her name but provided more than enough information for the Southern California press to pick the story up.

48. David Caute, *The Great Fear: The Anti-Communist Purge Under Truman and Eisenhower* (New York: Simon and Schuster, 1978), p. 143. The collapse of professional blacklisting was aided in part by humorist John Henry Faulk's suit against AWARE, Inc., and two key blacklisters, Laurence Johnson and Vincent Hartnett. Faulk became embroiled in the blacklists in December 1955 after he supported a reformist set of candidates (the so-called middle-of-the-road slate) for office in his union, the New York local of the American Federation of Television and Radio Artists (AFTRA). WCBS fired Faulk in August 1957 after AWARE circulated a bulletin attacking Faulk to WCBS sponsors General Foods and Colgate-Palmolive; newspaper columnists Walter Winchell, George Sokolsky, and Fulton Lewis, Jr.; HUAC; the FBI; Senator James Eastland; motion picture moguls; book publishers;

theater producers; and theatrical unions. HUAC, furthermore, criticized AFTRA's middle-of-the-road slate in its 1955 annual report and subpoenaed Faulk to testify on June 17, 1958. This subpoena, however, was postponed after Faulk's attorney, Louis Nizer, learned of AWARE's plans to host a reception ("Cocktails Against Communism") for the Committee that same day at New York City's Sheraton-McAlpin Hotel. Though Faulk never testified, he remained under Committee subpoena for five months and on the blacklist until 1962. The New York Supreme Court then upheld his claim for damages against AWARE, Hartnett, and Johnson. John Henry Faulk, *Fear on Trial* (New York: Simon and Schuster, 1964); Louis Nizer, *The Jury Returns* (Garden City, N.Y.: Doubleday, 1966), pp. 225–438. Faulk is presently pursuing another civil action based on FBI documents released under the Freedom of Information Act.

49. U.S., House, Subcommittee on Civil and Constitutional Rights of the Judiciary Committee, *FBI Oversight*, 94th Cong., 1st sess., 1975. For Douglas, see Donner, *Age of Surveillance*, p. 164n. For Condon, see memo, Fred J. Baumgardner to Alan H. Belmont, Nov. 13, 1953, FBI HUAC Files. For Marcantonio, see memo, Hoover to SAC New York, June 23, 1943, no. 17, Vito Marcantonio FBI Files (100-28126), JEH; "Facts Relating to Congressman Vito Marcantonio," Jan. 22, 1943, no. 17, ibid.; New York Field Office report, Nov. 25, 1950, no. 65, ibid. In addition to congressmen, other prominent personalities subjected to FBI surveillance included Supreme Court Justice William O. Douglas, financier Bernard Baruch, diplomat Sumner Welles, New Dealer Harry Hopkins, Harvard University president James Conant, Alabama gubernatorial nominee James E. Folson, Attorney General Tom Clark, Secretary of State Dean Acheson, Ambassador to the Soviet Union Joseph E. Davies, presidential candidate Adlai Stevenson, actors Fredric March, Edward G. Robinson, Harry Belafonte, and Zero Mostel, boxer Joe Louis, economist John Kenneth Galbraith, and reformer Helen Keller. The FBI, moreover, often leaked information from these files. In 1955 Bureau officials forwarded derogatory information on Galbraith to Senator Homer Capehart (R., Ind.) of the Committee on Banking and Currency. John Kenneth Galbraith, "My Forty Years with the F.B.I.," *Esquire*, Oct. 1977, p. 174.

50. Ungar, *FBI*, pp. 285–87, 354–55, 363; Sullivan, *The Bureau*, p. 53; Donner, *Age of Surveillance*, pp. 100, 103, 112; Theoharis, *Spying on Americans*, pp. 175–76. For Mundt's close relationship with Hoover and Nichols's successor, Cartha DeLoach, see the correspondence in Boxes 164(3), 165(3), 166(4), 167(3-4, 6-8), and 997(3), KEM.

51. Other committees receiving information from the FBI included the Joint Committee on Atomic Energy, the Senate Appropriations Committee, the Senate Armed Services Committee and its Preparedness Subcommittee, the Senate Committee on Labor and Public Welfare and its Subcommittee on Labor Management Relations, the Senate Foreign Relations Committee, and the House Judiciary Committee. FBI officials considered their "cooperation . . . pursuant to the law" only in the case of the Joint Committee on Atomic

Energy. Memo, Executives' Conference to Director, Oct. 14, 1953, FBI HUAC Files.

52. For FBI monographs and other literature, see SISS, *Statement by J. Edgar Hoover Concerning the 17th National Convention, Communist Party, U.S.A., December 10-13, 1959*, S.Doc. 80, 86th Cong., 2d sess., 1960 (Serial 12256); SISS, *Exposé of Soviet Espionage*, S.Doc. 114, 86th Cong., 2d sess., 1960 (Serial 12257); SISS, *The Current Communist Threat: A Statement by J. Edgar Hoover*, 87th Cong., 2d sess., 1962; SISS, *The Communist Party Line, Prepared by J. Edgar Hoover, Director FBI*, S.Doc. 59, 87th Cong., 1st sess., 1961 (Serial 12349). For the Pacifica Foundation, see Cook, *The FBI Nobody Knows*, pp. 49–50. For Levison, see Arthur M. Schlesinger, Jr., *Robert F. Kennedy and His Time* (Boston: Houghton Mifflin, 1978), pp. 368–69. For the McCarran squad, see Gary May, *China Scapegoat: The Diplomatic Ordeal of John Carter Vincent* (Washington, D.C.: New Republic Books, 1979), p. 235. For Javits, see Jacob K. Javits and Rafael Steinberg, *Javits: The Autobiography of a Public Man* (Boston: Houghton Mifflin, 1981), pp. 213, 221, 223, 232. Dodd, vice-chairman of SISS and chairman of the Juvenile Delinquency Subcommittee, was an ex-FBI agent who had virtually unlimited access to Bureau files. The FBI even helped Dodd's administrative assistant ghost-write his speeches. James Boyd, *Above the Law: The Rise and Fall of Senator Thomas J. Dodd* (New York: New American Library, 1968), pp. 109–10, 184.

53. Memo, Nichols to Tolson, Feb. 4, 1953, FBI HUAC Files. For Nichols on the "arrangement," see memo, Nichols to Tolson, Jan. 29, 1953, ibid. See also memo, Executives' Conference to Director, Oct. 14, 1953, ibid. For Nixon and Russell, see memo, Baumgardner to Belmont, Sept. 22, 1952, no. 1836, ibid. For the blind memorandums and the Attorney General's copies, see memo, D. Milton Ladd to Director, Sept. 24, 1952, ibid. Copies of some of these blind memorandums are filed in the FBI HUAC Files. See, for example, memo, Nichols to Tolson, Sept. 22, 1952, ibid., and the attached documents which refer to (1) demonstrations protesting HUAC's Chicago hearings and (2) "*suggestions which might be useful* to the McCarran Committee . . . [and its] scheduled hearings on [Communist] infiltration into the Mill, Mine and Smelters Workers Union. . . ."

54. *Washington Evening Star*, April 28, 1957, p. A-27. For Nichols on "personalities," see memo, Nichols to Tolson, Jan. 29, 1953, FBI HUAC Files. Hoover is quoted in memo, Hoover to Tolson, Ladd, and Nichols, Feb. 17, 1953, no. 1868, ibid. For the Chicago leaks, see the not-recorded memos, SAC Chicago to Director, July 3, 1952, ibid. For the electrical workers union, see airtel, SAC Pittsburgh to Director, March 2, 1953, no. 1875, ibid.

55. Letter, Mundt to Gene Hagbert, May 5, 1945, Box 678(2), KEM; letter, Hagbert to Mundt, April 30, 1945, ibid.; letter, Hoover to William I. Conway, Sept. 10, 1946, no. 1409, FBI HUAC Files; letter, Conway to Hoover, Sept. 4, 1946, no. 1409, ibid. See also memo, Clegg to Tolson, March 24, 1945, no. 1307, ibid.; memo, Alex Rosen to Tolson, April 6, 1945, no. 1316, ibid.; note, iee, July 17, 1945, no. 1324, ibid.; memo, R. C. Hendon to Tolson, July 18,

1945, no. 1324, ibid. The FBI also conducted loyalty investigations of applicant and incumbent employees for various state governors (including Earl Warren of California), the Red Cross, federal judges (among others, Supreme Court Chief Justice Fred Vinson and Supreme Court Justice Tom Clark), and the New York Police Department. Memo, Executives' Conference to Director, Oct. 14, 1953, FBI HUAC Files. For HUAC's staff expenses, see *Cong. Rec.*, 90th Cong., 1st sess., April 5, 1967, p. 8432. In 1971 Committee member and critic Robert F. Drinan, S.J. (D., Mass.) lamented a fifty-eight man staff "so well entrenched and so unaccountable . . . that they conduct business almost as if the members of the Committee were there only to give moral and financial support to the inquisitorial activities of the staff." Speech, "The Continued Injuries Done by the House Internal Security Committee," American University, Washington, D.C., Oct. 21, 1971.

56. Letter, Mundt to Legislative Reference Service, Library of Congress, Jan. 12, 1945, Box 680(1a), KEM; letter, Mundt to Finan, June 15, 1946, Box 679(3), KEM; letter, Finan to Mundt, June 12, 1946, ibid.

57 Edward J. Mowery, *HUAC and FBI: Targets for Abolition* (New York: Bookmailer, 1961), p. 12. See also letter, Mundt to Thomas, July 27, 1948, Box 683(9), KEM; letter, Thomas to Mundt, July 26, 1948, ibid. For the *100 Things* series, see H.Doc. 136, 82d Cong., 1st sess., 1951 (Serial 11521). The Senate Internal Security Subcommittee also distributed an incredible amount of anticommunist material—including 150,000 "names" (of persons, organizations, and publications) during its first five years and 180,000 copies of *The Communist Party of the United States of America—What It Is, How It Works—A Handbook for Americans*. See SISS, *Annual Report*, 84th Cong., 2d sess., 1957, pp. 5–8, 15.

58. *Cong. Rec.*, 79th Cong., 1st sess., Nov. 15, 1945, p. 10743. For HUAC's informal reports, see *Annual Report*, 80th Cong., 2d sess., 1948, pp. 21–24. For examples of HUAC's dissemination of formal and informal reports to members of Congress, newspaper reporters, and others, see René A. Wormser, *Foundations: Their Power and Influence* (New York: Devin-Adair, 1958), p. 117; *New York Times*, Feb. 27, 1956, p. 1 and Feb. 28, 1956, p. 1; letter, Russell to McCarthy, June 9, 1952, Communism-William Benton 1951–52, Westbrook Pegler Papers, HCH; Anne Braden, *House Un-American Activities Committee: Bulwark of Segregation* (Los Angeles: National Committee to Abolish HUAC, 1964), pp. 9–14; American Friends Service Committee, *The Police Threat to Political Liberty* (Philadelphia: American Friends Service Committee, 1979), pp. 98–99; Sweany deposition, pp. 78–79; letters, Wood to Wiley, Jan. 30 and March 3, 1952, Box 149(8), Alexander Wiley Papers, SHSW; *Cong. Rec.*, 93d Cong., 2d sess., April 1, 1974, p. 8928; ibid., 82d Cong., 2d sess., July 5, 1952, pp. 9537–39 and May 26, 1952, pp. 5959–60; ibid., 86th Cong., 2d sess., April 20, 1960, pp. 8362–63 and March 1, 1960, pp. 4031–37. For the Sioux Falls steel executive, see letter, M. L. Rysdon to Mundt, Aug. 2, 1949, Box 687(8), KEM; letter, Mundt to Rysdon, Aug. 5, 1949, ibid. For the National Conference of Bar Examiners, see letter,

Marjorie Merritt to Mundt (see also the accompanying "off-the-record" note), June 24, 1949, ibid.; letter, Mundt to Merritt, June 28, 1949, ibid. For Robnett, see letters, Mundt to Robnett, April 20, 1946, Box 679(3) and April 24, 1947, Box 681(3), KEM. Several members of Congress and newspapermen, including Senator Thurmond, also received FBI data regarding alleged CPUSA infiltration of the civil rights movement. See memo, Baumgardner to Sullivan, Oct. 3, 1961, FBI COINTELPRO-CPUSA Files.

IV. MAKING THE COLD WAR: INFLUENCING NATIONAL POLITICS

1. See Theoharis, *Seeds of Repression* and Freeland, *The Truman Doctrine.*
2. *Cong. Rec.*, 79th Cong., 2d sess., March 15, 1946, pp. 2330-31; ibid., March 27, 1946, pp. 2683-84, 2695; ibid., April 5, 1946, p. 3180; ibid., April 9, 1946, p. 3360; ibid., April 10, 1946, p. 3467; ibid., April 12, 1946, p. 3625-26; ibid., April 18, 1946, pp. 4007-8; ibid., May 2, 1946, pp. 4349-51, 4366-67; ibid., May 3, 1946, p. A2447; ibid., July 31, 1946, pp. 10525, 10529, 10531. See also *New York Times*, Feb. 15, 1946, p. 27; ibid., April 10, 1946, p. 21; ibid., April 19, 1946, p. 20; ibid., May 3, 1946, p. 23.
3. Spingarn is quoted in Demaris, *The Director*, p. 118. For Clark and Hoover, see Tom C. Clark Oral History, p. 108, HST; memo, Attorney General to Director, Dec. 5, 1946, ADV Loyalty Committee, A. Devitt Vanech Papers, HST; memo, Director to Attorney General, Dec. 3, 1946, ibid. For the dissemination of the FBI's reports, see memo, D. Milton Ladd to Director, Aug. 3, 1948, no. 3562, Alger Hiss FBI Files (65-56402), JEH; memos, H. B. Fletcher to Ladd, Aug. 6, 1948, no. X2 and July 29, 1948, no. X, William W. Remington FBI Files (74-1379), JEH; letter, Hoover to Harry Vaughan, Oct. 19, 1945, PSF-FBI C, HST; letter, Hoover to Vaughan, Nov. 8, 1945, PSF-FBI S, HST; letters, Hoover to George Allen, May 29, 1946 and June 7, 1946, PSF-FBI Atomic Bomb, HST. A congressional employee present at the special House Civil Service subcommittee hearing told Benjamin Ginzburg (see *Rededication to Freedom*, pp. 115-17) that the FBI leaked details of Bentley's story to the subcommittee.
4. For McCarran, see memo, Hoover to Tolson, Tamm, and Ladd, May 27, 1946, no. 27, Hiss FBI Files (101-2668); memo, Hoover to Attorney General, May 31, 1946, no. 23, ibid.; letter, TCC [Clark] to Hoover, June 3, 1946, no. 24, ibid. For the Hoover-Clark-Byrnes operation, see memo, Hoover to Tolson, Tamm, Ladd, and Clegg, March 19, 1946, Hoover O&C FBI Files-Alger Hiss (copies also to be available in Alger Hiss Papers, Harvard University Library, Cambridge); memos, Hoover to Tolson, Tamm, and Ladd, March 20 and 21, 1946, ibid. See also John Chabot Smith, "The Debate of the Century (Con'd)," *Harper's*, June 1978, pp. 81-85 and *Alger Hiss: The True Story* (New York: Holt, Rinehart and Winston, 1976), p. 141; Allen Weinstein, *Perjury: The Hiss-Chambers Case* (New York: Knopf, 1978), pp. 358-66.

5. James F. Byrnes, *All in One Lifetime* (New York: Harper, 1958), p. 323.

6. John F. Cronin, S. J., "The Problem of American Communism in 1945," Oct. 29, 1945, in CCCSC-Cronin, Francis P. Matthews Papers, HST. See also letter, Cronin to Emerson Schmidt, March 1, 1947, CCCSC-Cronin Correspondence, ibid.; Peter H. Irons, "The Cold War Crusade of the United States Chamber of Commerce," in Griffith and Theoharis, *The Specter*, p. 80. Mandel, a former Communist and business manager of the *Daily Worker*, had originally recruited Whittaker Chambers into the Communist party in the mid-1920s.

7. For Cronin's speech, see *Washington Post*, March 11 and 12, 1946. For Hoover, see Clark Oral History, p. 112. For Reece and Nixon, see Caute, *The Great Fear*, pp. 26–27. Martin is quoted in *New York Times*, Feb. 9, 1947, p. 2.

8. Irons, "Cold War Crusade," pp. 72–89. Matthews was later appointed Secretary of the Navy by Truman. FBI efforts to establish close liaison with Chamber of Commerce officials dated at least from 1941. See Nichols O&C FBI Files-Junior Chamber of Commerce.

9. See generally Irons, "Cold War Crusade," pp. 72–89. For the Chamber's concern about a "whitewash," see letters, Schmidt to Matthews, Dec. 16 and 26, 1946, CCCSC-Correspondence Ch. of Commerce Staff, Matthews Papers. For Ladd, see notes, On Meeting of Temporary Commission, Vol. II(1), President's Temporary Commission, Stephen J. Spingarn Papers, HST. For Wilson, see *Washington Daily News*, May 6, 1947. For Schmidt's HUAC appearance, see *Hearings on H.R. 1884 and H.R. 2122*, pp. 83–236. The third Chamber of Commerce pamphlet, *Communists Within the Labor Movement*, was written with the assistance not only of HUAC and the FBI but AFL official John Frey and Harry Read, a prominent member of the Association of Catholic Trade Unionists and an administrative assistant to the CIO's anticommunist secretary-treasurer, James Carey. James C. Foster, *The Union Politic: The CIO Political Action Committee* (Columbia: University of Missouri Press, 1975), p. 84. This pamphlet aided the successful drive for legislation requiring labor leaders to sign non-Communist affidavits.

10. Memo, Nichols to Tolson, Aug. 27, 1948, no. 1523, FBI HUAC Files.

11. Pearson, *Diaries*, pp. 58–59, 63; Clark Oral History, pp. 210–11. See also memos, Nichols to Tolson, Jan. 24 and 26, 1949, Nichols O&C FBI Files-Drew Pearson. In mid-July 1948 (two weeks before Bentley's testimony and Whittaker Chambers's first appearance before HUAC), Hearst reporter Howard Rushmore publicized much of the story. When testifying before an investigating committee in Washington state, Rushmore read from a classified FBI report which he apparently received from Larry Kerley, a disgruntled ex-FBI agent. He named Alger and Donald Hiss, Charles Kramer, Harry Dexter White, Nathan Witt, Nathan Gregory Silvermaster, Lee Pressman, Lawrence Duggan, and Harold Glasser as members of a "secret cell." Washington, *Second Report of the Joint Legislative Fact-Finding Committee on Un-American Activities*, 1948, pp. 191–93. For Kerley, see memo, Nichols to Tolson, Sept. 7, 1948, no. 1525, FBI HUAC Files. HUAC also had this information and was simply waiting for an opportune time to

open the spy hearings. A week before Chambers testified, Thomas wrote Mundt about the Committee's planned activities: "Since the Federal Grand Jury which has been sitting in New York has returned its indictments, I feel we are now free to proceed with the taking of open testimony from various witnesses who were subjects of this Grand Jury investigation." Thomas was particularly interested in "certain espionage activities against the Government." Letter, Thomas to Mundt, July 26, 1948, Box 683(9), KEM.

12. See, for example, memo, John L. Sullivan to the President, Aug. 5, 1948, PSF-FBI R, HST; memos, Fletcher to Ladd, Aug. 3, 1948, no. 82 and Aug. 4, 1948, no. 81, Remington FBI Files (121–6159); summary brief, re William Remington, July 22, 1948, no. X, ibid. (74–1379).

13. For Ferguson's alleged "double cross," see memo, Guy Hottell to Director, July 29, 1948, no. 3444, ibid. (65–56402).

14. Sullivan, *The Bureau*, pp. 95, 196; Garry Wills, *Nixon Agonistes: The Crisis of the Self-Made Man* (New York: New American Library, 1971), pp. 36–47; Nixon, *RN*, p. 58. See also William J. Gill, *The Ordeal of Otto Otepka* (New Rochelle, N.Y.: Arlington House, 1969), p. 32.

15. Memo, Ladd to Director, Dec. 9, 1948, no. 157, Hiss FBI Files. By the 1960s, if not much earlier, Nichols was indeed a close friend of Nixon and a campaign aide of sorts who was thought to have been in line for an administration job following the inauguration. Shortly before Nixon declared his candidacy, Nichols contacted John J. Ragan, whose twenty-four-year career with the FBI earned him the reputation as "the best wireman to come out of the Bureau." The former FBI Assistant Director asked Ragan to explore Nixon's Washington and New York law offices for taps and bugs. He received $75 a sweep, paid by personal checks signed by Nichols. Ragan went on to become Nixon's personal wireman and to tap syndicated columnist Joseph Kraft's Georgetown home in 1969. David Wise, *The American Police State* (New York: Random House, 1976), pp. 4, 9–10. Other assistance included an attempt in 1960 to sabotage John F. Kennedy's presidential campaign and the forwarding in 1972 of at least one FBI letterhead memorandum on George McGovern's campaign strategy to CREEP security chief James McCord. Sullivan, *The Bureau*, pp. 48–50; Donner, *Age of Surveillance*, p. 174.

16. In September 1949, for instance, Nichols "dropped by Nixon's Office on at least three occasions to take him to task for" his charge that HUAC "accomplished in three days what the FBI had not accomplished in 8 years in connection with the Hiss-Chambers matter." When Nixon finally contacted Nichols, he "apologized." Nixon said his statement was misinterpreted and promised to make amends by praising the Bureau in each and every speech he contemplated during his current campaign. Nichols then told Nixon that he had "stayed up until after midnight one night trying to find some basis whereby we could be of assistance to him, that when I told him we could not assist him this certainly did not mean we did not have information on Hiss and Chambers, and that I thought his crack was uncalled for." Though Nichols was "favorably impressed with Nixon's attitude," Tolson and Hoover

remained skeptical. "Nixon," as Tolson put it, "plays both sides against the middle." Memo, Nichols to Tolson, Sept. 29, 1948, no. 1531, FBI HUAC Files.

17. Memo, John Patrick Coyne to Ladd, Oct. 11, 1947, no. 482, FBI HUAC Files. For Nixon, see HUAC, *Hearings on H.R. 4422 and H.R. 4581, Proposed Legislation to Curb or Control the Communist Party of the U.S.*, 80th Cong., 2d sess., 1948, p. 35. Thomas is quoted in HUAC, *Hearings Regarding Communist Espionage in the U.S. Government*, 80th Cong., 2d sess., 1948, p. 561.

18. Memo, Nichols to Tolson, Dec. 2, 1948, no. 101, Hiss FBI Files.

19. Memo, Nichols to Tolson, Aug. 7, 1948, no. 3406, Remington FBI Files (65–56402). For Turner, see memo, Nichols to Tolson, Dec. 10, 1948, no. 213, Hiss FBI Files. For Lawrence, see the newspaper clippings in Int. Sec. Cong. Inv. Spy Trials, George M. Elsey Papers, HST. For the FBI's close contact with HUAC and the press, see generally memo, Nichols to Tolson, Sept. 7, 1948, no. 1525, FBI HUAC Files; memos, Hottel to Director, July 29, 1948, no. 3444 and Aug. 2, 1948, no. 3433, Remington FBI Files (65–56402); memos, Hottel to Director, Dec. 8, 1948, no. 136 and Dec. 21, 1948, no. 617, Hiss FBI Files; memo, Fletcher to Ladd, Dec. 8, 1948, no. 137, ibid.; memos, Nichols to Tolson, Dec. 7, 1948, no. 91 and no. 124, Dec. 3, 1948, no. 647, Dec. 9, 1948, no. 181 and no. 179, and Jan. 14, 1949, no. 1002, all ibid.; memos, Ladd to Director, Dec. 7, 1948, no. 92, Dec. 8, 1948, no. 89, and Dec. 14, 1948, no. 68, all ibid.

20. Memo, Truman to Attorney General, Dec. 16, 1948, PSF-General C, HST. For Ayers, see diary entry, Aug. 31, 1948, Eben Ayers Papers, HST. For the White House strategy, see memos, George M. Elsey to Clifford, Aug. 16 and 27, 1948, Loyalty Investigations(2), Clark Clifford Papers, HST; Democratic National Committee press release, Dec. 9, 1948, Communist Spy Probe, Democratic National Committee Files, HST; Department of Justice press release, Sept. 29, 1948, White House Assignment(1), Spingarn Papers.

21. Memos, Ladd to Director, Dec. 17, 1948, no. 352 and (for the Clark quote) Dec. 23, 1948, no. 622, Hiss FBI Files. See also Weinstein, *Perjury*, pp. 271–72, 275–76, 280, 301.

22. Thomas is quoted in Edith Tiger, ed., *In Re Alger Hiss*, 2 vols. (New York: Hill and Wang, 1979–1980), 1: 3. For Dewey, see Sullivan, *The Bureau*, pp. 41–44. For the DNC, see memo, William L. Batt, Jr., to J. Howard McGrath, Sept. 2, 1948, Dewey-Communism, Democratic National Committee Clipping File, HST. During the Roosevelt years, in contrast, the FBI investigated Dewey and his associates (including Edwin F. Jaeckle, chairman of the New York GOP Committee), occasionally forwarding derogatory information on Dewey to the White House. Letter, Hoover to Marvin H. McIntyre, June 5, 1940, PSF-Thomas E. Dewey, FDR; memo, Ladd to Director, June 29, 1944, Nichols O&C FBI Files-Edwin F. Jaeckle.

23. Nixon is quoted in Washington City News Service ticker, Oct. 3, 1952, no. 5403, Hiss FBI Files. See also memo, Ladd to Director, Oct. 9, 1952, no. 5403, ibid.; *New York Times*, Oct. 9, 1952, p. 25; *Washington Evening Star*, April 28, 1957, p. A-27. For the HUAC report, see *The Shameful Years*,

H.Rept. 1229, 82d Cong., 2d sess., 1952 (Serial 11575). The Bureau's assistance to HUAC and Nixon in these instances may have been indirect. Both were in possession of the FBI's memorandum of November 1945, "Soviet Espionage in the United States," which had been widely disseminated within the executive branch. Nichols claimed the memorandum, known within the Bureau as the "Nixon memo," was "loose." The Senate Internal Security Subcommittee had a copy and so did radio commentator Fulton Lewis, Jr., and Hearst reporter David Sentner—and HUAC, SISS, Lewis, and Sentner often received information in confidence from the FBI. Upon learning in late 1953 that the Hearst press planned to publish the memorandum, SISS counsel Robert Morris called Nichols and offered to contact Hearst executive Richard Berlin in an effort to "head this off." Memo, Nichols to Tolson, Nov. 12, 1953, FBI HUAC Files; memo, D. Milton Ladd to Director, Nov. 23, 1953, ibid. Less than a week later Hoover and Attorney General Herbert Brownell, Jr., appeared before SISS to discuss Harry Dexter White, the late Treasury Department official who was appointed by President Truman in January 1946 to an International Monetary Fund post despite the FBI's charge in the Nixon memo that he was a Soviet spy.

24. For the *coram nobis* petition, see Tiger, *In Re Alger Hiss.* The quote is in vol. 1, p. 18. For the abuse-of-power issues raised by the Hiss case, see the documentation in note 25.

25. For McCarran and Brooks, see Tiger, *In Re Alger Hiss,* 1: 102, 123. For the *coram nobis* petition, see also Athan Theoharis, "Abuse of Power: What the New Hiss Suit Uncovers," *Nation,* Oct. 7, 1978, pp. 336–40; Fred J. Cook, "The *Coram Nobis* Appeal: Alger Hiss—A New Ball Game," ibid., Oct. 11, 1980, pp. 340–43. For the Hiss Defense Fund, Chambers's book, and Andrews, see Morton Levitt and Michael Levitt, *A Tissue of Lies: Nixon vs. Hiss* (New York: McGraw-Hill, 1979), pp. 153–54, 177–80. For Bundy, see Leonard Mosley, *Dulles: A Biography of Eleanor, Allen, and John Foster Dulles and Their Family Network* (New York: Dial Press/James Wade, 1978), pp. 319–23. For HUAC's interest in defense witnesses, and so on, see memos, Nichols to Tolson, Jan. 11, 1950, no. 4478 and July 11, 1949, no. 3656, Hiss FBI Files; letter, Mundt to Isaac Don Levine, June 10, 1949, Box 687(8), KEM. For Griswold, see LHM, re Erwin Nathaniel Griswold, Dec. 14, 1951, PSF-FBI F, HST. For the book reviews, see letter, Hoover to Maxwell M. Rabb, June 7, 1957, OF5-F, DDE; letter, Mundt to Hoover, May 2, 1957, Box 937(4), KEM; letter, Hoover to Mundt, May 3, 1957, ibid. For Chambers's memoirs, see his *Witness* (New York: Random House, 1952). For Hiss's account, see his *In the Court of Public Opinion* (New York: Knopf, 1957). For Andrews's book, see Bert and Peter Andrews, *A Tragedy of History: A Journalists' Confidential Role in the Hiss-Chambers Case* (Washington, D.C.: Luce, 1962). Nichols also provided some assistance to reporters George Reedy and Jim Donovan, although their planned book on the Hiss case was never written. Interview with George Reedy, Milwaukee, April 20, 1982.

26. Memo, Clifford to the President, May 23, 1947, Internal Security-FELP

E.O. 9835, Elsey Papers. For Truman on Thomas, see Robert J. Donovan, *Conflict and Crisis: The Presidency of Harry S. Truman, 1945–1948* (New York: Norton, 1977), p. 292.

27. For the "clearly inspired" quote and the administration's commitment to this strategy, see diary entries, March 12, 13, 14, 15, and 19, 1947, Ayers Papers. For the FBI's reports on members of Congress, see letter, Hoover to George Allen, March 18, 1947, PSF-FBI Communist Data, HST; letters, Hoover to Allen, May 31 and July 29, 1946, PSF-FBI K, HST; letter, Hoover to Allen, Sept. 6, 1946, PSF-FBI P, HST; letter, Hoover to Allen, Sept. 12, 1946, PSF-FBI W, HST; letter, Hoover to Vaughan, May 29, 1946, PSF-FBI P, HST; letters, Hoover to Vaughan, March 18 and Oct. 8, 1947, PSF-FBI Communist Data, HST; letters, Hoover to Vaughan, March 7 and 12, 1946, PSF-FBI C, HST; letter, Hoover to Vaughan, July 22, 1949, CF-Justice Dept.(1), HST.

28. Clark is quoted in Department of Justice press release, Dec. 11, 1946, OF320-C, HST. See also the correspondence and other documentation in Justice Dept.-Freedom Train, Charles W. Jackson Files, HST. For the FBI's reports on Freedom Train critics, see memos, Director to Attorney General, Sept. 20, 23, 25, 26, and 30 and Oct. 2, 7, 14, and 24, 1947, and Feb. 17, 1948, all in Attorney General's Files-Freedom Train, Tom C. Clark Papers, HST.

29. Telegram, Thomas to Hoover, March 14, 1947, FBI Loyalty, Vanech Papers; memo, Director to Attorney General, March 18, 1947, ibid. For Hoover's eagerness to testify, see Demaris, *The Director*, pp. 120–21.

30. Memos, Nichols to Tolson, March 18, 1947, no. 1439 and March 19, 1947, no. 1440, FBI HUAC Files. For the "bally-hoo" quote, see memo, Tolson to Director, June 12, 1946, no. 1399, ibid.

31. Memo, Nichols to Tolson, March 25, 1947, no. 1451, ibid. For the Oak Ridge memorandum and Dennis, see memos, Nichols to Tolson, March 25, 1947, no. 1441 and March 26, 1947, no. 1457, ibid.; memo, Director to Attorney General, March 25, 1947, no. 1441, ibid.

32. Memo, Hoover to Tolson, Tamm, Ladd, and Nichols, March 24, 1947, no. 1431, ibid. The Committee again invited Hoover to testify three years later when holding hearings on the Mundt-Nixon Bill. The FBI Director responded by sending Tolson to see HUAC member Francis Walter and Ladd to see Deputy Attorney General Peyton Ford. Ladd told Ford that in the event Hoover did appear and was "asked any questions with reference to Communists in the Government or State Department etc., . . . [he] would have no alternative but to state the information contained in the Bureau's files." Needless to say, Hoover did not testify before HUAC on that occasion. Memos, Ladd to Director, March 4, 1950, no. 1636 and March 14, 1950, no. 1638, ibid.

33. HUAC, *Hearings on H.R. 4422 and H.R. 4581*, pp. 16–17, 22–23, 34. For the list, see memo, Director to Attorney General, March 27, 1947, FBI Loyalty, Vanech Papers. After learning from Robert Stripling that the CPUSA planned to send Benjamin Davis to testify at these same hearings, Nichols ordered the FBI Security Division to "prepare as soon as possible a

blind memorandum of public source material which can be furnished to Stripling." Memo, Nichols to Tolson, Feb. 18, 1948, no. 1495, FBI HUAC Files.

34. *SDSRIARA*, pp. 438–39. See also Michal R. Belknap, *Cold War Political Justice: The Smith Act, the Communist Party, and American Civil Liberties* (Westport, Conn.: Greenwood, 1977), pp. 46–47; memo, [McGohey] to [Clark], June 25, 1948, Smith Act-Correspondence, John F. X. McGohey Papers, HST. For Hoover's advice to Clark, see memos, Hoover to Tolson, Tamm, Ladd, and Nichols, April 1, 1947, no. 1438 and Jan. 13, 1948, no. 1492, FBI HUAC Files. For Clark's testimony, see *Hearings on H.R. 4422 and H.R. 4581*, pp. 20–21, 23. For Stripling, see Detroit News, Nov. 28, 1940, pp. 1–2. For the Dies Committee report, see Appendix I, *A Compilation of Original Sources Used as Exhibits to Show the Nature and Aims of the Communist Party, Its Connections with the U.S.S.R. and Its Advocacy of Force and Violence*, 76th Cong., 2d sess., 1940. For Hoover's order to index the Dies Committee report, see memo, Fred J. Baumgardner to D. Milton Ladd, May 12, 1948, no. 1510, FBI HUAC Files.

35. Memo, Sullivan to Belmont, Oct. 9, 1956, no. 47 (see also accompanying report, "Current Weaknesses of the Communist Party, USA," p. 88), FBI COINTELPRO-CPUSA Files. For Hoover on Judge Rifkind, see memo, Director to Attorney General, Sept. 17, 1948, Smith Act-Correspondence, McGohey Papers. For Clark, see Peter Steinberg, "Chartering the F.B.I.," *Nation*, Oct. 6, 1979, p. 301. For Hoover's report to the White House, see letter, Hoover to Vaughan, July 26, 1948, PSF-FBI Communist Data, HST. For federal employees, see Treasury Department Loyalty Board determination, re Martin R. Bradley, in Employee Review Board-B, John W. Snyder Papers, HST.

36. Letter, Clark to Thomas, Jan. 31, 1947, Attorney General's Files-J. Parnell Thomas, Clark Papers.

37. Lamont, *Freedom Is*, p. 20.

38. Letter, Hoover to Vaughan, Jan. 17, 1946, PSF-FBI Personal, HST.

39. For the contempt case, see I. F. Stone, "Is the Constitution Un-American?," *Nation*, Sept. 6, 1947, pp. 223–25; Carl Beck, *Contempt of Congress: A Study of the Prosecutions Initiated by the Committee on Un-American Activities, 1945–1957* (New Orleans: Hauser Press, 1959), pp. 25–33; HUAC, *Proceedings Against Dr. Edward K. Barsky and Others*, H.Rept. 1829, 79th Cong., 2d sess., 1946 (Serial 11023); HUAC, *Hearings on Joint Anti-Fascist Refugee Committee*, 79th Cong., 2d sess., 1946.

40. For the leak to Stripling, see memo, Ladd to Director, Feb. 6, 1947, no. 1422, FBI HUAC Files. For the Eisler case generally, see HUAC, *Hearings on Gerhart Eisler* and *Hearings Regarding Leon Josephson and Samuel Liptzen*, 80th Cong., 1st sess., 1947; Freeland, *The Truman Doctrine*, pp. 144–45; *Cong. Rec.*, 80th Cong., 1st sess., Feb. 18, 1947, p. 1135; Robert E. Stripling, *The Red Plot Against America*, ed. Bob Considine (Drexel Hill, Pa.: Bell, 1949), pp. 60–62. Clark is quoted in HUAC, *Hearings on H.R. 1884 and H.R. 2122*, p. 31.

41. Memos, Tamm to Director, March 13, 1947, no. 1429 and March 14, 1947, no. 1448X, FBI HUAC Files; memo, Hoover to Attorney General, March 13, 1947, no. 1455, ibid.

42. For the JAFRC's demise, see HUAC, *U.S. Communist Party Assistance to Foreign Communist Parties. (Veterans of the Abraham Lincoln Brigade.)*, 88th Cong., 1st sess., 1963, p. 649n. For Eisler's flight, see Caute, *The Great Fear*, pp. 233–34.

43. Letter, Hoover to Vaughan, March 15, 1947, PSF-FBI Communist Data, HST. For the FBI's reports on Rogge et al., see letter, Hoover to Vaughan, Nov. 13, 1947, PSF-FBI R, HST; letter, Hoover to Vaughan, June 21, 1948, PSF-FBI C, HST; letter, Ford to Connelly, July 9, 1948, CF-Justice Dept.(1), HST; letter, Tom [Clark] to Connelly, June 29, 1948, ibid.; memo, Hutchinson to Rowley, July 7, 1948, ibid. See also Philip Perlman interview, Dec. 15, 1954, Post-Pres. File-Memoirs, HST. FBI Assistant Director DeLoach later leaked to Senator Mundt at least one of the clemency petitions presented to Truman. Letter, DeLoach to McGaughey, Sept. 28, 1959, Box 162(9), KEM.

44. Beginning in 1947 both the Justice Department and the Democratic National Committee highlighted the prosecution of recalcitrant HUAC witnesses in an effort to document the Truman administration's anti-communist credentials. The DNC also pointed out that the FBI's budget had increased from less than $3 million per year under Herbert Hoover to more than $70 million under the Democrats. U.S., Department of Justice, *Annual Report of the Attorney General of the United States for the Fiscal Year Ended June 30, 1947* (Washington, D.C.: Government Printing Office, 1947), pp. 15–16; "The Democratic Record Against Communism in America," Dec. 9, 1953, in Anti-Communism, Charles S. Murphy Papers, HST.

45. Beck, *Contempt of Congress*, pp. 35–36. For the contempt cases, see *U.S v. Bryan*, 72 F.Supp. 58 (1947), 399 U.S. 323 (1949); *Bryan* v. *U.S.*, 174 F.2d 525 (1949), 183 F.2d 996 (1950), 340 U.S. 866 (1950); *Morford* v. *U.S.*, 176 F.2d 54 (1949), 184 F.2d 864 (1950), 339 U.S. 258 (1950); *U.S.* v. *Barsky*, 72 F.Supp. 165 (1947); *Barsky* v. *U.S.*, 167 F.2d 241 (1948), 334 U.S. 843 (1948); *Marshall* v. *U.S.*, 176 F.2d 473 (1949), 339 U.S. 933 (1950); *Eisler* v. *U.S.*, 170 F.2d 273 (1948), 338 U.S. 189 (1949), 338 U.S. 883 (1949); *U.S.* v. *Josephson*, 165 F.2d 82 (1948); *Josephson* v. *U.S.*, 333 U.S. 838 (1947), 335 U.S. 899 (1948); *Dennis* v. *U.S.*, 171 F.2d 986 (1948), 339 U.S. 162 (1950); *U.S.* v. *Dennis*, 72 F.Supp. 417 (1947).

46. 72 F.Supp. 58 (1947).

47. The Court of Appeals ruled that Eisler's petition had been received too late for consideration.

48. Lowenthal, *Federal Bureau of Investigation*, pp. 300–303. Holtzoff's sometimes cavalier attitude toward civil liberties is further highlighted by his July 1944 response to Hoover "that microphone surveillance is not equivalent to illegal search and seizure" and further "that evidence so obtained should be admissible" in court even when "an actual trespass is committed." *SDSRIARA*, p. 294 n74.

49. Diary entry, April 30, 1948, Ayers Papers. See also the entry of April 26, 1948, ibid. For the Hoover letter and Condon's response, see letter, Hoover to Secretary of Commerce, May 15, 1947, PSF-FBI C, HST; letter, Condon to William C. Foster, May 5, 1948, ibid.; note, TCC [Clark] to the President, May 3, 1948, ibid. See also HUAC, *Report to the Full Committee of the Special Subcommittee on National Security (Report on Dr. Edward U. Condon)*, 80th Cong., 2d sess., 1948; Goodman, *The Committee*, pp. 232, 234.

50. Letter, Chester Kamin to Thomas Sullivan, Sept. 2, 1970, Stamler Papers.

51. Notes, Dec. 2 and 3, 1953, Whitman File-Diary, Oct.–Dec. 1953, DDE. For Oppenheimer generally, see Philip M. Stern, *The Oppenheimer Case: Security on Trial* (New York: Harper and Row, 1969). For FBI reports to the White House on Oppenheimer, see letter, Hoover to Allen, May 29, 1946, PSF-FBI O, HST; letter, Hoover to Vaughan, Nov. 15, 1945, ibid.; letter, Hoover to Vaughan, Nov. 28, 1945, PSF-FBI M, HST; letter, Hoover to Vaughan, Feb. 28, 1947, PSF-FBI Atomic Bomb, HST. For the blind memorandum, see memo, Ladd to Director, Feb. 4, 1947, no. 135, J. Robert Oppenheimer FBI Files (100–17828), JEH. For Thomas, see memo, Hoover to Tolson, Tamm, Ladd, and Nichols, Oct. 30, 1947, no. 165X, ibid. For Walter, see memo, Nichols to Tolson, July 14, 1947, no. 157, ibid. For McCarthy and Cohn, see memo, Hoover to Tolson and Ladd, June 24, 1953, ibid.; memo, Hoover to Tolson, Ladd, Belmont, and Nichols, May 19, 1953, ibid.; memo, Nichols to Tolson, May 11, 1953, ibid.

52. Memo, re Proposed Change in Manual for Field Stenographer, Oct. 12, 1955, no. 7393, FBI Administrative Matters Files (66–1934).

53. HUAC voiced a similar complaint two years later: "The committee knows, as do the intelligence agencies of the executive branch, the identity of an individual who has turned over secret and confidential information for the use of the Soviet Union. Proof of this traitorous act, together with proof that this individual has perjured himself when he denies the accusation, is contained in the form of evidence which cannot be used in court . . . The committee is aware that this is not the only case in which prosecution is affected by the Federal Communications Act." HUAC, *Annual Report*, H.Rept, 3249, 81st Cong., 2d sess., 1950 (Serial 11385), p. 4.

54. Memo, Clark to the President, Dec. 21, 1948, PSF-General A, HST; "Suggested Passage for State of the Union Message," n.d. (ca. Dec. 1948), HUAC, Clark M. Clifford Files, HST. Truman's opposition to partisan investigations was qualified. When responding to criticism from those accusing his administration of betraying Chiang Kai-Shek, Truman directed the IRS and the Justice Department to investigate the so-called China lobby. The White House also tried to inspire a congressional investigation (for the purpose of "embarrassing . . . a sizeable group of Republicans in and out of Congress") and solicited FBI reports on China lobby czar Alfred Kohlberg. The Bureau, however, "cleared" Kohlberg—reporting that many non-FBI sources had accused him of being an agent of the Kuomintang but that confidential informants "T-1," "T-2," and "T-3" had all refuted this charge.

Memo, Truman to Secretary of the Treasury, June 11, 1951, PSF-China Lobby (China Lobby), HST; memo, Truman to Collector of Internal Revenue, June 11, 1951, ibid.; memo, Truman to Attorney General, June 11, 1951, ibid.; memos, Elting Arnold to E. I. McLarney, Aug. 15 and 20, 1951, PSF-China Lobby (Treasury Dept.), HST; memo, re Alfred Kohlberg, Aug. 31, 1951, PSF-China Lobby (Justice Dept.), HST; memo, Elsey to the President, March 28, 1951, Foreign Relations-China Lobby, Elsey Papers; memo, Elsey to Tannenwald, June 5, 1951, ibid.

55. Hoover regularly forwarded reports on the activities of HUAC's critics to the White House and to the Attorney General. See letters, Hoover to Vaughan, Jan. 5, 1949 and Oct. 18, 1947, PSF-FBI Communist Data, HST; letter, Hoover to Vaughan, April 3, 1947, PSF-FBI P, HST; letter, Clark to Connelly, July 23, 1946, PSF-FBI C, HST; memos, Director to Attorney General, July 19, 1945 and July 18, 1946, ibid.; memo, re Abraham Flaxner, May 22, 1946, PSF-FBI F, HST. Other aspects of the FBI's surveillance of the Committee's critics, however, were not forwarded to the White House. Hoover, for instance, apparently ordered a check of the Rockefeller Foundation after learning of a grant to Cornell University to study congressional investigating committees. Memo, H. B. Fletcher to Ladd, April 22, 1949, no. 1592, FBI HUAC Files; memo, Lee Pennington to Ladd, April 14, 1949, no. 1593, ibid.

56. Memo, Executives' Conference to Director, Oct. 14, 1953, ibid. The FBI supplied McCarthy and several of his key supporters (notably news-papermen Trohan, Sokolsky, Woltman, and Lewis) with "tips" and "leads" and summaries of particular Bureau files. "We gave McCarthy all we had," former FBI Assistant Director Sullivan recalled, "but all we had were fragments, nothing could prove his accusations." Sullivan, *The Bureau*, pp. 45–46, 267. See also Ralph de Toledano, *J. Edgar Hoover: The Man in His Time* (New Rochelle, N.Y.: Arlington House, 1973), p. 280; Trohan, *Political Animals*, p. 249; Thomas C. Reeves, *The Life and Times of Joe McCarthy: A Biography* (New York: Stein and Day, 1982), pp. 203–04, 245–46, 288, 517, 548. McCarthy's chief counsel, Roy Cohn, was also a personal friend of Hoover and Nichols. See Ungar, *FBI*, p. 278n; Roy Cohn, "Could He Walk on Water?," *Esquire*, Nov. 1972, pp. 117–19, 250–54.

57. Memo, Hoover to Tolson, Tamm, Ladd, and Clegg, March 19, 1946, Hoover O&C FBI Files-Alger Hiss, in Hiss Papers; memos, Hoover to Tolson, Tamm, and Ladd, March 20 and 21, 1946, ibid.

58. Memo, Nichols to Tolson, July 12, 1947, Oppenheimer FBI Files; memo, Nichols to Tolson, June 20, 1949, FBI NLG Files; memos, Fletcher to Ladd, Aug. 3, 1948, no. 82 and Aug. 4, 1948, no. 81, Remington FBI Files (121–6159); memo, Milton A. Jones to Nichols, April 2, 1947, no. 1156, FBI HUAC Files; memos, Nichols to Tolson, Nov. 18, 1947, no. 1486, March 1, 1948, no. 1497, Aug. 27, 1948, no. 1513, Nov. 23, 1948, no. 1550, Feb. 9, 1949, no. 1571, and June 24, 1949, no. 1615, all ibid. All the above memorandums are marked for destruction. The Nichols Official and Confidential files include unserialized documents regarding Bureau officials' interest in Truman's

nomination of James McGranery for Attorney General. Persona non grata to the Right for his role in the *Amerasia* case, McGranery was criticized severely by Frederick Woltman, and copies of this "cooperative and reliable" newspaper reporter's stories are contained in the Nichols files. These files also reveal that Nichols consulted with Senate Judiciary Committee Chairman Pat McCarran, SISS counsel Jay Sourwine, and then Assistant U.S. Attorney Roy Cohn during the McGranery confirmation hearings. In addition to his role in the *Amerasia* case, McGranery was thought to have blocked the planned perjury prosecution of Owen Lattimore, a State Department employee named by Senator McCarthy. There is no evidence in this file folder, however, to indicate that the FBI supported the attempt to block McGranery's confirmation. Memos, Nichols to Tolson, May 6, 8, 10, 14, 17, and 19, 1952, all in Nichols O&C FBI Files-James McGranery.

59. It is not known why the Nichols Official and Confidential file continues to contain documents marked for destruction or if the Do Not File files on Oppenheimer, Remington, Hiss, and NLG were deliberately transferred to the FBI's central files, which were serialized and therefore retrievable.

60. Interview with Robert McCaughey, Madison, South Dakota, Feb. 28, 1979. For an after-the-fact attempt to create such a phony paper record, see letter, Oxnam to Nichols, Oct. 14, 1955, Louis B. Nichols, Oxnam Papers; letter, Nichols to Oxnam, Oct. 19, 1955, ibid.; memo, Oxnam to File, Oct. 20, 1955, ibid. This procedure was described to me by Mr. McCaughey, who served as Mundt's administrative aide from 1945 until Mundt's death in 1974.

61. Letter, Williams to Mundt, May 20, 1954, Box 915(8), KEM; letter, Hoover to Mundt, June 14, 1954, ibid.; letter, Mundt to Fulbright, June 16, 1954, ibid.; letter, Mundt to Williams, May 29, 1954, ibid.; letter, Mundt to Nichols, June 5, 1954, Box 842(3), KEM; letter, Hoover to Mundt, July 2, 1954, Box 162(4), KEM. For the denials, see Whitehead, *The FBI Story*, p. 437; *New York Times*, March 15, 1954, p. 3; ibid., March 23, 1954, p. 10; ibid., March 25, 1954, pp. 12-14; ibid., May 12, 1954, p. 18. See also Stone, "J. Edgar Hoover," p. 4.

V. BUREAU ENEMIES: THE NATIONAL LAWYERS GUILD AND MAX LOWENTHAL

1. Percival R. Bailey, "The Case of the National Lawyers Guild, 1939-1958," in Athan Theoharis, ed., *Beyond the Hiss Case: The FBI, Congress, and the Cold War* (Philadelphia: Temple University Press, 1982), pp. 130-32.

2. For criticism of the FBI, see Cook, *The FBI Nobody Knows*, pp. 235-41; Whitehead, *The FBI Story*, pp. 204-17. Hoover reported to the White House on Norris's proposed criticism of the Bureau and forwarded a list of Boas's Communist front affiliations after learning of his plans to arrange a meeting with the President. FBI Rept. no. 511, Dec. 2, 1940 (summary only), OF10-B, FDR; letter, Hoover to Edwin Watson, April 13, 1940, no. 55, ibid.

3. *Cong. Rec.*, 78th Cong., 1st sess., Feb. 1, 1943, pp. 474–84. For the Dies Committee's Communist front charge, see Appendix IX, *Communist Front Organizations—With Special Reference to the National Citizens Political Action Committee*, 78th Cong., 2d sess., 1944, pt. 4, pp. 1267–79.

4. Bailey, "The Case of the NLG," pp. 134–35.

5. Letter, Hoover to Vaughan, Dec. 23, 1948, PSF-FBI N, HST.

6. Memo, Director to Attorney General, Feb. 24, 1950, Loyalty, Charles S. Murphy Files, HST.

7. For the Coplon affair, see Theoharis, *Spying on Americans*, pp. 100–01. Based on the record of government illegality unearthed during the New York trial, Coplon successfully appealed her conviction. The courts ordered a new trial and, after the Supreme Court denied the government's appeal, Coplon eventually won her freedom. *U.S.* v. *Coplon*, 185 F.2d 629 (2d Cir. 1950), 342 U.S. 920 (1952); *Coplon* v. *U.S.*, 191 F.2d 749 (D.C. Cir. 1951), 342 U.S. 926 (1952).

8. For Lawrence's, Brown's, and Childs's support, see the clippings in General Loyalty Files(2), Spingarn Papers. For Oxnam and Collier, see letter, Nichols to Oxnam, July 1, 1949, Louis B. Nichols, Oxnam Papers. While Nichols armed Oxnam with "objective" newspaper clippings, Lawrence may have received more substantial assistance. He embellished his attempt to defend FBI spying "in a period of Cold War" with a tale of how the Bureau might have prevented the Japanese attack on Pearl Harbor. Based on information the Bureau picked up in 1941 when monitoring communications between Hawaii and Japan, Lawrence said, the FBI went to the Federal Communications Commission, then headed by Bureau nemesis James L. Fly, with a request to review all messages filed by the Japanese consulate for transmission to Japan. The FCC, however, refused to allow the American communications companies in Hawaii to turn the messages over to the FBI.

9. Theoharis, *Spying on Americans*, p. 102. Assistant Attorney General Peyton Ford advised Truman to release the text of Roosevelt's wiretap directive of May 21, 1940, but the President refused. When investigating this matter, White House aide George Elsey discovered that Clark had deceived the President in 1946 when securing his approval for a wiretap directive. Quite simply, Clark edited FDR's earlier directive, giving the FBI much greater latitude to tap in national security cases. When approving his 1946 directive, Truman assumed that he was simply continuing Roosevelt's policy. Truman, however, did not rescind his directive upon learning in February 1950 of Clark's duplicity. Ibid., pp. 103–4. By that time, Clark was a justice on the United States Supreme Court.

10. For "June mail," see Athan Theoharis, "The Presidency and the Federal Bureau of Investigation: The Conflict of Intelligence and Legality," *Criminal Justice History International Annual* 2(1981): 136. See also the documents in FBI Administrative Matters Files (66-1372). For Bureau Bulletin No. 34, see Theoharis, *Spying on Americans*, p. 102, and "Bureaucrats Above the Law: Double Entry Intelligence Files," *Nation*, Oct. 22, 1977, pp. 393–97. Information relating to HUAC was also routinely recorded on the

administrative page. FBI field offices monitored the Committee's activities, compiling detailed reports on HUAC's proposed investigations prior to the convening of formal hearings. The reason why particular FBI field office reports were compiled and "submitted at this time" (because HUAC "will hold hearings" in the near future) was recorded only on the unserialized administrative page. See Baltimore Field Office Report, April 9, 1957, no. 2393, FBI Rosenberg-Sobell Committee Files (100–107111), JEH.

11. Memo, Director to Attorney General, Feb. 24, 1950, Loyalty, Murphy Files.

12. Letter, Hoover to Wilson, June 28, 1949, no. 157X, FBI NLG Files (100–7321). For Nichols on Wilson, see memo, Nichols to Tolson, June 28, 1949, no. 157X, ibid. For Durr, see letter, Durr to Truman, June 20, 1949, OF10-B, HST; letter, Truman to Durr, June 23, 1949, ibid.

13. Letters, Truman to McGrath, Dec. 6 and 17, 1949, The President, J. Howard McGrath Papers, HST. See also letter, Hoover to Vaughan, Jan. 14, 1950, PSF-FBI N, HST; letters, McGrath to Truman, Dec. 1 and 7, 1949, The President, McGrath Papers; letter, McGrath to Hoover, Dec. 1, 1949, ibid.; memo, Hoover to McGrath, Dec. 22, 1949, ibid.; Bailey, "The Case of the NLG," pp. 139–40.

14. Ibid., pp. 140–41. See also memo, Guy Hottel to Director, Dec. 13, 1949, no. 216, FBI NLG Files.

15. Memo, Guy Hottel to Director, May 10, 1950, no. 1661, FBI HUAC Files. For the Keeneys, see HUAC, *Testimony of Philip O. Keeney and Mary Jane Keeney and Statement Regarding Their Background*, 81st Cong., 1st sess., 1949.

16. For the NLG's charge, see Bailey, "The Case of the NLG," p. 143. For Coplon, see Sanche de Gramont, *The Secret War: The Story of International Espionage in World War II* (New York: G. P. Putnam's Sons, 1962), p. 76. The text of Rauh's speech is in National Defense-Internal Security(2), Spingarn Papers. For the NLG report, see "Report on Alleged Practices of the FBI," *Lawyers Guild Review* 10(Winter 1950): 185–96.

17. A copy of Wilson's story is filed in FBI NLG Files.

18. Bailey, "The Case of the NLG," pp. 143–44.

19. As of July 1978, according to a CIA study, there were thirteen major international Communist fronts, including the IADL. See U.S., House, Subcommittee on Oversight of the Permanent Select Committee on Intelligence, *The CIA and the Media*, 95th Cong., 1st and 2d sess., 1977–1978, pp. 560–627.

20. Bailey, "The Case of the NLG," p. 145.

21. HUAC, *National Lawyers Guild*, H.Rept. 3123, 81st Cong., 2d sess., 1950 (Serial 11384). For a comparison of the similar, often verbatim language of the FBI and HUAC reports, see Christy Macy and Susan Kaplan, comps., *Documents: A Shocking Collection of Memoranda, Letters and Telexes from the Secret Files of the American Intelligence Community* (New York: Penguin, 1980), pp. 25–28 (Doc. 1A–1C).

22. Bailey, "The Case of the NLG," p. 147. For the report, see *The National*

Committee to Defeat the Mundt Bill—A Communist Lobby, H.Rept. 3248, 81st Cong., 2d sess., 1950 (Serial 11385). Because information obtained by electronic surveillance was not considered public source information, the FBI apparently had HUAC launder the information by subpoenaing telegrams sent to and from the NLG office in Washington and telephone company records of long-distance calls.

23. Memos, Nichols to Tolson, July 12, 1950, no. 467, July 18, 1950, no. 477, and Aug. 29, 1950, FBI NLG Files; memo, Hottel to Director, June 16, 1950, no. 448, ibid.; letter, Harrison to McGrath, June 18, 1950, no. 448, ibid. See also Bailey, "The Case of the NLG," pp. 145–46. Whether or not the FBI assisted them in this instance, HUAC staff unearthed a NLG membership list and interviewed "over 40 employees of the Federal Government who are currently carried on the rolls of the National Lawyers Guild." HUAC, *National Lawyers Guild*, p. 21. The FBI, of course, also had a complete membership list and, as of December 26, 1949, concluded that 6.6 percent of Guild members were Communists. Bailey, "The Case of the NLG," p. 144.

24. FBI LHM, re Erwin Nathaniel Griswold, Dec. 14, 1951, PSF-FBI F, HST.

25. Harry S. Truman, *Public Papers of the Presidents of the United States: Harry S. Truman, 1950* (Washington, D.C.: Government Printing Office, 1965), p. 752. For the White House staff assistance, see letter, William J. Hopkins to Lowenthal, May 18, 1950, OF10–B, HST; memo, B. Bonsteel to Hopkins, n.d. (ca. May 1950), ibid.; note, ehl, to Miller, n.d. (ca. May 1950), ibid.; letter, Lowenthal to Hopkins, May 14, 1950, ibid. For Truman's opinion of the book, see letters, Truman to Lowenthal, June 22 and July 25, 1950, PSF-General (Max Lowenthal), HST; letter, Truman to Lowenthal, June 17, 1950, PPF-Max Lowenthal, HST. For Elsey, see memo, Elsey to Murphy, Spingarn and Bell, June 16, 1950, Loyalty Committee-Civil Rights(1), Spingarn Papers; George M. Elsey Oral History Interview, pp. 460–61, HST.

26. Letter, Lowenthal to Truman, Sept. 1, 1950, PSF-General (Max Lowenthal), HST; letter, Truman to Lowenthal, Sept. 8, 1950, ibid. For the hearings, see HUAC, *Hearings Regarding Communism in the United States Government*, 81st Cong., 2d sess., 1950, pt. 2, pp. 2959–85.

27. Letter, Hoover to Comrade [Trohan], Nov. 28, 1950, Correspondence-Hoover, Trohan Papers; letter, Trohan to Pegler, March 28, 1956, Communism-Max Lowenthal, Pegler Papers. For the media blitz, see, for example, *Washington Post*, Nov. 26, 1950, p. 7B; *Cong. Rec.*, 81st Cong., 2d sess., Nov. 30, 1950, pp. A7342–50. See also memo, Fred J. Baumgardner to Alan H. Belmont, Nov. 30, 1950, no. 1724X, FBI HUAC Files. The Crime Records Division harassed other authors who wrote critical books, including William W. Turner, Fred J. Cook, Bernard Conner, and Norman Ollestad. The Bureau smeared Lyle Stuart, Ollestad's publisher, in leaks describing him as a friend of Lowenthal's son and a "known homosexual." Though both accusations were false, Hoover wrote "Good stuff!" when first apprised of these plans to defend the Bureau. Donner, *Age of Surveillance*, p. 111n.

28. Letter, Dick to Truman, Jan. 22, 1951, OF10–B, HST; letter, Truman to

Dick, Jan. 30, 1951, ibid. For the FBI's dissemination, see Sullivan, *The Bureau*, p. 94. For the article, see Morris Ernst, "Why I No Longer Fear the FBI," *Reader's Digest*," Dec. 1950, pp. 135–39.

29. For the FBI's strategy and ultimate response to Fly, see memos, Nichols to Tolson, Dec. 13 and 30, 1949, Jan. 6 and 11, 1950, in Nichols O&C FBI Files-Morris Ernst; memo, M. A. Jones to Nichols, Dec. 15, 1949, ibid.; letter, Nichols to Ernst, Jan. 6, 1950, ibid.; note, [Hoover] to [Tolson, Clegg, Ladd, and Nichols], n.d. (ca. Nov. 13, 1949), ibid. See also Leo Rosten, "Is John Jones a Communist?," *Look*, Sept. 12, 1950, pp. 40–45; Morris Ernst, "Let's Help People Quit Being Reds," *Look*, July 4, 1950, pp. 13–18; James L. Fly, "The Case Against Wire Tapping," *Look*, Sept. 27, 1949, pp. 35–40. *Look* editors had worked closely with the FBI for some time. In early 1941, a *Look* executive forwarded to Hoover the results of a not-yet-published poll regarding congressional attitudes toward foreign policy issues, particularly neutrality issues. Hoover, in turn, forwarded this information to the White House. Letter, Hoover to Edwin Watson, May 12, 1941, PSF-Justice Dept., FDR. In 1947 the FBI assisted *Look* editors when they were compiling a picture book about the Bureau. Ungar, *FBI*, p. 375. Fly, on the other hand, was a frequent target of FBI leaks. In October 1939, a month after the outbreak of the European war, Fly, then FCC chairman, was charged with setting up an interdepartmental group to study international communications. The Bureau representative in this group, Edward A. Tamm, vehemently opposed the plan and, on October 27, FBI media contact Frank Waldrop published a critical article in the *Washington Times-Herald* entitled "FCC Revives the BLACK CHAMBER: Has Set Up Bureau to Decode Diplomatic and Business Cables." See letter, Hoover to Watson, Feb. 11, 1942, no. 1144, OF10-B, FDR; memo, Tamm to Director, Oct. 20, 1939, ibid.; memo, FDR to Watson, Feb. 3, 1942, ibid.; letter, Fly to FDR, Jan. 28, 1942, ibid.

30. For the FBI's interest in the "Ernst projects," see memos, Nichols to Tolson, Oct. 18, Nov. 2 and 17, 1949, Feb. 16 and April 4, 1950, all in Nichols O&C FBI Files-Morris Ernst. See also letter, Nichols to Oursler, March 13, 1950, ibid.; memos, Jones to Nichols, Dec. 15, 1949, Jan. 19 and March 9, 1950, all ibid.; letter, Oursler to Nichols, Dec. 7, 1949, ibid.; letter, Ernst to Nichols, Nov. 1, 1949, ibid.; letters, Hoover to Ernst, Oct. 20 and Nov. 4, 1949, ibid. For the article, see Morris Ernst, "Some Affirmative Suggestions for a Loyalty Program," *American Scholar* 19 (Autumn 1950): 452–60.

31. Letter, Ernst to Nichols, Sept. 21, 1950, Nichols O&C FBI Files-Morris Ernst; letter, Nichols to Ernst, Sept. 26, 1950, ibid. For *The Nation*, see letters, Hoover to Ernst, Aug. 3 and 30, 1943, ibid.; note, jm, Aug. 4, 1943, ibid. For the NLG, Fly, and Rundquist, see letter, Hoover to Ernst, Dec. 9, 1949, ibid.; memo, Nichols to Tolson, Oct. 31, 1949, no. 331, FBI ACLU Files (61–190), JEH; letter, Ernst to Rundquist, Oct. 24, 1951, ibid. For Ryan and Frank, see memo, Nichols to Tolson, Jan. 24, 1950, Nichols O&C FBI Files-Morris Ernst; memo, Nichols to Hoover, Dec. 15, 1950, ibid.

32. Thomas I. Emerson, "The National Lawyers Guild: Legal Bulwark of Democracy," *Lawyers Guild Review* 10(Fall 1950): 93–110.

33. Memo, Nichols to Tolson, Nov. 24, 1950, no. 591, FBI NLG Files. See also Bailey, "The Case of the NLG," p. 147.

34. Ibid., pp. 153–55, 172 n66. For Nichols's membership in the ABA committee, see Special Preparedness Subcommittee, Military Cold War Education, pt. 2, p. 603. For the ABA purge, aimed primarily at NLG attorneys and counsel for Smith Act defendants, see Jerold S. Auerbach, *Unequal Justice: Lawyers and Social Change in Modern America* (New York: Oxford University Press, 1976), pp. 231–62. The ABA also had a Special Committee on Education in the Contrast Between Liberty Under Law and Communism and a Standing Committee on Education Against Communism. Nor was Nichols the only FBI official favored by the ABA. For three years in a row, FBI Assistant Director Sullivan lectured at the Harvard Graduate School of Business Administration and his lectures were published by the ABA Standing Committee under the title "Freedom is the Exception." Ungar, *FBI*, p. 299. Sullivan often referred third parties to select ABA members for information on Communists and other radicals—for instance, in 1966, directing North Carolina Assistant Attorney General Ralph Moody to Morris I. Liebman, a member of an ABA anticommunist committee, and Dr. Frank Barnett, director of the National Strategy Information Center. Memo, Sullivan to DeLoach, May 16, 1966, FBI NCARL Files (100–433447).

35. Bailey, "The Case of the NLG," pp. 151–53. See also HUAC, *Communist Activities Among Professional Groups in the Los Angeles Area*, 82d Cong., 2d sess., 1952, pt. 1, pp. 2501–2629. For Ernst, see memo, Nichols to Tolson, Jan. 23, 1952, Nichols O&C FBI Files-Morris Ernst. For the ABA representative, see memo, SAC Los Angeles to Director, Sept. 8, 1952, FBI HUAC Files.

36. Memo, Executives' Conference to Director, Oct. 14, 1953, ibid.

37. Memo, Hoover to Tolson, Ladd, and Belmont, May 29, 1953, FBI NLG Files; memos, Nichols to Tolson, June 17, 1953 and Jan. 25, 1954, no. 108, Thomas I. Emerson FBI Files; memo, V. P. Keay to Belmont, Feb. 2, 1954, no. 109, ibid.; memo, Laughlin to Belmont, June 18, 1953, ibid.

38. Bailey, "The Case of the NLG," p. 162.

39. For the New York chapter, see memo, SAC New York to Director, Dec. 8, 1960, no. 2136, FBI NLG Files. A copy of this memorandum is filed in the COINTELPRO-CPUSA Files. For SISS, see memos, Belmont to L. V. Boardman, April 4 and May 15, 1958, FBI COINTELPRO-CPUSA Files. For the HUAC report, see *Communist Legal Subversion (The Role of the Communist Lawyer)*, H.Rept. 41, 86th Cong., 1st sess., 1959 (Serial 12158). Eighteen separate FBI field offices were involved in the leak to Sourwine. Memo, Director to SAC Baltimore et al., April 11, 1958, FBI COINTELPRO-CPUSA Files. To preclude future discovery, moreover, the documents recording this leak and the yellow file copies of the blind memorandums made available to Sourwine were purposefully filed in the central COINTELPRO file and not in the targeted attorneys' individual case files.

40. HUAC, *National Lawyers Guild*, pp. 3–4.

VI. COLD WAR JUSTICE: THE TRIALS OF WILLIAM WALTER REMINGTON

1. Memo, Ladd to Director, Feb. 3, 1949, no. 90, William W. Remington FBI Files (121-6159), JEH.

2. See, for example, teletype, Hoover to SAC New York, June 12, 1950, no. 8 (74-1379), ibid.; memo, Ladd to Director, Oct. 12, 1950, no. 341 (74-1379), ibid.; memo, Ladd to Director, May 4, 1951, no. 1191 (121-6159), ibid. When Remington was later indicted for perjury and Hoover received word that the trial date had been delayed, he wrote: "Again adjourned! H." An additional delay led to this comment: "Some more stalling by the govt. H." Washington City News Service ticker, Nov. 3, 1950, no. 425 (74-1379), ibid.; teletype (marked "URGENT"), SAC New York to Director and SACs Washington and Boston, Nov. 9, 1950, no. 492 (74-1379), ibid.

3. For biographical information on Remington, see New York Field Office Report, Sept. 8, 1950, no. 306 (74-1379), ibid.

4. Teletype, SAC Knoxville to Director and SAC Washington, April 7, 1950, no. 165 (121-6159), ibid.; memo, Ladd to Director, Jan. 31, 1951, no. 1720 (74-1379), ibid. When preparing for Remington's libel suit, Bentley's attorney, Godfrey P. Schmidt, who later presided over the AWARE blacklisting enterprise, also sent an investigator to Tennessee. (By her own account, Bentley did not even meet Remington until March 1942.) Schmidt was "pleased" with the results and, after the suit was settled, turned his information over to HUAC. Goodman, *The Committee*, pp. 286-87.

5. Washington Field Office Report, April 27, 1950, no. 434 (121-6159), Remington FBI Files; memo, Alan H. Belmont to Ladd, March 24, 1950, no. 34X (101-1185), ibid. HUAC's investigator called on Kirkpatrick in this instance because the witness he was trying to locate, Elizabeth Winston Todd, was then assistant director of network operations at CBS. The FBI learned of this episode when George Crandall, director of press information at CBS, alerted the Bureau's New York office.

6. Letter, Hoover to Richardson, April 13, 1950, no. 255 (121-6159), ibid. For Cronin, see memo, Laughlin to Belmont, March 15, 1950, no. 34, (101-1185), ibid. For Hoover's order, see memo, H. B. Fletcher to Ladd, Feb. 6, 1950, no. 25X (101-1185), ibid. For Nichols, see memo, Nichols to Tolson, April 5, 1950, no. 104X (121-6159), ibid.

7. Washington Field Office Report, April 27, 1950, no. 434 (121-6159), ibid. For Appell and Ladd on HUAC's failure to locate McConnell and Bridgman, see memo, Ladd to Director, Jan. 31, 1951, no. 1720 (74-1379), ibid. For Russell, see memo, C. H. Stanley to Belmont, April 14, 1950, no. 177 (121-6159), ibid.; teletype, Guy Hottel to Director, April 12, 1950, no. 168 (121-6159), ibid. For Hoover's order, see teletype, Hoover to SACs New York and Knoxville, April 14, 1950, no. 176 (121-6159), ibid. According to FBI Assistant Director Alan H. Belmont, McConnell knew Remington to be a Communist during the 1930s but "can not produce evidence to support this knowledge" and thus "will not make that statement for fear of being subject to libel." Memo, Belmont to Ladd, April 26, 1950, no. 205 (121-6159), ibid.

During follow-up interviews, additional "negative information such as BRIDGMAN's failure to recall Post Office Box 1692 at Knoxville" was set out on the administrative page. Memo, SAC Boston to Director, June 26, 1950, no. 30 (74–1379), ibid.

8. Memo, Belmont to Ladd, April 26, 1950, no. 105 (121–6159), ibid.; memo, Hottel to Director, May 5, 1950, no. 110 (121–6159), ibid.

9. Memo, Hottel to Director, April 14, 1950, no. 258 (121–6159), ibid. For the Remington hearings, see HUAC, *Hearings Regarding Communism in the United States Government*, 81st Cong., 2d sess., 1950, pts. 1–2. Russell's contact with the Washington Field Office was Raphael I. Nixon. See memo, Hottel to Director, July 29, 1948, no. 3444 (65–56402), Remington FBI Files. Nixon left the FBI in late 1951 or early 1952 to succeed Benjamin Mandel as HUAC's research director. Mandel, in turn, moved over to the Senate Internal Security Subcommittee.

10. For example, see Washington Field Office Report, July 21, 1950, no. 58 (74–1379), ibid.

11. Teletype, Hottel to Director, April 26, 1950, no. 285 (121–6159), ibid.; memo, Belmont to Ladd, April 28, 1950, no. 342 (121–6159), ibid.

12. Memo, Director to Ford, May 3, 1950, no. 342 (121–6159), ibid. For Barstow's testimony, see HUAC, *Hearings Regarding Communism in the United States Government*, pt. 1, pp. 1893–1905.

13. Memo, SJS [Spingarn] to Murphy, April 27, 1950, Loyalty, Charles S. Murphy Files, HST; letter, Remington to Sawyer, June 9, 1950, copy in Washington Field Office Report, July 21, 1950, no. 58 (74–1379), Remington FBI Files; Charles Sawyer, *Concerns of a Conservative Democrat* (Carbondale: Southern Illinois University Press, 1968), pp. 182–83.

14. Memo, Director to Ford, May 3, 1950, no. 349 (121–6159), Remington FBI Files; memo, Ladd to Director, Jan. 31, 1951, no. 1720 (74–1379), ibid. See also Cook, *The FBI Nobody Knows*, p. 319.

15. Memo, Director to SAC New York, Oct. 17, 1950, no. 3854 (65–56402), Remington FBI Files; teletype, SAC New York to Director and SACs Washington and Philadelphia, Jan. 13, 1951, no. 1319 (74–1379), ibid. See also Herbert L. Packer, *Ex-Communist Witnesses: Four Studies in Fact Finding* (Stanford: Stanford University Press, 1962), pp. 84–86. For Bentley's soap opera–like memoirs (nearly half the book consists of melodramatic dialogue), see *Out of Bondage* (New York: Devin-Adair, 1951).

16. Both Hand and Brunini are quoted in Packer, *Ex-Communist Witnesses*, pp. 87–89.

17. Washington Field Office Report, May 24, 1950 (74–1379), Remington FBI Files. For Ann's refusal to sign, see memo, SAC Washington to Director, June 1, 1950, no. 2 (74–1379), ibid. For her reluctance to testify, see memo, Hottel to Director, Aug. 4, 1950 (74–1379), ibid. For Donegan, see memo, Laughlin to Belmont, May 31, 1950, no. 135 (121–6159), ibid.

18. Cook, *The FBI Nobody Knows*, pp. 314, 316, 324–25. See also memo, Director to SAC New York, July 17, 1947, no. 2695 (65–56402), Remington FBI Files; Washington Field Office Report, May 24, 1950 (74–1379), ibid. For

an insightful if sometimes impressionistic portrait of Ann Remington, see Murray Kempton, *Part of Our Time: Some Monuments and Ruins of the Thirties* (New York: Simon and Schuster, 1955), pp. 222–30. Remington first met Bentley through Joe North, editor of *New Masses* and a friend of Ann Remington's mother, Elizabeth Moss. Moss introduced Remington to North and the *New Masses* editor introduced the Remingtons to Jacob Golos, Bentley's lover and reputed master spy. Later, Golos took them to meet Bentley, who was introduced as "Helen Johnson."

19. Noonan is quoted in Cook, *The FBI Nobody Knows*, p. 324.

20. Ibid., p. 327. Four years later, on January 1, 1955, New Hampshire Attorney General Louis G. Wyman filed a report based on an eighteen month investigation of CPUSA activities at Dartmouth. Though a prolific redhunter in his own right, Wyman's report cited the very testimony that Chanler had been unable to put into the trial record. Ibid., pp. 328–29.

21. For Rosenman and the Dartmouth source, see teletypes, SAC Boston to Director and SACs Washington, Newark, and New York, Oct. 14 and 18, 1950, no. 342 (74-1379), Remington FBI Files. For Stotes, see teletype, SAC Boston to Director, May 1, 1950, no. 326 (121-6159), ibid. For Donegan, see memo, SAC New York to Director, Oct. 24, 1950 (74-1379), ibid.

22. For Hopkins, see teletype, SAC New York to Director and SAC Boston, Dec. 26, 1950, no. 847 (74-1379), ibid. For Clapp, see teletype, SAC New York to Director and SAC Washington, Dec. 26, 1950, no. 845 (74-1379), ibid. For the indices check, see teletype, SAC New York to Director and SACs Washington and Boston, Dec. 27, 1950, no. 839 (74-1379), ibid.

23. For Hart, see memo, SAC Milwaukee to Director, Oct. 6, 1950, no. 302 (74-1379), ibid. See also teletype, SAC New York to Director and SAC Washington, Oct. 16, 1950, no. 349 (74-1379), ibid.

24. Letter, Hoover to [deleted], Nov. 15, 1950, no. 531 (74-1379), ibid. For Zein, Bielaski, and Rauh, see memo, SAC Milwaukee to Director, Oct. 17, 1950, no. 372 (74-1379), ibid. The Rauh memorandum is discussed in memo, Belmont to Ladd, Nov. 15, 1950 (74-1379), ibid.

25. Washington Field Office Report, July 21, 1950, no. 58 (74-1379), ibid.; memo, Stanley to Belmont, Sept. 5, 1950 (74-1379), ibid.

26. Lawrence's interest and working relationship with Nichols is recorded in teletype, Hoover to SAC New York, Jan. 22, 1951, no. 1611 (74-1379), ibid.; memos, Director to SAC New York, Nov. 2, 1950, no. 456 and Nov. 14, 1950, no. 532 (74-1379), ibid.; memos, Nichols to Tolson, Oct. 21 and 31, 1950, Nov. 6, 1950, no. 532, Dec. 2, 1950, no. 621, and Dec. 30, 1950, no. 957 (74-1379), all ibid. When testifying before a House subcommittee in 1977, *U.S. News and World Report* deputy editor Joseph Fromm discussed his conviction "that a responsible journalist cannot serve two masters . . . [a] conviction . . . reinforced in my case by a policy that David Lawrence . . . enforced that barred cooperation between any member of the staff of *U.S. News and World Report* and the CIA or, indeed, any intelligence organization, beyond the legitimate relationship between journalists and news sources." Subcommittee on Oversight, *The CIA and the Media*, pp. 99, 119–20.

27. Memo, Director to McInerney, Oct. 27, 1951, no. 1973 (74–1379), Remington FBI Files; memo, Director to Assistant Attorney General, Jan. 22, 1953, no. 2177 (74–1379), ibid. For Velde and the Marshall Foundation, see also New York Field Office Report, March 5, 1951 (74–1379), ibid.; memo, Stanley to Belmont, Jan. 22, 1953, no. 2177 (74–1379), ibid.; *Cong. Rec.*, 82d Cong., 1st sess., Oct. 17, 1951, pp. 13397–98.

28. Memo, SAC Washington to Director, March 31, 1955, no. 2231 (74–1379), Remington FBI Files. For the Circuit Court of Appeals and the Supreme Court rulings, see 191 F.2d 246 (1951); 342 U.S. 895 (1951); 343 U.S. 907 (1952); 208 F.2d 567 (1953); 347 U.S. 913 (1954).

29. Memo, Hottel to Director, June 4, 1947, no. 2494 (65–56402), Remington FBI Files. For Remington's anticommunism, see Cook, *The FBI Nobody Knows*, pp. 317–18.

30. A "technical surveillance" (wiretap) on Remington's phone from November 1945 to November 1947 revealed no information indicating membership in the CPUSA or espionage activities. For the tap, see memo, Hoover to Attorney General, Nov. 17, 1945, no. 27X (65–56402), Remington FBI Files; memo, Hottel to Director, Nov. 14, 1947, no. 2956 (65–56402), ibid.

VII. THE FBI, HUAC, AND COLD WAR LIBERALISM

1. *SDSRIARA*, p. 430; *IARA*, p. 66.

2. Mary S. McAuliffe, *Crisis on the Left: Cold War Politics and American Liberals, 1947–1954* (Amherst: University of Massachusetts Press, 1978), passim. The writings of the major theorists of Cold War liberalism include Reinhold Niebuhr, *The Irony of American History* (New York: Charles Scribner's Sons, 1952) and *Christian Realism and Political Problems* (New York: Charles Scribner, 1953); Sidney Hook, *Political Power and Personal Freedom* (New York: Criterion, 1959) and *Heresy, Yes—Conspiracy, No* (New York: John Day, 1953); Arthur M. Schlesinger, Jr., *The Vital Center* (Boston: Houghton Mifflin, 1949).

3. Thus, Cold War liberals Schlesinger, Hook, Irving Kristol, Daniel Bell, Elmer Rice, David Riesman, and Richard Rovere could find, if only for a short time, common ground with such conservatives as Whittaker Chambers, James Burnham, John Dos Passos, James T. Farrell, Ralph de Toledano, and John Chamberlain in the CIA-funded ACCF. McAuliffe, *Crisis on the Left*, pp. 115–29; Diana Trilling, *We Must March My Darlings* (New York: Harcourt Brace Jovanovich, 1977), p. 61.

4. Even perennial Socialist party candidate Norman Thomas, who had access to CIA funds as executive board chairman of the ACCF, complained to President Eisenhower that loyalty investigators were confusing Socialists with Communists. Thomas, who was particularly concerned about the activities of a State Department security official and former FBI agent, Scott McLeod, was nonetheless indifferent to the substance of the charges that McLeod and others had raised. Thomas objected principally because charges

of disloyalty were being made against Socialists as well as Communists. Memo, re meeting with Norman Thomas, Oct. 27, 1953, Whitman File-Norman Thomas, DDE; letter, Thomas to Eisenhower, Aug. 18, 1953, ibid.; letter, Thomas to Dulles, Sept. 10, 1953, ibid.

5. Diana Trilling, "A Communist and His Ideals," *Partisan Review* 18(July-Aug. 1951): 433; Robert M. La Follette, Jr., "Turn the Light on Communism," *Collier's*, Feb. 8, 1947, p. 74; Arthur M. Schlesinger, Jr., *What About Communism?* (New York: Public Affairs Committee, 1950), pp. 19, 23-24, 27-28; letter, Rovere to Schlesinger, Sept. 30, 1952, Correspondence, Richard Rovere Papers, SHSW; letter, Rovere to Irving Kristol, July 25, 1953, ibid.

6. For the NAACP's anticommunism, see Wilson Record, *Race and Radicalism: The NAACP and the Communist Party in Conflict* (Ithaca, N.Y.: Cornell University Press, 1964), pp. 154-57, 161-64. For the FBI report to the White House, see letter, Hoover to Harry Vaughan, Jan. 12, 1950, PSF-FBI Communist Data, HST. See also memo, SJS [Spingarn] to Clifford, Dec. 19, 1949, OF596-B, HST; letter, Wilkins to Clifford, Dec. 20, 1949, ibid. For the FBI's surveillance of the NAACP, see *SDSRIARA*, pp. 416-17, 450-51.

7. In the early 1950s Reuther allowed the CIA to launder $50,000 through the UAW—money that was given to Reuther's brother Victor to help organize anticommunist unions in Germany. Ronald Radosh, *American Labor and United States Foreign Policy* (New York: Random House, 1969), pp. 438-39. Ironically, Victor Reuther's name was on the CIA's HTLINGUAL (New York City mail intercept project) "watch list" and the Agency opened his mail in the late 1960s. See the CIA documents regarding Reuther and HTLINGUAL at the Center for National Security Studies, Washington, D.C.

8. Sigler claimed there were 15,000 active Communists in Michigan, an estimate seven times greater than the FBI's tabulation. He also named fifteen organizations as Communist fronts, including the NAACP and the Detroit Council for Youth Services. Among others, the board of directors of the Council for Youth Services included the Detroit Police Chief and several other high-ranking city officials. Sigler later "cleared" the NAACP, explaining that he had confused it with another group having the same initials. He also received an apology from the State Police detective who had inadvertently mixed the files on the Detroit Youth Assembly with those on the Council for Youth Services. Jacobs, "The Conduct of Local Political Intelligence," pp. 122-24.

9. David M. Oshinsky, "Labor's Cold War: The CIO and the Communists," in Griffith and Theoharis, *The Specter*, pp. 143-44; James R. Prickett, "Communism and Factionalism in the UAW, 1939-1947," *Science and Society* 32(No. 3, 1968): 276. For Woltman, see Max M. Kampelman, *The Communist Party vs. the C.I.O.* (New York: Praeger, 1959), pp. 74, 92 n26.

10. In 1940, when Secretary of Labor Frances Perkins wanted to appoint Reuther to head the Labor Department's Safety Advice Board, President Roosevelt blocked the appointment after hearing from the FBI. Memos, FDR to Attorney General, May 29, 1940, PSF-Justice Dept. (Robert Jackson),

FDR; memo, Hoover to Attorney General, May 22, 1940, ibid.; letter, Jackson to Marguerite LeHand, May 24, 1940, ibid.; letter, Hoover to Edwin Watson, May 23, 1940, no. 85, OF10-B, FDR.

11. William D. Andrew, "Factionalism and Anti-Communism: Ford Local 600," *Labor History* 20(Spring 1979): 228–29, 231, 251, 255; John W. Anderson Oral History Interview, pp. 149–50, ALH. Other unions also sought HUAC's assistance. When the Committee visited Chicago in 1959, officials of the International Association of Machinists (IAM) worked with HUAC staff in an effort to check a reform movement in Lodge 113. The *Chicago American* reported that IAM assigned several investigators to assist HUAC, and Lodge 113 president Albert Dency was removed after he received a Committee subpoena. IAM official A. J. Hayes then placed Lodge 113 under an administrator. See "The Machinists Union and the Un-American Activities Committee," June 1, 1959, in Box 1, Oscar Paskal Papers, ALH; HUAC, *Communist Infiltration of Vital Industries and Current Communist Techniques in the Chicago, Ill., Area*, 86th Cong., 1st sess., 1959, pp. 599–601.

12. *Cong. Rec.*, 76th Cong., 3d sess., Jan. 23, 1940, p. 570. For AFL officials' close relationship with HUAC member Karl Mundt, see letter, Woll to Mundt, April 24, 1947, Box 681(3), KEM; letter, Mundt to Woll, April 30, 1947, ibid.; letter, Meany to Mundt, May 26, 1947, Box 679(5), KEM; letter, Harry Holloway, Jr. to Philip Murray, May 5, 1947, ibid.

13. For Democratic red-baiting, see Caute, *The Great Fear*, p. 38; Richard M. Fried, "Electoral Politics and McCarthyism: The 1950 Campaign," in Griffith and Theoharis, *The Specter*, pp. 198–201; Athan Theoharis, "The Rhetoric of Politics: Foreign Policy, Internal Security, and Domestic Politics in the Truman Era, 1945–1950," in Barton Bernstein, ed., *Politics and Policies of the Truman Administration*, (Chicago: Quadrangle, 1972), pp. 221–22.

14. Quoted in Justus D. Doenecke, *Not to the Swift: The Old Isolationists in the Cold War Era* (Lewisburg, Penna.: Bucknell University Press, 1979), p. 216.

15. Confidential Memo for the President, Nov. 19, 1947, Clark M. Clifford Papers, HST.

16. Diary entries, March 17 and 18, 1948, Eben Ayers Papers, HST. See also Daniel Yergin, *Shattered Peace: The Origins of the Cold War and the National Security State* (Boston: Houghton Mifflin, 1977), pp. 275–302. For FBI reports to the White House on "Wallace and his Communists," see letters, Hoover to Harry Vaughan, Oct. 23, 1946, June 25, July 31, Aug. 18, and Dec. 19, 1947, and Jan. 27, 1948, all in PSF-FBI W, HST; letters, Hoover to Vaughan, Jan. 19 and 27, and March 16, 1948, in PSF-FBI Communist Data, HST; letters, Hoover to George Allen, Sept. 20 and 25, 1946, and March 18, 1947, ibid.; letter, Hoover to Vaughan, March 3, 1948, PSF-FBI S, HST; letter, Hoover to Vaughan, March 11, 1948, PSF-FBI Personal, HST; letter, Hoover to Vaughan, April 3, 1947, PSF-FBI P, HST; letter, Hoover to Allen, Sept. 20, 1946, PSF-FBI Argentina, HST; letter, Hoover to Allen, Sept. 23, 1946, PSF-FBI N, HST; memo, Director to Attorney General, Feb. 12, 1948, CF-Justice Dept.(1), HST.

17. Executive committee minutes, March 18, 1948, Series 2, Box 36, ADA

Papers, SHSW. See also Clifton Brock, *Americans for Democratic Action* (Washington, D.C.: Public Affairs Press, 1962), p. 52.

18. Biddle is quoted in U.S., House, Select Committee on Lobbying, *Lobbying, Direct and Indirect*, pt. 6, *Americans for Democratic Action*, 81st Cong., 2d sess., 1950, p. 12. For the dissemination of anticommunist literature and ADA red-baiting, see executive committee minutes, May 1, 1948, Series 2, Box 34, ADA Papers. See also John S. Rosenberg, "The Boys of '48: The A.D.A.'s Long Shadow," *Nation*, Feb. 23, 1980, pp. 208-10.

19. *Cong. Rec.*, 80th Cong., 2d sess., May 5, 1948, pp. A2754-58; Karl M. Schmidt, *Henry Wallace: Quixotic Crusade 1948* (Syracuse, N.Y.: Syracuse University Press, 1960), p. 159. For other examples, see Curtis D. Mac-Dougall, *Gideon's Army*, 3 vols. (New York: Marzani and Munsell, 1965), 2: *The Decision and the Organization*, pp. 379, 561; Richard J. Walton, *Henry Wallace, Harry Truman, and the Cold War* (New York: Viking, 1976), pp. 274-321. See also the Public Relations File in Series 7, Boxes 105-6, ADA Papers, passim.

20. Interview with Curtis D. MacDougall, Evanston, Illinois, April 17, 1979.

21. John Morton Blum, ed., *The Price of Vision: The Diary of Henry A. Wallace, 1942-1946* (Boston: Houghton Mifflin, 1973), pp. 332, 361, 406; Sullivan, *The Bureau*, p. 37; Jonathan Daniels, *White House Witness, 1942-1945* (Garden City, N.Y.: Doubleday, 1975), pp. 174-75. At the time FBI officials were secretly working to discredit Wallace, they also attempted to ingratiate themselves with the Vice-President. In 1942 Hoover alerted Wallace to CPUSA activities in the Joint Anti-Fascist Refugee Committee upon learning that the JAFRC had asked him to speak at a dinner. Similarly, when a delegation from the Women's Auxiliary of the National Maritime Union scheduled a meeting with the Vice-President, Hoover again alerted Wallace to CPUSA plans to publicize the meeting in the *Daily Worker*. Letters, Hoover to Wallace, Oct. 10 and 23, 1942, Hol-Hor, Henry Wallace Papers, FDR.

22. MacDougall, *Gideon's Army*, vol. 1: *The Components of the Decision*, p. 127; Athan Theoharis, "The Politics of Scholarship: Liberals, Anti-Communism, and McCarthyism," in Griffith and Theoharis, *The Specter*, pp. 269-70. For the Dies Committee attack on UDA, see *Annual Report*, H.Rept. 2277, 77th Cong., 2d sess., 1942 (Serial 10664).

23. Theoharis, "Politics of Scholarship," pp. 269-70; ADA press release, July 12, 1950, Series 5, Box 16, ADA Papers. Marcantonio, who had represented the East Harlem district for eight terms, lost the election.

24. Letter, Biddle to ADA board members, July 17, 1951, Series 5, Box 16, ibid.; executive committee minutes, June 25, 1951, Series 2, Box 35, ibid. For ADA on HUAC, see Brock, *Americans for Democratic Action*, p. 143.

25. Carey McWilliams, "The Witch Hunt's New Phase," *New Statesman and Nation*, Oct. 27, 1951, p. 455; Diana Trilling, "A Memorandum on the Hiss Case," *Partisan Review* 17 (May-June 1950): 500 and *We Must March*, pp. 46n, 51, 56-57; Sidney Hook, *Common Sense and the Fifth Amendment* (New York: Criterion, 1957), p. 141.

26. Schlesinger, *Vital Center*, pp. 125, 204, 217 and "What Made Them Turn Red?," *Look*, Aug. 1, 1950, p. 68; UAW press release, May 2, 1954, Box 227, Workers Defense League Papers, ALH.

27. Goodman, *The Committee*, pp. vii–viii, ix–x. For Ernst and the tax question, see Morris Ernst, "What Makes an Un-American," *Saturday Review*, Sept. 1, 1945, pp. 14–15; letter, Ernst to FDR, June 10, 1942, PSF-Morris Ernst, FDR. See also memo, Tamm and Tolson to the Director, Dec. 12, 1941, Hoover O&C FBI Files-Dies Committee.

28. *Harper's*, March 1954, p. 31.

29. When the press publicized ACLU official Roger Baldwin's denial of Dies's charge, the FBI Director wrote: "This is to laugh! H." See the notation on the *Washington Post* clipping, Jan. 5, 1939, no. 40X6, FBI HUAC Files (61-7582).

30. Memo, Hoover to Tolson, Tamm, and Nichols, Nov. 28, 1940, no. 576, ibid.; memo, Attorney General to the President, Nov. 28, 1940, OF320 (Dies Committee 1940-41), FDR. For the "deal," see Lamont, *Freedom Is*, pp. 268–70, 273; letters, Jackson to Lewis (Dies offered a similar deal to CIO president John L. Lewis), Feb. 7, 8, and 9, 1940, all in Correspondence, Gardner Jackson Papers, FDR; letter, Jackson to Ernst, Nov. 28, 1939, ibid.; transcript, President's Conference with Dies, Nov. 29, 1940, OF320 (Dies Committee 1940-41), FDR. Ernst was both a close friend and informal adviser to Roosevelt, providing him with a steady stream of political "tidbits" (advice and intelligence regarding FDR's supporters and opponents). Roosevelt, in turn, often acted on Ernst's suggestions. For example, see memo, FDR to HM [Morgenthau], May 7, 1942, PSF-Morris Ernst, FDR.

31. HUAC, *Hearings on H.R. 4422 and H.R. 4581, Proposed Legislation to Curb or Control the Communist Party of the United States*, 80th Cong., 2d sess., 1948, p. 229. For Flynn, see Corliss Lamont, ed., *The Trial of Elizabeth Gurley Flynn* (New York: Horizon Press, 1968).

32. Letter, Dorothy Dunbar Bromley, Arthur Garfield Hays, Quincy Howe, Elmer Rice, and Roger Baldwin to Thomas, Oct. 29, 1947, Box 681(1), KEM; Corliss Lamont, *Yes to Life: Memoirs of Corliss Lamont* (New York: Horizon Press, 1981), pp. 110–12. See also McAuliffe, *Crisis on the Left*, pp. 87–101, 167 n7.

33. Ibid., pp. 87–107.

34. Ibid., pp. 91–94; Merlyn S. Pitzele, "Is There a Blacklist?," *New Leader*, May 12, 1952, pp. 21–23.

35. *New York Times*, Aug. 4, 1977, p. 1.

36. Memos, Nichols to Tolson, July 27, 1955, Dec. 23, 1955, no. 573, and Jan. 4, 1956, no. 574, all in FBI ACLU Files.

37. Memo, Nichols to Tolson, Oct. 17, 1955, ibid.

38. For Pennington, see memo, Nichols to Tolson, May 12, 1954, no. 473, ibid. For Mandel, see letter (copy to Mandel), Ferman to Nichols, March 13, 1957, no. 652, ibid. For Roosevelt, see memo, Gordon A. Nease to Tolson, July 29, 1958, ibid. For Ferman's role as informer, see memos, Nichols to Tolson, Nov. 24, 1953, no. 442, Dec. 16, 1953, and Jan. 7, 1954, no. 454, all ibid. Pennington, who regularly passed information to HUAC, worked for the

Notes to pp. 187–195

Legion until 1956. He claimed to have "70,000 confidential contacts" who fed him information on subversives; he was also a CIA informer and a close friend of James McCord. After the Watergate burglary, Pennington helped McCord destroy documents linking McCord to the Agency. Wise, *The American Police State*, pp. 255–56.

39. For FDR, see Steele, "Franklin D. Roosevelt," p. 24 n32. For *The Nation* and the *New York Daily News*, see memo, Foxworth to Director, Dec. 31, 1941, Nichols O&C FBI Files-Morris Ernst. For Truman, see letter, William D. Hassett to Ernst, Nov. 10, 1945, OF263 (1945–47), HST; letter, Ernst to Hassett, Nov. 8, 1945, ibid. For Ernst's testimony, see HUAC, *Hearings on H.R. 4422 and H.R. 4581*, pp. 279, 294–96. For Remington, see memo, Nichols to Tolson, May 25, 1949, no. 19X1, William W. Remington FBI Files (101–1185), JEH. For McCarthy, see memo, Nichols to Tolson, March 29, 1952, Nichols O&C FBI Files-Morris Ernst.

40. For the FBI's assistance, see letter, Hoover to Ernst, Feb. 29, 1952, no. 389, FBI ACLU Files; letter, Ernst to Nichols, Feb. 13, 1952, no. 388, ibid.; letters, Nichols to Ernst, Feb. 21 and July 16, 1952, Nichols O&C FBI Files-Morris Ernst; letter, Ernst to Nichols, Feb. 5, 1952, ibid. See also memos, Nichols to Tolson, June 4 and July 16, 1951, and June 11, 1952, all ibid.; memo, Nichols to Director, March 6, 1952, ibid. For the book, see Morris L. Ernst and David Loth, *Report on the American Communist* (New York: Holt, 1952).

41. Memo, Nichols to Tolson, Nov. 9, 1956, FBI ACLU Files.

42. For the Newspaper Guild, see letter, Ernst to Nichols, Feb. 13, 1952, no. 388, ibid.; letter, Hoover to Ernst, Feb. 29, 1952, no. 389, ibid. For the ACLU executive board minutes, see memo, Nichols to Tolson, Feb. 15, 1952, ibid. For the Do Not File document, see memo, Hoover to Tolson, Ladd, Nichols, and Belmont, Nov. 20, 1950, Nichols O&C FBI Files-Morris Ernst.

43. Memo, Nichols to Tolson, Oct. 17, 1955, FBI ACLU Files. For Fly, see memo, Nichols to Tolson, Feb. 15, 1952, ibid.; letter, Hoover to Ernst, Feb. 29, 1952, no. 389, ibid.

44. For Nichols's opinion, see memo, Nichols to Tolson, Nov. 24, 1953, no. 442, ibid. For the *Counterattack* leak, see Jerold L. Simmons, "Operation Abolition: The Campaign to Abolish the House Un-American Activities Committee, 1938–1965" (Ph.D. diss., University of Minnesota, 1971), p. 156.

45. Letter, Hoover to [deleted], May 26, 1959, no. 767, FBI ACLU Files.

46. Memo, SAC San Francisco to Director, June 10, 1955, ibid.; memo, SAC Los Angeles to Director, Aug. 31, 1960, FBI NCARL Files (100–433447).

47. Hoover, Tolson, and DeLoach are quoted in memos, DeLoach to Tolson, Oct. 14, 1959, no. 791 and Sept. 3, 1959, no. 785, FBI ACLU Files. For Whalen, see memo, M. A. Jones to DeLoach, Sept. 3, 1959, no. 785X, ibid.

48. Schlesinger, *The Vital Center*, p. 129.

VIII. COUNTERINTELLIGENCE

1. Schlesinger, *Robert F. Kennedy and His Time*, p. 275.
2. Quoted in memo, Louis B. Nichols to Clyde Tolson, Jan. 29, 1953, FBI

352

HUAC Files. For the concern with "investigations of the present Administration," see cabinet minutes, Jan. 30, Feb. 6 and 12, 1953, Whitman File-Cabinet Minutes, DDE.

3. For McLeod, see Ross Y. Koen, *The China Lobby in American Politics* (New York: Macmillan, 1960), pp. 240-41. For the agreement and Persons on "strong pressure," see memo, Nichols to Tolson, March 7, 1953, no. 1885, FBI HUAC Files. Adams is quoted in memo, Adams to Dodge, March 2, 1953, Whitman File-Legislative Meetings 1953(3), DDE. For Eisenhower and Hoover, see *New York Times*, Feb. 26, 1953, p. 16 and April 5, 1953, p. 32. For the HUAC hearings, see *Communist Methods of Infiltration (Education)*, 83d Cong., 1st and 2d sess., 1953-1954, pts. 1-9. For Hoover's order, see Sigmund Diamond, "The Arrangement: The FBI and Harvard University in the McCarthy Era," in Theoharis, *Beyond the Hiss Case*, pp. 362-64.

4. Cabinet minutes, June 11, 1954, Whitman File-Cabinet Minutes, DDE. The CPUSA did not always cultivate federal employees. FBI informers William D. and Peggy Ames, for instance, both worked at the Naval Air Station in Alameda, California, at the time of their expulsion from the party in September 1950. When revealing their status as undercover Bureau operatives, they advised HUAC that "we were dropped from the party rolls for inactivity, and, both of us being in the Federal civil service, they felt that we were not part of the hardened core of the party." HUAC, *Investigation of Communist Activities in the San Francisco Area*, 83d Cong., 1st sess., 1953, pt. 4, pp. 3400-401.

5. E.O. 10491, *Federal Register* 18(Oct. 16, 1953): 6583; statement by the President, Aug. 24, 1954, OF133-E-1 (1954), DDE. Hoover had long favored an immunity bill. See memo, Edward A. Tamm to Director, Nov. 22, 1940, no. 513, FBI HUAC Files (61-7582).

6. See SAC Letter No. 57-26, May 7, 1957, in FBI Security Index Files, JEH. For the Supreme Court decisions, see *Rogers* v. *U.S.*, 340 U.S. 367 (1951); *Hoffman* v. *U.S.*, 341 U.S. 479 (1951). For the Bureau's interest in the strategy of prospective HUAC witnesses, see memo, Director to Warren Olney III, Nov. 11, 1953, FBI HUAC Files.

7. Cabinet minutes, April 2, 1954, Whitman File-Cabinet Minutes, DDE.

8. Some of the most important Supreme Court rulings included *Slochower* v. *Board of Education*, 350 U.S. 551 (1956); *Communist Party* v. *Subversive Activities Control Board*, 351 U.S. 115 (1956); *Cole* v. *Young*, 351 U.S. 536 (1956); *Pennsylvania* v. *Nelson*, 350 U.S. 497 (1956); *Watkins* v. *U.S.*, 354 U.S. 178 (1957); *Yates et al.* v. *U.S.*, 354 U.S. 298 (1957); *Jencks* v. *U.S.*, 353 U.S. 657 (1957); *Sweezy* v. *New Hampshire*, 354 U.S. 234 (1957); *Schware* v. *Board of Bar Examiners of New Mexico*, 353 U.S. 232 (1957); *Nowak* v. *U.S.*, 356 U.S. 660 (1958).

9. Caute, *The Great Fear*, pp. 138, 156-57; Walter F. Murphy, *Congress and the Court: A Case Study in the American Political Process* (Chicago: University of Chicago Press, 1962), pp. 139-41; Donald J. Kemper, *Decade of Fear: Senator Hennings and Civil Liberties* (Columbia: University of Missouri Press, 1965), p. 178. For Nichols, see Pearson, *Diaries*, pp. 516-17.

10. For the COINTELPROs, see Theoharis, *Spying on Americans*, pp.

133–55; Donner, *Age of Surveillance*, pp. 177–240; *SDSRIARA*, pp. 3–77. See also Geoffrey Rips, *The Campaign Against the Underground Press* (San Francisco: City Lights Books, 1981).

11. One COINTELPRO operation in Chicago involved an anonymous letter to Blackstone Ranger leader Jeff Fort. Intended to "drive a wedge between the Blackstone Rangers," a street gang, and the highly politicized Black Panther party, the FBI-authored letter falsely informed Fort that the Panthers "blame you for blocking their thing and there's supposed to be a hit out for you." The letter contained a stark suggestion ("I know what I'd do if I was you") and was drafted to provoke "retaliatory action which could disrupt the BPP [Black Panther party] or lead to reprisals against its leadership." When preparing this letter, the Chicago Field Office conceded that the well-armed Rangers were susceptible to "violent type activity," including "shooting." They were also aware of a Chicago Police Intelligence Unit estimate linking Fort's Rangers and rival gangs to nearly 300 Chicago-area murders between 1965 and 1969. Senior FBI officials, nonetheless, approved the mailing. *SDSRIARA*, pp. 195–98.

12. See memo, Fred J. Baumgardner to Alan H. Belmont, Jan. 8, 1958, FBI COINTELPRO-CPUSA Files. To Hoover, the collapse of the party was simply a ruse: "The Communist Party of the United States is not out of business; it is not dead; it is not even dormant. It is, however, well on its way to achieving its current objective, which is to make you believe that it is shattered, ineffective, and dying." Quoted in HUAC, *Communist Infiltration Activities in the South*, 85th Cong., 2d sess., 1958, p. 2754.

13. As FBI liaison with the White House, DeLoach supervised the processing of requests for name checks—receiving, for instance, a list of some 400 names on a single day in 1965. Acting on the basis of FBI reports, Office of Economic Opportunity (OEO) head Sargent Shriver and other Johnson administration officials, in turn, sought to fire or suspend antiwar activists—including a Peace Corps trainee and a consultant to a Harlem youth group that received OEO funds. President Johnson, moreover, directed DeLoach to brief conservative congressmen and journalists on Vietnam War critics. On one occasion, when forwarding to the President a *Chicago Tribune Sunday Magazine* article by Walter Trohan on the New Left, White House aide Marvin Watson noted that the FBI had given Trohan all of the information for the article. Memo, Marvin [Watson] to the President, July 10, 1967, WHCF, EX HU6, LBJ. For the name checks, see memo, Mildred [Stegall] to Watson, Oct. 1, 1965, WHCF, EX PE6, LBJ; memo, James R. Jones to Stegall, April 27, 1966, WHCF, EX ND14–4, LBJ; memo, Shriver to the President, Aug. 14, 1967, CF, HU4, LBJ; memo, Tom Kelly to Bob Emond, April 12, 1968, CF, JL, LBJ. For DeLoach's close relationship with Johnson, see WHCF, Name File-Cartha DeLoach, LBJ.

14. For DeLoach's career, see Ungar, *FBI*, pp. 280, 283, 287, 293–95, 313. For the *Rational Observer*, see Macy and Kaplan, comps., *Documents*, pp. 149–50 (doc. 51a). While Nichols left behind only a very meager paper record of his leaking activities, DeLoach frequently sent blind memorandums to

friendly journalists accompanied by flashy cover letters ("Hi Comrade: This is certainly a person who should be exposed"). Note, DeLoach to Trohan, June 9, 1961, Correspondence-DeLoach, Trohan Papers.

15. Memo, SAC Chicago to Director, April 29, 1965, no. 9–526, FBI COINTELPRO-CPUSA Files; *SDSRIARA*, p. 25.

16. For the FBI's assistance to HUAC in preparing charts, see interview with Francis J. McNamara, Bethesda, Maryland, June 13, 1979.

17. See, for example, memo, Baumgardner to Sullivan, April 29, 1964, no. 34–722, FBI COINTELPRO-CPUSA Files; memo, SAC New York to Director, April 8, 1964, no. 34–677, ibid.; airtel, Director to SAC New York, April 8, 1964, no. 34–670, ibid.; airtel, SAC New York to Director, April 3, 1964, no. 34–676, ibid.; memos, SAC Cleveland to Director, July 12, 1962, no. 11–40 and June 20, 1962, no. 11–36, ibid.

18. Memos, SAC Boston to Director, Sept. 14, 1962, no. 5–46, Dec. 14, 1961, no. 5–12, and Nov. 16, 1961, no. 5–5, all ibid.; airtel, Director to SAC Boston, Nov. 13, 1961, no. 5–3, ibid.; airtel, SAC Boston to Director, Nov. 9, 1961, no. 5–3, ibid. The Bureau routinely identified members of dissident groups as police informers (the so-called "snitch jacket" technique) by working with HUAC and the Senate Internal Security Subcommittee. In one instance in October 1959, the FBI had SISS subpoena a number of alleged Communist party members in Philadelphia. With a single exception—the subject of the snitch jacket—they were all called to testify. The FBI Field Office then anonymously contacted local CPUSA leaders to ask why this individual had not been called. The Bureau effort to identify this individual as an informer succeeded and he was expelled from the party. Ironically, he was in reality an informer for a private anticommunist group who had been hindering the activities of the FBI's own informers. Memo, SAC Philadelphia to Director, Nov. 3, 1959, ibid.; memo, Director to SAC Philadelphia, Nov. 12, 1959, ibid. See also *SDSRIARA*, p. 60.

19. This practice dated at least from December 1955. See memo, SA Deane to SAC New York, Dec. 21, 1955, no. 1891, FBI Rosenberg-Sobell Committee Files (100–107111), JEH; memo, SAC New York to Director, Jan. 20, 1956, no. 1905, ibid.

20. See, for example, memo, SAC Buffalo to Director, Oct. 23, 1957, no. 439, FBI COINTELPRO-CPUSA Files; memo, Director to SAC Buffalo, Nov. 1, 1957, ibid.; memos, SAC Pittsburgh to Director, April 23, 1959, no. 1024, Feb. 25, 1959, no. 923, March 31, 1959, no. 982, and March 3, 1959, no. 977, all ibid.; airtel, Director to SAC Pittsburgh, April 27, 1959, no. 1024, ibid.; memos, SAC Cleveland to Director, June 13, 1962, no. 11–34 and June 20, 1962, no. 11–37, ibid.; memo, Baumgardner to Sullivan, June 19, 1962, no. 11–35, ibid.; airtel, SAC Seattle to Director, July 13, 1959, no. 1161, ibid.

21. For Sporn and the FBI in Buffalo, see teletype, Director to SAC Buffalo, April 28, 1964, no. 6–86, ibid.; memos, SAC Buffalo to Director, April 15, 1964, no. 6–86, May 12, 1964, no. 6–89, June 11, 1964, and Jan. 11, 1965, all ibid.; airtel, SAC Buffalo to Director, March 18, 1964, ibid.; memos, Baumgardner to Sullivan, April 28, 1964, no. 6–85 and June 9, 1964, no. 6–97,

ibid. For the HUAC hearing, see *Communist Activities in the Buffalo, N.Y., Area,* 88th Cong., 2d sess., 1964.

22. Memo, Director to SAC San Francisco, April 11, 1967, no. 47–490, COINTELPRO-CPUSA Files.

23. The FBI favored "HCUA" over "HUAC," a not quite proper acronym which some supporters of the Committee thought to be pejorative.

24. Memo, Baumgardner to Belmont, Jan. 19, 1961, no. 22–36, FBI COINTELPRO-CPUSA Files. For the Buffalo teachers, see memo, Baumgardner to Belmont, April 22, 1960, no. 1645, ibid. For the Legion, see memos, SAC Newark to Director, Dec. 18, 1961, no. 31–24 and Nov. 30, 1961, no. 34–19, ibid. For *Labor Today,* see memo, Baumgardner to Sullivan, July 2, 1962, ibid.; memos, Director to SAC Detroit, July 3, 1962, no. 15–43 and Feb. 14, 1963, no. 15–70, ibid. For the *Baltimore News-Post,* see memo, Baumgardner to Belmont, Aug. 18, 1959, ibid. For the NAACP official, see memo, Baumgardner to Belmont, June 7, 1960, no. 1729, ibid. For the Boy Scouts, see memo, Baumgardner to Sullivan, Oct. 17, 1961, ibid.

25. Letter, Hoover to SAC San Francisco, Jan. 6, 1939, no. 45, FBI HUAC Files. The FBI meticulously indexed all published HUAC hearings and reports. As early as March 1941 this index consisted of 15,000 three-by-five cards. Memo, R. C. Hendon to Tolson, March 7, 1941, no. 958, ibid.

26. Letter, Louis Russell to Mundt, March 29, 1950, Box 686(6), KEM. The FBI, which rarely had more than four agents reviewing HUAC files, was sometimes overwhelmed by eighteen or more Civil Service Commission Investigators who, because monopolizing "desk space," created a "volume" (productivity) problem for the Bureau. FBI officials considered this a "deplorable situation." Memos, SAC Washington to Director, March 15, 1951, no. 1741 and Feb. 27, 1951, no. 1774, FBI HUAC Files; memo, Nichols to Tolson, March 13, 1951, no. 1745, ibid.

27. J. Edgar Hoover, "Role of the FBI in Federal Employee Security Program," *Northwestern University Law Review* 49(July–Aug. 1954): 335.

28. Philip Perlman interview, Dec. 15, 1954, in Post-Pres. File-Memoirs, HST. For examples, see Adam Yarmolinsky, *Case Studies in Personnel Security* (Washington, D.C.: Bureau of National Affairs, 1955), pp. 1, 14–15, 86, 197–99, 256, 289, 291, 296. For the subcommittee, see United Press clipping, March 19, 1947, in Employee Loyalty Program, Raymond R. Zimmerman Files, HST.

29. Memos, J. C. Strickland to Ladd, Jan. 8, 1945, no. 1295 and Feb. 20, 1945, no. 1299, FBI HUAC Files. See also Dies, *Martin Dies' Story,* p. 112; Harold L. Nelson, *Libel in News of Congressional Investigating Committees* (Minneapolis: University of Minnesota Press, 1961), pp. 67–71; Carr, *The House Committee on Un-American Activities,* p. 338 n25.

30. Ibid., p. 338–39n; *New York Times,* March 24, 1950, p. 3.

31. For the widespread use of Appendix IX, see Vern Countryman, *Un-American Activities in the State of Washington: The Work of the Canwell Committee* (Ithaca, N.Y.: Cornell University Press, 1951), p. 87; Barrett, *The Tenney Committee,* pp. 21–22n; Abraham Lincoln National Republican

Club, "The Puzzling Record of Senator Paul H. Douglas," n.d. (ca. Oct. 1950), in Smear Tactics, Charles S. Murphy Papers, HST; Miller, *The Judges and the Judged*, p. 82; Buckley and Bozell, *McCarthy and His Enemies*, p. 81; Iverson, *The Communists and the Schools*, p. 245; Nelson, *Libel*, pp. 69, 155 n45.

32. For Pennington, see letter, Belmont Farley to Mundt, Dec. 28, 1948, Box 686(3), KEM. For Hoover on the *Guide*, see J. Edgar Hoover, *Masters of Deceit* (New York: Holt, Rinehart and Winston, 1958), p. 95. See also SISS, *Revitalizing of the Communist Party in the Philadelphia Area*, pt. 2, *Communist Illusion and Democratic Reality*, 86th Cong., 1st sess., 1959. p. 105; memo, Stanley to Belmont, July 12, 1951, FBI HUAC Files.

33. See, for example, memo, Director to SAC New York, March 7, 1957, no. 2341, FBI Rosenberg-Sobell Committee Files. Other intelligence community members also relied heavily on HUAC publications. According to Rear Admiral Vernon L. Lowrance, Navel Intelligence regularly purchased Committee publications "in volume" and distributed them to field offices around the world. Special Preparedness Subcommittee, *Military Cold War Education*, pt. 5, p. 2095. In the mid-1950s, the CIA funded a Georgetown University project to distribute abroad and stockpile various reports of the House Select Committee on Communist Aggression. Letter, J. S. Earman to Kersten, April 4, 1955, Series 12, Box 1, Charles J. Kersten Papers, Marquette University, Milwaukee; letters, Kersten to Allen Dulles, March 29 and Dec. 5, 1955, ibid.; memo, re Action Program to Exploit House Reports on Communist Aggression, March 28, 1955, ibid.; memo, Kersten to Dulles, Dec. 5, 1955, ibid.

34. *SDSRIARA*, p. 435. The *Guide* became increasingly valuable to the FBI during the Eisenhower years—chiefly because no organizations were formally added to the Attorney General's list after 1955.

35. FBI procedures for using the *Guide* are referred to in memo, Supervisor Marchessault to SAC New York, April 17, 1956, no. 2009, FBI Rosenberg-Sobell Committee Files; memo, SA Carone to SAC New York, April 25, 1957, no. 2408, ibid.; memo, Director to SAC New York, Feb. 13, 1959, no. 3404, ibid. The Bureau continued this practice into the 1970s. One FBI Crime Records Division memorandum of November 1970, apparently prepared for the use of House Internal Security Committee Chairman Ichord, cited Lillian Hellman's associations with thirty-nine "subversive" groups. Eighteen had been cited by Truman- and Eisenhower-era attorneys general, fifteen by HUAC, and six by the California Committee on Un-American Activities. Memo, M. A. Jones to Thomas E. Bishop, Nov. 18, 1970, no. 1, FBI CPJ Files (62–113909).

36. *SDSRIARA*, pp. 12 n54.

37. Memo, Belmont to Director, Aug. 26, 1959, FBI COINTELPRO-CPUSA Files.

38. Memo, Executives' Conference to Director, Oct. 14, 1953, FBI HUAC Files. The state and local police blind memorandums dissemination policy is referred to in this same document.

39. Ibid. For Cohen, see memo, SAC Chicago to Director, Dec. 26, 1951, no. 117, Milton Cohen FBI Files (100-3303); memo, Director to SAC Chicago, Jan. 8, 1952, ibid. Cohen was again investigated in 1959 under yet another informal program directing FBI agents to harass radicals by following them and, at the appropriate time, "interviewing" them. The Chicago SAC described Cohen's interview in a report to Bureau headquarters: "The agents surveilled COHEN to a place three blocks from his residence and with no other persons in the immediate area, he was approached . . . COHEN immediately stated, 'No, I won't talk to you.' The agents proceeded on foot with COHEN for a short distance attempting to persuade him to converse with them. He would make no other statement, however, and the contact was therefore terminated." Characterized as "sullen" and "hostile," Cohen was subpoenaed six years later by HUAC and identified as a Communist by an FBI informer. Memo, SAC Chicago to Director, Jan. 19, 1959, ibid.

40. David K. Dunaway, "Songs of Subversion," *Village Voice*, Jan. 21, 1980, p. 40. The FBI also leaked information on the Weavers, who made their debut at a benefit for the Foley Square Smith Act defendants and were noted for such tunes as "If I Had a Hammer" and "Goodnight Irene," to the Senate Internal Security Subcommittee. Either the FBI or Governor Lausche provided similar assistance to *New York World-Telegram* reporter Frederick Woltman.

41. Memos, SAC Boston to Director, Feb. 3 and March 17, 1953, no. 1882, FBI HUAC Files; teletype, Hoover to SAC Boston, March 10, 1953, ibid.; teletype, SAC Boston to Director, March 16, 1953, ibid.; memo, Nichols to Tolson, March 19, 1953, no. 1891, ibid.; memo, Belmont to Ladd, March 17, 1953, no. 1907, ibid. For Diamond and Bellah, see Navasky, *Naming Names*, p. 58. The five Harvard faculty members were Law School Dean Erwin N. Griswold, Latin Language and Literature Professor Mason Hammond, Graduate School of Public Administration Dean Edward S. Mason, Physics Professor Edward M. Purcell, and Law School Professor Arthur E. Sutherland.

42. Airtels, SAC Philadelphia to Director, Nov. 9, 1953, no. 2080 and Nov. 10, 1953, no. 2029, FBI HUAC Files.

43. For Fuoss and Kunzig, see memos, SAC Philadelphia to Director, Feb. 26, 1953, no. 1880 and Oct. 10, 1952, no. 1840, ibid; teletype, Hoover to SAC Philadelphia, Oct. 10, 1952, ibid.; airtels, Hoover to SAC Philadelphia, Nov. 3, 1953 no. 2000, ibid.; teletype, SAC Philadelphia to Director, Oct. 20, 1953, no. 1987, ibid. For SISS, see memo, Joseph A. Sizzo to Belmont, Oct. 26, 1953, ibid.

44. Including Abraham Egnal, Louis Ivens, Joseph Ehrenreich, Sadie T. Atkinson, Thomas Deason, William G. Solar, Sophie Elfont, Caroline K. Perloff, Samuel Drasin, Eleanor Fleet, Angella Intille, Solomon Hass, and Goldie Watson.

45. HUAC, *Investigation of Communist Activities in the Philadelphia Area*, 83d Cong., 2d sess., 1954, pt. 5, p. 6798.

46. This FBI policy is referred to in airtel, Hoover to SACs Los Angeles and San Francisco, March 13, 1953, no. 1881, FBI HUAC Files; memo, SAC Los Angeles to Director, March 27, 1953, no. 1889, ibid.

47. See memo, Baumgardner to Belmont, Dec. 22, 1960, no. 2177, FBI COINTELPRO-CPUSA Files. See also memo, DeLoach to John P. Mohr, Dec. 29, 1960, no. 81, FBI NCARL Files (100-433447).

48. For the Panthers, see Ungar, *FBI*, p. 122. For King, see *SDSRIARA*, pp. 63, 131-83; *Report of the Department of Justice Task Force to Review the FBI Martin Luther King, Jr., Security and Assassination Investigations* (Washington, D.C.: Government Printing Office, 1977), pp. 132-42. See also memo, Jones to Bishop, May 22, 1968, Hoover O&C FBI Files-Martin Luther King. For DeLoach and the Passport Office, see memos, Bland to Sullivan, June 6 and Aug. 22, 1961, FBI Security Index Files, JEH; memos, [deleted] to [deleted], Oct. 12 and 19, 1961, ibid.; FBI LHM, re Jeremiah Stamler . . . (Passport Sanction), March 18, 1964, FBI HUAC Files.

49. Sullivan, *The Bureau*, p. 93.

50. For the Fund, see Thomas C. Reeves, *Freedom and the Foundation: The Fund for the Republic in the Era of McCarthyism* (New York: Knopf, 1969); Frank K. Kelly, *Court of Reason: Robert Hutchins and the Fund for the Republic* (New York: Free Press, 1981).

51. For the media assault, see Reeves, *Freedom and the Foundation*, pp. 105, 124-26, 130-31, 136-37, 146, 157, 233; Ungar, *FBI*, pp. 298-99; Fulton Lewis, Jr., *The Fulton Lewis Jr. Report on the Fund for the Republic* (Washington, D.C.: Special Reports, 1956); Donner, *Age of Surveillance*, p. 111. For the Stanford grant, see letter, Hoover to Herbert Hoover, Sept. 8, 1955 (see also accompanying memo), PPI-J. Edgar Hoover, HCH. For Cogley's report, see *Report on Blacklisting*, vol. 1: *Movies* and vol. 2: *Radio-Television*.

52. Memos, Nichols to Tolson, June 17, 1955, no. 537, Sept. 6, 1955, and June 11, 1955, no. 530, FBI ACLU Files (61-190), JEH. Fearless enough to have joined the ill-fated Joint Anti-Fascist Refugee Committee in 1949, thirteen years later Ferry accused Hoover of "being as responsible as any person for keeping the Red poltergeist hovering in the national consciousness." The chairman of the Republican National Committee condemned Ferry's "virtually traitorous" remark. But "as for John Edgar Hoover," *Time* magazine reported, "he followed his usual policy—and said not a word in his own defense." In fact, Hoover and DeLoach leaked information regarding Ferry to several media allies and worked closely with Trohan "to set the record straight." Letter, Hoover to Trohan, Aug. 15, 1962, Correspondence-Hoover, Trohan Papers. For Ferry, see Jack Levin, "Hoover and the Red Scare," *Nation*, Oct. 20, 1962, p. 232; "Opinion: 'Leave It to Experts,'" *Time*, Aug. 17, 1962, pp. 18-19.

53. HUAC, *Investigation of So-Called Blacklisting in Entertainment Industry—Report of the Fund for the Republic, Inc.*, 84th Cong., 2d sess., 1956, pt. 1, p. 5221. See also Ungar, *FBI*, pp. 298-99; HUAC press release, March 30, 1958, in Jeremiah Stamler Papers, SHSW. For another Committee

investigation of the Fund, see *Investigation of the Award by the Fund for the Republic, Inc. (Plymouth Meeting, Pa.)*, 84th Cong., 2d sess., 1956.

54. For the SSS, which relied on FBI reports (11,818 in all, including COINTELPRO reports) and access to HUAC files to select dissident groups and individuals rather than suspected tax law violators for audits between 1969 and 1973, see the SSS documents on file in the Center for National Security Studies, Washington, D.C.; U.S., Senate, Subcommittee on Constitutional Rights of the Judiciary Committee, *Political Intelligence in the IRS: The Special Service Staff*, 93d Cong., 2d sess., 1974; U.S., Congress, Joint Committee on Internal Revenue Taxation, *Investigation of the Special Service Staff of the Internal Revenue Service*, 94th Cong., 1st sess., 1975. SSS director Paul Wright's recommendation to the chief of the IRS audit division that he review the tax exemption of the Meiklejohn Civil Liberties Library, a San Francisco–based organization that provided legal materials to attorneys involved in civil liberties cases, provides an example of how investigative subjects were selected. Wright attempted to inspire this audit in March 1971 after receiving FBI reports indicating (1) that the Library was to sponsor "the Thomas Paine Law School"; (2) that three instructors scheduled to participate in this school had been members of the National Lawyers Guild; (3) that HUAC had cited the Guild as a Communist front; and (4) that the Meiklejohn Library president—as of January 2, 1948—might have been a CPUSA member. *SDSRIARA*, pp. 887-88.

55. In January 1948 the Treasury Department announced that it was investigating the tax status of every group on the Attorney General's list. By the end of the year, at least sixteen groups lost their exemptions. Treasury Dept. press release, Feb. 4, 1948, Attorney General's List, Eleanor Bontecou Papers, HST; Fund for the Republic, *Digest of the Public Record of Communism in the United States* (New York: Fund for the Republic, 1955), p. 77.

56. Letter, Mundt to Creigh, March 22, 1947, Box 681(3), KEM; letter, Mundt to Rankin, April 19, 1947, ibid.; letter, Hoover to Pegler, April 26, 1947, Communism-John Roy Carlson, Pegler Papers.

57. For the Reece Committee, see Wormser, *Foundations*; U.S., Congress, House, Special Committee to Investigate Tax-Exempt Foundations, *Hearings on Tax-Exempt Foundations*, 83d Cong., 2d sess., 1954; idem, *Tax-Exempt Foundations*, H.Rept. 2681, 83d Cong., 2d sess., 1954 (Serial 11748). For FBI assistance to the Reece Committee, see Donner, *Age of Surveillance*, p. 324; letter, [deleted] to Hoover, Dec. 13, 1952, no. 90, Thomas I. Emerson FBI Files (101-3315).

58. Memos, Belmont to L. V. Boardman, Oct. 15, 1957, no. 414 and Oct. 19, 1956, no. 65, FBI COINTELPRO-CPUSA Files; memo, Director to Attorney General, March 3, 1958, ibid.; memo, Hoover to IRS Commissioner, Oct. 23, 1956, ibid. The FBI-IRS relationship contrasts starkly with the pre–Cold War period. "The data filed with the Internal Revenue Bureau for income tax purposes," Clyde Tolson and Edward A. Tamm advised Hoover in 1941, "is [sic] considered by that Bureau as being ultra-confidential and is only

accessible, even to the Federal Bureau of Investigation, upon request of the Attorney General to the Secretary of the Treasury in individual cases." Memo, Tolson and Tamm to Director, Dec. 21, 1941, Hoover O&C FBI Files-Martin Dies.

59. See J. Edgar Hoover, "The Crime of the Century," *Reader's Digest*, May 1951, pp. 149-68.

60. Quoted in memo, Nichols to Tolson, April 11, 1956, Nichols O&C FBI Files-Harry S. Truman. This unserialized file folder on Truman includes derogatory information, including Truman's sponsorship in 1944 of an alleged kleptomaniac for a federal civil service job (which Hoover considered "a shocking commentary") and a *New York Daily News* story that was killed in 1952 for fear of libel. Made available to Nichols by a confidential source, this story accused Truman of accepting loans and cash gifts from wealthy Missourians.

61. Memo, Baumgardner to Belmont, Dec. 11, 1959, no. 1405, FBI COINTELPRO-CPUSA Files. For the FBI's surveillance and interest in the HUAC probe, see memos, SAC New York to Director, Aug. 18, 1955, no. 1801 and June 3, 1955, no. 1735, FBI Rosenberg-Sobell Committee Files; airtel, Director to SAC Chicago, July 15, 1955, no. 1772, ibid.; memo, Supervisor [deleted] to SAC New York, March 25, 1958, no. 2895, ibid.; memo, SA McAndrews to SAC New York, May 17, 1955, no. 1722, ibid.; memo, SA Minihan to SAC New York, n.d. (ca. May 1955), no. 1723, ibid.; memo, ASAC Moore to SAC New York, April 28, 1955, no. 1714, ibid.; memo, SAC Washington to Director, Aug. 19, 1955, no. 1802A, ibid.; memo, Baumgardner to Belmont, Dec. 11, 1959, no. 1405, FBI COINTELPRO-CPUSA Files. For the HUAC hearings and report, see *Investigation of Communist Activities (The Committee to Secure Justice in the Rosenberg Case and Affiliates)*, 84th Cong., 1st sess., 1955, pts. 1-2; *Trial by Treason—The National Committee to Secure Justice for the Rosenbergs and Morton Sobell*, H.Doc. 206, 85th Cong., 1st sess., 1957 (Serial 12016).

62. Quoted in memo, DeLoach to Mohr, Dec. 23, 1960, no. 2173, FBI COINTELPRO-CPUSA Files. See also Baumgardner to Belmont, Dec. 30, 1959, no. 1467, Dec. 11, 1959, no. 1405, and Dec. 16, 1960, no. 2189, ibid.; memos, Director to SAC New York, Dec. 15, 1959, no. 1405 and Oct. 4, 1960, no. 1954, ibid.; memo, SAC New York to Director, Nov. 19, 1959, no. 3773, FBI Rosenberg-Sobell Committee Files; memo, Director to SAC New York, Dec. 3, 1959, no. 3787, ibid. The Bureau also forwarded *Trial by Treason* and other information to Monsignor Edwin B. Broderick in New York City in an effort to counter the Rosenberg-Sobell Committee's planned attempt to circulate a clemency petition among Catholic priests in the New York area. Airtel, Director to SAC New York, Jan. 19, 1960, no. 1465, FBI COINTELPRO-CPUSA Files; memo, SAC New York to Director, Jan. 21, 1960, ibid.

63. Memo, SA Marchessault to SAC New York, May 17, 1954, no. 1478, FBI Rosenberg-Sobell Committee Files; memo, SA McAndrews to SAC New York, Aug. 17, 1954, no. 1560, ibid. For Kaufman, see also Ungar, *FBI*, p. 260;

Vern Countryman, "Out, Damned Spot," *New Republic*, Oct. 8, 1977, p. 16; Garrow, *The FBI and Martin Luther King*, p. 23.

64. All quoted in memo, SAC New York to File, May 14, 1958, no. 2985A, FBI Rosenberg-Sobell Committee Files. For Bishop's account, see *Cong. Rec.*, 92d Cong., 2d sess., April 19, 1972, p. 13496. Conversely, at DeLoach's direction, the Cleveland Field Office furnished derogatory information on Walter Schneir, co-author of *Invitation to an Inquest* (Garden City, N.Y.: Doubleday, 1965), to a contact at radio station WKYC because Schneir and Sobell's wife Helen were scheduled to appear in an audience participation show. Memo, Jones to DeLoach, Nov. 8, 1965, FBI Rosenberg-Sobell Committee Files.

65. Similarly, not all journalists accepted material from the FBI. Benjamin Bradlee of *Newsweek*, *Atlanta Constitution* publisher Ralph McGill, Lou Harris of the *Augusta Chronicle*, John Herbers of the *New York Times*, Chicago columnist Mike Royko, and David Kraslow of the *Los Angeles Times* all refused to accept derogatory personal information on Martin Luther King, Jr. Garrow, *The FBI and Martin Luther King*, pp. 127, 130–31, 135.

66. For press coverage of the burglary and the FBI's probe, see the following issues of the *New York Times*: April 8, 1971, p. 22; ibid., April 10, 1971, p. 30; ibid., April 12, 1971, p. 18; ibid., April 13, 1971, p. 23; ibid., April 14, 1971, p. 54; ibid., May 2, 1971, p. 66; ibid., May 12, 1971, p. 26; ibid., May 13, 1971, p. 18; ibid., May 18, 1971, p. 16; ibid., June 6, 1971, p. 22; ibid., July 10, 1971, p. 9; ibid., July 24, 1971, p. 11; ibid., Feb. 27, 1972, p. 21; ibid., March 12, 1972, p. 27. See also the *Washington Post*, issues of March 23, 1971, p. A–3; ibid., March 24, 1971, pp. A–1, A–11; ibid., March 25, 1971, pp. A–1, A–5; ibid., March 26, 1971; A–2; ibid., March 27, 1971, A–4. For the Media papers, see "The Complete Collection of Political Documents Ripped-Off from the FBI Office in Media, Pa.," *WIN* 8 (March 1972). See also Citizens' Commission to Investigate the FBI Papers, SHSW.

67. See, for example, Richard H. Blum, ed., *Surveillance and Espionage in a Free Society: A Report by the Planning Group on Intelligence and Security to the Policy Council of the Democratic National Committee* (New York: Praeger, 1972); Pat Watters and Stephen Gillers, eds., *Investigating the FBI* (Garden City, N.Y.: Doubleday, 1973).

68. For the Army, see *SDSRIARA*, pp. 802–03. For the "KGB," see Donner, *Age of Surveillance*, p. 109. For McGovern, Kennedy, and Muskie, see *Cong. Rec.*, 92d Cong., 1st sess., Feb. 1, 1971, pp. 1195–201; ibid., Feb. 10, 1971, pp. 2507–8; ibid., March 1, 1971, pp. 4414–15; ibid., April 14, 1971, pp. 10313–16.

69. Ibid., April 5, 1971, p. 9470; ibid., April 22, 1971, pp. 11561–66; ibid., April 15, 1971, p. 10490. For press coverage of Boggs's charges and the congressional response, see *New York Times*, April 6, 1971, p. 1; ibid., April 8, 1971, pp. 1, 23; ibid., April 20, 1971, p. 34; ibid., April 21, 1971, p. 46; ibid., April 24, 1971, p. 26.

70. Donner, *Age of Surveillance*, p. 493 n54. Boggs knew of what he spoke. When serving as a Warren Commission member he received FBI documents

containing derogatory information on the Commission's critics—including photographs of their sexual activities. Ibid., p. 114.

71. For the administration's efforts, see *New York Times*, April 5, 1971, p. 15; ibid., April 6, 1971, p. 27; ibid., April 8, 1971, p. 1; ibid., April 17, 1971, p. 1; ibid., April 24, 1971, pp. 1, 26; ibid., March 24, 1971, p. 24; *Cong. Rec.*, 92d Cong., 1st sess., April 22, 1971, pp. 11561–66; Ungar, *FBI*, p. 488; *Washington Post*, March 10, 1971, pp. A-1, A-7 and March 25, 1971, pp. A-1, A-5; *Milwaukee Journal*, March 25, 1971, p. 6 and April 16, 1971, p. 1; "The FBI Story," *New Republic*, April 10, 1971, pp. 5–7. For the White House request, see *SDSRIARA*, p. 551.

72. *Washington Post*, April 20, 1971, pp. A-1, A-9; Ungar, *FBI*, p. 358; *Cong. Rec.*, 92d Cong., 1st sess., April 5, 1971, pp. 9470, 9480; ibid., April 6, 1971, pp. 9746–47; ibid., April 7, 1971, pp. 10059–60; ibid., April 22, 1971, pp. 11567–72; ibid., May 10, 1971, pp. 14156–83, 14011; *New York Times*, April 11, 1971, p. 17; ibid., April 16, 1971, pp. 1, 12; ibid., April 19, 1971, pp. 28–29. For Ford, see Turner, *Hoover's F.B.I.*, pp. 100–103. For Nixon on Hoover's retirement, see Nixon, *RN*, pp. 596–99. When *Time* columnist Hugh Sidey publicized the rumor that Nixon might fire Hoover, the FBI Director responded by ordering a file check on Sidey. Memo, Jones to Bishop, Oct. 18, 1971, FBI CPJ Files.

73. *New York Times*, April 19, 1971, p. 1; *Washington Post*, April 20, 1971, p. A-9. Though concerned about executive privilege in 1971, Congress' concern was mainly a response to Vietnam, the Pentagon Papers, and then National Security Adviser Henry Kissinger's penchant for secrecy and unilateralism. See U.S., Senate, Subcommittee on Separation of Powers of the Committee on the Judiciary, *Hearings on Executive Privilege*, 92d Cong., 1st sess., 1971.

74. See Watters and Gillers, eds., *Investigating the FBI*.

75. Routing slip, n.d. (ca. May 1971), no. 6, FBI CPJ Files. Invitations to participate in the conference were rejected by Attorney General Mitchell, the Society of Former Special Agents of the FBI, and FBI Director Hoover. When drafting Hoover's letter of regrets to Duane Lockard, the Crime Records Division summarized "at some length . . . many of the major accomplishments of this Bureau since the Director took over and state[d] them in a manner which we believe will commend itself to readers among the American public." By publicizing the Hoover-Lockard correspondence, the FBI hoped "to pull the teeth of the conference," to "*force* the conference, if that can be done at all, to recognize the overall worth of this Bureau." Memo, D. J. Dalbey to Tolson, Oct. 6, 1971, no. 7, ibid. For the correspondence, see *Cong. Rec.*, 92d Cong., 1st sess., Nov. 2, 1971, pp. 38792–94.

76. Memo, Director to Attorney General, April 30, 1971, no. 4, FBI CPJ Files; memos, Jones to Bishop, May 5, 1971, no. 6 and Oct. 1, 1971, no. 8, ibid.

77. *Cong. Rec.*, 92d Cong., 1st sess., Oct. 28, 1971, pp. 38091–92 and Nov. 19, 1971, p. 42222. See also memo, Jones to Bishop, Nov. 18, 1971, no. 1, FBI CPJ Files.

78. Memos, Jones to Bishop, Sept. 28, 1971, no. 10 and Oct. 1, 1971, no. 8,

FBI CPJ Files; memo, Alex Rosen to Sullivan, Sept. 24, 1971, no. 10, ibid.; memos, C. Bolz to Bates, Oct. 13, 1971, no. 14 and Oct. 19, 1971, no. 18, ibid.

79. Memo, Bishop to Felt, Oct. 29, 1971, FBI CPJ Files. Other newspapermen, such as *New York Times* reporter Robert Smith, were identified by the Bureau as "unfriendly" and denied any information. Memo, Bishop to Felt, Oct. 15, 1971, no. 17, ibid.

80. Memo, Jones to Bishop, Nov. 3, 1971, no. 43, FBI CPJ Files; *Cong. Rec.*, 92d Cong., 1st sess., Oct. 28, 1971, p. 38169 and Nov. 2, 1971, pp. 38917–20. The FBI also forwarded Buckley's column to Attorney General Mitchell, Assistant Attorney General Robert C. Mardian, and White House aide John Ehrlichman. In the Senate, Strom Thurmond put the Buckley column and Robert Allen's FBI-assisted column into the *Cong. Rec.* (92d Cong., 1st sess., Oct. 27, 1971, pp. 37686–87).

81. Memos, Jones to Bishop, Nov. 3, 1971, no. 43, Nov. 8, 1971, no. 59, and Nov. 9, 1971, no. 52, FBI CPJ Files.

82. *Cong. Rec.*, 92d Cong., 1st sess., Nov. 9, 1971, pp. 40073–79. The CRD briefed yet another congressman, former FBI agent Frank E. Denholm (D., S.D.) several months later. Memo, Jones to Bishop, Feb. 29, 1972, FBI CPJ Files.

83. Robert Wall, "Special Agent for the FBI," *New York Review of Books*, Jan. 27, 1972, pp. 12–18; *SDSRIARA*, p. 550.

84. For Stern's petition and the released documents, see *DIOISP*, pp. 3831–3913, 3540–44.

85. For the Petersen report and its impact, see *SDSRIARA*, pp. 73–74, 553–54; *HIA*, vol. 6, *FBI*, pp. 270–71; *IARA*, p. 271 n20; Ungar, *FBI*, p. 571; U.S., House, Subcommittee on Civil and Constitutional Rights of the Committee on the Judiciary, *Hearings on FBI Counterintelligence Programs*, 93d Cong., 2d sess., 1974, pp. 9–15, 44–47, passim. See also *New York Times*, Nov. 16, 1974, p. 23; ibid., Nov. 18, 1974, p. 20; ibid., Nov. 19, 1974, p. 27; ibid., Nov. 24, 1974, sec. IV, p. 3; ibid., Dec. 5, 1974, p. 52.

86. Quoted in Demaris, *The Director*, p. 324.

87. See the comments of Ichord, Ashbrook, and HISC staff in *DIOISP*, pp. 3328, 3338, 3343; HISC, *Annual Report*, H.Rept. 771, p. 39 and *Annual Report*, H.Rept. 1646, 93d Cong., 2nd sess., 1974 (Serial 13063-1), pp. 47–48.

88. *DIOISP*, pp. 3533, 3472, 3475–84. For Maroney's "expertise," see Richard D. Cotter, "Notes Toward a Definition of National Security," *Washington Monthly*, Dec. 1975, pp. 8–9. Maroney appeared to be equally ignorant about the IRS Special Service Staff—even though the IDIU helped the SSS select dissidents for tax audits.

89. For the Justice Department's apparent laissez faire attitude see, for examples, *DIOISP*, pp. 3533, 3365; *IARA*, p. 135 n673; Cotter, "Notes," p. 9. For the grand jury system, see U.S., House, Subcommittee on Immigration, Citizenship, and International Law of the Committee on the Judiciary, *Hearings on Grand Jury Reform*, 95th Cong., 1st sess., 1977, pts. 1–2.

90. For the comments of Nittle and Ichord (and the similar comments of Committee witnesses), see *DIOISP*, pp. 3439, 3446, 3487–88, 3491–92, 3515, 3630–31, passim. The Bureau used COINTELPRO techniques not only

against Communists and other left-of-center dissidents. Though its assault on the far Right was sometimes ambivalent—for instance, the FBI disseminated John Birch Society literature in an effort to discredit civil rights activists—under COINTELPRO-White Hate Group the Bureau investigated seventeen Ku Klux Klan organizations and nine other coteries. In 1965 and 1966 the FBI actively supported HUAC's investigation of the KKK by directing the Committee to an "available" ex-agent who was hired to direct the probe; by leaking information on Klan supporters to journalists and then referring these journalists to HUAC for additional information; by working closely with the Committee to protect the security of its informants; by leaking information to the Committee; and by disseminating HUAC's published hearings and reports on the Klan to "reliable news media." In one case, the Knoxville SAC proposed that HUAC subpoena a local Klansman who was described in Marine Corps records as a "depressed, listless and expressionless low-grade moron" with "a mental age rating of 10.6." When KKK officials arrived in Washington, D.C., in response to Committee subpoenas, the FBI arranged to have press photographers greet them. For those Klansmen who testified in executive session, the Bureau attempted to create the impression among their colleagues that they were informers. And for those KKK members who would not be subpoenaed but were "susceptible to believing that they would be called," the FBI sought to "heighten their expectations" by mailing at least seventy-five packets of "tourist-type literature" from the Washington area. See FBI COINTELPRO-White Hate Group Files, JEH, passim. Despite this assault, Robert Shelton, Imperial Wizard of the United Klans of America, felt the worst harassment came from the HUAC hearings (which were also based on access to IRS records) and his subsequent indictment for contempt of Congress. Patsy Sims, *The Klan* (New York: Stein and Day, 1978), p. 120. For the IRS, see letter, Edwin E. Willis to Johnson, Feb. 1, 1967, WHCF, FE14-1, LBJ.

IX. FRIENDLY WITNESSES

1. Memo, Director to SAC Cincinnati, Aug. 7, 1950, no. 1688, FBI HUAC Files. For Kunzig, see HUAC, *Investigation of Communist Activities in the San Francisco Area*, 83d Cong., 1st sess., 1953, pt. 4, pp. 3382–83.
2. Quoted in Donner, *Age of Surveillance*, p. 134.
3. In Los Angeles alone in 1953, some 670 persons were named as Communists before the Committee. By early February 1954, the FBI had plowed through 639 (or 95.3%) of these names, reviewing files and compiling updated reports where appropriate. Memo, SAC Los Angeles to Director, Feb. 9, 1954, no. 2168, FBI HUAC Files.
4. Donner, *Age of Surveillance*, p. 59.
5. Letter, Hoover to Edwin Watson, June 3, 1940 (see also accompanying memo of June 2, 1940), no. 109, OF10-B, FDR; letter, Hoover to Harry Hopkins, July 18, 1942, no. 2216-A, ibid.
6. *SDSRIARA*, pp. 233–35; Donner, *Age of Surveillance*, p. 137.

7. *Chicago Tribune*, Jan. 21, 1978, p. 4; *Washington Post*, Jan. 21, 1978, p. 1; Jay Peterzell, "The Breitel Report: New Light on FBI Use of Informants," *First Principles*, Oct. 1980, p. 2. The information relating to the Chicago informers was released during the recently-settled consolidated law suit, *Alliance to End Repression* v. *O'Grady*, 74 c 3268; *ACLU* v. *City of Chicago*, 75 c 3295; and *Chicago Lawyers Committee for Civil Rights Under Law* v. *City of Chicago*, 76 c 1982 (N.D., Ill., 1981). The information regarding the Socialist Workers party was compiled by Special Master Charles D. Breitel at the direction of District Court Judge Thomas P. Greisa during the ongoing lawsuit, *Socialist Workers Party et. al.* v. *Attorney General et al.*, 73 c 3160 (S.D., N.Y.).

8. FBI agents rarely worked undercover, although they did occasionally infiltrate New Left groups during the 1960s and early 1970s. See Cyril Payne, *Deep Cover: An FBI Agent Infiltrates the Radical Underground* (New York: Newsweek Books, 1980). Infiltration was practiced more frequently in the 1940s when the Bureau was active in Latin America. By October 25, 1940, at least fifteen corporations and other enterprises serviced the FBI's needs in Latin America, by carrying agents on their payrolls and providing other services. The FBI worked closely with Standard Oil, Pan American Airways, United Fruit, National City Bank, Montgomery Ward, Dun and Bradstreet, American Metal, American Express, the Smithsonian Institution, the Pan American News Service, and the Rockefeller Foundation. Letter, Hoover to Watson, Oct. 25, 1940 (see also accompanying memo of Oct. 24, 1940), no. 408, OF10-B, FDR. See also memo, Hoover to Edward A. Tamm and Hugh H. Clegg, June 27, 1940, Nichols O&C FBI Files-Harold Hochschild; letter, Hoover to Henry M. Morgenthau, Jr., July 12, 1940, ibid. The FBI remained active in Latin America during the immediate postwar period. Thereafter, its activities were more sporadic and specialized—as when President Johnson had Hoover dispatch an FBI squad to the Dominican Republic in May 1965 on special assignment. See Administrative Histories, vol. 13, FBI, LBJ.

9. Herbert A. Philbrick, *I Led 3 Lives*, with a Foreword by Efrem Zimbalist, Jr. (New York: McGraw-Hill, 1953; reprint ed., Washington, D.C.: Capitol Hill Press, 1972).

10. HUAC, *Investigation of Communist Activities in the San Francisco Area*, pt. 5, p. 3490.

11. Levin, "Hoover and the Red Scare," p. 233; Donner, *The Un-Americans*, p. 176; Turner, *Hoover's F.B.I.*, p. 188. Velde is quoted in HUAC, *Investigation of Communist Activities in the Pacific Northwest Area*, pt. 10, *Portland*, 83d Cong., 2d sess., 1954, pp. 6704–05. For the FBI survey, see SISS, *Interlocking Subversion in Government Departments*, 83d Cong., 1st sess., 1953, p. 23. For the FBI's "up-to-date" reports, see memo, SAC Philadelphia to Director, Oct. 28, 1952, no. 1852, FBI HUAC Files; memo, Director to SAC Newark, Nov. 25, 1952, no. 1853, ibid.

12. Airtel, SAC Charlotte to SAC Chicago, April 8, 1963, no. 132, FBI CCDBR Files (100–37762).

13. Angela Calomiris, *Red Masquerade* (Philadelphia: Lippincott, 1950),

p. 45 and passim; Marion Miller, *I Was a Spy* (Indianapolis: Bobbs-Merrill, 1960).

14. For Dietze, Cvetic, and the raid, see *New York Times*, March 25, 1950, p. 1 and March 26, 1950, p. 25; *Pittsburgh Sun-Telegraph*, March 6, 1950, p. 1 and March 9, 1950, p. 2; *Pittsburgh Press*, March 11, 1950, p. 1; *Pittsburgh Post-Gazette*, March 11, 1950, pp. 1, 5. See also HUAC, *Annual Report*, H.Rept. 3249, 81st Cong., 2d sess., 1950 (Serial 11385), p. 26; HUAC, *Exposé of the Communist Party of Western Pennsylvania*, pt. 3, *Based Upon Testimony of Matthew Cvetic and Documents of Communist Party of Western Pennsylvania*, 81st Cong., 2d sess., 1950, pp. 3073–3142, 3154–63.

15. Donner, *Age of Surveillance*, pp. 435–37. For the Chicago police, see Louis Wille, "Sniffing Out Subversion," *Chicago Journalism Review*, Feb. 1969, p. 10. As these burglaries suggest, private-sector and state and local police red squads supplemented the FBI's investigative assistance to the Committee. During the 1950s, the New York State Police routinely compiled dossiers on individuals at the Committee's request. New York, *Report of the New York State Assembly Special Task Force on State Police Non-Criminal Files, State Police Surveillance*, 1977, p. 19.

16. For Cvetic's career, see Matthew Cvetic, *The Big Decision* (Hollywood: By the Author, 1959); Caute, *The Great Fear*, p. 216–20; Hymen Lumer, *The Professional Informer* (New York: New Century, 1955), p. 9; Frank J. Donner, "The Informer," *Nation*, April 10, 1954, p. 307. HUAC staff sometimes assisted Cvetic's activities as a professional anticommunist. In December 1954, they arranged for him to testify, along with eight other informers, at Carl Braden's state sedition trial in Kentucky. Braden, a copyreader for the *Louisville Courier-Journal*, and his "accomplices" were indicted on a charge of seditiously inciting racial conflict (shootings, fiery crosses, bomb threats) by buying a home in a white area and reselling it to Andrew Wade IV, a black electrical contractor. Two HUAC investigators were also sent to Kentucky to help the prosecution prepare for trial. Unable to raise bail of $40,000 pending appeal, Braden, who was sentenced to fifteen years, spent eight months in prison. In 1956, all charges against him were dismissed. Anne Braden, *The Wall Between* (New York: Monthly Review Press, 1958).

17. For Budenz, see Donner, "The Informer," p. 307; Jack Anderson, *Confessions of a Muckraker* (New York: Random House, 1979), pp. 201–02; Caute, *The Great Fear*, pp. 109, 123, 576 n27; Lumer, *Professional Informer*, pp. 5–6.

18. Murray Kempton, *America Comes of Middle Age* (Boston: Little, Brown, 1963), p. 14; Donner, "The Informer," p. 305. For Budenz's testimony, see Robert A. Devine, *American Immigration Policy, 1924–1952* (New Haven, Conn.: Yale University Press, 1957), p. 161. Johnson is quoted in Lumer, *Professional Informer*, p. 8.

19. Kempton, *America Comes of Middle Age*, p. 321; Rovere, *The American Establishment*, pp. 113–32. The Montana for D'Ewart Committee also hired Matusow in 1952 to assist in the campaign against liberal Senator

James E. Murray, an ADA member and one of only seven Democrats to vote against the McCarran Act. Citing HUAC files to connect Murray to thirteen red fronts, the D'Ewart Committee published an expensive brochure entitled *Senator Murray and the Red Web Over Congress.*

20. For Oxnam's role in the Matusow affair, see his correspondence with Matusow, McGrath, Brownell, and Velde in HUAC, Oxnam Papers.

21. Quoted in Caute, *The Great Fear,* p. 137. For Walter's charge, see *New York Times,* Feb. 4, 1955, p. 8. For Williams, see memo, ASAC Moore to SAC New York, April 28, 1955, no. 1714, FBI Rosenberg-Sobell Committee Files (100–107111), JEH.

22. For Hoover, see Bales, comp., *J. Edgar Hoover Speaks,* p. 133. For Jackson, see *Cong. Rec.,* 84th Cong., 1st sess., July 5, 1955, pp. A4878–79. For Eisenhower, see cabinet minutes, March 18, 1955, Whitman File-Cabinet Minutes, DDE; memo, Eisenhower to Attorney General, Nov. 4, 1953, Whitman File-Diary, DDE. See also Harvey Matusow, *False Witness* (New York: Cameron and Kahn, 1955); Caute, *The Great Fear,* pp. 133–38.

23. *SDSRIARA,* pp. 262–63. Investigative sources, including HUAC executive session hearings, were also given "T" symbols.

24. Whether to withhold files from persons filing FOIA requests or to justify noncompliance with court-ordered discovery, FBI officials have consistently refused access to informant files. According to a 1976 affidavit of FBI Assistant Director James B. Adams, the FBI guarantees its informers anonymity: "In each and every case the confidential informant must be and is assured that his identity will not be revealed. Disclosure in some cases may endanger the informant's life . . . " According to the *FBI Manual of Instructions,* however, informers were to be groomed for public testimony: "Contacting agent must condition informant for the fact that he may at a future date be called upon to testify to information that he has furnished on security matters. Proper indoctrination of informant is essential . . . in security cases." Peterzell, "The Breitel Report," p. 2.

25. For examples, see Subfile E, Rosenberg-Sobell Committee Files.

26. For Clardy's meeting with Picard and Kaess, see *Detroit News,* Oct. 21, 1953, p. 29 and Nov. 7, 1953, p. 2.

27. HUAC, *Investigation of Communist Activities in the State of Michigan,* pts. 2–3, *Detroit,* 83d Cong., 2d sess., 1954, pp. 5085, 5132, 5146, 5148–49.

28. In the U.S. Court of Appeals, *Saul Wellman et al.* v. *U.S.,* Brief for Appellants, pp. 68, 70–72, in Series 4, Box 30, Civil Rights Congress of Michigan Papers, ALH. For the FBI-Ford Investigation Section relationship, see memo, Ladd to Director, Jan. 29, 1952, FBI HUAC Files. The eight prosecution witnesses received, in total, $74,800 from the Ford Motor Company, $7,090 from the City of Detroit and the State of Michigan, and $90,760 from the FBI and possibly other federal agencies. For two of these informers, FBI payments constituted their main source of income.

29. McNamara interview. The FBI may have provided informers and HUAC staff with the names of people they wanted identified as Communists

regardless of the informer's first-hand knowledge. When HUAC investigator William Wheeler asked FBI informer Leonard B. Wildman to identify numerous people as CPUSA members, Wildman conceded that he had "forgot a lot of names" but noted that "the FBI and the Immigration Department submitted a lot of names to me." When Wheeler asked Wildman to identify a "Joe Burner," he responded: "That was the Bernard or something I think I mentioned earlier. I have been trying to think of that name because I turned it over to the FBI. I thought it was Bernard, but it is Burner. I wasn't certain of it. But Joe Burner, I think—gosh, I was thinking it was George Burner." How Wheeler came up with Joe Burner's name, unless the FBI told him, is a mystery. HUAC, *Investigation of Communist Activities in the Pacific Northwest Area*, pt. 1, pp. 6016, 6020, 6030.

30. *Detroit Times*, Feb. 13, 1952, p. 1; HUAC, *Investigation of Communist Activities in the Newark, N.J., Area*, 84th Cong., 1st sess., 1955, pts. 1-2, pp. 993-94; HUAC, *Investigation of Communist Activities in the State of Michigan*, pt. 8, *Flint*, passim.

31. Memo, Belmont to Ladd, Feb. 20, 1952, no. 1792, FBI HUAC Files. For Hoover on Wheeler, see the notation on teletype, SAC Boston to Director and SAC New York, Jan. 30, 1950, no. 1630, ibid. For Hoover on the Committee's "good work," see memo, Hoover to Attorney General, July 17, 1950, no. 1672, ibid.

32. Memos, Belmont to Ladd, Feb. 20, 1952, no. 1792, Feb. 22, 1952, no. 1801, and Feb. 25, 1952, no. 1794, ibid. For Hoover on "panic and unrest," see memo, Director to Attorney General, March 27, 1950, no. 1646, ibid.

33. Memo, E. H. Winterrowd to Ladd, March 31, 1950, no. 1648, ibid.

34. Memo, SAC Detroit to Director, April 11, 1952, no. 1809, ibid. For Hoover on "ultimate security," see the notation on memo, Ladd to Director, April 26, 1950, no. 1658, ibid. For Ford, see memo, Peyton [Ford] to Mickey [Ladd], Aug. 16, 1950, no. 1689, ibid.

35. See Hoover's notation on memo, Ladd to Director, May 2, 1952, ibid. For Nichols and Russell, see memo, Nichols to Tolson, April 11, 1952, no. 1808, ibid. For the Committee's access to FBI informants in Chicago, see memo, Baumgardner to Belmont, April 28, 1952, ibid.

36. Memo, SAC Pittsburgh to Director, May 29, 1958, FBI COINTELPRO-CPUSA Files (100-3-104), JEH; memo, Director to SAC Pittsburgh, June 17, 1958, no. 623, ibid. For the HUAC hearings, see *Current Strategy and Tactics of Communists in the United States (Greater Pittsburgh Area)*, *Problems of Security in Industrial Establishments Holding Defense Contracts (Greater Pittsburgh Area)*, and *Problems Arising in Cases of Denaturalization and Deportation of Communists (Greater Pittsburgh Area)*, 86th Cong., 1st sess., 1959, pts. 1-3.

37. Memo, SAC Los Angeles to Director, Oct. 16, 1958, FBI COINTELPRO-CPUSA Files. For HUAC's earlier investigation, see *The Southern California District of the Communist Party (Structure-Objectives-Leadership)*, 86th Cong., 1st sess., 1959, pts. 1-2. These hearings were held in September 1958.

38. See HUAC, *The Southern California District of the Communist Party,* pt. 3; HUAC, *Western Section of the Southern California District of the Communist Party,* 86th Cong., 1st sess., 1959, pts. 1–3.

39. Memo, Director to SAC Los Angeles, Oct. 31, 1958, no. 777, FBI COINTELPRO-CPUSA Files. The FBI also tried to inspire congressional investigations on the state level. In February 1971, the Philadelphia Field Office anonymously mailed information regarding the Black Panther party's alleged welfare abuses to five state senators who had all previously called for a probe of state welfare programs. Memo, SAC Philadelphia to Director, Feb. 16, 1971, FBI COINTELPRO-Black Extremist Files (100–448006), JEH; airtel, Director to SAC Philadelphia, Feb. 24, 1971, ibid.

40. Memo, SAC Los Angeles to Director, April 29, 1960, FBI COINTELPRO-CPUSA Files; airtel, SAC Los Angeles to Director, April 7, 1960, ibid. Only recorded copies of these heavily deleted documents were filed in the COINTELPRO files. The original or serialized copies were filed in the informer files (134 series), suggesting that the informer files record a substantial number of FBI leaks to HUAC.

41. Memo, SAC Cleveland to Director, Dec. 14, 1959, no. 1379, ibid.; memo, Director to SAC Cleveland, Dec. 23, 1959, no. 1379, ibid.

42. The Brown quote is in Julia Brown, *I Testify,* with an Introduction by Herbert Philbrick (Belmont, Mass.: Western Islands, 1966), pp. 183–84, 192. For the FBI's interest in Brown's HUAC appearance and attempts to exploit her testimony, see teletype, SAC Cleveland to SAC Los Angeles, Nov. 20, 1961, no. 549, FBI CCDBR Files; teletype, SAC Los Angeles to SAC Chicago, Nov. 20, 1961, no. 549, ibid.; airtel, SAC Cleveland to SAC Chicago, Nov. 20, 1961, no. 550, ibid.; memos, SAC Cleveland to Director, July 12, 1962, no. 11–40, July 3, 1962, no. 11–39, June 13, 1962, no. 11–38, and June 20, 1962, no. 11–36, all in FBI COINTELPRO-CPUSA Files; memos, Director to SAC Cleveland, June 20, 1962, no. 11–37 and June 13, 1962, no. 11–34, ibid.; memo, Baumgardner to Sullivan, June 19, 1962, no. 11–35, ibid.

43. These results are recorded in memos, SAC Cleveland to Director, July 13, 1961, no. 2712, July 12, 1962, no. 11–40, and June 20, 1962, no. 11–36, all ibid.

44. Memos, SAC Minneapolis to Director, July 15, 1964, no. 43–108, Aug. 18, 1964, no. 43–109, and Nov. 27, 1964, no. 43–116, all ibid.

45. Memo, SAC Boston to Director, July 14, 1965, no. 5–173, ibid.

46. Memos, SAC Los Angeles to Director, Aug. 15, 1966, no. 26–263 and June 30, 1966, ibid. According to the SAC, the Citizens Information blacklister had been in contact with the local FBI office prior to acting against the unfriendly HUAC witness. She reportedly described her organization as "a non-partisan group composed of volunteer workers who researched HCUA publications in order to document organizations for college students." George Murphy (R., Cal.), then a United States Senator, also contacted the FBI office seeking information on the controversial HUAC witness and her husband. The Bureau apparently declined to assist Murphy and instead referred him to HUAC, "where the derogatory information concerning the [deleted] originated."

47. HUAC, *Current Strategy and Tactics of Communists (Greater Pittsburgh Area)*, pt. 1, pp. 326, 354–55; Cook, *The FBI Nobody Knows*, p. 44. See also In the Supreme Court of the United States, October Term 1968, *Jeremiah Stamler, M.D., and Yolanda Hall, Plaintiffs-Appellants* v. *Hon. Edwin E. Willis, et. al., Defendants-Appellees*, Appendices 4 and 5 to Jurisdictional Statement, p. 60, in Stamler Papers; Caute, *The Great Fear*, pp. 119, 221–22.

48. Warren Olney III, "The Use of Former Communists as Witnesses," *Vital Speeches of the Day*, Aug. 15, 1954, p. 649. The Poskonka quote is in HUAC, *Communist Infiltration of Vital Industries and Current Communist Techniques in the Chicago, Ill, Area*, 86th Cong., 1st sess., 1959, pp. 643–44.

49. Airtel, Director to SAC Boston, Dec. 14, 1960, no. 2120, FBI COINTELPRO-CPUSA Files.

50. HUAC and its successor continued to serve as a way station of sorts for FBI operatives. Responding to a question in a civil suit, the FBI described Louise Rees, an *Information Digest* investigator and a HISC staff member from January 1974 until the Committee expired in January 1975, "as an FBI informant from August 1973 to February 1976" who "reported on domestic security matters." Donner, *Age of Surveillance*, p. 449.

51. Airtels, SAC San Francisco to Director, April 21, 1969, no. 99 and April 30, 1969, no. 95, FBI Revolutionary Communist Party Files (105-184369); airtels, Director to SAC San Francisco, May 2, 1969, no. 96 and June 10, 1969, ibid. For the Goffs's testimony and the report, see HISC, *Investigation of Attempts to Subvert the United States Armed Services*, 92d Cong., 1st sess., pt. 1, 1971, pp. 6423–75; HISC, *America's Maoists: Revolutionary Union, Venceremos Organization*, H.Rept. 1166, 92d Cong., 2d sess., 1972 (Serial 12976-1A). The FBI also leaked information on the Revolutionary Union to the Senate Internal Security Subcommittee. HISC West Coast investigator William Wheeler, moreover, was referred to a *San Francisco Examiner* reporter, Ed Montgomery, for additional leads and the names of "possible witnesses." Airtel, Director to SAC San Francisco, Sept. 30, 1969, FBI Revolutionary Union Files.

X. OPERATION ABOLITION

1. F. Edward Hébert, *"Last of the Titans": The Life and Times of Congressman F. Edward Hébert of Louisiana* (Lafayette: Center for Louisiana Studies, 1976), pp. 273–74, 320–24. For the congressional debates on the Dies Committee, see Gellermann, *Martin Dies*. Hébert, fiercely conservative and staunchly opposed to the New Deal, consulted with FBI Assistant Director Nichols before joining the Committee. Described by Nichols as "very pro-FBI and . . . . extremely reliable," Hébert first emerged as a Bureau friend during his years as city editor of the *New Orleans Item*. Hébert frequently received information from the FBI on a confidential basis both as a newspaperman and a HUAC member, and one of the Bureau's earlier leaks may have involved Huey Long. Memos, Louis B. Nichols to Clyde Tolson, Nov. 18, 1947, no. 1486 and Dec. 8, 1947, no. 1489, FBI HUAC Files.

2. Mowery, *HUAC and FBI*, p. 11.

3. Memo, Nichols to Tolson, Sept. 18, 1957, FBI ACLU Files (61–190), JEH; memo, Gordon A. Nease to Tolson, July 29, 1958, ibid.; letters, Ferman to Nichols, Dec. 19, 1956, no. 633 and March 13, 1957, no. 652, ibid. Ferman was selected to write the lone "anti-HUAC" essay, "A Comment by a Civil Libertarian," in Buckley, *The Committee and Its Critics*.

4. Francis Biddle, *The Fear of Freedom* (Garden City, N.Y.: Doubleday, 1942), p. 123; Irving Brant, *The Bill of Rights: Its Origin and Meaning* (New York: Bobbs-Merrill, 1965), p. 465. For the roll call analysis, see Lewis A. Kaplan, "The House Un-American Activities Committee and Its Opponents: A Study in Congressional Dissonance," *Journal of Politics* 30(Aug. 1968): 647–71. With the exception of Henry B. Gonzalez (D., Tex.) and John V. Lindsay (R., N.Y.), HUAC's congressional opponents were all northern Democrats.

5. See Murray Kempton, "The Lord of the Flies," *New Republic*, June 22, 1963, pp. 9–10.

6. Quoted in Frank J. Donner, "HUAC: The Dossier-Keepers," *Studies on the Left* 2(No. 1, 1961): 23.

7. The Bureau routinely investigated activists who opposed the Committee. David R. Luce, for one, was placed on the Security Index chiefly because of his criticism of HUAC. FBI files note his 1954 letter to the editor of the *Michigan Daily* criticizing University of Michigan administrators for their decision to fire professors who refused to cooperate with the Committee. Later, in 1959, when an SAC recommended removing Luce from the Security Index, senior FBI officials challenged this recommendation. Luce, they advised, "has been a prolific writer of letters to newspapers protesting against the House Committee on Un-American Activities, McCarthyism, and the Smith Act trials." (Similarly, the FBI file on Catholic radical Dorothy Day noted her opposition to the Smith and McCarran Acts and occasions where she "had spoken against" HUAC.) Five years later, in anticipation of Luce's scheduled trip abroad, the FBI prepared a letterhead memorandum on Luce and his anti-HUAC activities and disseminated it to the CIA, the State Department, and the legal attaches in London and Bonn. See David R. Luce FBI Files, Milwaukee.

8. HUAC, *Operation Abolition* (see also the accompanying letter, Hoover to Walter, Nov. 2, 1957), 85th Cong., 1st sess., 1957.

9. *Cong. Rec.*, 86th Cong., 1st sess., Jan. 15, 1959, p. 695. For JFK, see memo, SAC Boston to Director, March 13, 1958, Hoover O&C FBI Files-John F. Kennedy.

10. For these leaks, see memo, F. J. Baumgardner to Alan H. Belmont, Aug. 25, 1960, no. 14, FBI NCARL Files (100–433447); memo, DeLoach to John P. Mohr, Dec. 29, 1960, no. 81, ibid.; memos, Baumgardner to Sullivan, July 16, 1962, Sept. 4, 1962, no. 23, Nov. 23, 1962 (serial no. 434 recorded in FBI CCPAF Files [100–387548], Jan. 29, 1963 (serial no. 442 recorded in FBI CCPAF Files), Jan. 30, 1963, Feb. 17, 1964, no. 433, Feb. 20, 1964, no. 435, Feb. 26, 1964, no. 444, Nov. 3, 1964, no. 551, Nov. 20, 1964, no. 563, Dec. 14,

1964, no. 571, and Jan. 13, 1965, no. 582, all ibid.; airtels, SAC Los Angeles to Director, Jan. 3, 1963, no. 321, Jan. 10, 1964, no. 415, Jan. 15, 1964, no. 412, and Feb. 25, 1964, no. 442, all ibid.; airtel, SAC Pittsburgh to Director, Jan. 23, 1964, no. 437, ibid.; memo, SAC Chicago to Director, Dec. 8, 1964, no. 568, ibid.; airtel, SAC Washington to Director, Jan. 11, 1965, no. 579, ibid.

11. Memo, Baumgardner to Belmont, Jan. 11, 1961, no. 2229, FBI COINTELPRO-CPUSA Files (100-3-104), JEH.

12. For the NCAHUAC, see Jerold L. Simmons, "Operation Abolition: The Campaign to Abolish the House Un-American Activities Committee, 1938-1965" (Ph.D. diss., University of Minnesota, 1971); National Committee Against Repressive Legislation Papers, SHSW.

13. Airtel, SAC Los Angeles to Director, June 16, 1960, FBI NCARL Files; airtel, Director to SAC Los Angeles, June 23, 1960, ibid.

14. For FBI dissemination of information on NCAHUAC, see memos, Baumgardner to Belmont, Aug. 25, 1960, no. 14, Nov. 3, 1960, and May 22, 1961, no. 129, ibid.; Los Angeles Field Office Report, Nov. 30, 1960, ibid. For the Legion, see letter, Donald I. Sweany, Jr. (National Americanism Commission research specialist) to William J. Haese (American Legion National Security Commission), April 6, 1961, Series 8, Box 2, Kersten Papers.

15. For Walter and Scherer, see *Cong. Rec.*, 86th Cong., 1st sess., Jan. 19, 1959, pp. A1958–59 and Jan. 9, 1959, pp. 364–65; ibid., 87th Cong., 2d sess., May 1, 1962, pp. 7466–68. For HUAC's dossiers, see Series 8, Box 2, Kersten Papers, passim.

16. For the FBI's interest in the pamphlet, see airtel, Director to SAC Los Angeles, Jan. 21, 1964, no. 412, FBI NCARL Files; airtels, SAC Los Angeles to Director, Jan. 23, 1964, no. 419 and April 24, 1964, no. 476, ibid.; memo, SAC Louisville to Director, March 4, 1964, no. 448, ibid.; memos, SAC Memphis to Director, April 23, 1964, no. 474 and May 28, 1964, ibid. For the LHM, see memo, Baumgardner to Sullivan, May 1, 1964, no. 471, ibid. Unlike the Bradens, many civil rights activists were reluctant to criticize the committee publicly or call for its abolition. As late as December 1963 the leadership of the Student Non-Violent Coordinating Committee, concerned that SNCC members would be subpoenaed to testify about Communist infiltration of the civil rights movement, was deeply divided on the HUAC issue. Clayborne Carson, *In Struggle: SNCC and the Black Awakening of the 1960s* (Cambridge, Mass.: Harvard University Press, 1981), pp. 106-07.

17. Memo, Thomas E. Marum to Oran H. Waterman, June 11, 1962, FBI NCARL Files; memos, F. L. Williamson to Waterman, Sept. 20, 1963, March 19 and Feb. 23, 1966, ibid.; memo, Robert A. Crandall to Waterman, Oct. 18, 1972, ibid.; memo, Yeagley to Director, July 12, 1963, ibid.; memo, Director to SAC Chicago, July 23, 1966, ibid. The Justice Department considered proceeding against NCARL only in December 1970 when Assistant Attorney General Robert Mardian requested an interview with several FBI informers and inquired about their availability for public testimony at SACB hearings. Memo, Mardian to Director, Dec. 2, 1970, ibid.

18. Airtel, Director to SAC Chicago, May 10, 1966, ibid. See also airtel,

SAC Los Angeles to Director, June 21, 1962, ibid.; airtel, Director to SAC Memphis, April 27, 1971, ibid.

19. For Wilkinson's testimony, see HUAC, *Communist Infiltration and Activities in the South*, 85th Cong., 2d sess., 1958, pp. 2681–87.

20. For the FBI's interest in Wilkinson's mail, see memo, SAC Charlotte to Director, Aug. 29, 1961, no. 476, FBI CCDBR Files (100–37762). For the blind memorandum, see memo, Baumgardner to Sullivan, Oct. 12, 1962 (serial no. 52–4 recorded in FBI COINTELPRO-CPUSA Files), copy in FBI NCARL Files. For Ronstadt, see HUAC, *The Communist Party's Cold War Against Congressional Investigation of Subversion. Report and Testimony of Robert Carrillo Ronstadt (April 25, 1962)*, 87th Cong., 2d sess., 1962, pp. 1484–85, 1489–91.

21. Airtel, SAC Minneapolis to Director, Aug. 13, 1964, FBI NCARL Files. For the FBI's "urgent" interest, see teletype, SAC Baltimore to Director, June 24, 1964, no. 513, ibid.

22. For the standing order, see airtel, Director to SACs Chicago et al., April 30, 1962, no. 196, ibid. For academic freedom, see airtel, Director to SACs Los Angeles, Omaha, and Minneapolis, Oct. 9, 1962 (serial no. 26–52 recorded in FBI COINTELPRO-CPUSA Files), copy in FBI NCARL Files. For surveillance of Wilkinson's lectures, see Minneapolis Field Office Report, July 31, 1962, FBI NCARL Files. For local police red squads see memo, SAC Detroit to Director, Nov. 4, 1963, ibid. For Global Books, see memo, SAC Detroit to Director, Nov. 14, 1962, ibid.

23. Omaha Field Office Report, April 4, 1962, ibid. Similarly, a Dec. 5, 1966 airtel from the Detroit SAC to the Director, cross-referenced to a Nov. 8, 1966 airtel from the Los Angeles SAC recommending disruption of Wilkinson's schedule, reported: "FRANK WILKINSON did not speak at Albion College as scheduled on November 17, 1966." It is impossible to ascertain from documents released thus far whether this was the result of Bureau intervention. In any event, local FBI offices were eager to take credit for Wilkinson's difficulties.

24. This operation is described in airtels, SAC Detroit to Director, May 22, 1962, no. 205 and May 22, 1962 (serial no. 3765 recorded in FBI COINTELPRO-CPUSA Files), copy in FBI NCARL Files.

25. For the proposal and DeLoach's notation, see airtel, SAC Washington to Director, May 2, 1962, no. 198, FBI NCARL Files.

26. For Wilkinson and the FBI at Knox College, see airtel, Director to SACs Chicago et al., Sept. 27, 1962 (serial no. 9–80 recorded in FBI COINTELPRO-CPUSA Files), copy in FBI NCARL Files; airtel, SAC Springfield to Director, Oct. 12, 1962, no. 202, FBI NCARL Files; Springfield Field Office LHM, Oct. 25, 1962, ibid.; teletype, SAC Chicago to Director, Oct. 11, 1962, no. 1291, Richard Criley FBI Files (100–32864); radiogram, Director to SACs Chicago and Springfield, Oct. 12, 1962, no. 1274, ibid. For Tower, see memo, Baumgardner to Sullivan, Oct. 12, 1962 (serial no. 52–4 recorded in FBI COINTELPRO-CPUSA Files), copy in FBI NCARL Files; radiogram, Director to SACs Chicago and Springfield, Oct. 12, 1962 (serial

no. 52-2 recorded in FBI COINTELPRO-CPUSA Files), copy in FBI NCARL Files. For Trohan, see letter, Deke [DeLoach] to Comrade [Trohan], Oct. 12, 1962, Correspondence-DeLoach, Trohan Papers. De-Loach's letter, written on plain white paper, was not filed in the NCARL File or in the COINTELPRO-CPUSA File.

27. Memo, SAC Cincinnati to Director, May 19, 1964, FBI NCARL Files. University of Cincinnati officials allowed a spokesman for a local right-wing group headed by M. G. Lowman, Circuit Riders, Inc., to present HUAC's side of the argument. Because Circuit Riders' activities were chronicled in FBI COINTELPRO reports, it seems likely that this organization may have received some type of assistance from the Bureau.

28. Airtel, SAC Omaha to Director, Nov. 2, 1965 (see also accompanying LHM), ibid.

29. For these and other examples, see *SDSRIARA*, pp. 17, 57-58, 88 n27, 247.

30. For the FBI in Buffalo, see airtel, SAC Los Angeles to Director, April 9, 1964, FBI NCARL Files; airtels, SAC Buffalo to Director, April 16, 1964, no. 6-83 and April 20, 1964, no. 6-88, FBI COINTELPRO-CPUSA Files; memo, Baumgardner to DeLoach, April 23, 1964, no. 6-84, ibid.; memo, Baumgardner to Sullivan, April 22, 1964, no. 6-87, ibid.; radiograms, Director to SAC Buffalo, April 24, 1964, no. 6-88 and April 22, 1964, no. 6-83, ibid.

31. For the FBI letters and pamphlet, see memos, SAC Pittsburgh to Director, Sept. 30, 1963, no. 39-62, Oct. 28, 1963, no. 39-67, and Nov. 13, 1963, no. 39-68, ibid; memo, Director to SAC Pittsburgh, Oct. 3, 1963, no. 39-63, ibid. For DeLoach, see memo, Baumgardner to Sullivan, Oct. 7, 1963, ibid. For Wilkinson in Minneapolis and Cleveland, see memo, Director to SAC New York, Sept. 18, 1962, no. 34-280, ibid. The New York SAC was ordered to destroy his copy of this last document, which highlighted several examples of what senior FBI officials considered to be especially effective counter-intelligence operations.

32. The Youngstown quote is from memo, Director to SAC Cleveland, Oct. 8, 1963, no. 11-108, ibid. For the FBI in Cleveland, see also memos, SAC Cleveland to Director, May 22, 1962, no. 11-30, March 14, 1963, no. 11-76, and Oct. 11, 1963, no. 11-109, ibid.; memo, Baumgardner to Sullivan, May 16, 1962, no. 11-25, ibid.; airtels, SAC Cleveland to Director, May 9, 1962 and Oct. 4, 1963, no. 11-108, ibid.; airtel, Director to SAC Cleveland, Feb. 21, 1963, no. 11-72, ibid.

33. Memo, SAC Cleveland to Director, Dec. 2, 1964, ibid.; memo, Director to SAC Cleveland, Nov. 6, 1964, no. 11-184, ibid.; airtel, SAC Cleveland to Director, Oct. 28, 1964, no. 11-184, ibid. See also *IARA*, p. 247.

34. For Ruby, see *SDSRIARA*, p. 49 n204. For Wilkinson and the OFC, see Cleveland Field Office LHM, Oct. 22, 1963, FBI NCARL Files; Cleveland Field Office Report, March 14, 1963, ibid. A week before Wilkinson's appearance at Oberlin College, a COINTELPRO report noted that a student prominent in the activities of the "13th Ohio District Committee to Abolish the HCUA" was asked to leave school because he did not meet the academic

requirements. Memo, SAC Cleveland to Director, Feb. 13, 1963, FBI COINTELPRO-CPUSA Files. Apparently, the FBI arranged an article in the *Elyria Chronicle Telegram* ("HUAC Opponent Leaves OC") to publicize this expulsion.

35. For the FBI's assistance to Wood, see airtel, SAC Cleveland to Director, Jan. 21, 1963, no. 11-67, FBI COINTELPRO-CPUSA Files; memos, SAC Cleveland to Director, Aug. 30, 1961, no. 2835, July 13, 1961, no. 2712, and July 31, 1961, ibid.; memo, Sullivan to Belmont, July 21, 1961, no. 2748, ibid. For Mowery, see Donner, *Age of Surveillance*, p. 112.

36. Including the Wisconsin Committee for Constitutional Freedom, the Women's International League for Peace and Freedom, Citizens for Constitutional Rights, the Washington Area Committee to Abolish HUAC, the Minnesota Committee to Defend the Bill of Rights, the Chicago Committee to Defend the Bill of Rights, and the New York Council to Abolish the Un-American Activities Committee.

37. Airtel, Director to SAC Salt Lake City, May 27, 1963, FBI NCARL Files.

38. Memo, SA [deleted] to SAC Chicago, Dec. 2, 1960, FBI CCDBR Files.

39. Memo, Baumgardner to Belmont, Jan. 11, 1961, no. 2229, FBI COINTELPRO-CPUSA Files; airtel, Director to SAC Milwaukee, Dec. 21, 1961, no. 2132, ibid.

40. Milwaukee Field Office Report, Oct. 13, 1961, FBI NCARL Files.

41. Memos, SAC Cleveland to Director, July 13, 1961, no. 2712 and July 31, 1961, FBI COINTELPRO-CPUSA Files; memo, Sullivan to Belmont, July 21, 1961, no. 2748, ibid.

42. Memo, SAC Cleveland to Director, Aug. 30, 1961, no. 2835, ibid.

43 Memos, SAC Chicago to Director, June 21, 1962, no. 1196 and April 23, 1962, no. 1145, Criley FBI Files.

44. For the FBI's consideration and implementation of this action, see airtel, SAC Chicago to Director, May 14, 1962, no. 1165, ibid.; memo, SAC Cleveland to Director, May 22, 1962, no. 11-30, FBI COINTELPRO-CPUSA Files; memo, Baumgardner to Sullivan, May 16, 1962, no. 11-25, ibid.; airtel, Director to SAC Cleveland, May 15, 1962, no. 11-22, ibid.; airtel, SAC Cleveland to Director, May 9, 1962, no. 11-22, ibid.; memo, Director to SAC New York, Sept. 18, 1962, no. 34-280, ibid.

45. Memos, SAC Chicago to Director, June 21, 1962, no. 1196, Aug. 3, 1962, July 18, 1962, no. 1200, and Nov. 15, 1962, no. 1302, all in Criley FBI Files. See also memo, [deleted] to [deleted], July 6, 1962, ibid.; memos, Director to SAC Chicago, June 7, 1962, no. 1180, July 9, 1962, no. 1280, Aug. 20, 1962, no. 1228, and Sept. 6, 1962, no. 1239, all ibid.; airtel, SAC Chicago to Director, May 14, 1962, no. 1166, ibid.; memos, SAC Chicago to Director, Aug. 3, 1962, no. 9-63 and Aug. 31, 1962, FBI COINTELPRO-CPUSA Files. These anonymous mailings were meticulously executed. FBI headquarters ordered the Chicago Field Office to mail their characterization of the CCDBR from a place "where a formerly active Communist Party member, such as [deleted], would normally deposit his mail and at a time he could reasonably be expected to do so."

46. For Broyles, see memo, SAC Chicago to Director, Aug. 3, 1962, Criley FBI Files; memo, Director to SAC Chicago, Aug. 20, 1962, no. 1228, ibid. For Rosenzweig, see memo, SAC Chicago to Director, Aug. 31, 1962, no. 1236, ibid.; memo, Director to SAC Chicago, Sept. 6, 1962, no. 1239, ibid.

47. For the INS, see FBI NCARL Files, passim. For the SSS, see form letter request for FBI reports, Paul H. Wright (Special Service Staff) to FBI, Oct. 16, 1970, ibid. For the Oberlin student, see memo, SAC New York to Director, April 22, 1963, ibid. For the Army file, see Donner, *Age of Surveillance*, p. 299. For Army censorship, see Special Preparedness Subcommittee, *Military Cold War Education*, pt. 5, pp. 2106-08. For Abzug, see Goldstein, *Political Repression*, p. 478. Even before the Special Service Staff was established in 1969, the FBI obtained confidential access to CCDBR bank account records and used this information to make "inquiries" to the IRS. And for whatever reasons, in 1965 the IRS audited CCDBR income tax returns. Memo, SA [deleted] to SAC Chicago, Nov. 24, 1961, FBI CCDBR Files; Chicago Field Office Report, Jan. 12, 1965, no. 115 (recorded in FBI CCDBR headquarters file 100-433419), copy in FBI CCDBR Files.

48. Subcommittee on Oversight, *The CIA and the Media*, pp. 189, 192, 232, 399. The FBI also investigated Warren Commission critics. In February 1964 an FBI-authored news story regarding a *National Guardian*-sponsored meeting on the Warren Commission was sent to "a cooperative news media source." Quoting from HUAC documents, the FBI's news story described the *Guardian* as "a virtual official propaganda arm of Soviet Russia." *HIA*, vol. 6, *FBI*, p. 762. Walter Winchell had described the *Guardian* in similar terms the previous month and dismissed Lane as an "agitator" seeking to abolish HUAC. Cedric Belfrage and James Aronson, *Something to Guard: The Stormy Life of the National Guardian, 1948-1967* (New York: Columbia University Press, 1978), p. 298.

49. *Chicago Sun-Times*, Feb. 3, 1979, p. 10 and Feb. 5, 1979, p. 29; memo, Chicago Field Office, Jan. 10, 1966 (re CCDBR and marked "Not for File"). The document authorizing this burglary was not filed with official FBI records but kept in the SAC's personal safe. Normally, such documents were routinely destroyed to preclude outside knowledge of such "clearly illegal" (the phrase is the FBI's) techniques. Instead, this document was produced during the Alliance to End Repression red squad suit in Chicago.

50. Airtel, SAC Washington to Director, Dec. 15, 1960, FBI NCARL Files.

51. For Porter, see Los Angeles Field Office Report, July 20, 1965, ibid. For Roosevelt and Conyers, see Chicago Field Office LHMs, Jan. 12, 1961 and April 8, 1965, ibid. For Hoover's directive, see memo, Director to SAC Los Angeles, Oct. 15, 1962, no. 242, ibid. For Maverick, see airtel, SAC San Antonio to Director, April 27, 1964, ibid. For FBI officials' interest in congressional voting, see memo, Baumgardner to Sullivan, Jan. 30, 1963, ibid.

52. For the HUAC leak, see airtel, SAC Washington to Director, Jan. 11, 1965, no. 579, ibid.; airtel, Director to SAC Washington, n.d. (ca. Nov. 30, 1964), ibid. For Allen, see memo, Baumgardner to Sullivan, Jan. 10, 1962, ibid. For Sickles, see airtel, SAC Washington to Director, Nov. 25, 1964, ibid.

53. Airtel, SAC New York to Director, Dec. 16, 1960, no. 57, ibid.; memo,

W. D. Griffith to Quinn Tamm, Dec. 21, 1960, no. 80, ibid.; memo, Baumgardner to Belmont, Dec. 22, 1960 (see also accompanying blind memorandum, serial no. 2177 recorded in FBI COINTELPRO-CPUSA Files), copy in FBI NCARL Files; memo, DeLoach to Mohr, Dec. 29, 1960, no. 81, FBI NCARL Files; memo, Baumgardner to Belmont, Jan. 16, 1961 (see also Walter's accompanying press release), no. 2233, FBI COINTELPRO-CPUSA Files. The NCAHUAC and its New York affiliate did not always see eye to eye, though the FBI never doubted they were both following the Communist party line. For the Bureau's highly inaccurate account of factionalism within the anti-HUAC movement and efforts to promote this factionalism, see New York Field Office Report, Sept. 24, 1964, FBI NCARL Files. This was not the first time HUAC had used the matching addressograph technique. A Committee report of 1956 noted that the National Committee to Secure Justice for Morton Sobell had used the same plates as the *National Guardian*. HUAC, *Trial by Treason*, p. 39. Whether the FBI alerted HUAC in 1956 is not known. It should be noted, however, that to establish NYCAUAC use of the *Worker's* plates in 1960 the FBI had to conduct detailed laboratory tests.

54. Memo, Baumgardner to Belmont, Jan. 16, 1961, no. 2233, FBI COINTELPRO-CPUSA Files.

55. Letter, Yates to [constituent], Dec. 6, 1960, HUAC 1960, Sidney R. Yates Papers, HST; letter, Roosevelt to all members of the House, Dec. 31, 1960, HUAC 1961, ibid.

56. Memo, Baumgardner to Belmont, Jan. 9, 1961, no. 8, FBI CCDBR Files.

57. See Hoover's notation on memo, Baumgardner to Sullivan, Dec. 14, 1961, no. 157, FBI NCARL Files.

58. Quoted in memo, Baumgardner to Sullivan, Jan. 10, 1962, no. 158, ibid. See also airtel, SAC Washington to Director, Jan. 8, 1962, no. 156, ibid.; airtel, SAC Chicago to Director, Dec. 19, 1961, ibid.; Washington Field Office LHM, Jan. 16, 1963, ibid.

59. Teletype, SAC Washington to Director and SACs Los Angeles et al., Jan. 7, 1965, no. 581, ibid. See also memo, Baumgardner to Sullivan, Jan. 13, 1965, no. 582, ibid. The congressmen included Edwards, Hawkins, Burton, Roosevelt, Ryan, Lindsay, Conyers, Robert L. Leggett (D., Cal.), Benjamin S. Rosenthal (D., N.Y.), Charles C. Diggs (D., Mich.), and William S. Moorhead (D., Pa.). William A. Barrett (D., Pa.) was later added to the FBI's list.

60. For the resolutions, see the two documents cited in note 59. For Gude and Celler, see Washington Field Office LHMs, Dec. 29, 1966 and March 14, 1969, ibid. For Edwards, see Washington Field Office Report, May 4, 1967, ibid. For Foley et al., see Washington Field Office LHM, March 27, 1969, ibid.

61. Letter, [Hoover] to Persons, Jan. 3, 1961, ibid.; letter, [Hoover] to Jenkins, Feb. 28, 1964, ibid. For the FBI's surveillance of the luncheon, see, for example, airtel, SAC Pittsburgh to Director, Jan. 23, 1964, no. 437, ibid.;

memo, Baumgardner to Sullivan, Feb. 26, 1964, no. 444, ibid.; Washington Field Office Report, April 21, 1964, ibid. President Johnson was a personal friend of Aubrey Williams and presented, in 1964, another NCAHUAC founder, Alexander Meiklejohn, with the Presidential Freedom Award. Such recognition infuriated conservative anticommunists and at least one FBI leak to HUAC appears to have concerned Meiklejohn. Memo, Baumgardner to Sullivan, Nov. 3, 1964, no. 551, ibid. Nevertheless, by 1968 Johnson was an active if behind-the-scenes supporter of the Committee—no doubt because HUAC supported his efforts to smear critics of the Vietnam War as Communist stooges. See memo, [Harold] Barefoot Sanders to the President, Feb. 29, 1968, WHCF, EX FG411/U–Z, LBJ.

62. At least one COINTELPRO–New Left operation involved the NCAHUAC. Airtel, SAC Boston to Bureau, June 2, 1970, FBI COINTELPRO–New Left Files (100–449698), JEH. The FBI kept its investigation of NCARL open until April 14, 1975, in an effort to determine whether Wilkinson planned to file suit under the Freedom of Information Act.

63. Memo, Brennan to Sullivan, Jan. 4, 1967, FBI NCARL Files.

CONCLUSION

1. The San Francisco demonstrations were immortalized in a film, *Operation Abolition*, commissioned by HUAC and made from subpoenaed news films. In addition, the Committee and the FBI distributed 250,000 copies of Hoover's *Communist Target—Youth* (86th Cong., 2d sess., 1960), a report that dismissed the student demonstrators as Communist dupes. The Bureau also launched at least one formal counterintelligence action to disrupt "Communist Plans to Enlarge the San Francisco Demonstration." Memo, F. J. Baumgardner to Alan H. Belmont, July 1, 1960, no. 1777, FBI COINTELPRO–CPUSA Files (100–3–104), JEH. The HUAC film and other attempts to disparage the demonstrators, however, backfired. Students for a Democratic Society organizer Clark Kissinger and other activists were grateful for *Operation Abolition* because it showed police clubbing students. George Thayer, *The Farther Shores of Politics: The American Political Fringe* (New York: Simon and Schuster, 1968), p. 401.

2. For the FBI's interest in the Chicago demonstrations, see teletype, SAC Chicago to Director, May 24, 1965, FBI CCDBR Files (100–37762); memo, Baumgardner to Sullivan, May 25, 1965, ibid.; memo, SA [deleted] to SAC Chicago, June 21, 1965, ibid.; Chicago Field Office Report, July 12, 1965, ibid.; memo, SA [deleted] to SAC Chicago, June 16, 1966, Quentin Young FBI Files; report, SA [deleted], May 13, 1965, ibid. For press coverage, see *New York Times*, May 25, 1965, p. 16; ibid., May 26, 1965, p. 9; ibid., May 28, 1965, p. 9; ibid., May 30, 1965, sec. IV, p. 2; ibid., Aug. 4, 1965, p. 14.

3. There is some evidence that a few FBI agents and officials, possibly including Cartha DeLoach, experimented with a new tactic. Because the

Communist smear was no longer taken quite so seriously in the 1960s and was sometimes totally inappropriate, the Bureau sought to discredit select critics by linking them to the Mafia rather than to the CPUSA. One self-described victim of such a strategy, former Congressman Cornelius Gallagher (D., N.J.), had in 1965-1966 chaired a special House Government Operations Committee inquiry on "Investigative Activities of Federal Civilian Agencies." *Cong. Rec.*, 92d Cong., 2d sess., April 19, 1972, pp. 13491-97. Gallagher was later convicted of tax evasion charges and named by South Korean rice dealer Tongsun Park as the recipient of $221,000. Former San Francisco Mayor Joseph L. Alioto also claimed he was the smeared in a *Look* magazine article, based on FBI leaks, charging him with being "enmeshed in . . . La Cosa Nostra." U.S., Senate, Subcommittee on Constitutional Rights of the Judiciary Committee, *Federal Data Banks, Computers and the Bill of Rights*, 92d Cong., 1st sess., 1971, pt. 1, pp. 492-530.

4. McNamara interview.

5. *U.S.* v. *U.S. District Court*, 407 U.S. 297 (1972); *Alderman* v. *U.S.*, 394 U.S. 165 (1969).

6. For the Justice Department correspondence and the Committee's comments, see HISC, *Annual Report*, H.Rept. 301, 93d Cong., 1st sess., 1973 (Serial 13022-4), p. 168; HISC, *Annual Report*, H.Rept. 771, pp. 116-18 and *Annual Report*, H.Rept. 1646, 93d Cong., 2d sess., 1974 (Serial 13063-1), pp. 123-25. For a detailed discussion of the Stamler, Hall, and Cohen case, see Kenneth O'Reilly, "The Stamler Challenge: Congressional Investigative Power and the First Amendment," *Congressional Studies* 7(Spring 1979): 57-72. See also Thomas P. Sullivan, Chester M. Kamin, and Arthur M. Sussman, "The Case Against HUAC: The Stamler Litigation," *Harvard Civil Rights-Civil Liberties Law Review* 11 (Spring 1976): 243-62; Hans Zeisel and Rose Stamler, "The Evidence: A Content Analysis of the HUAC Record," ibid., pp. 263-98.

7. Memo, D. Milton Ladd to Director, Oct. 22, 1941, no. 1021, FBI HUAC Files (61-7582); memo, Edward A. Tamm to Director, Oct. 27, 1941, Hoover O&C FBI Files-Martin Dies. Though Committee wiretapping dated from the late 1930s, the only documented electronic surveillance occurred in 1972 when Herbert Romerstein, chief investigator for HISC's Republican minority, and Richard Norusis, former civilian chief of a United States Army intelligence unit, were caught bugging a room at the Midland Hotel in Chicago where an alleged Communist group had scheduled a conference. Romerstein and Norusis reportedly remained to complete their mission. Donner, *Age of Surveillance*, p. 402.

8. Memos, Larry Temple to the President, Jan. 10 and 13, Feb. 6, April 30, May 4, 10, and 28, and June 19, 1968, all in White House Aide Files-Larry Temple (SACB), LBJ; note, LBJ, Aug. 27, 1968, WHCF, EX FG285, LBJ; memo, Temple to the President, Jan. 19, 1968, CF, FG285, LBJ.

9. Letter, Marlin W. Johnson to Edward V. Hanrahan, Aug. 22, 1967, Milton Cohen FBI Files (100-3303).

10. For the Johnson case, see *Cong. Rec.*, 91st Cong., 2d sess., Sept. 23,

1970, p. 33276; HISC, *New Mobilization Committee to End War in Vietnam*, 91st Cong., 2d sess., 1970, pt. 2, pp. 4231, 4283. For FBI surveillance of New Mobe, see *SDSRIARA*, pp. 320, 338; *HIA*, vol. 6, *FBI*, pp. 782-84; Morton Halperin et al., *The Lawless State* (New York: Penguin, 1976), p. 121; Nelson Blackstock, *COINTELPRO: The FBI's Secret War on Political Freedom* (New York: Vintage, 1976), pp. 154, 167-68; Donner, "The Theory and Practice of American Political Intelligence," p. 34. CIA files, moreover, contain a copy of a HISC staff study on New Mobe.

11. Theoharis, *Spying on Americans*, pp. 9-11, 281 n1.

12. The Pike Committee did not fare as well. Following unauthorized disclosure of portions of its report to the *Village Voice*, the House voted to suppress the Pike Committee's final report. See J. Leiper Freeman, "Investigating the Executive Intelligence: The Fate of the Pike Committee," *Capitol Studies* 5(Fall 1977): 103-18; I. F. Stone, "The Schorr Case: The Real Dangers," *New York Review of Books*, April 1, 1976, pp. 6-11.

13. HISC, *Terrorism*, 93d Cong., 2d sess., 1974, pts. 1-4. See also the following Committee reports: *Political Kidnappings, 1968-1973*, 93d Cong., 1st sess., 1973; *Symbionese Liberation Army* and *Terrorism*, 93d Cong., 2d sess., 1974.

14. *Cong. Rec.*, 94th Cong., 1st sess., Jan. 14, 1975, pp. 20-33; Kenneth O'Reilly, "Watergate Fallout: The Quiet Death of the Un-Americans," *USA Today*, Jan. 1980, pp. 58-59; Robert Morris, *Self Destruct: Dismantling America's Internal Security* (New Rochelle, N.Y.: Arlington House, 1979), pp. 56-60; "Liberal Democrats Scrap Internal Security Committee," *Human Events*, Jan. 25, 1975, pp. 3-4; "Rodino Pulls Plug on Anti-Red Probes," ibid., May 31, 1975, p. 3. The congressional internal security committees did not suffer alone. The SACB and the Justice Department's Internal Security Division were abolished in 1973, and the Attorney General's list of subversive organizations was formally discarded in 1974.

15. *SDSRIARA*, pp. 968-69. For FBI officials' interest in obtaining results and maintaining secrecy rather than conforming to statutory regulations, see ibid., pp. 3, 10-11, 15-17, 64, 108, 135, 257, 302, 307-10, 343-44, 355, 360-61, 670, 675-76; *IARA*, pp. 11, 13-14, 61-62, 64, 109-11, 127 n635, 137-63, 285-86; *HIA*, vol. 6, *FBI*, pp. 24, 357, 684.

16. The Bureau apparently leaked derogatory information on Long, whose Senate probe paralleled Congressman Gallagher's (see note 3), to *Life* magazine. The FBI also investigated the members of the Long Subcommittee, compiling a briefing book (with a tab for each senator) that was filed in Hoover's unserialized official and confidential file. *HIA*, vol. 6, *FBI*, pp. 161-62, 477, 830-35; *SDSRIARA*, pp. 307-10, 661, 665-68; Donner, *Age of Surveillance*, p. 256.

17. U.S., House, Subcommittee of the Committee on Appropriations, *Departments of State, Justice, and Commerce*, 92d Cong., 1st sess., 1971, pt. 1, p. 660.

18. Jay Peterzell, "The Heritage Report: Unleashing the Dogs of McCarthyism," *Nation*, Jan. 17, 1981, pp. 33, 51-52.

19. For Francis and SST, see Frank J. Donner, "The New F.B.I. Guidelines: Rounding Up the Usual Suspects," *Nation*, Aug. 7–14, 1982, pp. 110–15.
20. "Campus Police," ibid., April 24, 1982, pp. 482–83.
21. *New York Times*, Feb. 10, 1982, p. 31.
22. Alan Wolfe, "How Reagan Uses Truth: Ignorance as Public Policy," *Nation*, April 3, 1982, p. 398.
23. For more recent Bureau efforts to refurbish its tarnished image, including assistance to the short-lived ABC television series *Today's FBI* (1981–1982) starring Mike Connors, see Nat Hentoff, "Annals of Mythology/This Is Your New FBI," *Village Voice*, Oct. 21–27, 1981, p. 8.

Selected Bibliography

RECORDS OF THE FEDERAL BUREAU OF INVESTIGATION

FBI records for the Bureau's formative years are available in the National Archives. All other FBI records and files are accessible only through the Freedom of Information Act. When reviewing FOIA requests, the FBI deletes data it is not required by law to release (such as security-classified information or the names of informants) and then releases to the requestor photocopies of the specified documents. All deletions are subject to appeal through the Department of Justice and ultimately the courts. Additional photocopies of those files and records which the FBI deems of sufficient general interest are made available to the public in the FOI/Privacy Acts reading room at FBI headquarters.

Records Available in the National Archives

Record Group 65. Records of the Bureau of Investigation, 1908–1922 (microfilm).

FBI Files Available in the J. Edgar Hoover FBI Building

American Civil Liberties Union
COINTELPRO-Black Extremist
COINTELPRO-CPUSA
COINTELPRO-New Left
COINTELPRO-White Hate Group
German-American Bund (report only)
Alger Hiss
Vito Marcantonio
J. Robert Oppenheimer
William Walter Remington
Rosenberg-Sobell Committee
Security Index

Selected Bibliography

FBI Files To Be Deposited at the Marquette University Library

Administrative Matters
  Subfile 66-1372
  Subfile 66-1934
  Subfile 66-9330
J. Edgar Hoover Unserialized Official and Confidential Files
  Martin Dies Folder
  John F. Kennedy Folder
  Martin Luther King, Jr., Folder
House Committee on Un-American Activities
Louis B. Nichols Unserialized Official and Confidential Files
  American Civil Liberties Union Folder
  American Youth Congress Folder
  Mrs. Courtney Ryley Cooper Folder
  Dies Committee Folder
  Morris Ernst Folder
  Otto N. Frankfurter Folder
  Herbert Hoover Folder
  Harold Hochschild Folder
  Edwin F. Jaeckle Folder
  Junior Chamber of Commerce Folder
  Justice Department Folder
  John H. Kerr Folder
  Carol King Folder
  Walter Krivitsky Folder
  John L. Lewis Folder
  James McGranery Folder
  Harry McMullin Folder
  Paul Mallon Folder
  New York Daily News Folder
  Val O'Farrell Folder
  Drew Pearson Folder
  John D. Rockefeller III Folder
  Harry S Truman Folder
  Earl Warren Folder

Other FBI Files

Chicago Committee to Defend the Bill of Rights. Chicago.
Milton Cohen. Chicago.
Committee for Public Justice. New York City.
Richard Criley. Chicago and Carmel, California.
Thomas I. Emerson. New Haven, Connecticut.
David R. Luce. Milwaukee.
Curtis D. MacDougall. Evanston, Illinois.

National Committee Against Repressive Legislation (formerly National Committee to Abolish HUAC). Los Angeles.
National Lawyers Guild. New York City.
Revolutionary Communist Party (formerly Revolutionary Union). San Francisco.
Quentin D. Young. Chicago.

OTHER GOVERNMENT RECORDS

Central Intelligence Agency Records. HTLINGUAL Files (photocopies). Center for National Security Studies. Washington, D.C.
Internal Revenue Service Records. Special Service Staff Files (photocopies). Center for National Security Studies. Washington, D.C.
Record Group 60. General Records of the Department of Justice. Numerical Files. National Archives. Washington, D.C.

MANUSCRIPTS

Major Archives

Archives of Labor History and Urban Affairs. Wayne State University. Detroit.
    American Federation of Teachers Papers
    Civil Rights Congress of Michigan Papers
    Ganley-Wellman Papers
    Nat Ganley Papers
    Donald Montgomery Papers
    Stanley Nowak Papers
    Harvey O'Connor Papers
    Oscar Paskal Papers
    Workers Defense League Papers
Dwight D. Eisenhower Library. Abilene, Kansas.
    Dwight D. Eisenhower Papers
        Official File
        Ann Whitman File
    John Foster Dulles Papers
Herbert Hoover Library. West Branch, Iowa.
    Karl Baarslag Papers
    Herbert Hoover Papers
        Cabinet Offices
        Foreign Affairs
        Post-Presidential Individual Name File
        President's Secretary's File
        Subject File

Selected Bibliography

Westbrook Pegler Papers
Walter Trohan Papers
Lyndon B. Johnson Library. Austin, Texas.
    Lyndon B. Johnson Papers
        Administrative Histories
        Appointments File
        Confidential File
        White House Aide Files
        White House Central File
Library of Congress, Washington, D.C.
    John P. Frey Papers
    Katharine A. Kellock Papers
    G. Bromley Oxnam Papers
Franklin D. Roosevelt Library. Hyde Park, New York.
    Francis Biddle Papers
    Stephen T. Early Papers
    Harry L. Hopkins Papers
    Gardner Jackson Papers
    Lowell Mellett Papers
    Henry M. Morgenthau, Jr., Papers
    Eleanor Roosevelt Papers
    Franklin D. Roosevelt Papers
        Confidential File
        Official File
        President's Personal File
        President's Secretary's File
    Harold D. Smith Papers
    Henry Wallace Papers
State Historical Society of Wisconsin. Madison.
    American Communications Association Papers (Local 10, New York City)
    Americans for Democratic Action Papers
    American League for Peace and Democracy Papers (Madison branch)
    Louise R. Berman Papers
    Marquis Childs Papers
    Citizens Commission to Investigate the FBI Papers
    Elizabeth Poe Kerby Papers
    National Committee Against Repressive Legislation Papers
    Richard Rovere Papers
    David J. Saposs Papers
    Jeremiah Stamler Papers
    Alexander Wiley Papers
    Women Strike for Peace Papers
Harry S. Truman Library. Independence, Missouri.
    Eben Ayers Papers
    Eleanor Bontecou Papers
    Tom C. Clark Papers

Clark M. Clifford Papers
Democratic National Committee Clipping File
Democratic National Committee Files
George M. Elsey Papers
John F. X. McGohey Papers
J. Howard McGrath Papers
Francis P. Matthews Papers
Charles S. Murphy Papers
John W. Snyder Papers
Stephen J. Spingarn Papers
Harry S Truman Papers
    Clark M. Clifford Files
    Confidential File
    Charles W. Jackson Files
    Charles S. Murphy Files
    Official File
    Post-Presidential File
    President's Personal File
    President's Secretary's File
    Raymond R. Zimmerman Files
A. Devitt Vanech Papers
Sidney R. Yates Papers

Other Manuscripts

Chicago Committee to Defend the Bill of Rights Papers. Chicago Historical
    Society.
Homer S. Cummings Papers. University of Virginia Library. Charlottesville.
Alger Hiss Papers. To be deposited at the Harvard University Library.
    Cambridge, Massachusetts.
Charles J. Kersten Papers. Marquette University Library. Milwaukee.
Mayor's Papers. Burton Historical Collection. Detroit Public Library.
    Detroit.
Karl E. Mundt Papers. Karl E. Mundt Archival Library Dakota State College.
    Madison, South Dakota.

GOVERNMENT DOCUMENTS

Publications of the House Committee on Un-American Activities

Dies Committee, HUAC, and HISC hearings and reports are too volum-
inous to cite here. For the most complete listing available, see Appendix II, in
Kenneth O'Reilly, "The Bureau and the Committee: A Study of J. Edgar
Hoover's FBI, the House Committee on Un-American Activities, and the
Communist Issue" (Ph.D. dissertation, Marquette University, 1981), pp.

580–605. A comprehensive (2,338-page) index of names, organizations, and publications cited in Dies Committee and HUAC hearings and reports is also available. See U.S., Congress, House, Committee on Un-American Activities, *Cumulative Index to Publications of the Committee on Un-American Activities, 1938–1954*, 84th Cong., 1st sess., 1955 and *Supplement to Cumulative Index to Publications of the Committee on Un-American Activities, 1955–1968*, 91st Cong., 2d sess., 1970.

INTERVIEWS AND ORAL HISTORIES

Anderson, John W. Archives of Labor History and Urban Affairs. Wayne State University. Detroit.

Clark, Tom C. Harry S Truman Library. Independence, Missouri.

Criley, Richard. Carmel, California. April 5, 1979.

Elsey, George M. Harry S Truman Library. Independence, Missouri.

Hess, Karl. Washington, D.C. October 1, 1979.

McCaughey, Robert. Madison, South Dakota. February 28, 1979.

MacDougall, Curtis D. Evanston, Illinois. April 17, 1979.

McNamara, Francis J. Bethesda, Maryland. June 13, 1979.

Reedy, George. Milwaukee. April 20, 1982.

Romerstein, Herbert. Washington, D.C. June 8, 1979.

Wilkinson, Frank. Washington, D.C. June 12, 1979.

OTHER UNPUBLISHED SOURCES

Carlson, Lewis H. "J. Parnell Thomas and the House Committee on Un-American Activities, 1938–1948." Ph.D. dissertation, Michigan State University, 1967.

Drinan, S.J., Robert F. "The Continued Injuries Done by the House Internal Security Committee." Speech, American University, Washington, D.C., October 21, 1971.

Heimoski, Frank J. "Address to the Law Enforcement Intelligence Unit Eastern Regional Conference." Speech, Chicago, November 1, 1963.

Jacobs, James B. "The Conduct of Local Political Intelligence." Ph.D. dissertation, Princeton University, 1977.

Marden, David L. "The Cold War and American Education." Ph.D. dissertation, University of Kansas, 1976.

O'Reilly, Kenneth. "The Bureau and the Committee: A Study of J. Edgar Hoover's FBI, the House Committee on Un-American Activities, and the Communist Issue." Ph.D. dissertation, Marquette University, 1981.

Simmons, Jerold L. "Operation Abolition: The Campaign to Abolish the House Un-American Activities Committee, 1938–1965." Ph.D. dissertation, University of Minnesota, 1971.

Index

Abt, John, 103
Abzug, Bella, 219, 275
Acheson, Dean, 112, 325n49
Adams, Alva B., 24
Adams, James B., 368n24
Adams, Sherman, 195
Adamson, Ernie, 119
Addams, Jane, 14, 271
Addes, George, 173-74
Adler, Solomon, 153
Agriculture, Department of, 56, 289
Air Force, 237, 320n18
Alioto, Joseph L., 380n3
Allen, Bob, 211, 223, 224, 320n14
Allen, Donna, 276, 279
Allen, Robert, 364n80
Alliance to End Repression: red squad
    suit, 377n49
Amerasia, 112, 338n58
America First Committee, 24
American Bar Association (ABA), 88,
    145-46, 147, 198; anticommunist
    committees, 144, 343n34
American Business Consultants (ABC),
    89-90
American Citizens Political Awakening
    Association, 19
American Civil Liberties Union (ACLU),
    61, 70, 82, 141-42, 143, 145, 171, 194,
    212, 256; anticommunism of, 182-84;
    Bureau of Investigation surveillance of,
    17, 18, 19, 21; and the Dies Committee,
    181-82; and the FBI, 184-93; FBI
    surveillance of, 67; Los Angeles
    affiliate, 190-91; Northern California
    affiliate, 191, 192; Seattle affiliate, 190.
    *See also names of ACLU officials and
    staff*
American Coalition of Patriotic, Civic,
    and Fraternal Societies, 49

American Committee for Cultural Free-
    dom (ACCF), 171, 347n3
American Committee for the Protection
    of the Foreign Born, 234
American Defense Society, 18
American Federation of Labor (AFL), 15,
    48, 59, 174-75, 329n9
American Federation of Television and
    Radio Artists (AFTRA), 324-25n48
American Friends Service Committee,
    259
American Labor party (ALP), 83
American League for Peace and
    Democracy, 44, 64, 70, 314n54
American Legion, 33, 37, 115, 145, 189,
    205, 232, 237, 252, 266, 352n38; and
    ACLU, 185-86; anticommunism of,
    35, 87, 88-89; and FBI, 89, 203, 214,
    323n36; and Hollywood, 88; and
    HUAC opponents, 259; National
    Americanism Commission, 70, 88-89,
    185, 186; National Public Relations
    Commission, 88; Radical Research
    Committee, 53
American Magazine, 32, 123
American Mercury, 84, 85
American Patriots, Inc., 43
American Protective League (APL), 17
American Security Council (ASC), 86-87,
    88
American Slav Congress, 234, 235
American Student Union, 51
American Veterans Committee, 166
American Youth Congress (AYC): and
    CPUSA, 52-53; FBI burglary of, 53,
    64; FBI surveillance of, 52; and Eleanor
    Roosevelt, 51-53
Americans Battling Communism, 235
Americans for Democratic Action
    (ADA), 89, 137, 193, 368n9; anticom-

389

397

Wherry, Kenneth, 102
White, Harry Dexter, 329n11
White Slave Traffic Act (Mann Act), 26-27
Whitehead, Don, 39, 80, 81, 95, 321n20
Whitley, Rhea, 43, 48
Whitney, R. M., 18
Wickersham, George W., 27
Widener, Alice, 224
Wier, William, 255
Wigglesworth, Richard, 102
Wildman, Leonard B., 369n29
Wiley, Alexander, 99
Wilkins, Roy, 172-73
Wilkinson, Frank, 85-86, 186, 262-70, 273, 276-77, 293, 374n23, 375n34, 379n62
William Sloane Associates, 141
Williams, Aubrey, 259, 267, 280, 379n61
Williams, Edward Bennett, 320n18
Williams, George, 215, 238
Williams, J. D., 128
Willkie, Wendell, 63
Wills, Garry, 107
Wilson, Charles H., 219
Wilson, H. H., 222
Wilson, Lyle, 80, 95, 105, 135-36, 138
Winchell, Walter, 32, 40, 76, 80, 105, 128, 141, 164-65, 324n47, 377n48
Winrod, Gerald, 40
Winston, Henry, 269
Wisconsin Committee for Constitutional Freedom, 270-71, 376n36

Witness (Chambers), 112
Witt, Nathan, 238-39, 329n11
Wolfe, Alan, 294
Woll, Matthew, 174
Woltman, Frederick, 80, 83, 141, 174, 175, 212, 337n56, 358n40
Women Strike for Peace, 282
Women's International League for Peace and Freedom (WILPF), 201, 251, 268, 269, 271-72, 376n36
Wood, John S., 137, 154, 204-5, 255, 318n2
Woodrum, Clifton A., 312n46
Woods, Leta, 269-70, 271
Worker, The, 277, 378n53
Workers Alliance Congress (WAC), 60
World Council of Churches, 83
Wright, Paul, 360n54
Wyman, Louis G., 346n20

Yalta, 6, 126
Yankwich, Leon R., 94
Yeagley, J. Walter, 261
Young Communist League, 49
Young Republican League, 265

Zapp, Manfred, 69
Ziegler, Ronald, 220
Zien, Burton J., 162-63
Zoll, Allen, 205